O9-AHT-586

# FOCUS ON LITERATURE

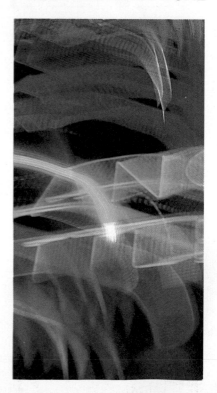

HOUGHTON MIFFLIN COMPANY    BOSTON
Atlanta  Dallas  Geneva, Illinois  Hopewell, New Jersey  Palo Alto  Toronto

FOCUS ON LITERATURE

# ACTION

PHILIP McFARLAND

FRANCES FEAGIN

SAMUEL HAY

STELLA S.F. LIU

FRANK McLAUGHLIN

NORMA WILLSON

# CREDITS

From The New Yorker: Moore, Rosalie. "Catalogue," reprinted by permission; © 1940, 1968, The New Yorker Magazine, Inc.

Alegría, Ricardo E. "The Envious Animals" (originally titled "The Renegades") from *Barinques*, edited by Babin and Steiner. Published by Random House, Inc. Reprinted by permission of the author, Ricardo Alegría.

Armour, Richard. "Good Sportsmanship," from *Nights with Armour*. Copyright © 1958 by Richard Armour. Used with permission of McGraw-Hill Book Company.

Benét, Rosemary Carr. "Nancy Hanks," from *A Book of Americans* by Rosemary and Stephen Vincent Benét. Holt, Rinehart and Winston, Inc. Copyright 1933 by Stephen Vincent Benét. Copyright renewed, 1961, by Rosemary Carr Benét. Reprinted by permission of Brandt & Brandt.

Blaine, Scott. "Hockey," reprinted from *Scholastic Scope* © 1972 by Scholastic Magazine, Inc.

Bonosky, Phillip. "The Wishing Well," Adapted and reprinted by permission of the author.

Buck, Pearl. "The Big Wave," reprinted by permission of Harold Ober Associates Incorporated. Copyright 1947 by the Curtis Publishing Company. Copyright 1948 by Pearl S. Buck.

Burke, Norah. "Polar Night," reprinted by permission of Scholastic Magazine, Inc. From *Story* Magazine, copyright 1953 by *Story* Magazine, Inc.

Chang, Isabelle. "The Artist," from *Tales from Old China* by Isabelle Chang. Copyright © 1969 by Isabelle Chang. Reprinted by permission of Random House, Inc.

Chase, Richard. "Jack's Hunting Trip," from *The Jack Tales* by Richard Chase. Copyright 1943 and renewed © 1971 by Richard Chase. Reprinted by permission of Houghton Mifflin Company.

Coatsworth, Elizabeth. "Daniel Webster's Horses" and "Who Is Sad?" ©Copyright Elizabeth Coatsworth. By kind permission of Mark Peterson on behalf of Elizabeth Coatsworth.

Courlander, Harold. "Jean Britisse," from *The Piece of Fire and Other Haitian Tales* copyright © 1964 by Harold Courlander. Reprinted by permission of Harcourt Brace Jovanovich, Inc.

Davies, W.H. "Sheep," copyright © 1963 by Jonathan Cape Ltd. Reprinted from *The Complete Poems of W.H. Davies*, by permission of Wesleyan University Press.

Library of Congress Catalog Card Number: 76-53136

ISBN: 0-395-24966-X

Layefsky, Virginia. ''Moonlight—Starlight,'' reprinted by permission of the author.

Lewis, Oscar. ''Roberto,'' from *The Children of Sanchez* by Oscar Lewis. Copyright © 1961 by Oscar Lewis. Reprinted by permission of Random House, Inc.

Lin Yutang. ''The Tiger,'' retold by Lin Yutang. Copyright © 1952 by Lin Yutang. From *Famous Chinese Short Stories* by Lin Yutang, used by permission of The John Day Company, publisher.

Linderman, Frank. ''Interview with a Crow Chief,'' excerpted and reprinted by permission of Wilda Linderman and Verne Linderman. Originally published under the title *American: The Life Story of a Great Indian* by Frank B. Linderman. The John Day Publishing Company 1930.

Macmillan, Cyrus. ''Strong Wind the Invisible,'' published as ''The Indian Cinderella'' in *Canadian Wonder Tales* by Cyrus Macmillan. Published by the Bodley Head and Clark Irwin Canada.

Mannix, Daniel P. ''Bat Quest,'' copyright by Daniel P. Mannix. Excerpted and reprinted by permission of Harold Matson Co., Inc.

McCord, Jean. ''The Long Way Around,'' copyright © 1968 by Jean McCord. From *Deep Where the Octopi Lie*. Slightly adapted and used by permission of Atheneum Publishers.

McGinley, Phyllis. ''A Choice of Weapons,'' from *Times Three* by Phyllis McGinley. Copyright 1954 by Phyllis McGinley. Originally appeared in *The New Yorker*. Reprinted by permission of The Viking Press.

McLeod, Irene Rutherford. ''Lone Dog,'' from *Songs to Save a Soul* by Irene Rutherford McLeod. By permission of the Author's Literary Estate and Chatto & Windus.

Merriam, Eve. ''Conversation with Myself,'' from *It Doesn't Always Have to Rhyme* by Eve Merriam. Reprinted by permission of Eve Merriam c/o International Creative Management. Copyright by Eve Merriam.

Millay, Edna St. Vincent. ''The Buck in the Snow,'' from *Collected Poems,* Harper & Row. Copyright, 1928, 1955, by Edna St. Vincent Millay and Norma Millay Ellis.

Nash, Ogden. ''The Panther,'' from *Verses From 1929 On* by Ogden Nash. Copyright 1940 by Ogden Nash. ''The Guppy,'' from *Verses* by Ogden Nash. Copyright 1944 by Ogden Nash. By permission of Little, Brown and Co.

Nathan, Robert. ''Dunkirk,'' copyright 1941 and renewed by Robert Nathan. Reprinted from *The Green Leaf: The Collected Poems of Robert Nathan,* by permission of Alfred A. Knopf, Inc.

Noyes, Alfred. ''The Highwayman,'' from *Collected Poems In One Volume* by Alfred Noyes. Copyright 1906, renewed 1934 by Alfred Noyes. Reprinted by permission of J. B. Lippincott Company.

O'Hara, Mary. ''My Friend Flicka,'' adapted and abridged from *My Friend Flicka* by Mary O'Hara. Copyright 1941 © renewed 1969 by Mary O'Hara. Slightly adapted and reprinted by permission of J. B. Lippincott Company.

Paredes, Américo. ''The Rabbit and the Coyote,'' from *Folktales of Mexico* by Américo Paredes. © University of Chicago, 1970. Adapted and reprinted by permission of the publisher.

Petry, Ann. ''A Glory over Everything,'' from *Harriet Tubman* by Ann Petry. Copyright 1955 by Ann Petry. Reprinted by permission of Thomas Y. Crowell Company, Inc., publisher.

Quinn, Anthony. ''Grandmother and the Workmen,'' from *The Original Sin: A Self-Portrait* by Anthony Quinn. Copyright © 1972 by Anthony Quinn. By permission of Little, Brown and Co.

Reynolds, Quentin. ''Secret for Two,'' by permission of the Estate of Quentin Reynolds.

Ritchey, Barbara. ''Question,'' copyright © 1972 by the National Council of Teachers of English. Reprinted by permission of the publisher and the author.

Roethke, Theodore. ''The Sloth,'' from *The Collected Poems of Theodore Roethke* copyright 1950 by Theodore Roethke. Reprinted by permission of Doubleday & Company, Inc.

Credits continued on page 528.

**Philip McFarland** teaches at Concord Academy in Massachusetts, where he has served for a number of years as Chairman of the English Department. He earned his B.A. at Oberlin College in Ohio, and he received a Master's Degree and First Class Honors in English Literature at Cambridge University in England. Mr. McFarland has published a novel and is the co-author of several high-school textbooks in both composition and literature.

**Frances Feagin** is a teacher of English at Albany High School in Albany, Georgia. She received her B.A. and M.Ed. from Mercer University in Macon, Georgia. She has had extensive teaching experience at the secondary level, including five years as Supervisor of English, and has been involved in the continuing study and revision of local curricula.

**Samuel Hay** is Director of the Africana Studies and Research Center at Purdue University in Indiana. A graduate of Bethune-Cookman College, he received an M.A. from Johns Hopkins University and a Ph.D. from Cornell University. He has taught English, Drama, and Speech at high schools in Florida and Maryland. Dr. Hay is a playwright and the author of numerous articles on black literature.

**Stella S.F. Liu** is an Associate Professor of Education at Wayne State University in Detroit, Michigan. Dr. Liu received her B.A. from Yenching University in China and her Ph.D. from the University of California at Berkeley; she is a recipient of an outstanding dissertation award from the International Reading Association. Dr. Liu has had extensive experience as a teacher, reading specialist, and reading coordinator at both the elementary and secondary levels.

**Frank McLaughlin,** co-founder and editor of *Media and Methods* magazine, is an Associate Professor at Fairleigh Dickinson University in New Jersey. A graduate of St. Joseph's College in Philadelphia, Mr. McLaughlin received his M.A. from Villanova University. Formerly an English teacher and department chairman, he continues to work in high schools as coordinator of teaching interns. He has written numerous articles for *Media and Methods* and other publications.

**Norma Willson** is Chairwoman of the English Department at West High School in Torrance, California. A graduate of Kansas State College, she received an M.A. from the University of Southern California. She is a frequent speaker at national and state conferences on topics relating to the image of women in society and education, particularly in textbooks.

**Marcella Johnson** is Instructional Supervisor and Specialist in Communication Skills for the Instructional Planning Division of the Los Angeles Unified School District. As consultant for the Focus on Literature Series, she reviewed the selections written by and about members of minority groups.

# ConTenTs

## MYSTERY & SUSPENSE

# ANIMALS

# ACTION & BRAVERY

# CONFLICTS

# MYTHS & TALES

# TURNING POINTS

MYSTERY & SUSPENSE

Harry came into the motel room as I was putting my shoulder holster on. "Forget it, Ralph," he said.

I looked at him. "Forget it? What do you mean, forget it?"

He took off his coat and tossed it on the bed. "The bank's closed," he said.

"It can't be closed," I said. "This is Tuesday."

"Wrong," he said. He flipped his automatic out of his holster and tossed it on the bed. "It can be closed," he said. "Everything can be closed. This is Griffin's Day."

"This is *what's* Day?"

"Griffin's," he said. He shrugged out of his shoulder holster and tossed it on the bed. "Kenny Griffin's Day," he said.

"I give up," I said. "What's a Kenny Griffin?"

"Astronaut," he said. He opened his shirt collar and tossed himself onto the bed. "Comes from this burg," he said. "It's his Homecoming Day. They're having a big parade for him."

"By the bank?" I asked.

"What difference?" He moved his automatic out from under his hip, adjusted his pillow, and shut his eyes. "The bank's closed anyway," he said.

I cocked my head, and from far away I heard band music. "Well, if that isn't nice," I said.

"They're gonna give him the key to the city," Harry said.

"That is real nice," I said.

"Speeches, and little kids giving him flowers."

"That's so nice I can't stand it," I said.

"He was in orbit," Harry said.

"He should of stayed in orbit," I said.

"So we'll do it tomorrow," said Harry.

"I know," I said. "But it's just irritating."

It was more irritating to me than to Harry, because, after all, I was the planner. I hated it when a plan went wrong or had to be changed around, no matter how minor the change. Like planning a caper on Tuesday and having to do it on Wednesday instead. A small alteration, an unimportant shift, but we'd have to stay in this town one day longer than expected, which increased the chances of identification at some later date. We'd have to change our airline reservations, which maybe some smart clerk would think about afterward. We'd show up at the Miami hotel a day late, which would tend to make us conspicuous there, too. Nothing vital, sure, nothing desperate, but it only takes a tiny leak to sink a mighty battle-ship. I remember reading that on a poster once when I was a kid, and it made a big impression on me.

I am the natural planner type. I had cased this bank and this town for three weeks *before* making my plan, and then for another five days *after* it was set. I worked out just the right method, the right time, the right getaway, the right everything.

The one thing I didn't work out was one of those astro-nauts hailing from this town and deciding on *my* day he'll come on back again. As I later said to Harry, why couldn't he of just phoned?

So we did it on Wednesday. We went to the bank at pre-cisely two fifty-four, flipped the masks up over our faces, and announced, "This is a stickup. Everybody freeze."

Everybody froze. While I watched the people and the door, Harry went behind the counter and started filling the bag.

Actually, Wednesday worked just as well as Tuesday so far as the mechanics of the plan were concerned. On all three mid-week days, Tuesday and Wednesday and Thursday, all but three of the bank employees were at lunch at two fifty-four P.M., having to take a later-than-normal lunch because the bank was at its busiest during usual lunch hours. On the days I had checked it, there had never been any more than three customers here at this time, and the average had been only slightly over one. Today, for instance, there was just one, a small and elderly lady who carried an umbrella despite the bright sun outside.

The rest of the plan would work as well on Wednesday as on Tuesday, too. The traffic lights I'd timed worked the same every day of the week, the plane schedule out at the airport was the same as yesterday, and the traffic we could expect on the Belt Highway was no different, either. Still, I did hate to have things changed on me.

Harry was done filling the bag at one minute to three, which was a full minute ahead of time. We both stood by the door and waited, and when the second hand was done with its sweep once more, Harry put his gun away, flipped his mask off, picked up the bag and went out to where we'd parked the stolen Ford in front of the fire hydrant.

I now had forty seconds. I was looking everywhere at once, at my watch, at the three employees and the little old lady customer and at Harry out front in the Ford. If he didn't manage to get it started in time, we'd have to wait another minute and ten seconds.

But he did. After thirty-one seconds he gave me the sign. I nodded, let nine more seconds go by and dashed out of the bank. Eighteen running paces while I stuffed the gun away and stripped off the mask, and then I was in the car and it was rolling.

There was a traffic light at the corner. "Twenty-two miles an hour," I said, looking at that light, seeing it red down there in front of us.

"I know," said Harry. "Don't worry, I know."

The light turned green just as we reached the intersection. We sailed on through. I looked back, and saw people just erupting from the bank.

Midway down this block there was an alley on the right that led through to the next block. Harry made the turn, smooth and sweet, into a space hardly any wider than our car, and ahead of us was the MG. Harry hit the brakes, I grabbed the bag, and we jumped out of the Ford. Harry opened the Ford's hood and grabbed a handful of wires and yanked. Then he shut the hood and ran to the MG.

I was already in it, putting on the beard and the sunglasses and the cap and the yellow turtleneck sweater. Harry put on his beard and sunglasses and beret and green sports jacket. He started the engine, I stared at the second hand of my watch.

"Five," I said. "Four. Three. Two. One. Go!"

We shot out of the alley, turned left, made the light just before it went to red, turned right, made the lights perfectly for three blocks, then hit the Schuyler Avenue ramp to the Belt Highway.

"You watch the signs," Harry said. "I'll watch the traffic."

"Naturally," I said.

Almost every city has one of these by-pass highways now, a belt that makes a complete circuit of the city. Not only can travelers passing through use it to avoid getting involved in city traffic, but local citizens can use it for high-speed routing from one part of the city to the other. This one, called the Belt Highway, was an elevated road all the way around, giving a fine view of the town and the countryside.

But it was neither the town nor the surrounding country-

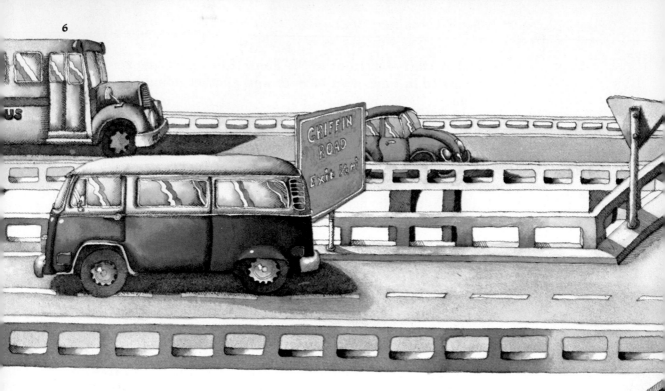

side I was interested in at the moment. Right now my primary concern was the Airport Road exit. As Harry steered us through the light midweek afternoon traffic, I watched the signs.

One thing I have to admit, they did put up plenty of signs. Like for the first exit we came to, which was called Callisto Street Exit. First there was a sign that said, "Callisto Street Exit, ¼ Mile." A little after that, there was a sign that said, "Callisto Street Exit, Keep Right." And then finally, at the exit itself, a sign with an arrow pointing to the down-ramp and the words, "Callisto Street Exit."

Of course, all of this was mostly geared for local citizens, so there wasn't any sign telling you where Callisto Street itself might take you, but if you knew it was Callisto Street you wanted, there wasn't a chance in the world that you'd miss it.

Harry buzzed us along in the white MG, just exactly at the fifty-mile-an-hour speed limit, and I watched the exits go by, with the standard three signs for each one: Woodford Road, Eagle Avenue, Griffin Road, Crowell Street, Five Mile Road, Esquire Avenue. . . .

I looked at my watch. I said, "Harry, are you going too slow? You're supposed to go fifty."

Harry was insulted; he prides himself on being one of the best drivers in the business. "I *am* going fifty," he said, and gestured for me to take a look at the speedometer myself.

But I was too intent on watching for signs. Airport Road I wanted; Airport Road. I said, "It shouldn't be taking anywhere near *this* long, I know."

"I'm doing fifty—and I *been* doing fifty."

I looked at my watch, then back out at the highway. "Maybe the speedometer's busted. Maybe you're only doing forty."

"I'm doing fifty," Harry said. "I can *tell.* I know what fifty feels like, and I'm doing fifty."

"If we miss that plane," I said, "we're in trouble."

"We won't miss it," said Harry grimly, and hunched over the wheel.

"The cops will be asking questions all around the neighborhood back there now," I said. "Sooner or later they'll find somebody that saw this car come out of the alley. Sooner or later they'll be looking for us in *this* car and with *these* descriptions."

"You just watch the signs," said Harry.

So I watched the signs. Remsen Avenue, De Witt Boulevard, Green Meadow Park, Seventeenth Street, Glenwood Road, Powers Street. . . .

Harry said, "You must of missed it."

I said, "Impossible. I've read every sign. Every sign. Your speedometer's off."

"It isn't."

Earhart Street, Willoughby Lane, Firewall Avenue, Broad Street, Marigold Hill Road. . . .

I looked at my watch. "Our plane just took off," I said.

"You keep looking at your watch," Harry said. "That's how come you missed it."

"I did not miss it," I said.

"Here comes Schuyler Avenue again," he said. "Isn't that where we got on?"

"How did I miss it?" I cried. "Hurry, Harry! We'll get it this time! They'll have a plane going *somewhere!*"

Harry crouched over the steering wheel.

They stopped us halfway around the circuit again. Some smart cop had seen us—the description was out by now, of course—and radioed in, and they set up a nice little road block across their elevated highway, and we drove right around to it and stopped, and they put the arm on us.

As I was riding in the back of a police car, going in the opposite direction of the Belt now, I asked the detective I was handcuffed to, "Do you mind telling me what you did with Airport Road?"

He grinned at me and pointed out the window, saying, "There it is."

The sign he pointed at said, "Griffin Road, ¼ Mile."

I said, "Griffin Road? I wanted *Airport* Road."

"That's it," he said. "We changed the name yesterday, in honor of Kenny Griffin. You know, the astronaut. We're all real proud of Kenny around here."

"I better not say anything against him then," I said.

DISCUSSION

1. In what ways does the return of Kenny Griffin to his hometown set up obstacles to the scheme of Harry and Ralph?

2. The mood of the narrator, Ralph, who tells the story, is calm. How does his mood add to the effectiveness of the story?

3. **Plot.** The arrangement of events in a story is called the plot. It is the bare outline of what happens in the order that each event occurs. What are the important events in this story; in other words, what is the plot?

For further activities, see page 24.

# The Dinner Party

MONA GARDNER

The country is India. A colonial official and his wife are giving a large dinner party. They are seated with their guests—army officers and government attachés and their wives, and a visiting American naturalist—in their spacious dining room, which has a bare marble floor, open rafters, and wide glass doors opening onto a veranda.

A spirited discussion springs up between a young girl who insists that women have outgrown the jumping-on-a-chair-at-the-sight-of-a-mouse era and a colonel who says that they haven't.

"A woman's unfailing reaction in any crisis," the colonel says, "is to scream. And while a man may feel like it, he has that ounce more of nerve control than a woman has. And that last ounce is what counts."

The American does not join in the argument but watches the other guests. As he looks, he sees a strange expression come over the face of the hostess. She is staring straight ahead, her muscles contracting slightly. With a slight gesture she summons the servant standing behind her chair and whispers to him. The servant's eyes widen, and he quickly leaves the room.

Of the guests, none except the American notices this or sees the servant place a bowl of milk on the veranda just outside the open doors.

The American comes to with a start. In India, milk in a bowl means only one thing—bait for a snake. He realizes there must be a cobra in the room. He looks up at the rafters—the likeliest place—but they are bare. Three corners of the room are empty, and in the fourth the servants are waiting to serve the next course. There is only one place left—under the table.

His first impulse is to jump back and warn the others, but he knows the commotion would frighten the cobra into striking. He speaks quickly, the tone of his voice so arresting that it sobers everyone.

"I want to know just what control everyone at this table has. I will count three hundred—that's five minutes—and not one of you is to move a muscle. Those who move will forfeit fifty rupees. Ready!"

The twenty people sit like stone images while he counts. He is saying ". . . two hundred and eighty . . ." when, out of the corner of his eye, he sees the cobra emerge and make for the bowl of milk. Screams ring out as he jumps to slam the veranda doors safely shut.

"You were right, Colonel!" the host exclaims. "A man has just shown us an example of perfect control."

"Just a minute," the American says, turning to his hostess. "Mrs. Wynnes, how did you know that cobra was in the room?"

A faint smile lights up the woman's face as she replies: "Because it was crawling across my foot."

DISCUSSION

1.   How does the hostess Mrs. Wynnes show greater self-control than the American naturalist?

2.   At what point in the story do you know where the cobra is?

3.   The colonel's line "a woman's unfailing reaction in any crisis is to scream" (page 11) is a generalization. It assumes that *all* women react the way he has perhaps seen *one* woman react. How does this false generalization help to emphasize later events in the story?

4.   Setting.   The setting of a story is the time and place where the action takes place. How important is the setting in this story? For example, would a setting in a New York apartment at the present time be equally effective for this story?

# THE MIDNIGHT VISITOR

## ELSIE KATTERJOHN

CHARACTERS:    ADAMS, an American secret agent    MAX, a foreign agent
                   FOWLER, a young American writer    HENRI, a Frenchman

THE SCENE    A small, sixth-floor room in a gloomy hotel in Paris. The room is dark except for a shaft of light from a partly open transom above the door to the hall at stage right. The dim light reveals the usual collection of shabby hotel-room furniture. At stage left are two doors: one at left center is closed and blocked off by a desk placed squarely against it; the closet door at lower left is slightly ajar. At upper center are shabby velveteen curtains that hide all but a narrow vertical strip of the window behind. Traffic noises from the street six stories below sound faintly in the background.

THE TIME    The present. It is nearly midnight.

       As the curtains open, a dark figure moves stealthily about the room. He holds a small flashlight which he shines into the closet, among the papers on the desk, and into the chest of drawers across the room. After a moment, footsteps and voices are heard in the hall. Suddenly alert, the dark figure snaps off his flashlight. His form is seen once against the darker black of the window; then he disappears into the closet.
       Through the open transom is heard a jingling of keys. As the door opens, Adams is talking. He wheezes as he talks.

ADAMS [ushering his companion into the room ahead of him]: Of course you are disappointed! You were told that I was a secret agent, a spy—that I deal in espionage and danger. You wanted to meet me because you are a writer—and young and romantic. [He presses a light switch inside the door. When the stage is lighted, Adams is seen to be very fat and his wrinkled business suit is badly in need of cleaning. He looks anything but a secret agent.] No doubt you expected mysterious figures in the night, the crack of pistols, maybe even drugs in the wine. [Closing the door, he chuckles at the embarrassment of his guest, a good-looking, neatly dressed young man who seems more boyish than his 28 years.]

FOWLER: No, not really. Well—[with a self-conscious laugh] a couple of mysterious figures, maybe.

ADAMS [tossing his battered hat onto the bed]: Instead, you have spent a dull evening in a second-rate music hall with a sloppy fat man.

FOWLER [protesting]: Oh, it wasn't so bad.

ADAMS: And do I get messages slipped furtively into my hand by dark-eyed beauties? On the contrary, all I get is one ordinary telephone call making an appointment in my room. Admit it, my friend, you have been bored.

FOWLER: No, not bored—just a bit——

ADAMS: Ah yes, you are completely disillusioned. An evening wasted and you have nothing to write about—not even a small paragraph to put into that notebook of yours. [Fowler looks at notebook he is still holding in his hand, smiles sheepishly, and puts it into his pocket.] But take cheer, my friend. After all, this is Paris. You may yet see some drama tonight.

But come—see my view—even from a shabby hotel room on the sixth floor it is still quite a view. [He walks to window and pulls open the draperies a few more inches. The night presses blackly against the glass.] Oh, too bad, the fog is even thicker now. But still you can make out the Eiffel tower in the distance there. [Chuckling] Even a foggy night in Paris is better than a clear night in Des Moines, no?

FOWLER [taking a few steps toward the window and glancing only briefly at the distant view]: Mr. Adams, excuse me if I am prying, but—you mentioned—well—that phone call. . . .

ADAMS: Ah, Mr. Fowler, you are observant. Very observant. And such devotion to your work shall not go unrewarded. Was that phone call important? Yes, my friend, it was very important. That is why we have cut short a bit our evening on the town, and why, in fact, I have brought you back here with me. Perhaps I will show you that I do not waste my time completely. Yes, the call had to do with a certain paper—a very important paper—for which several men have risked their lives. You shall see this paper presently. It will come to me here in the next-to-last step of its journey into official hands. [Confidentially] You realize, of course, that I could not let you witness this event if it were not for your uncle's very persuasive letter. But how can one disappoint a dear old friend? [Closing the draperies and returning to a position down center] Some day soon this paper may well affect the course of history. Now in this thought there is drama, is there not?

Suddenly the door to the closet opens and out steps a man with a small automatic in his hand. He is slender, not very tall, and his rather pointed features suggest the crafty expression of a fox.

ADAMS: Max!

MAX [speaking with an indefinable European accent]: Good evening, Mr. Adams.

ADAMS [wheezing]: Max, you gave me a start! I thought you were in Berlin. What are you doing here? [He backs away.]

MAX: I was in Berlin, yes. But I, too, had a telephone call—earlier in the week. So here I am. I will have your weapon, please. [Adams puts on a look of innocence.] Your gun, please, which I know you are never without. Give it to me. [Adams shrugs, hands over gun he takes from shoulder holster. Fowler looks amazed, not having suspected that Adams was armed.] Thank you. Now—the report—[Again Adams pretends innocence.] The report on our new missiles that is being delivered to you tonight? [With exaggerated politeness] We merely thought it would be safer in our hands than in yours.

ADAMS: But—even I didn't know until the phone call tonight—[He smiles weakly, then shrugs.] Well, you always were known for your timing——

MAX [with a tight smile]: Just so. Please sit down. We may as well be comfortable. You, too, young man. [He shrewdly appraises Fowler, who remains standing, still dazed at the turn of events.]

ADAMS [backs to armchair at center stage and sinks down heavily]: Max, I just can't get over your being *here.* [To Fowler] As you may have gathered, Max and I have known each other a long time. In fact, I might say [glances at Max] we are old business associates. [Fowler smiles nervously, nods.] Max, I'm sorry not to be more hospitable, but I can't say I am exactly happy to see you. The last time we met—two years ago, wasn't it? In Geneva? [Adams is obviously playing for time.] I was expecting you then—but now—why, I don't even have comfortable accommodations to offer you—certainly nothing like that delightful little villa in Geneva. You remember it—the one with the stained glass windows and the balconies?

MAX: Yes, I recall your hospitality at that villa—including the gendarmes.[1] Thank you! But this room will serve for our transaction.

ADAMS: Oh, well, I suppose the quarters [Indicating room] are adequate, but really, the management here is impossible! [To Fowler] I was assured—*assured* that this hotel was safe, and yet this is the second time in a month—the *second* time, mind you—that somebody has gotten into my room off that confounded balcony!

MAX: Balcony? No [taking key from pocket and holding it up], I used a passkey. I did not know about the balcony. It might have saved me some trouble had I known.

ADAMS [in surprise and irritation]: A passkey? A passkey! Well, that is the limit. Max, I'm truly annoyed. I expected the balcony, but a passkey—why, this is ridiculous. At least the balcony called for a little ingenu-

---

[1] *gendarmes* (zhän'därmz): French police.

ity. The ironic thing is that it is not even my balcony. It belongs to the next apartment. [Glancing toward Fowler] This room,
you see, used to be part of a larger unit, and that door there
[Indicates sealed door] used to connect with the living room. *It* had
the balcony, which extends under *my* window, too. You can get
onto it from the empty room two doors down—and someone
did, last month. Nothing was lost that time—but the management promised me they would block it off. [Shrugs wearily.] But
they haven't done it. No matter, I guess——

MAX: As you say, no matter. [Glancing at Fowler, who stands stiffly a few feet from Adams, Max
waves the gun with a commanding gesture.] Please sit down. [Fowler
perches on edge of bed.] We have a wait of half an hour at least, I
think.

ADAMS: Thirty-one minutes. The appointment was for twelve-thirty. [Moodily] I
wish I knew how you learned about that report, Max.

MAX [smiling, but only with his mouth]: I may say, the interest is mutual. We would like
to know how the report was gotten out of our country. How-
ever, no harm has been done. I will have it back.

There is a sudden rapping on the door. Fowler jumps.

MAX [sharply]: Who——?

ADAMS [calmly]: The gendarmes. I thought that so important a paper as the one we
are waiting for might well be given a little extra protection tonight—from the police.

MAX [in an angry whisper, flourishing the gun]: You—! [Bites his lip uncertainly as the rapping is
repeated.]

ADAMS: What will you do now, Max? If I do not answer, they have instructions to
enter anyway. The door is unlocked. And they will not hesitate
to shoot. [Max starts toward closet door.] Nor will they neglect to
search the room. You would be quite a prize for. . . .

MAX [interrupting in a sharp whisper]: Quiet!

His face twisted with rage, Max has been glancing about the room. He abruptly changes direction and
backs swiftly toward window at upper center. The gun in his right hand is still leveled at the other two.
With his left arm, he reaches behind him and pushes open the window. Then he swings his left leg
over the sill. The street noises are louder now.

MAX: Don't move till I'm gone! You have outsmarted me this time—but we
haven't seen the last of each other, I think! [Smugly] So thoughtful of you to inform me of this convenient exit. Au revoir![2]

The rapping on the door becomes louder, more insistent.

---

[2] *Au revoir* (ō rə-vwár'): French, until we meet again; good-bye.

HENRI [from outside]: M'sieu![3] M'sieu Adams!

Max, who has twisted his body so that his gun still covers the fat man and his guest, grasps the window frame with his left hand and then swings his right leg up and over the sill. He pushes free with his left hand and drops out of sight.

Adams' body relaxes visibly. With seeming casualness, he goes to the window and closes it, then crosses the room and opens the door.

ADAMS: Ah, Henri——[A waiter enters with a tray on which are a bottle and two glasses.]

HENRI: Pardon, M'sieu, the cognac you ordered for when you returned. [He sets the tray on a small table and deftly uncorks the bottle.]

ADAMS: Merci, Henri. [Hands him a coin.]

HENRI: Merci, M'sieu. [He leaves.]

FOWLER [staring after him, stammering]: But—the police—

ADAMS: There were no police. Only Henri, whom I was expecting.

FOWLER: But the man on the balcony—Max—won't he—?

ADAMS: No, he will not return. [He reaches for the bottle of cognac.] You see, my young friend, there is no balcony.

Fowler stands frozen as the meaning of this last statement sinks in; then he dashes to the window, flings it open, and looks down. Among the street noises that filter up through the open window, an ambulance siren rises and grows steadily louder.

ADAMS [filling the glasses]: Come, have your drink. Maybe now, after all, you have something to write about.

He raises his glass as the CURTAINS CLOSE.

[3] *M'sieu* (mə-syœ'): from the French *Monsieur,* mister or sir.

DISCUSSION

1.   The battle of wits between Adams and Max increases the suspense in the play. Mention two or three instances that would seem to give the advantage to Max. For example, Max takes possession of Adams's gun.

2.   Although the main action concerns Max and Adams, in what ways is Fowler an important character?

3.   **Surprise ending.**   A surprise ending is one that the reader does not expect. When Adams says, "You see, my young friend, there is no balcony," the reader is as surprised as Fowler was. What other clue does Adams give that leads the reader to think that Max will be successful in his attempts to steal the reports on new missiles?

For further activities, see page 24.

# Eldorado

EDGAR ALLAN POE

Gaily bedight,
A gallant knight
In sunshine and in shadow
Had journeyed long,
Singing a song,                                    5
In search of Eldorado.

But he grew old—
This knight so bold—
And o'er his heart a shadow
Fell, as he found                                  10
No spot of ground
That looked like Eldorado.

And, as his strength
Failed him at length,
He met a pilgrim shadow:                            15
"Shadow," said he,
"Where can it be—
This land of Eldorado?"

"Over the mountains
Of the moon,                                       20
Down the valley of the Shadow
Ride, boldly ride,"
The shade replied,
"If you seek Eldorado!"

*Eldorado:* legendary city of great wealth in Spanish
America; any place of abundance, wealth, or opportunity.    1.  *bedight:* dressed.

DISCUSSION

1.   This poem shows a lifelong search. What is the knight seeking?
Does he succeed in his quest?

2.   At about what age is the knight in each section? Find a descriptive
line in each that expresses the mood of the knight at that particular period in his life.

Ghost ships have fascinated men of the sea since ancient times. Stories about them range from the ghastly to the humorous, like most other ghost stories. The ones that seem most intriguing, however, are not those about doom and terror, but about life and hope, especially when they come out of a war.

During the Second World War sailors in the Pacific theater of operations often went on such long and lonely voyages that after a time it seemed as though they would never come home again. The unlucky ones never did. Generally, ships sailed in long convoys, merchant ship after merchant ship, like trains of vessels on the water strung out almost as far as the eye could see. Occasionally, however, they sailed alone. It was dangerous, for a single, unescorted vessel could easily be picked off by an enemy submarine or bomber, and disappear without a trace. One such ship that we will call here the *S/S Mallory Knight* not only succeeded in eluding the enemy, but was once saved from destruction by the ghost of another ship.

It happend in the Southwest Pacific. The *S/S Mallory Knight,* being a fairly fast ship, was ordered to carry a vital cargo of electronic equipment to a secret destination in the Philippine Islands. As they approached South Point, a treacherous area off Guimaras Island, the captain was forced to stop the engines and remain outside the barrier reefs until he could check his bearings and make certain of a safe passage through the treacherous Guimara Straits. They dared not show any lights, radio silence was a necessity, and yet it was not wise to remain stationary for too long a time.

Unfortunately, the chart for that particular area was missing. The captain was faced with a

# The Light at South Point

### EDWARD ROWE SNOW

choice. He could proceed slowly, hoping against hope that he did not rip out the bottom on jagged reefs just beneath the surface of the sea, or he could wait until daybreak and take visual soundings. Either way he was in trouble. As he paced the bridge, desperately trying to make up his mind, the second mate came running in from the starboard wing. He had incredible news. A ship beyond South Point had blinked a message to them, providing all the coordinates for a safe passage through. "Thank God!" exclaimed the skipper. "Acknowledge the message and ask her to identify herself."

A few minutes later the mate returned and said that the ship was English. She was the *Regent Panther* out of Liverpool. This was duly noted in the log book, then the captain rang Slow Speed Ahead on the engine telegraph, and personally stood wheel watch until the *S/S Mallory Knight* was safely through South Point.

By the time they had successfully negotiated the passage it was dawn and, of course, the *Regent Panther* was nowhere to be seen. But it was not until months later, after the voyage had been completed, that the captain of the *S/S Mallory Knight* learned the whole truth of how he had been saved. He was in New York having dinner with several other captains, one of whom happened to be English. After hearing the story about the passage through South Point, the Englishman frowned and asked, "When did you say that happened?"

"Last fall, just before we sailed back to San Francisco. Why do you ask?"

"Well," replied the English captain politely, "I'm afraid you've got your information wrong. Last fall was still 1943. And I happen to know that the *Regent Panther* sank off South Point twenty years ago. You see, my father was her skipper, and he went down with all hands."

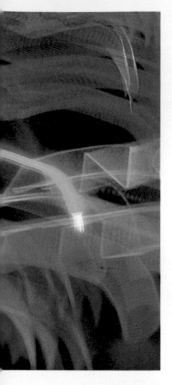

## VOCABULARY

### Just One of Those Days (page 2)

Good authors choose exact words to convey the appropriate mood, or feeling. Substitute a verb for each of the verbs in bold type in these sentences that *changes* the effect of the sentence. For example, "I *accepted* the chance" lacks the enthusiasm of "I *jumped* at the chance." On separate paper, write your sentences with the new verbs and be ready to explain the change in mood.

1. "Wrong," he said. He *flipped* his automatic out of his holster and tossed it on the bed.
2. "Griffin's," he said. He *shrugged* out of his shoulder holster and tossed it on the bed.
3. I *cocked* my head, and from far away I heard band music.
4. I am the natural planner type. I had *cased* this bank and this town for three weeks.
5. The light turned green just as we reached the intersection. We *sailed* on through.

### The Midnight Visitor (page 13)

In writing a play, the dramatist gives directions that will help the character to speak the written lines in a specific manner. *Speak* and *act* the following line: "So here I am. I will have your weapon, please" in two different ways. In one version you might be determined; in another, uncertain.

Following are directions for acting and/or speaking. Try each, making up whatever words you need.

1. answer a question with *a self-conscious laugh*
2. answer a question by *protesting*
3. look at something in your hand and *smile sheepishly*
4. *look innocent*
5. *smile weakly*

## COMPOSITION

### Just One of Those Days (page 2)

Rewrite one section of the story, changing the calm, assured mood of Harry and Ralph. The part beginning with "It was irritating" and ending with "Why couldn't he just of phoned?" would be a good one (page 4).

## The Midnight Visitor (page 13)

Fowler is a "young and romantic" writer (page 13). Imagine that you are in his place and write a paragraph or two describing the impression that Adams makes on him. Remember that he is somewhat disappointed with Adams as a secret agent—until the very end of the play.

## READING

### Just One of Those Days (page 2)

Ralph thought he had planned everything in detail for the bank robbery. On separate paper, list the numbers of the items in which his information is correct.

1. Ralph knew the bank was closed for Griffin's Day.
2. He knew Tuesday was Kenny Griffin's day.
3. He knew who Kenny Griffin was.
4. He had cased the bank before the robbery.
5. He had timed the traffic lights.
6. He knew how long the traffic light would be red.
7. He knew where Airport Road exit was.
8. He knew Airport Road was changed to Griffin Road.

### The Light at South Point (page 22)

On separate paper, list the number of each event in the order that it appeared in the story.

1. The chart for that area was missing.
2. A ship beyond South Point blinked a message that it was safe to pass.
3. The captain noted the message from the *Regent Panther* in the log book.
4. *S/S Mallory Knight* was ordered to carry a vital cargo to a secret destination in the Philippine Islands.
5. The captain was forced to stop the engines to make certain of a safe passage through the Guimara Straits.
6. The English captain said that the *Regent Panther* had sunk off South Point twenty years ago.
7. They came through the passage safely and the *Regent Panther* was nowhere to be seen.
8. The captain learned the truth of the *Regent Panther* months later.
9. The ship identified herself as the *Regent Panther*.

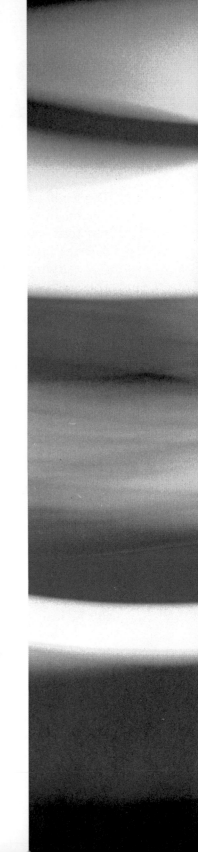

# The Highwayman

ALFRED NOYES

PART ONE

The wind was a torrent of darkness among the gusty trees,
The moon was a ghostly galleon tossed upon cloudy seas,
The road was a ribbon of moonlight over the purple moor,
And the highwayman came riding—
    Riding—riding—    5
The highwayman came riding, up to the old inn-door.

He'd a French cocked hat on his forehead, a bunch of lace at his chin,
A coat of the claret velvet, and breeches of brown doeskin;
They fitted with never a wrinkle, his boots were up to the thigh.
And he rode with a jeweled twinkle,    10
    His pistol butts a-twinkle,
His rapier hilt a-twinkle, under the jeweled sky.

Over the cobbles he clattered and clashed, in the dark innyard.
He tapped with his whip on the shutters, but all was locked and barred.
He whistled a tune to the window, and who should be waiting there    15
But the landlord's black-eyed daughter,
    Bess, the landlord's daughter,
Plaiting a dark red love-knot into her long black hair.

And dark in the dark old innyard, a stable-wicket creaked
Where Tim the ostler listened. His face was white and peaked;    20
His eyes were hollows of madness, his hair like moldy hay;
But he loved the landlord's daughter,
    The landlord's red-lipped daughter.
Dumb as a dog he listened, and he heard the robber say,

"One kiss, my bonny sweetheart. I'm after a prize tonight,    25
But I shall be back with the yellow gold before the morning light;
Yet, if they press me sharply and harry me through the day,
Then look for me by moonlight,

2. *galleon:* ship of the fifteenth and sixteenth centuries.  19. *stable-wicket:* stable-gate.  20. *ostler:* stableman.

Watch for me by moonlight,

I'll come to thee by moonlight, though hell should bar the way!"    30

He rose upright in the stirrups; he scarce could reach her hand,
But she loosened her hair in the casement! His face burnt like a brand
As the black cascade of perfume came tumbling over his breast,
And he kissed its waves in the moonlight

(O sweet black waves in the moonlight!);    35

Then he tugged at his rein in the moonlight and galloped away to the west.


PART TWO

He did not come in the dawning; he did not come at noon.
And out of the tawny sunset, before the rise of the moon,
When the road was a gypsy's ribbon, looping the purple moor,
A redcoat troop came marching—    40

Marching—marching—

King George's men came marching, up to the old inn-door.

They said no word to the landlord; they drank his ale instead;
But they gagged his daughter and bound her to the foot of her narrow bed.
Two of them knelt at her casement, with muskets at their side.    45
There was death at every window,

And hell at one dark window,

For Bess could see through her casement the road that *he* would ride.

They had bound her up to attention, with many a sniggering jest;
They had bound a musket beside her, with the muzzle beneath her breast.    50
"Now keep good watch!" and they kissed her. She heard the dead man say,
*Look for me by moonlight,*

*Watch for me by moonlight,*

*I'll come to thee by moonlight, though hell should bar the way!*

She twisted her hands behind her, but all the knots held good.    55
She writhed her hands till her fingers were wet with sweat or blood.
They stretched and strained in the darkness, and the hours crawled by like years,
Till now, on the stroke of midnight,

Cold on the stroke of midnight,

The tip of one finger touched it! The trigger at least was hers!    60

---

32. *casement:* hinged windows opening outward; *brand:* firebrand, a flaming piece of wood.

The tip of one finger touched it; she strove no more for the rest!
Up she stood to attention, with the muzzle beneath her breast.
She would not risk their hearing; she would not strive again;
For the road lay bare in the moonlight,
      Blank and bare in the moonlight,                            65
And the blood of her veins in the moonlight throbbed to her love's refrain.

*Tlot-tlot, tlot-tlot!* Had they heard it? The horse-hoofs ringing clear!
*Tlot-tlot, tlot-tlot* in the distance! Were they deaf that they did not hear?
Down the ribbon of moonlight, over the brow of the hill,
The highwayman came riding—                                  70
      Riding—riding—
The redcoats looked to their priming! She stood up, straight and still.

*Tlot-tlot* in the frosty silence! *Tlot-tlot* in the echoing night!
Nearer he came and nearer! Her face was like a light.
Her eyes grew wide for a moment; she drew one last deep breath.            75
Then her finger moved in the moonlight,
      Her musket shattered the moonlight,
Shattered her breast in the moonlight, and warned him—with her death.

72. *priming:* preparing guns for firing.

He turned; he spurred to the west; he did not know who stood
Bowed, with her head o'er the musket, drenched with her own blood.  80
Not till the dawn he heard it, and his face grew gray to hear
How Bess, the landlord's daughter,
    The landlord's black-eyed daughter,
Had watched for her love in the moonlight, and died in the darkness there.

Back he spurred like a madman, shouting a curse to the sky,  85
With the white road smoking behind him and his rapier brandished high!
Blood-red were his spurs in the golden noon, wine-red was his velvet coat,
When they shot him down on the highway,
    Down like a dog on the highway,
And he lay in his blood on the highway, with a bunch of lace at his throat.  90

*And still of a winter's night, they say, when the wind is in the trees,*
*When the moon is a ghostly galleon tossed upon cloudy seas,*
*When the road is a ribbon of moonlight over the purple moor,*
*A highwayman comes riding—*
    *Riding—riding—*  95
*A highwayman comes riding, up to the old inn-door.*

*Over the cobbles he clatters and clangs, in the dark innyard.*
*He taps with his whip on the shutters, but all is locked and barred.*
*He whistles a tune to the window, and who should be waiting there*
*But the landlord's black-eyed daughter,*  100
    *Bess, the landlord's daughter,*
*Plaiting a dark red love-knot into her long black hair.*

**DISCUSSION**   1.  Bess warns the highwayman "with her death" (line 78). How did the highwayman react when he learned of her sacrifice?

2.  Lines 91–102 repeat much that is given in lines 1–18. Why do you think the author began and ended the poem in the same way? Why did he choose a different style of type for the end?

For further activities, see page 59.

# MOONLIGHT — STARLIGHT

## VIRGINIA LAYEFSKY

The genesis of the idea for the party was in an old Halloween costume Anne Carey found packed in a box in the attic. It had been made thirty years ago for a seven-year-old Anne by her mother. She had been a woman who threw nothing away.

After Anne inherited the large Victorian spaces her mother had swept and garnished most of her life, she often came upon pieces of her own life—up until her marriage at least—neatly labeled and stored here or there. She was apt to find them on those first days of her husband's occasional absences when she used house cleaning as a balm for initial loneliness.

The costume she found that day was so beautifully sewn and carefully packed that its state of preservation was remarkable. When she shook out its folds, the coins which her mother had sewn individually on the bodice long ago clinked with a special sound that set up a painful little echo of disappointment in her forgetful heart. Though she remembered clearly then the smell of chrysanthemums and sewing-machine oil in her mother's room the day the costume was fitted, she could not have said why the sound of the coins oppressed her with such a profound sense of loss.

It had to do with the party she had lost, of course. It was to have been her very own. The games had been planned and the decorations made. Invitations had already been sent when, due to the death by drowning of two small cousins in upstate New York, the party was canceled. The accident had happened the day before they were to leave to visit Anne. She had been broken-hearted, not for the cousins whom she had never seen but for the party which was canceled. In time she was able to forget everything about it but the sense of loss, which persisted unacknowledged up to today when she opened the box to find the costume still waiting there.

And that was the reason why Halloween became the occasion for the only really large children's party Anne Carey ever gave. She made a costume, less carefully done, for her nine-year-old son and dressed her daughter in the gypsy outfit she herself was to have worn long ago.

The party was a resounding success. Children, remembering it, asked her for months afterwards to give another, but she never did. Nor did she tell the reasons why it became the last children's party of any kind that she ever gave. . . .

The arrangements seemed so simple at first. She told her son Bobby he could invite the entire fourth grade with all its younger brothers and sisters.

Games and refreshments were no problem. Now that Anne thought of it, she remembered the entire program of the beautiful party planned long ago. The bobbing for apples, followed by pin-the-tail-on-the-donkey and musical chairs, marched through her mind in a succession almost as orderly and magical now as then. There would be none of the professional entertainment that had figured recently in some of the more ambitious neighborhood parties. What she wanted was a real, old-fashioned Halloween party.

It was something she was to repeat often during the week to the friends who called her with warnings and advice.

Had she a first-aid kit? She would probably need one. And be sure to omit the booby prizes—children who won them were apt to weep, considering them a disgrace.

The warnings began to include, unpleasantly often, the names of the Usher children. Everyone hoped they had not been invited, although on being questioned no one seemed able to tell Anne more than that they were considered strange, the rather menacing unknown quantity in the local algebra of human relationships. They were not much liked by other children.

And then, everyone knew how strange the parents were, living off by themselves as they did, never associating with anyone.

Had she seen the father's work? Gruesome decadent stuff that no one who hadn't a morbid streak would think of painting. And according to rumors, it was just as well they did keep to themselves. It seemed Usher had a sense of humor that, to say the least, was sardonic. It could be, they had heard, very ugly at times.

By that time, however, it was too late. The older child—the girl—was in the fourth grade. She and her brother had been invited along with the rest.

On Halloween Anne with her two children stood in the golden porch light welcoming their guests. The children, in various disguises, began to come shortly after dark. They all seemed to arrive at the same time, coming out of the gloomy, old-fashioned lane like a small army of faceless grotesques. Every child was masked.

For an instant Anne felt invaded by a force of nameless, not necessarily friendly strangers. Only the shadows of parents coming from the obscurity into familiarity assured her that beneath the grinning skull or monstrous face was a dimple or a freckled nose she knew.

The party had become a reality at last. Each adult whispered instructions of various sorts to each small mystery at his side before setting it free to join its wriggling, hopping contemporaries. As they took leave of Anne with compliments and thanks, there was an unmistakable look of relief on most of their departing faces. She had said she could manage alone, even with her husband absent on business for his firm.

By eight o'clock, when the party hats had been passed out, and the last parent had gone, almost everyone who had been invited was there.

The party began in good order. They all pinned the tail on the donkey. Waiting patiently, good-children-all-in-a-line, each child was blindfolded and sent with cardboard tail in hand toward the donkey on the wall. Only one very young black cat—anonymous to Anne—cried because it had pinned its particular tail to the donkey's nose. It was quite easily comforted.

The second game passed gaily, even hilariously. The children unmasked as they went to the big tin washbowl full of apples floating on top of the water that filled it. At the sight of laughter on small faces freed so recently from the horrors which had hidden them from sight, Anne was charmed with a sudden feeling of felicity.

The children, hands held behind their backs, bobbed for the apples. She watched them, holding to her moment with the sweet satisfaction of fulfillment.

Down to the last detail, from the sound of the children's shrill, excited voices to the orange-and-black crepe paper and balloons, the festive smell of candle wax heating the pulpy pumpkins, she had her party at last.

It was well that she held to the moment, listening to the laughter, seeing the children's warm cheeks and tender, perspiring necks, her own daughter's thrilled awareness of her multicolored petticoats. For shortly after that the party began to change.

It started during the next game, which was musical chairs, and at first it was almost imperceptible. Perhaps because it was the third rather strenuous game of the evening, Anne noticed some of the children showing signs of being overtired. Some of the smaller ones' cheeks were too flushed or pale.

They had put the chairs in a row themselves, working rather wildly with some petty wrangling. There were quarrels in the air before they even started. And at the same time, something else, an odd feeling of restlessness and distraction as though their minds were somewhere else.

Watching them march around the chairs, and the way each scrambled for a place once the music stopped, Anne decided she never had liked the game. It demanded a ruthlessness in the end that she found unpleasant, disliking the ultimate winner.

She was glad when it was over and she had settled the children to making funny men and animals out of the marshmallows, gumdrops and toothpicks she had set out on card tables.

A drooping rabbit's ear, a cat's tail hanging from its owner down the back of a chair, a worn sneaker sticking out beneath a ghost's shroud seemed charming to her still. And yet, she felt less delighted than before.

The room became quiet enough for her to hear the children's labored breathing as they concentrated on their efforts. As they reached for the colored candies to fit them awkwardly on the toothpicks, Anne was not able to get rid of the slight depression settling over her. There was that furtive, restless quality creeping about the room as though all the small figures bending over their nonsense were less intent than they pretended to be. There was a sense of shifting, of lifting the head to listen, though no child did these things.

In the near silence she heard the wind rising outside. It was then, too, that she heard the front gate creak as it opened.

No child looked up. As Anne listened for the footsteps which should have sounded on the porch afterward, each child seemed to concentrate more obliviously than before.

When Anne crossed the room to the entrance hall, she felt
she was being watched. It was such a strong feeling she turned
to look back. No one had even seen her go.

Nothing but the wind, rushing into the hall like some be-
lated guest, met her at the open door. Behind it, in darkness
that crept away from the porch light, she could see no one.

It was when her eyes searched the old garden at the side of
the house that she saw them. They were standing by a small
stone sundial Anne's grandfather had set there years ago. A boy
and a girl, hand in hand, they stood looking at her, motionless
as it was.

Not until she called to them inviting them inside did they
move forward. As they came through the dark, up the porch
steps, Anne felt at last how truly starless the night was, how like
these particular parents to send them out alone.

They passed in silence through the door she held open for them. Once inside the hall, they waited, making no move towards the living room, standing always together in their peculiar stillness. Anne, for some reason unknown, not only closed but bolted the door.

They were staring wordlessly up at her when she turned back to them. She found herself struggling with a feeling of aversion for them, since now that they had arrived she realized how relieved she had been earlier at their absence.

The girl was a head taller than her brother, though both were identically costumed. Neither of them was masked, yet it was only one face that both turned to her, the boy's being simply a smaller version of the girl's.

To Anne they had the look of having been drawn by their father instead of procreated in the usual way. She thought she even recognized Usher's personal style in the deliberate exaggeration of line and the faintly corrupt, half-graceful proportions of that face with its twofold glance.

The eyes, in particular, were as overly large as the ones he painted. They were a flat, tobacco brown. It was to the expression in them that she owed her feeling of aversion. For both pairs held a fixed, impersonal intentness that was less unchildlike, she thought, than inhuman.

Still, they were only children, just come to a strange house. Anne, feeling slightly guilty, pointed the way to the living room.

They walked ahead of her, docilely enough, not seeming to notice when Anne, following them, suddenly stopped still. She had noticed at last what they were wearing. She felt a sense of affront, of somehow being publicly insulted. If friends had called Usher's humor unpleasant and sardonic, she had not known up until then what those words could mean. For even to Anne, no authority on such matters, it was obvious he had sent them dressed in costumes representing the grave clothes of children of a past generation. Both wore on their heads wreaths of stiff formal leaves, and were dressed in folds of white cloth from shoulder to foot. The costumes were draped delicately and, from a distance at least, looked as beautifully sewn as her own child's dress. That each detail had the stamp of conscious artistic effort only added to the cynical horror of the idea.

Though the other children looked up as they entered the room, they remained sitting at their tables. Anne, sensing the general withdrawal on their part, came closer to her new guests, intending to reassure them. Close enough to the boy, in fact, to feel she had seen the worst, ultimate point of the joke. For the material of their costumes had the limp suppleness of age. The hand-sewn lace on them was yellow.

After their initial drawing back the children began to speak again, to laugh, get up from the tables and show her what they had made.

They began a game of blindman's bluff. It was not one of the games planned for the evening, but Anne took advantage of it to go away to privacy for a few moments.

She stood alone in the gaily decorated dining room with its rows of shining, waiting plates. She frowned, moving her lips slightly like a child over a mathematics problem, wondering uneasily how the children of such a father might be expected to behave. A need to see what was happening, as urgent as the need for privacy had been a few minutes before, sent her to the door of the room.

What she saw reassured her. The two children, along with the others, crouched, hiding from the blindfolded child who groped after them with outstretched hands. She saw the boy shrink away in his turn from the blindman, giggling softly. His eyes were shining childishly. She reproached herself.

Yet the party was changed. The mood of it began to resemble more nearly the wild "play-outs" of her childhood's summer nights, when the long, soft dusk encouraged a feeling of lawlessness, of perilous emotions, a sort of childish debauch. There was a feverish, tense look on some of their faces.

Anne had gone to the kitchen before the party went out of control. The children had begun to choose their own games by that time, and had been playing a comparatively quiet one when she left the room. It was an ancient game, a sort of ritual she remembered having played herself, known as old witch.

> "I'm going downtown to smoke my pipe
> And I won't be back till Saturday night
> And if you dare let the old witch in
> I'll beat you red—white—and blue!"

A small voice chanted the words behind her as she entered the kitchen. For a time she busied herself pouring cider, warming plates, mentally counting heads, as she concentrated on her own activities.

Until the lights went out.

The entire house was suddenly dark. Someone, she knew, had pulled a switch. When she called out anxiously she was answered by her son's cheerful voice.

They had decided, he called, to play moonlight-starlight.

The name, heard aloud, made a chill run over Anne. She hadn't thought of it for years. As a child it had been the only game she had feared and hated. She felt intolerable anxiety as she wondered, while knowing at once, who had suggested it. The party was out of hand.

She groped across the kitchen to the drawer that held her husband's flashlight, disguising her unreasonable fear with irritation at her son for pulling the switch without permission.

Someone had taken and forgotten to return the flashlight. As she turned away, trying to think where she had put candles, she was remembering against her will the way the game was played.

For moonlight-starlight was an outdoor game, another part of the summer nights. Children played it only after dark.

Anne remembered it well. The child who was "it," the ghost, hid in some dark and secret place. Each child, separate and alone, had to wander in search of it. On finding it they, too, became ghosts. Until at last only one child was left to wander alone, watched by all the secret ghosts, who would, in the end, pounce upon it.

There were no candles. She set out in darkness.

The switch box was located across the living room in an alcove which had been built as a small conservatory with french doors opening into the garden. Even in the blackness of the hall, Anne knew exactly where it was.

The house, except for small sounds and sudden scamperings, was silent. It seemed to take a long time to walk the length of the hall. In darkness the house grew larger, as large as she had thought it as a child. And now, more nearly child than adult, she walked forward with dread.

At any time now "it," changed from the familiar playmate to some nameless horror, could jump suddenly upon her from its hiding place. For, like it or not, she, too, was a player now.

Her hand touched the living-room wall and she groped forward, angry with herself for the way she shrank against it. She had reached the doors leading to the conservatory before she heard the whispering. It came from inside the room and there was a quality in it that froze her motionless, hardly breathing.

For a few seconds her faculties were turned inward on her own pounding heart. It was only gradually, as she realized she had not been noticed, that she calmed somewhat. She found she was able to see dimly the three small figures standing inside. The white garments of two of them even shone slightly, though so little light came from the night which waited outside in the garden.

When she was able to hear something besides her own pulse she listened to the phrase the two in white whispered again and again, distinguishing, at last, the words.

"Come out . . . come out into the dark . . . come with us. . . ."

They whispered it together, excited, persuasive, with an urgent, secret sibilance that held an increasing seductiveness at each repetition.

The third child, so enticed, whimpered once and stood quiet between them after that. It had been the small sound of an animal so full of fear as to be beyond outcry.

It released Anne from the fear that held her. For the voice had been her daughter's.

Though she leaped forward she made no attempt to reach her child. Her urge was the primitive, overwhelming one for light to chase away the darkness. The hands that had fumbled so often before moved with the speed and sureness of fear which is beyond panic.

And the taller of the two, the girl, swayed gently toward her with smiling teeth at the same second lights blazed throughout the house and her own child was in her arms.

They stood alone in the glass-enclosed room. Other players who had been wandering about downstairs blinked their eyes in the sudden light, calling reproachful questions.

Every child had come back into the living room before Anne, with trembling hands, shut the french doors which had been swinging open in the wind from the garden. No child asked where two of the guests had gone.

No one mentioned them at all through the final stages of the party. Anne, having had to choose between illness and anger, chose rightly. It was anger that sustained her through the refreshments, the collecting of coats and the arrival, thanks, and good-byes of parents.

It was faithful through the night. She went to bed angry and it was with her when she woke the next morning. She guarded it carefully as she planned the call she would make to Usher that day, since if she lost it she feared what might take its place.

In the end, it was Mrs. Usher who called Anne first. She had a pleasant voice, crisp and courteous though rather impersonal sounding.

She called, she said, to explain why her children had not been able to attend the party. They had had fever all day and she believed it might be developing into a light case of chicken pox. Both she, and they, had been so disappointed. She had made their costumes herself; they were to have gone as a cat and a mouse.

The voice seemed to fade out on the next few sentences. At the first words Anne heard there had been a slight, sickening wrench somewhere inside her. It was a relatively mild one, considering that it was the displacement of whatever held her being secure in its particular place in the universe.

The voice wanted to know if most of the other children had been able to make it. Some of them, it knew, had had to come a long way.

The invitations had been on orange paper. She remembered them. Her mother had let her cut out and address them herself, guiding her hand as it made fat wavering letters on the envelopes. She had been so proud that they were to go all the way to upstate New York.

Anne's voice, when she answered, was steadier than the room, still wheeling crazily around herself and the telephone.

Yes, she said, some of the children had had to come a very long way.

Children would do almost anything not to miss a party, the voice said.

Yes, Anne said. All the children had come.


DISCUSSION    1.    The game played at the end of the party was one that Anne had hated and feared as a child. How does she feel in watching it as an adult?

2.    The late visitors to the Halloween party are first thought to be the Usher children. How does Anne's conversation with Mrs. Usher tell us who they really are?

3.    Through Anne's memories, the author weaves an experience of Anne's childhood into her adult life. What features of the party of the present are like the party planned in her childhood?

For further activities, see page 58.

# Daniel Webster's Horses

ELIZABETH COATSWORTH

If when the wind blows
   Rattling the trees,
Clicking like skeletons'
   Elbows and knees,

You hear along the road      5
   Three horses pass,
Do not go near the dark
   Cold window-glass.

If when the first snow lies
   Whiter than bones,      10
You see the mark of hoofs
   Cut to the stones,

Hoofs of three horses
   Going abreast—
Turn about, turn about,      15
   A closed door is best!

Upright in the earth
   Under the sod
They buried three horses,
   Bridled and shod,      20

Daniel Webster's horses—
   He said as he grew old,
"Flesh, I loved riding,
   Shall I not love it cold?

"Shall I not love to ride      25
   Bone astride bone,
When the cold wind blows
   And snow covers stone?

"Bury them on their feet,
   With bridle and bit.      30
They were good horses.
   See their shoes fit."

23. *Flesh:* alive.   24. *cold:* when I am dead.

## DISCUSSION

1.  Daniel Webster makes a strange request for the burial of his horses. How does he wish them to be buried? Why?

2.  **Word choice.**  Writers choose words carefully. If they want us to see, hear, or feel, they use words that appeal to the senses. For example, in the first stanza we can hear the wind "Rattling the trees, / Clicking like skeletons' / Elbows and knees." Pick out similar lines that create vivid pictures.

# The Telltale Heart

EDGAR ALLAN POE

True!—nervous—very, very dreadfully nervous I had been and am; but why *will* you say that I am mad? The disease had sharpened my senses—not destroyed, not dulled them. Above all was the sense of hearing acute. I heard all things in the heaven and in the earth. I heard many things in hell. How, then, am I mad? Hearken! and observe how healthily, how calmly I can tell you the whole story.

It is impossible to say how first the idea entered my brain; but once conceived, it haunted me day and night. Object there was none. Passion there was none. I loved the old man. He had never wronged me. He had never given me insult. For his gold I had no desire. I think it was his eye! Yes, it was this! He had the eye of a vulture—a pale blue eye, with a film over it. Whenever it fell upon me, my blood ran cold; and so by degrees—very gradually—I made up my mind to take the life of the old man, and thus rid myself of the eye forever.

Now this is the point. You fancy me mad. Madmen know nothing. But you should have seen *me.* You should have seen how wisely I proceeded—with what caution, with what foresight, with what dissimulation[1] I went to work! I was never kinder to the old man than during the whole week before I killed him. And every night, about midnight, I turned the latch of his door and opened it—oh, so gently! And then, when I had made an opening sufficient for my head, I put in a dark lantern, all closed, closed, so that no light shone out, and then I thrust in my head. Oh, you would have laughed to see how cunningly I thrust it in! I moved it slowly—very, very slowly, so that I might not disturb the old man's sleep. It took me an hour to place my whole head within the opening so far that I could see him as he lay upon his bed. Ha!—would a madman have been so wise as this? And then, when my head was well in the room, I undid the lantern cautiously—oh, so cautiously—cautiously (for the hinges creaked), I undid it just so much that a single thin ray fell upon the vulture eye. And this I did for seven long nights—every night just at midnight—but I found the eye al-

---

[1] *dissimulation:* pretense in order to deceive.

ways closed; and so it was impossible to do the work, for it was
not the old man who vexed me, but his Evil Eye. And every
morning, when the day broke, I went boldly into the chamber,
and spoke courageously to him, calling him by name in a hearty
tone, and inquiring how he had passed the night. So you see he
would have been a very profound old man, indeed, to suspect
that every night, just at twelve, I looked in upon him while he
slept.

Upon the eighth night I was more than usually cautious in
opening the door. A watch's minute hand moves more quickly
than did mine. Never before that night had I *felt* the extent of
my own powers, of my sagacity. I could scarcely contain my
feelings of triumph. To think that there I was, opening the
door, little by little, and he not even to dream of my secret
deeds or thoughts. I fairly chuckled at the idea; and perhaps he
heard me, for he moved on the bed suddenly, as if startled. Now
you may think that I drew back—but no. His room was as
black as pitch with the thick darkness (for the shutters were
close fastened, through fear of robbers), and so I knew that he
could not see the opening of the door, and I kept pushing it on
steadily, steadily.

I had my head in, and was about to open the lantern, when
my thumb slipped upon the tin fastening, and the old man
sprang up in bed, crying out, "Who's there?"

I kept quite still and said nothing. For a whole hour I did
not move a muscle, and in the meantime I did not hear him lie
down. He was still sitting up in the bed, listening—just as I
have done night after night, hearkening to the deathwatches[2] in
the wall.

---

[2] *deathwatches:* beetles that live in old woodwork. Their ticking sound was thought to be a
warning of death.

Presently I heard a slight groan, and I knew it was the groan of mortal terror. It was not a groan of pain or of grief—oh no!—it was the low, stifled sound that arises from the bottom of the soul when overcharged with awe. I knew the sound well. Many a night, just at midnight, when all the world slept, it has welled up from my own bosom, deepening with its dreadful echo the terrors that distracted me. I say I knew it well. I knew what the old man felt, and pitied him, although I chuckled at heart. I knew that he had been lying awake ever since the first slight noise, when he had turned in the bed. His fears had been ever since growing upon him. He had been trying to fancy them causeless, but could not. He had been saying to himself, "It is nothing but the wind in the chimney—it is only a mouse crossing the floor," or "It is merely a cricket which has made a single chirp." Yes, he had been trying to comfort himself with these suppositions, but he had found all in vain. *All in vain,* because Death, in approaching him, had stalked with his black shadow before him and enveloped the victim. And it was the mournful influence of the unperceived shadow that caused him to feel—although he neither saw nor heard—to *feel* the presence of my head within the room.

When I had waited a long time, very patiently, without hearing him lie down, I resolved to open a little—a very, very little—crevice in the lantern. So I opened it—you cannot imagine how stealthily, stealthily—until, at length, a single dim ray, like the thread of the spider, shot from out the crevice and fell full upon the vulture eye.

It was open—wide, wide open—and I grew furious as I gazed upon it. I saw it with perfect distinctness—all a dull blue, with a hideous veil over it that chilled the very marrow in my bones; but I could see nothing else of the old man's face or person, for I had directed the ray, as if by instinct, precisely upon the spot.

And now—have I not told you that what you mistake for madness is but over-acuteness of the senses?—now, I say, there came to my ears a low, dull, quick sound, such as a watch makes when enveloped in cotton. I knew *that* sound well, too. It was the beating of the old man's heart. It increased my fury, as the beating of a drum stimulates the soldier into courage.

But even yet I refrained and kept still. I scarcely breathed. I held the lantern motionless. I tried how steadily I could maintain the ray upon the eye. Meantime the hellish tattoo of the

heart increased. It grew quicker and quicker, and louder and louder every instant. The old man's terror *must* have been extreme! It grew louder, I say, louder every moment!—Do you mark me well? I have told you that I am nervous; so I am.—And now at the dead hour of the night, amid the dreadful silence of that old house, so strange a noise as this excited me to uncontrollable terror. Yet, for some minutes longer I refrained and stood still. But the beating grew louder, louder! I thought the heart must burst. And now a new anxiety seized me—the sound would be heard by a neighbor! The old man's hour had come! With a loud yell, I threw open the lantern and leaped into the room. He shrieked once—once only. In an instant I dragged him to the floor and pulled the heavy bed over him. I then smiled gaily, to find the deed so far done. But, for many minutes, the heart beat on with a muffled sound. This, however, did not vex me; it would not be heard through the wall. At length it ceased. The old man was dead. I removed the bed and examined the corpse. Yes, he was stone, stone dead. I placed my hand upon the heart and held it there many minutes. There was no pulsation. He was stone dead. His eye would trouble me no more.

If still you think me mad, you will think so no longer when I describe the wise precautions I took for the concealment of the body. The night waned, and I worked hastily but in silence. First of all I dismembered the corpse. I cut off the head and the arms and the legs.

I then took up three planks from the flooring of the chamber and deposited all between the scantlings.[3] I then replaced the boards so cleverly, so cunningly, that no human eye—not even *his*—could have detected anything wrong. There was nothing to wash out—no stain of any kind, no blood spot whatever. I had been too wary for that. A tub had caught all—ha! ha!

When I had made an end of these labors, it was four o'clock—still dark as midnight. As the bell sounded the hour, there came a knocking at the street door. I went down to open it with a light heart—for what had I *now* to fear? There entered three men, who introduced themselves, with perfect suavity, as officers of the police. A shriek had been heard by a neighbor during the night; suspicion of foul play had been aroused; information had been lodged at the police office, and they (the officers) had been deputed to search the premises.

I smiled—for *what* had I to fear? I bade the gentlemen welcome. The shriek, I said, was my own in a dream. The old man, I mentioned, was absent in the country. I took my visitors all over the house. I bade them search—search *well*. I led them, at length, to *his* chamber. I showed them his treasures, secure, undisturbed. In the enthusiasm of my confidence I brought chairs into the room, and desired them *here* to rest from their fatigues, while I myself, in the wild audacity of my perfect triumph, placed my own seat upon the very spot beneath which reposed the corpse of the victim.

The officers were satisfied. My *manner* had convinced them. I was singularly at ease. They sat, and while I answered cheerily, they chatted of familiar things. But ere long I felt myself getting pale and wished them gone. My head ached, and I fancied a ringing in my ears; but still they sat and still chatted. The ringing became more distinct; it continued and became more distinct. I talked more freely to get rid of the feeling, but it continued and gained definitiveness—until at length I found that the noise was *not* within my ears.

No doubt I now grew *very* pale—but I talked more fluently, and with a heightened voice. Yet the sound increased—and

---

[3] *scantlings:* timbers.

what could I do? It was a *low, dull, quick sound—much such a sound as a watch makes when enveloped in cotton.* I gasped for breath—and yet the officers heard it not. I talked more quickly, more vehemently—but the noise steadily increased. I arose and argued about trifles, in a high key and with violent gesticulations, but the noise steadily increased. Why *would* they not be gone? I paced the floor to and fro with heavy strides, as if excited to fury by the observations of the men—but the noise steadily increased. What *could* I do? I foamed—I raved—I swore! I swung the chair upon which I had been sitting, and grated it upon the boards, but the noise arose over all and continually increased. It grew louder—louder—*louder!* And still the men chatted pleasantly, and smiled. Was it possible they heard not? No, no! They heard!—They suspected!—They *knew!*—They were making a mockery of my horror!—This I thought, and this I think. But anything was better than this agony! Anything was more tolerable than this derision! I could bear those hypocritical smiles no longer! I felt that I must scream or die! And now—Again—Hark!—Louder! Louder! Louder! *Louder!*

"Villains!" I shrieked, "dissemble [4] no more! I admit the deed! Tear up the planks!—here, here!—It is the beating of his hideous heart!"

---

[4] *dissemble:* pretend.

DISCUSSION

1. "Why *would* they not be gone?" the man telling this story wonders. The policemen do not seem to hear the sound of the beating heart; so what causes them to linger? Why does the narrator finally confess to the murder?

2. **Point of view.** The narrator of a story determines the point of view; that is, *who* tells the story. The author may stand outside the story and view what happens from a distance or enter into the story and tell what happens as it would appear to one of the characters. This story, for example, is told from the point of view of the murderer himself. We know only what he lets us know or what we can guess from his words and actions. Suppose that one of the police officers had told the story. What differences would there have been?

For further activities, see page 58.

# EXAMINATION DAY

HENRY SLESAR

The Jordans never spoke of the exam, not until their son, Dickie, was twelve years old. It was on his birthday that Mrs. Jordan first mentioned the subject in his presence, and the anxious manner of her speech caused her husband to answer sharply.

"Forget about it," he said. "He'll do all right."

They were at the breakfast table, and the boy looked up from his plate curiously. He was an alert-eyed youngster, with flat blond hair and a quick, nervous manner. He didn't understand what the sudden tension was about, but he did know that today was his birthday, and he wanted harmony above all. Somewhere in the little apartment there were wrapped, beribboned packages waiting to be opened, and in the tiny wall-kitchen, something warm and sweet was being prepared in the automatic stove. He wanted the day to be happy, and the moistness of his mother's eyes, the scowl on his father's face, spoiled the mood of fluttering expectation with which he had greeted the morning.

"What exam?" he asked.

His mother looked at the tablecloth. "It's just a sort of Government intelligence test they give children at the age of twelve. You'll be getting it next week. It's nothing to worry about."

"You mean a test like in school?"

"Something like that," his father said, getting up from the table. "Go read your comic books, Dickie."

The boy rose and wandered toward that part of the living room which had been "his" corner since infancy. He fingered the topmost comic of the stack, but seemed uninterested in the colorful squares of fastpaced action. He wandered toward the window, and peered gloomily at the veil of mist that shrouded the glass.

"Why did it have to rain *today?*" he said. "Why couldn't it rain tomorrow?"

His father, now slumped into an armchair with the Government newspaper, rattled the sheets in vexation. "Because it just did, that's all. Rain makes the grass grow."

"Why, Dad?"

"Because it does, that's all."

Dickie puckered his brow. "What makes it green, though? The grass?"

"Nobody knows," his father snapped, then immediately regretted his abruptness.

Later in the day, it was birthday time again. His mother beamed as she handed over the gaily colored packages, and even his father managed a grin and a rumple-of-the-hair. He kissed his mother and shook hands gravely with his father. Then the birthday cake was brought forth, and the ceremonies concluded.

An hour later, seated by the window, he watched the sun force its way between the clouds.

"Dad," he said, "how far away is the sun?"

"Five thousand miles," his father said.

Dick sat at the breakfast table and again saw moisture in his mother's eyes. He didn't connect her tears with the exam until his father suddenly brought the subject to light again.

"Well, Dickie," he said, with a manly frown, "You've got an appointment today."

"I know, Dad. I hope——"

"Now it's nothing to worry about. Thousands of children take this test every day. The Government wants to know how smart you are, Dickie. That's all there is to it."

"I get good marks in school," he said hesitantly.

"This is different. This is a——special kind of test. They give you this stuff to drink, you see, and then you go into a room where there's a sort of machine——"

"What stuff to drink?" Dickie said.

"It's nothing. It tastes like peppermint. It's just to make sure you answer the questions truthfully. Not that the Government thinks that you won't tell the truth, but this stuff makes *sure.*"

Dickie's face showed puzzlement, and a touch of fright. He looked at his mother and she composed her face into a misty smile.

"Everything will be all right," she said.

"Of course it will," his father agreed. "You're a good boy, Dickie; you'll make out fine. Then we'll come home and celebrate. All right?"

"Yes, sir," Dickie said.

They entered the Government Educational Building fifteen minutes before the appointed hour. They crossed the marble floors of the great pillared lobby, passed beneath an archway and entered an automatic elevator that brought them to the fourth floor.

There was a young man wearing an insignia-less tunic, seated at a polished desk in front of Room 404. He held a clipboard in his hand, and he checked the list down to the J's and permitted the Jordans to enter.

The room was as cold and official as a courtroom, with long benches flanking metal tables. There were several fathers and sons already there, and a thin-lipped woman with cropped black hair was passing out sheets of paper.

Mr. Jordan filled out the form, and returned it to the clerk. Then he told Dickie: "It won't be long now. When they call your name, you just go through the doorway at that end of the room." He indicated the portal with his finger.

A concealed loudspeaker crackled and called off the first name. Dickie saw a boy leave his father's side reluctantly and walk slowly toward the door.

At five minutes of eleven, they called the name of Jordan.

"Good luck, son," his father said, without looking at him. "I'll call for you when the test is over."

Dickie walked to the door and turned the knob. The room inside was dim, and he could barely make out the features of the gray-tunicked attendant who greeted him.

"Sit down," the man said softly. He indicated a high stool beside his desk. "Your name's Richard Jordan?"

"Yes, sir."

"Your classification number is 600–115. Drink this, Richard."

He lifted a plastic cup from the desk and handed it to the boy. The liquid inside had the consistency of buttermilk, tasted only vaguely of the promised peppermint. Dickie downed it, and handed the man the empty cup.

He sat in silence, feeling drowsy, while the man wrote busily on a sheet of paper. Then the attendant looked at his watch, and rose to stand only inches from Dickie's face. He unclipped a pen-like object from the pocket of his tunic, and flashed a tiny light into the boy's eyes.

"All right," he said. "Come with me, Richard."

He led Dickie to the end of the room, where a single wooden armchair faced a multi-dialed computing machine. There was a microphone on the left arm of the chair, and when the boy sat down, he found its pinpoint head conveniently at his mouth.

"Now just relax, Richard. You'll be asked some questions, and you think them over carefully. Then give your answers into the microphone. The machine will take care of the rest."

"Yes, sir."

"I'll leave you alone now. Whenever you want to start, just say 'ready' into the microphone."

"Yes, sir."

The man squeezed his shoulder, and left.

Dickie said, "Ready."

Lights appeared on the machine, and a mechanism whirred. A voice said:

"Complete this sequence. One, four, seven, ten. . . ."

Mr. and Mrs. Jordan were in the living room, not speaking, not even speculating.

It was almost four o'clock when the telephone rang. The woman tried to reach it first, but her husband was quicker.

"Mr. Jordan?"

The voice was clipped; a brisk, official voice.

"Yes, speaking."

"This is the Government Educational Service. Your son, Richard M. Jordan, Classification 600–115, has completed the Government examination. We regret to inform you that his intelligence quotient has exceeded the Government regulation, according to Rule 84, Section 5, of the New Code."

Across the room, the woman cried out, knowing nothing except the emotion she read on her husband's face.

"You may specify by telephone," the voice droned on, "whether you wish his body interred by the Government or would you prefer a private burial place? The fee for Government burial is ten dollars."

**DISCUSSION**

1. Usually we like to make high grades on examinations. What penalty does Richard pay for too high a score?

2. Why do you suppose the Government made and enforced Rule 84, Section 5?

3. What evidence is there earlier in the story that Richard might "fail" the examination?

For further activities, see page 59.

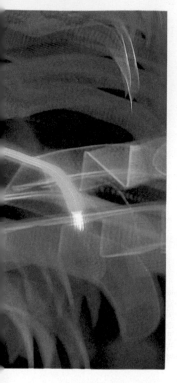

## VOCABULARY

### Moonlight—Starlight (page 31)

On separate paper, match the number of the word with the letter of the definition at the right.

| | | | |
|---|---|---|---|
| 1. | gruesome | a. | having no pity |
| 2. | tense | b. | providing merriment |
| 3. | inhuman | c. | marked by suspense |
| 4. | ruthless | d. | inspiring horror |
| 5. | hilarious | e. | lacking kindness |

### The Telltale Heart (page 46)

Poe used many descriptive adverbs in his writing. Following are sentences or parts of sentences from the story with the adverbs omitted but listed following the sentences. On separate paper, write the word that belongs in each blank space. When you finish, check your answers with the story.

1. Nervous, very, very——nervous (page 46).
2. To see how——I thrust it in (p. 46).
3. I had waited for a long time very——(p. 48).
4. I opened it—you cannot imagine how——(p. 48).
5. I talked more——(p. 50).

patiently     dreadfully     fluently     cunningly     stealthily

## COMPOSITION

### Moonlight—Starlight (page 31)

Think of several games you played in your childhood. Choose one that you could use as the basis of a story that has ghostly qualities. Write the story and share it with your classmates.

### The Telltale Heart (page 46)

Describe the final scene of "The Telltale Heart" from the point of view of one of the policemen. Let us hear his reactions to what he sees, including details of the house and behavior of the murderer.

# READING

## The Highwayman (page 26)

Following is a list of details. On separate paper, write T (true) for each item that is mentioned in the poem and F (false) for each that is not.

1. The wind was a torrent of darkness.
2. The highwayman came riding up to the new motel.
3. He was dressed in a fancy way.
4. The landlord had a blue-eyed daughter.
5. Tim was a stableman who loved the landlord's daughter.
6. The highwayman said he would come back to the inn by moonlight.
7. The redcoats were prepared to fire.
8. The landlord's daughter was killed.
9. The highwayman did not go back to find Bess.
10. The highwayman was shot down.

## The Telltale Heart (page 46)

Look back at the story and on separate paper make two lists. In the first jot down all the descriptive words or expressions that picture the haunting eye. In the second, list those that make you hear the beating heart.

When you have finished, decide which had the greater effect on the narrator—the eye or the heart.

## Examination Day (page 53)

On separate paper, mark each statement T(true) or F (false). Also give the information from the story that led to your decision.

1. When people were too smart, the government killed them.
2. Anyone could take the government test.
3. When Dickie turned twelve, his parents were thrilled.
4. The test was "cheat-proof."
5. No clues were given to suggest that Dickie was smart.
6. The test was given to twelve-year-olds.
7. The unhappiness of Dickie's parents was related to his birthday.
8. The government played a significant role in people's lives.
9. Dickie was unaware of his parents' concern.
10. Dickie's test score determined his fate.

# COMPOSITION

Sometimes you know you *ought* to write to someone, but you can't think of anything to say. On the other hand, it seems easy enough to write a note to explain to your parents that you're going to be with the Murrays at the baseball game at Wrigley Field this afternoon and should be home by six. When you have something definite in mind, you have a better chance of writing clearly and well.

Good writing is good writing whether it appears as a note on a kitchen table, or a set of instructions for assembling a bicycle, or a newspaper editorial, or a job application, or a journal entry, or a recipe, or a letter, or an assignment. Good writing, in class or out, knows what it is about. It is clear. It is specific. And it keeps to the point.

Clear, specific, and unified writing is easier when you are interested in your subject and eager to write about it. Consequently, your own writing will be better if it draws on what you do know and care about. Even when writing purely from your imagination, use what you know and feel comfortable with. For example, in describing a monster from another world that you have created, assemble it from parts of your own experience. Give the monster eyes like the headlights of a car (you know what headlights look like), repulsive skin like a cockroach's. Give it the size of a bear rearing on its hind legs and the color of an oil slick. Your writing will be good because it is specific, vivid, and clear. And it will be much more interesting than a vague description such as "A hideous monster appeared. It was horrible to look at."

When you write, then, about mystery and suspense or about anything else, as often as possible *draw on what you know.* Remember rooms you have sat in, skills you have mastered, emotions you have felt. Recall streets you have crossed, people you have met, skies you have gazed at, parks you have wandered through. Think of sounds, tastes, and smells you have experienced. All these experiences that have filled *your* life so far provide you with your best materials for writing.

**CHOOSING
A SUBJECT**

## ABOUT THE SELECTIONS

1. Which of the prose selections in this section did you enjoy most? Write a brief paper of a paragraph or two that explains why you liked that one best. Was it because of the suspense? What details were included to add to the tension? Did you like the selection for its humor, or for the way it uses words? Point out where it seems funniest or uses words most cleverly. Remember: be specific.

2. In which selection did you meet the most memorable people? Most memorable are by no means always the most pleasant. Perhaps the murderer in "The Telltale Heart" stands out in your mind. Or maybe you remember most vividly the two eerie children at the party in "Moonlight—Starlight." In a paragraph explain what specific details of dress, manner, and speech the author has included to make you see and remember that person.

3. Each of these selections creates an atmosphere of its own. For instance, the atmosphere of "The Light at South Point" is affected by the tension of war and the loneliness of the ocean. Which of the selections seems most successfully to develop atmosphere—the "feel" of the surroundings? In a paragraph briefly explain what the atmosphere of the selection is. Mention specific details (weather, time of day) that help create that atmosphere.

4. Three poems in the section present rides on horseback. In a paragraph compare the three: "Eldorado," "The Highwayman," and "Daniel Webster's Horses." Which most successfully echoes the *sound* of horses in motion? What letters, syllables, or words help express that sound?

## ON YOUR OWN

1. Reread the descriptions of the following rooms: the dining room in India (page 10), the sixth-floor room in the Paris hotel (page 13), Room 404 in "Examination Day" (page 53). Each room affects the reader differently because of the different specific details mentioned in the description. In a paragraph describe a room you know well, but avoid mentioning every detail you can think of about it. Instead, select the four or five details that will, in just a few sentences, let us picture the room and its atmosphere clearly.

2. Think of a room you know well and then imagine that it has been transformed in some way. Picture it cobwebby and empty of furniture, or gutted by fire, or fallen into ruins with the windows broken. Then describe it in a way that gives the transformed room a sense of mystery or horror—a room where something suspenseful might happen. Remember: start with what you know well.

3. The way people speak tells us a lot about them. Consider the way the madman talks in "The Telltale Heart" or how the secret agent speaks in "The Midnight Visitor." Briefly record an imaginary speaker's words in a way that lets the reader come to know her or him merely by what is said, and how. (You might find it easier to have your imaginary speaker talking on a telephone.)

4. What is the most exciting thing that has ever happened to you? Write a paragraph that describes the event. Include specific details that will help the reader feel what you felt while living through the excitement.

ANIMALS

# A Secret for Two

QUENTIN REYNOLDS

Montreal is a very large city, but, like all large cities, it has some very small streets. Streets, for instance, like Prince Edward Street, which is only four blocks long, ending in a *cul-de-sac*.[1] No one knew Prince Edward Street as well as did Pierre Dupin, for Pierre had delivered milk to the families on the street for thirty years now.

During the past fifteen years the horse which drew the milk wagon used by Pierre was a large white horse named Joseph. In Montreal, especially in that part of Montreal which is very French, the animals, like children, are often given the names of saints. When the big white horse first came to the Provincale Milk Company, he didn't have a name. They told Pierre that he could use the white horse henceforth. Pierre stroked the softness of the horse's neck; he stroked the sheen of its splendid belly, and he looked into the eyes of the horse.

"That is a kind horse, a gentle and a faithful horse," Pierre said, "and I can see a beautiful spirit shining out of the eyes of the horse. I will name him after good St. Joseph, who was also kind and gentle and faithful and a beautiful spirit."

Within a year Joseph knew the milk route as well as Pierre. Pierre used to boast that he didn't need reins—he never touched them. Each morning Pierre arrived at the stables of the Provincale Milk Company at five o'clock. The wagon would be loaded and Joseph hitched to it. Pierre would call *"Bon jour, vieille ami,"*[2] as he climbed into his seat and Joseph would turn his head and the other drivers would smile and say that the

[1] *cul-de-sac* (French, kŭl-dǐ-săk'): dead-end street.
[2] *Bon jour, vieille ami* (French, bôn zhür' vyā yä-mē'): good morning, old friend.

horse would smile at Pierre. Then Jacques, the foreman, would say, "All right, Pierre, go on," and Pierre would call softly to Joseph, *"Avance, mon ami,"*[3] and this splendid combination would stalk proudly down the street.

The wagon, without any direction from Pierre, would roll three blocks down St. Catherine Street, then turn right two blocks along Roslyn Avenue; then left, for that was Prince Edward Street. The horse would stop at the first house, allow Pierre perhaps thirty seconds to get down from his seat and put a bottle of milk at the front door and would then go on, skipping two houses and stopping at the third. So down the length of the street. Then Joseph, still without any direction from Pierre, would turn around and come back along the other side. Yes, Joseph was a smart horse.

Pierre would boast at the stable of Joseph's skill. "I never touch the reins. He knows just where to stop. Why, a blind man could handle my route with Joseph pulling the wagon."

So it went on for years—always the same. Pierre and Joseph both grew old together, but gradually, not suddenly. Pierre's huge walrus mustache was pure white now and Joseph didn't lift his knees so high or raise his head quite as much. Jacques, the foreman of the stables, never noticed that they were both getting old until Pierre appeared one day carrying a heavy walking stick.

"Hey, Pierre," Jacques laughed. "Maybe you got the gout, hey?"

*"Mais oui,*[4] Jacques," Pierre said uncertainly. "One grows old. One's legs get tired."

"You should teach the horse to carry the milk to the front door for you," Jacques told him. "He does everything else."

He knew every one of the forty families he served on Prince Edward Street. The cooks knew that Pierre could neither read nor write, so instead of following the usual custom of leaving a note in an empty bottle, if an additional quart of milk was needed they would sing out when they heard the rumble of his wagon wheels over the cobbled street, "Bring an extra quart this morning, Pierre."

Pierre had a remarkable memory. When he arrived at the

---

[3] *Avance, mon ami* (French, ə-väns′ mō nä-mē′): go ahead, my friend.
[4] *Mais oui* (French, mä wē′): but yes.

stable he'd always remember to tell Jacques, "The Paquins took an extra quart this morning; the Lemoines bought a pint of cream."

Jacques would note these things in a little book he always carried. Most of the drivers had to make out the weekly bills and collect the money, but Jacques, liking Pierre, had always excused him from this task. All Pierre had to do was to arrive at five in the morning, walk to his wagon, which was always in the same spot at the curb, and deliver his milk. He returned some two hours later, got stiffly from his seat, called a cheery *"Au 'voir"* to Jacques and then limped slowly down the street.

One morning the president of the Provincale Milk Company came to inspect the early morning deliveries. Jacques pointed Pierre out to him and said, "Watch how he talks to that horse. See how the horse listens and how he turns his head toward Pierre? See the look in that horse's eyes? You know, I think those two share a secret. I have often noticed it. It is as though they both sometimes chuckle at us as they go off on their route. Pierre is a good man, Monsieur President, but he gets old. Would it be too bold for me to suggest that he be retired and be given perhaps a small pension?" he added anxiously.

"But of course," the president laughed. "I know his record. He has been on this route now for thirty years and never once has there been a complaint. Tell him it is time he rested. His salary will go on just the same."

But Pierre refused to retire. He was panic-stricken at the thought of not driving Joseph every day. "We are two old men," he said to Jacques. "Let us wear out together. When Joseph is ready to retire—then I, too, will quit."

Jacques, who was a kind man, understood. There was something about Pierre and Joseph which made a man smile tenderly. It was as though each drew some hidden strength from the other. When Pierre was sitting in his seat, and when Joseph was hitched to the wagon, neither seemed old. But when they finished their work, then Pierre would limp down the street slowly, seeming very old indeed, and the horse's head would drop and he would walk very wearily to his stall.

Then one morning Jacques had dreadful news for Pierre when he arrived. It was a cold morning and still pitch-dark. The air was like iced wine that morning and the snow which had

fallen during the night glistened like a million diamonds piled together.

Jacques said, "Pierre, your horse, Joseph, did not wake this morning. He was very old, Pierre, he was twenty-five, and that is like seventy-five for a man."

"Yes," Pierre said, slowly. "Yes. I am seventy-five. And I cannot see Joseph again."

"Of course you can," Jacques soothed. "He is over in his stall, looking very peaceful. Go over and see him."

Pierre took one step forward then turned. "No . . . no . . . you don't understand, Jacques."

Jacques clapped him on the shoulder. "We'll find another horse just as good as Joseph. Why, in a month you'll teach him to know your route as well as Joseph did. We'll. . . ."

The look in Pierre's eyes stopped him. For years Pierre had worn a heavy cap, the peak of which came low over his eyes, keeping the bitter morning wind out of them. Now Jacques looked into Pierre's eyes and he saw something which startled him. He saw a dead, lifeless look in them. The eyes were mirroring the grief that was in Pierre's heart and his soul. It was as though his heart and soul had died.

"Take today off, Pierre," Jacques said, but already Pierre was hobbling off down the street, and had one been near one would have seen tears streaming down his cheeks and have heard half-smothered sobs. Pierre walked to the corner and stepped into the street. There was a warning yell from the driver of a huge truck that was coming fast and there was the scream of brakes, but Pierre apparently heard neither.

Five minutes later an ambulance driver said, "He's dead. Was killed instantly."

Jacques and several of the milk-wagon drivers had arrived and they looked down at the still figure.

"I couldn't help it," the driver of the truck protested, "he walked right into my truck. He never saw it, I guess. Why, he walked into it as though he was blind."

The ambulance doctor bent down. "Blind? Of course the man was blind. See those cataracts?[5] This man has been blind for five years." He turned to Jacques, "You say he worked for you? Didn't you know he was blind?"

[5] *cataracts:* disease causing blindness or partial blindness.

DISCUSSION

1.  We know by the last line that Pierre is blind. Did you suspect the truth earlier? Look back in the story for clues that the author has given. For example, on page 66 Pierre says, "Why, a blind man could handle my route with Joseph pulling the wagon."

2.  What qualities does the horse have that make the name *Joseph* just right for him?

3.  There is an unusually close bond between Pierre and Joseph. Find several examples from the story that show this clearly.

4.  What did other characters in the story think of Pierre and Joseph? How do you know?

# LONE DOG

### IRENE RUTHERFORD MCLEOD

I'm a lean dog, a keen dog, a wild dog, and lone;
I'm a rough dog, a tough dog, hunting on my own;
I'm a bad dog, a mad dog, teasing silly sheep;
I love to sit and bay the moon, to keep fat souls from sleep.

I'll never be a lap dog, licking dirty feet,                    5
A sleek dog, a meek dog, cringing for my meat,
Not for me the fireside, the well-filled plate,
But shut door, and sharp stone, and cuff, and kick, and hate.

Not for me the other dogs, running by my side,
Some have run a short while, but none of them would bide.   10
O mine is still the lone trail, the hard trail, the best,
Wide wind, and wild stars, and hunger of the quest!

## DISCUSSION

1.  This poem describes a particular kind of dog. Pick several phrases showing the kind of life it enjoys.

2.  **Stanza.**  In some poems, like this one, lines are grouped together and printed as a unit. This unit is called a stanza, and the form of the first stanza is usually repeated throughout the poem. This poem has three stanzas. Why do you think the author chose to use stanzas rather than a solid block of twelve lines?

For further activities, see page 109.

# Rikki-tikki-tavi

RUDYARD KIPLING

This is the story of the great war that Rikki-tikki-tavi fought single-handed, through the bathrooms of the big bungalow in Segowlee cantonment. Darzee, the tailorbird, helped him, and Chuchundra, the muskrat, who never comes out into the middle of the floor, but always creeps round by the wall, gave him advice; but Rikki-tikki did the real fighting.

He was a mongoose, rather like a little cat in his fur and his tail, but quite like a weasel in his head and his habits. His eyes and the end of his restless nose were pink; he could scratch himself anywhere he pleased, with any leg, front or back, that he chose to use; he could fluff up his tail till it looked like a bottle brush, and his war cry, as he scuttled through the long grass, was: "Rikk-tikk-tikki-tikki-tchk!"

One day, a high summer flood washed him out of the burrow where he lived with his father and mother, and carried him, kicking and clucking, down a roadside ditch. He found a little wisp of grass floating there, and clung to it till he lost his senses. When he revived, he was lying in the hot sun on the middle of a garden path, very draggled indeed, and a small boy was saying: "Here's a dead mongoose. Let's have a funeral."

"No," said his mother; "let's take him in and dry him. Perhaps he isn't really dead."

They took him into the house, and a big man picked him up between his finger and thumb, and said he was not dead but half-choked; so they wrapped him in cotton wool, and warmed him, and he opened his eyes and sneezed.

"Now," said the big man (he was an Englishman who had just moved into the bungalow), "don't frighten him, and we'll see what he'll do."

It is the hardest thing in the world to frighten a mongoose, because he is eaten up from nose to tail with curiosity. The motto of all the mongoose family is, "Run and find out"; and Rikki-tikki was a true mongoose. He looked at the cotton wool, decided that it was not good to eat, ran all round the table, sat up and put his fur in order, scratched himself, and jumped on the small boy's shoulder.

"Don't be frightened, Teddy," said his father. "That's his way of making friends."

"Ouch! He's tickling under my chin," said Teddy.

Rikki-tikki looked down between the boy's collar and neck, snuffed at his ear, and climbed down to the floor, where he sat rubbing his nose.

"Good gracious," said Teddy's

mother, "and that's a wild creature! I suppose he's so tame because we've been kind to him."

"All mongooses are like that," said her husband. "If Teddy doesn't pick him up by the tail, or try to put him in a cage, he'll run in and out of the house all day long. Let's give him something to eat."

They gave him a little piece of raw meat. Rikki-tikki liked it immensely, and when it was finished he went out into the veranda and sat in the sunshine and fluffed up his fur to make it dry to the roots. Then he felt better.

"There are more things to find out about in this house," he said to himself, "than all my family could find out in all their lives. I shall certainly stay and find out."

He spent all that day roaming over the house. He nearly drowned himself in the bathtubs, put his nose into the ink on a writing table, and burnt it on the end of the big man's cigar, for he climbed up in the big man's lap to see how writing was done. At nightfall he ran into Teddy's nursery to watch how kerosene lamps were lighted, and when Teddy went to bed, Rikki-tikki climbed up too; but he was a restless companion, because he had to get up and attend to every noise all through the night, and find out what made it. Ted-

dy's mother and father came in, the last thing, to look at their boy, and Rikki-tikki was awake on the pillow. "I don't like that," said Teddy's mother; "he may bite the child." "He'll do no such thing," said the father. "Teddy's safer with that little beast than if he had a bloodhound to watch him. If a snake came into the nursery now——"

But Teddy's mother wouldn't think of anything so awful.

Early in the morning Rikki-tikki came to early breakfast in the veranda riding on Teddy's shoulder, and they gave him banana and some boiled egg; and he sat on all their laps one after the other, because every well-brought-up mongoose always hopes to be a house-mongoose some day and have rooms to run about in, and Rikki-tikki's mother (she used to live in the General's house at Segowlee) had carefully told Rikki what to do if ever he came across white men.

Then Rikki-tikki went out into the garden to see what was to be seen. It was a large garden, only half cultivated, with bushes as big as summer houses of Marshal Niel roses, lime and orange trees, clumps of bamboos, and thickets of high grass. Rikki-tikki licked his lips. "This is a splendid hunting ground," he said, and his tail grew bottle-brushy at the thought of it, and he

scuttled up and down the garden, snuffing here and there till he heard very sorrowful voices in a thorn-bush.

It was Darzee, the tailorbird, and his wife. They had made a beautiful nest by pulling two big leaves together and stitching them up the edges with fibers, and had filled the hollow with cotton and downy fluff. The nest swayed to and fro, as they sat on the rim and cried.

"What is the matter?" asked Rikki-tikki.

"We are very miserable," said Darzee. "One of our babies fell out of the nest yesterday, and Nag ate him."

"H'm!" said Rikki-tikki, "that is very sad—but I am a stranger here. Who is Nag?"

Darzee and his wife only cowered down in the nest without answering, for from the thick grass at the foot of the bush there came a low hiss—a horrid cold sound that made Rikki-tikki jump back two clear feet. Then inch by inch out of the grass rose up the head and spread hood of Nag, the big black cobra, and he was five feet long from tongue to tail. When he had lifted one-third of himself clear of the ground, he stayed balancing to and fro exactly as a dandelion tuft balances in the wind, and he looked at Rikki-tikki with the wicked snake's eyes that never change their expression, whatever the snake may be thinking of.

"Who is Nag?" said he. "I am Nag. The great god Brahm[1] put his mark upon all our people when the first co-

bra spread his hood to keep the sun off Brahm as he slept. Look, and be afraid!"

He spread out his hood more than ever, and Rikki-tikki saw the spectacle mark on the back of it that looks exactly like the eye part of a hook-and-eye fastening. He was afraid for the minute; but it is impossible for a mongoose to stay frightened for any length of time, and though Rikki-tikki had never met a live cobra before, his mother had fed him on dead ones, and he knew that all a grown mongoose's business in life was to fight and eat snakes. Nag knew that too, and at the bottom of his cold heart he was afraid.

"Well," said Rikki-tikki, and his tail began to fluff up again, "marks or no marks, do you think it is right for you to eat fledglings out of a nest?"

Nag was thinking to himself, and watching the least little movement in the grass behind Rikki-tikki. He knew that mongooses in the garden meant death sooner or later for him and his family, but he wanted to get Rikki-tikki off his guard. So he dropped his head a little, and put it on one side.

"Let us talk," he said. "You eat eggs. Why should not I eat birds?"

"Behind you! Look behind you!" sang Darzee.

Rikki-tikki knew better than to waste time in staring. He jumped up in the air as high as he could go, and just under him whizzed by the head of Nagaina, Nag's wicked wife. She had crept up behind him as he was talking, to make an end of him; and he heard her savage hiss as the stroke missed. He

---

[1] *Brahm* (bräm): in the Hindu religion, the creator of the world; usually known as Brahma (brä′mə).

came down almost across her back, and if he had been an old mongoose he would have known that then was the time to break her back with one bite; but he was afraid of the terrible lashing return stroke of the cobra. He bit, indeed, but did not bite long enough, and he jumped clear of the whisking tail, leaving Nagaina torn and angry.

"Wicked, wicked Darzee!" said Nag, lashing up as high as he could reach toward the nest in the thorn bush; but Darzee had built it out of reach of snakes, and it only swayed to and fro.

Rikki-tikki felt his eyes growing red and hot (when a mongoose's eyes grow red, he is angry), and he sat back on his tail and hind legs like a little kangaroo, and looked all round him, and chattered with rage. But Nag and Nagaina had disappeared into the grass. When a snake misses its stroke, it never says anything or gives any sign of what it means to do next. Rikki-tikki did not care to follow them, for he did not feel sure that he could manage two snakes at once. So he trotted off to the gravel path near the house, and sat down to think. It was a serious matter for him.

If you read the old books of natural history, you will find they say that when the mongoose fights the snake and happens to get bitten, he runs off and eats some herb that cures him. That is not true. The victory is only a matter of quickness of eye and quickness of foot—snake's blow against mongoose's jump—and as no eye can follow the motion of a snake's head when it strikes, that makes things much more wonderful than any magic herb. Rikki-tikki knew he was a young mongoose, and it made him all the more pleased to think that he had managed to escape a blow from behind. It gave him confidence in himself, and when Teddy came running down the path, Rikki-tikki was ready to be petted.

But just as Teddy was stooping, something flinched a little in the dust, and a tiny voice said: "Be careful. I am death!" It was Karait, the dusty brown snakeling that lies for choice on the dusty earth; and his bite is as dangerous as the cobra's. But he is so small that nobody thinks of him, and so he does the more harm to people.

Rikki-tikki's eyes grew red again, and he danced up to Karait with the peculiar rocking, swaying motion that he had inherited from his family. It looks very funny, but it is so perfectly balanced a gait that you can fly off from it at any angle you please; and in dealing with snakes this is an advantage. If Rikki-tikki had only known, he was doing a much more dangerous thing than fighting Nag, for Karait is so small, and can turn so quickly, that unless Rikki bit him close to the back of the head, he would get the return stroke in his eye or lip. But Rikki did not know: his eyes were all red, and he rocked back and forth, looking for a' good place to hold. Karait struck out. Rikki jumped sideways and tried to run in, but the wicked little dusty gray head lashed within a fraction of his shoulder, and he had to jump over the body, and the head followed his heels close.

Teddy shouted to the house: "Oh, look here! Our mongoose is killing a snake"; and Rikki-tikki heard a scream from Teddy's mother. His father ran out with a stick, but by the time he came up, Karait had lunged out once too far, and Rikki-tikki had sprung, jumped on the snake's back, dropped his head far between his forelegs, bitten as high up the back as he could get hold, and rolled away. That bite paralyzed Karait, and Rikki-tikki was just going to eat him up from the tail, after the custom of his family at dinner, when he remembered that a full meal makes a slow mongoose, and if he wanted all his strength and quickness ready, he must keep himself thin.

He went away for a dust bath under the castor-oil bushes, while Teddy's father beat the dead Karait. "What is the use of that?" thought Rikki-tikki. "I have settled it all"; and then Teddy's mother picked him up from the dust and hugged him, crying that he had saved Teddy from death, and Teddy's father said that he was a providence, and Teddy looked on with big scared eyes. Rikki-tikki was rather amused at all the fuss, which, of course, he did not understand. Teddy's mother might just as well have petted Teddy for playing in the dust. Rikki was thoroughly enjoying himself.

That night, at dinner, walking to and fro among the wine glasses on the table, he could have stuffed himself three times over with nice things; but he remembered Nag and Nagaina, and though it was very pleasant to be patted and petted by Teddy's mother, and to sit on Teddy's shoulder, his eyes would get red from time to time, and he would go off into his long war-cry of *"Rikk-tikk-tikki-tikki-tchk!"*

Teddy carried him off to bed, and insisted on Rikki-tikki sleeping under his chin. Rikki-tikki was too well bred to bite or scratch, but as soon as Teddy was asleep, he went off for his nightly walk round the house, and in the dark he ran up against Chuchundra, the muskrat, creeping round by the wall. Chuchundra is a brokenhearted little beast. He whimpers and cheeps all the night, trying to make up his mind to run into the middle of the room, but he never gets there.

"Don't kill me," said Chuchundra, almost weeping. "Rikki-tikki, don't kill me."

"Do you think a snake killer kills muskrats?" said Rikki-tikki scornfully.

"Those who kill snakes get killed by snakes," said Chuchundra, more sorrowfully than ever. "And how am I to be sure that Nag won't mistake me for you some dark night?"

"There's not the least danger," said Rikki-tikki; "but Nag is in the garden, and I know you don't go there."

"My cousin Chua, the rat, told me—" said Chuchundra; and then he stopped.

"Told you what?"

"H'sh! Nag is everywhere, Rikki-tikki. You should have talked to Chua in the garden."

"I didn't—so you must tell me. Quick, Chuchundra; or I'll bite you!"

Chuchundra sat down and cried till the tears rolled off his whiskers. "I am a very poor man," he sobbed. "I never had spirit enough to run out into the middle of the room. H'sh! I mustn't tell you anything. Can't you *hear*, Rikki-tikki?"

Rikki-tikki listened. The house was as still as still, but he thought he could just catch the faintest *"scratch-scratch"* in the world—a noise as faint as that of a wasp walking on a windowpane—the dry scratch of a snake's scales on brickwork.

"That's Nag or Nagaina," he said to himself; "and he is crawling into the bathroom sluice. You're right, Chuchundra; I should have talked to Chua."

He stole off to Teddy's bathroom but there was nothing there, and then to Teddy's mother's bathroom. At the bottom of the smooth plaster wall there was a brick pulled out to make a sluice for the bath water, and as Rikki-tikki stole in by the masonry curb where the bath is put, he heard Nag and Nagaina whispering together outside in the moonlight.

"When the house is emptied of people," said Nagaina to her husband, *"he* will have to go away, and then the garden will be our own again. Go in quietly, and remember that the big man who killed Karait is the first one to bite. Then come out and tell me, and we will hunt for Rikki-tikki together."

"But are you sure that there is anything to be gained by killing the people?" said Nag.

"Everything. When there were no people in the bungalow, did we have any mongoose in the garden? So long as the bungalow is empty, we are king and queen of the garden; and remem-

ber that as soon as our eggs in the melon bed hatch (as they may tomorrow), our children will need room and quiet."

"I had not thought of that," said Nag. "I will go, but there is no need that we should hunt for Rikki-tikki afterward. I will kill the big man and his wife, and the child if I can, and come away quietly. Then the bungalow will be empty, and Rikki-tikki will go."

Rikki-tikki tingled all over with rage and hatred at this, and then Nag's head came through the sluice, and his five feet of cold body followed it. Angry as he was, Rikki-tikki was very frightened as he saw the size of the big cobra. Nag coiled himself up, raised his head, and looked into the bathroom in the dark, and Rikki could see his eyes glitter.

"Now, if I kill him here, Nagaina will know; and if I fight him on the

open floor, the odds are in his favor. What am I to do?" said Rikki-tikki-tavi.

Nag waved to and fro, and then Rikki-tikki heard him drinking from the biggest water jar that was used to fill the bath. "That is good," said the snake. "Now, when Karait was killed, the big man had a stick. He may have that stick still, but when he comes in to bathe in the morning he will not have a stick. I shall wait here till he comes. Nagaina—do you hear me?—I shall wait here in the cool till daytime."

There was no answer from outside, so Rikki-tikki knew Nagaina had gone away. Nag coiled himself down, coil by coil, round the bulge at the bottom of the water jar, and Rikki-tikki stayed still as death. After an hour he began to move, muscle by muscle, toward the jar. Nag was asleep, and Rikki-tikki looked at his big back, wondering which would be the best place for a good hold. "If I don't break his back at the first jump," said Rikki, "he can still fight; and if he fights—O Rikki!" He looked at the thickness of the neck below the hood, but that was too much for him; and a bite near the tail would only make Nag savage.

"It must be the head," he said at last; "the head above the hood; and, when I am once there, I must not let go."

Then he jumped. The head was lying a little clear of the water jar, under the curve of it; and, as his teeth met, Rikki braced his back against the bulge of the red earthenware to hold down the head. This gave him just one second's purchase, and he made the most of it. Then he was battered to and fro as a rat is shaken by a dog—to and fro on the floor, up and down, and round in great circles; but his eyes

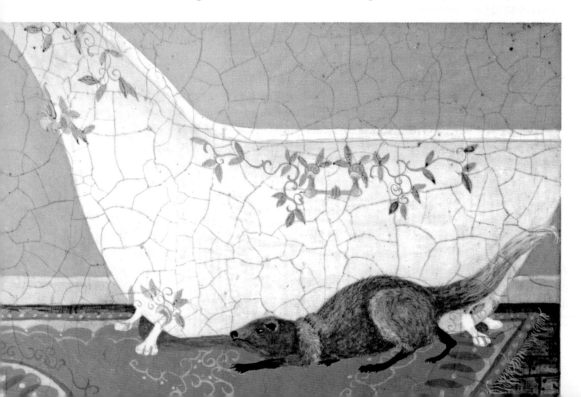

were red, and he held on as the body cart-whipped over the floor, upsetting the tin dipper and the soap dish and the flesh brush, and banged against the tin side of the bath. As he held he closed his jaws tighter and tighter, for he made sure he would be banged to death, and, for the honor of his family, he preferred to be found with his teeth locked. He was dizzy, aching, and felt shaken to pieces when something went off like a thunderclap just behind him; a hot wind knocked him senseless, and red fire singed his fur. The big man had been wakened by the noise, and had fired both barrels of a shotgun into Nag just behind the hood.

Rikki-tikki held on with his eyes shut, for now he was quite sure he was dead; but the head did not move, and the big man picked him up and said: "It's the mongoose again, Alice; the little chap has saved *our* lives now." Then Teddy's mother came in with a very white face, and saw what was left of Nag, and Rikki-tikki dragged himself to Teddy's bedroom and spent half the rest of the night shaking himself tenderly to find out whether he really was broken into forty pieces, as he fancied.

When morning came he was very stiff, but well pleased with his doings. "Now I have Nagaina to settle with, and she will be worse than five Nags, and there's no knowing when the eggs she spoke of will hatch. Goodness! I must go and see Darzee," he said.

Without waiting for breakfast, Rikki-tikki ran to the thorn bush where Darzee was singing a song of triumph at the top of his voice. The news of Nag's death was all over the garden,

for the sweeper had thrown the body on the rubbish heap.

"Oh, you stupid tuft of feathers!" said Rikki-tikki angrily. "Is this the time to sing?"

"Nag is dead—is dead—is dead!" sang Darzee. "The valiant Rikki-tikki caught him by the head and held fast. The big man brought the bang-stick, and Nag fell in two pieces! He will never eat my babies again."

"All that's true enough; but where's Nagaina?" said Rikki-tikki, looking carefully round him.

"Nagaina came to the bathroom sluice and called for Nag," Darzee went on; "and Nag came out on the end of a stick—the sweeper picked him up on the end of a stick and threw him upon the rubbish heap. Let us sing about the great, the red-eyed Rikki-tikki!" and Darzee filled his throat and sang.

"If I could get up to your nest, I'd roll all your babies out!" said Rikki-tikki. "You don't know when to do the right thing at the right time. You're safe enough in your nest there, but it's war for me down here. Stop singing a minute, Darzee."

"For the great, the beautiful Rikki-tikki's sake I will stop," said Darzee. "What is it, O Killer of the terrible Nag?"

"Where is Nagaina, for the third time?"

"On the rubbish heap by the stables, mourning for Nag. Great is Rikki-tikki with the white teeth."

"Bother my white teeth! Have you ever heard where she keeps her eggs?"

"In the melon bed, on the end nearest the wall, where the sun strikes nearly all day. She hid them there weeks ago."

"And you never thought it worthwhile to tell me? The end nearest the wall, you said?"

"Rikki-tikki, you are not going to eat her eggs?"

"Not eat exactly; no. Darzee, if you have a grain of sense you will fly off to the stables and pretend that your wing is broken, and let Nagaina chase you away to this bush. I must get to the melon bed, and if I went there now she'd see me."

Darzee was a featherbrained little fellow who could never hold more than one idea at a time in his head; and just because he knew that Nagaina's children were born in eggs like his own, he didn't think at first that it was fair to kill them. But his wife was a sensible bird, and she knew that cobras' eggs meant young cobras later on; so she flew off from the nest, and left Darzee to keep the babies warm, and continue his song about the death of Nag. Darzee was very like a man in some ways.

She fluttered in front of Nagaina by the rubbish heap, and cried out, "Oh, my wing is broken! The boy in the house threw a stone at me and broke it." Then she fluttered more desperately than ever.

Nagaina lifted up her head and hissed, "You warned Rikki-tikki when I would have killed him. Indeed and truly, you've chosen a bad place to be lame in." And she moved toward Darzee's wife, slipping along over the dust.

"The boy broke it with a stone!" shrieked Darzee's wife.

"Well! It may be some consolation to you when you're dead to know that I shall settle accounts with the boy. My husband lies on the rubbish heap this morning, but before night the boy in the house will lie very still. What is the use of running away? I am sure to catch you. Little fool, look at me!"

Darzee's wife knew better than to do that, for a bird who looks at a snake's eyes gets so frightened that she cannot move. Darzee's wife fluttered on, piping sorrowfully, and never leaving the ground, and Nagaina quickened her pace.

Rikki-tikki heard them going up the path from the stables, and he raced for the end of the melon patch near the wall. There, in the warm litter about the melons, very cunningly hidden, he found twenty-five eggs, about the size of a bantam's eggs, but with whitish skin instead of shell.

"I was not a day too soon," he said; for he could see the baby cobras curled up inside the skin, and he knew that the minute they were hatched they could each kill a man or a mongoose. He bit off the tops of the eggs as fast as he could, taking care to crush the young cobras, and turned over the litter from time to time to see whether he had missed any. At last there were only three eggs left, and Rikki-tikki began to chuckle to himself, when he heard Darzee's wife screaming:

"Rikki-tikki, I led Nagaina toward the house, and she has gone into the veranda, and—oh, come quickly—she means killing!"

Rikki-tikki smashed two eggs, and tumbled backward down the melon

bed with the third egg in his mouth, and scuttled to the veranda as hard as he could put foot to the ground. Teddy and his mother and father were there at early breakfast; but Rikki-tikki saw that they were not eating anything. They sat stone still, and their faces were white. Nagaina was coiled up on the matting by Teddy's chair, within easy striking distance of Teddy's bare leg, and she was swaying to and fro singing a song of triumph.

"Son of the big man that killed Nag," she hissed, "stay still. I am not ready yet. Wait a little. Keep very still, all you three. If you move I strike, and if you do not move I strike. Oh, foolish people, who killed my Nag!"

Teddy's eyes were fixed on his father, and all his father could do was to whisper, "Sit still, Teddy. You mustn't move. Teddy, keep still."

Then Rikki-tikki came up and cried: "Turn round, Nagaina; turn and fight!"

"All in good time," said she, without moving her eyes. "I will settle my account with you presently. Look at your friends, Rikki-tikki. They are still and white; they are afraid. They dare not move, and if you come a step nearer I strike."

"Look at your eggs," said Rikki-tikki, "in the melon bed near the wall. Go and look, Nagaina."

The big snake turned half round, and saw the egg on the veranda. "Ah-h! Give it to me," she said.

Rikki-tikki put his paws one on each side of the egg, and his eyes were blood-red. "What price for a snake's egg? For a young cobra? For a young king cobra? For the last—the very last of the brood? The ants are eating all the others down by the melon bed."

Nagaina spun clear round, forgetting everything for the sake of the one egg; and Rikki-tikki saw Teddy's father shoot out a big hand, catch Teddy by the shoulder, and drag him across the little table with the teacups, safe and out of reach of Nagaina.

"Tricked! Tricked! Tricked! *Rikk-tck-tck!*" chuckled Rikki-tikki. "The boy is safe, and it was I—I—I that caught Nag by the hood last night in the bathroom." Then he began to jump up and down, all four feet together, his head close to the floor. "He threw me to and fro, but he could not shake me off. He was dead before the big man blew him in two. I did it. *Rikki-tikki-tck-tck!* Come then, Nagaina. Come and fight with me. You shall not be a widow long."

Nagaina saw that she had lost her chance of killing Teddy, and the egg lay between Rikki-tikki's paws. "Give me the egg, Rikki-tikki. Give me the last of my eggs, and I will go away and never come back," she said, lowering her hood.

"Yes, you will go away, and you will never come back; for you will go to the rubbish heap with Nag. Fight, widow! The big man has gone for his gun! Fight!"

Rikki-tikki was bounding all round Nagaina, keeping just out of reach of her stroke, his little eyes like hot coals. Nagaina gathered herself together, and flung out at him. Rikki-tikki jumped up and backward. Again and again and again she struck, and each time her head came with a whack on the matting of the veranda, and she gathered herself together like a watch spring. Then Rikki-tikki danced in a circle to get behind her, and Nagaina spun round to keep her head to his head, so that the rustle of her tail on the matting sounded like dry leaves blown along by the wind.

He had forgotten the egg. It still lay on the veranda, and Nagaina came nearer and nearer to it, till at last, while Rikki-tikki was drawing breath, she caught it in her mouth, turned to the veranda steps, and flew like an arrow down the path, with Rikki-tikki behind her. When the cobra runs for her life, she goes like a whiplash flicked across a horse's neck.

Rikki-tikki knew that he must catch her, or all the trouble would begin again. She headed straight for the long grass by the thorn bush, and as he was running Rikki-tikki heard Darzee still singing his foolish little song of triumph. But Darzee's wife was wiser. She flew off her nest as Nagaina came along, and flapped her wings about Nagaina's head. If Darzee had helped they might have turned her; but Nagaina only lowered her hood and went on.

Still, the instant's delay brought Rikki-tikki up to her, and as she plunged into the rat hole where she and Nag used to live, his little white teeth were clenched on her tail, and he went down with her—and very few mongooses, however wise and old they may be, care to follow a cobra into its hole. It was dark in the hole; and Rikki-tikki never knew when it might open out and give Nagaina room to turn and strike at him. He held on savagely, and struck out his feet to act as brakes on the dark slope of the hot, moist earth.

Then the grass by the mouth of the hole stopped waving, and Darzee said: "It is all over with Rikki-tikki! We must sing his death song. Valiant Rikki-tikki is dead! For Nagaina will surely kill him underground."

So he sang a very mournful song that he made up on the spur of the minute, and just as he got to the most touching part the grass quivered again, and Rikki-tikki, covered with dirt, dragged himself out of the hole leg by leg, licking his whiskers. Darzee stopped with a little shout. Rikki-tikki shook some of the dust out of his fur and sneezed. "It is all over," he said. "The widow will never come out again." And the red ants that live between the grass stems heard him, and began to troop down one after another to see if he had spoken the truth.

Rikki-tikki curled himself up in the grass and slept where he was— slept and slept till it was late in the afternoon, for he had done a hard day's work.

"Now," he said, when he awoke, "I will go back to the house. Tell the Coppersmith, Darzee, and he will tell the garden that Nagaina is dead."

The Coppersmith is a bird who makes a noise exactly like the beating of a little hammer on a copper pot; and the reason he is always making it is because he is the town crier to every Indian garden, and tells all the news to everybody who cares to listen. As Rikki-tikki went up the path, he heard his "attention" notes like a tiny dinner gong; and then the steady *"Ding-dong-tock!* Nag is dead—*dong!* Nagaina is dead! *Ding-dong-tock!"* That set all the birds in the garden singing, and the frogs croaking; for Nag and Nagaina used to eat frogs as well as little birds.

When Rikki got to the house, Teddy and Teddy's mother (she still looked very white, for she had been fainting) and Teddy's father came out and almost cried over him; and that night he ate all that was given him till he could eat no more, and went to bed on Teddy's shoulder, where Teddy's mother saw him when she came to look late at night.

"He saved our lives and Teddy's life," she said to her husband. "Just think, he saved all our lives!"

Rikki-tikki woke up with a jump, for all the mongooses are light sleepers.

"Oh, it's you," said he. "What are you bothering for? All the cobras are dead; and if they weren't, I'm here."

Rikki-tikki had a right to be proud of himself; but he did not grow too proud, and he kept that garden as a mongoose should keep it, with tooth and jump and spring and bite, till never a cobra dared show its head inside the walls.

# DARZEE'S CHANT

*(Sung in honor of Rikki-tikki-tavi)*

Singer and tailor am I—
  Doubled the joys that I know—
Proud of my lilt through the sky,
  Proud of the house that I sew—
Over and under, so weave I my music—
  so weave I the house that I sew.   5

Sing to your fledglings again,
  Mother, oh lift up your head!
Evil that plagued us is slain,
  Death in the garden lies dead.
Terror that hid in the roses is impotent—
  flung on the dung-hill and
  dead!   10

Who hath delivered us, who?
  Tell me his nest and his name.
Rikki, the valiant, the true,
  Tikki, with eyeballs of flame,
Rik-tikki-tikki, the ivory fanged, the hunt-
  er with eyeballs of flame.   15

Give him the Thanks of the Birds,
  Bowing with tail feathers spread!
Praise him with nightingale words—
  Nay, I will praise him instead.
Hear! I will sing you the praise of the
  bottle-tailed Rikki, with eyeballs
  of red!   20

(Here Rikki-tikki interrupted, and the rest of the song is lost.)

**DISCUSSION**

1. It takes the full cooperation of animals and people to rid the garden of cobras. Darzee's wife, for example, pretends a broken wing to distract Nagaina. Give two or three examples of this close cooperation.

2. Rikki-tikki is the only animal in the story that kills another. Why do we still like him?

3. Rikki-tikki's instincts equip him well to fight snakes, but in one instance his quick thinking saves three lives. How does he trick Nagaina with the egg?

4. Compare the relationships between Darzee and his wife and between Nag and Nagaina. Which character is stronger in each couple?

For further activities, see page 108.

# OLD BEN

## JESSE STUART

One morning in July when I was walking across a clover field to a sweet-apple tree, I almost stepped on him. There he lay coiled like heavy strands of black rope. He was a big bull blacksnake. We looked at each other a minute, and then I stuck the toe of my shoe up to his mouth. He drew his head back in a friendly way. He didn't want trouble. Had he shown the least fight, I would have soon finished him. My father had always told me there was only one good snake—a dead one.

When the big fellow didn't show any fight, I reached down and picked him up by the neck. When I lifted him he was as long as I was tall. That was six feet. I started calling him Old Ben as I held him by the neck and rubbed his back. He enjoyed having his back rubbed and his head stroked. Then I lifted him into my arms. He was the first snake I'd ever been friendly with. I was afraid at first to let Old Ben wrap himself around me. I thought he might wrap himself around my neck and choke me.

The more I petted him, the more affectionate he became. He was so friendly I decided to trust him. I wrapped him around my neck a couple of times and let him loose. He crawled down one arm and went back to my neck, around and down the other arm and back again. He stuck out his forked tongue to the sound of my voice as I talked to him.

"I wouldn't kill you at all," I said. "You're a friendly snake. I'm taking you home with me."

I headed home with Old Ben wrapped around my neck and shoulders. When I started over the hill by the pine grove, I met my cousin Wayne Holbrook coming up the hill. He stopped suddenly when he saw me. He started backing down the hill.

"He's a pet, Wayne," I said. "Don't be afraid of Old Ben."

It was a minute before Wayne could tell me what he wanted. He had come to borrow a plow. He kept a safe distance as we walked on together.

Before we reached the barn, Wayne got brave enough to touch Old Ben's long body.

"What are you going to do with him?" Wayne asked. "Uncle Mick won't let you keep him!"

"Put him in the corncrib," I said. "He'll have plenty of delicate food in there. The cats we keep at this barn have grown fat and lazy on the milk we feed em."

I opened the corncrib door and took Old Ben from around my neck because he was beginning to get warm and a little heavy.

"This will be your home," I said. "You'd better hide under the corn."

Besides my father, I knew Old Ben would have another enemy at our home. He was our hunting dog, Blackie, who would trail a snake, same as a possum or mink. He had treed blacksnakes, and my father had shot them from the trees. I knew Blackie would find Old Ben, because he followed us to the barn each morning.

The first morning after I'd put Old Ben in the corncrib, Blackie followed us. He started toward the corncrib holding his head high, sniffing. He stuck his nose up to a crack in the crib and began to bark. Then he tried to tear a plank off.

"Stop it, Blackie," Pa scolded him. "What's the matter with you? Have you taken to barking at mice?"

"Blackie is not barking at a mouse," I said. "I put a blacksnake in there yesterday!"

"A blacksnake?" Pa asked, looking unbelievingly. "A blacksnake?"

"Yes, a pet blacksnake," I said.

"Have you gone crazy?" he said. "I'll move a thousand bushels of corn to get that snake!"

"You won't mind this one," I said. "You and Mom will love him."

My father said a few unprintable words before we started back to the house. After breakfast, when Pa and Mom came to the barn, I was already there. I had opened the crib door and there was Old Ben. He'd crawled up front and was coiled on a sack. I put my hand down and he crawled up my arm to my neck and over my shoulder. When Mom and Pa reached the crib, I thought Pa was goint to faint.

"He has a pet snake," Mom said.

"Won't be a bird or a young chicken left on this place," Pa said. "Every time I pick up an ear of corn in that crib, I'll be jumping."

"Pa, he won't hurt you," I said, patting the snake's head.

"He's a natural pet, or somebody has tamed him. And he's not going to bother birds and young chickens when there are so many mice in this crib."

"Mick, let him keep the snake," Mom said. "I won't be afraid of it."

This was the beginning of a long friendship.

Mom went to the corncrib morning after morning and shelled corn for her geese and chickens. Often Old Ben would be lying in front on his burlap sack. Mom watched him at first from the corner of her eye. Later she didn't bother to watch him any more than she did a cat that came up for his milk.

Later it occurred to us that Old Ben might like milk, too. We started leaving milk for him. We never saw him drink it, but his pan was always empty when we returned. We know the mice didn't drink it, because he took care of them.

"One thing is certain," Mom said one morning when she went to shell corn. "We don't find any more corn chewed up by the mice and left on the floor."

July passed and August came. My father got used to Old Ben, but not until he had proved his worth. Ben had done something our nine cats couldn't. He had cleaned the corncrib of mice.

Then my father began to worry about Old Ben's going after water, and Blackie's finding his track. So he put water in the crib.

September came and went. We began wondering where our pet would go when days grew colder. One morning in early October we left milk for Old Ben, and it was there when we went back that afternoon. But Old Ben wasn't there.

"Old Ben's a good pet for the warm months," Pa said. "But in the winter months, my cats will have to do the work. Maybe Blackie got him!"

"He might have holed up for the winter in the hayloft," I told Pa after we had removed all the corn and didn't find him. "I'm worried about him. I've had a lot of pets—ground hogs, crows, and hawks—but Old Ben's the best yet."

November, December, January, February, and March came and went. Of course we never expected to see Old Ben in one of those months. We doubted if we ever would see him again.

One day early in April I went to the corncrib, and Old Ben lay stretched across the floor. He looked taller than I was now.

His skin was rough and his long body had a flabby appearance.
I knew Old Ben needed mice and milk. I picked him up, petted
him, and told him so. But the chill of early April was still with
him. He got his tongue out slower to answer the kind words I
was saying to him. He tried to crawl up my arm but he couldn't
make it.

That spring and summer mice got scarce in the corncrib
and Old Ben got daring. He went over to the barn and crawled
up into the hayloft, where he had many feasts. But he made
one mistake.

He crawled from the hayloft down into Fred's feed box,
where it was cool. Old Fred was our horse.

There he lay coiled when the horse came in and put his
nose down on top of Old Ben. Fred let out a big snort and
started kicking. He kicked down a partition, and then turned
his heels on his feed box and kicked it down. Lucky for Old Ben
that he got out in one piece. But he got back to his crib.

Old Ben became a part of our barnyard family, a pet and
darling of all. When children came to play with my brother and
sisters, they always went to the crib and got Old Ben. He enjoyed the children, who were afraid of him at first but later
learned to pet this kind old reptile.

Summer passed and the late days of September were very
humid. Old Ben failed one morning to drink his milk. We knew
it wasn't time for him to hole up for the winter.

We knew something had happened.

Pa and I moved the corn searching for him. Mom made a
couple of trips to the barn lot to see if we had found him. But

all we found was the rough skin he had shed last spring.

"Fred's never been very sociable with Old Ben since he got in his box that time," Pa said. "I wonder if he could have stomped Old Ben to death. Old Ben could've been crawling over the barn lot, and Fred saw his chance to get even!"

"We'll see," I said.

Pa and I left the crib and walked to the barn lot. He went one way and I went the other, each searching the ground.

Mom came through the gate and walked over where my father was looking. She started looking around, too.

"We think Fred might've got him," Pa said. "We're sure Fred's got it in for him over Old Ben getting in his feed box last summer."

"You're accusing Fred wrong," Mom said. "Here's Old Ben's track in the sand."

I ran over to where Mom had found the track. Pa went over to look, too.

"It's no use now," Pa said softly. "Wouldn't have taken anything for that snake. I'll miss him on that burlap sack every morning when I come to feed the horses. Always looked up to me as if he understood."

The last trace Old Ben had left was in the corner of the lot near the hogpen. His track went straight to the woven wire fence and stopped.

"They've got him," Pa said. "Old Ben trusted everything and everybody. He went for a visit to the wrong place. He didn't last long among sixteen hogs. They go wild over a snake. Even a biting copperhead can't stop a hog. There won't be a trace of Old Ben left."

We stood silently for a minute looking at the broad, smooth track Old Ben had left in the sand.


DISCUSSION     1.  By the end of the story, the narrator's "pa" likes Old Ben. What accounts for his change of mind?

2.  How can you be fairly certain that the horse, Fred, isn't responsible for Ben's death?

3.  Most people are afraid of snakes. Why do you think this is so?

# THE SLOTH

## THEODORE ROETHKE

In moving-slow he has no peer.
You ask him something in his ear;
He thinks about it for a Year;

And then, before he says a Word
There, upside down (unlike a bird)    5
He will assume that you have heard—

A most EX-as-per-at-ing Lug.
But should you call his manner Smug,
He'll sigh and give his branch a Hug;

Then off again to Sleep he goes,    10
Still swaying gently by his Toes,
And you just know he knows he knows.

DISCUSSION

1. The speaker in this poem notes that the sloth is slow and gentle. What expressions emphasize these characteristics?

2. Find lines that you think show the speaker's like or dislike of the sloth.

3. **Rhyme.** The repetition of the same sound or sounds, usually at the ends of lines, is called rhyme. Point out the four different rhymes that Roethke uses in this poem.

# Love Song for a Jellyfish

SANDRA HOCHMAN

How amazed I was, when I was a child,
To see your life on the sand.
To see you living in your jelly shape,
Round and slippery and dangerous.
You seemed to have fallen
Not from the rim of the sea,
But from the galaxies.
Stranger, you delighted me. Weird object of
The stinging world.

DISCUSSION

1. The speaker in the poem is "delighted" with the jellyfish. Why?

2. Mention several other members of the "stinging world." Can humans also sting? How?

After two years in Mexico, Daniel Mannix
and his wife Jule thought they knew every
kind of animal in Mexico. But they still had
to learn about vampire bats.

# BAT QUEST

DANIEL P. MANNIX

I first heard about the vampires through Dr. Alfredo Tellez Giron. Dr. Giron had isolated "derriengue fever" in vampires and
shown that they were causing the death of thousands of cattle.
The vampires were also known to carry rabies. Most interesting
to us was that possibly vampires had migrated north and
crossed the Texas border. The skull of a vampire bat was report-
edly found in a cave in the Big Bend area of Texas. Together
with Charles Mohr, then with the Academy of Natural Sciences
in Philadelphia, we decided to explore caves in northern Mexico
and find how close the vampire colonies were to the border.

Charles Mohr's interest in the bats was purely scientific,
but Jule and I determined to keep a few as pets and see if we
could tame them. No one seemed to know much about the
weird creatures. We couldn't understand why a sleeper attacked
by a vampire never seemed to wake up, how the bats went
about delivering their nocturnal raids, or how an animal as
small as a bat could apparently show considerable intelligence
in plotting his forays. Perhaps by keeping pet vampires we
could answer some of these questions.

Vampires are comparatively small bats. Their bodies are
only about three inches long and they have a wingspread of little more than a foot. A single vampire can only drink about a
tablespoon of blood, but a horde of them can cause a sleeper to
lose enough blood to weaken him. They are found only in this
hemisphere and were first reported by the conquistadores. European scientists thought these men were simply repeating a native legend until Charles Darwin proved the existence of the
vampires by sleeping out in the jungle and letting himself be
bitten. But not until it was discovered that the vampires could
transmit disease was any real interest taken in them.

We discovered our first vampires in the cave of Los Sabinos, about 200 miles south of the border. At the time this was the northernmost colony of vampires ever reported, although since then another colony has been found 50 miles closer to the United States. The village of Los Sabinos consisted of half a dozen thatched huts deep in the jungle, a few people, and several sheep, pigs, and goats. I spent some time talking to the Indians as I was curious to find out what sort of people would voluntarily live next to a community of vampire bats. The villagers discussed the bats as calmly as New Jerseyites would talk about mosquitoes. The bats came every night to feed on their stock—and on them. The villagers retired to their huts as soon as the sun went down and carefully filled in every chink. If anyone forgot a chink, when he awoke the next morning he was dripping blood from half a dozen little wounds. When the animals got bitten so badly they became weak, the villagers took them into the huts too.

I asked if they'd ever thought of moving. They had, but this was a good, high spot in the jungle with a spring of excellent water. There were no ticks, mosquitoes, or polluted wells. What were a few vampires?

Two Indians, a father and a son, offered to act as guides to the cave. I noticed them calmly testing a 150-foot fiber rope of a type usually used by climbers preparing to ascend the Matterhorn.

"How high is the roof of this cave?" Jule asked.

"How high is the sky, señora?" the son replied carelessly.

The Indians insisted on taking along a double handful of the rough, home-dipped candles that hung in bunches from the ceilings of the huts.

"The candles don't give as much light as our miner's headlamps," Charlie Mohr pointed out.

"The candles don't have batteries that go dead, either," said the old man stubbornly.

The Indians told us that no one knew how deep the cave might be. "Several people have tried to reach the end, señors," he explained. "Maybe some succeeded. Nobody knows because they never came out again."

The entrance to the cave was shrouded by a forest of curiously twisted trees that looked like the papier-mâché[1] creation

---

[1] *papier-mâche* (pä′pər-mə-shã′): molding material made from shredded paper and glue.

of a Hollywood murder-mystery set. Our guides led the way down a steep slope into a natural amphitheater, hung with jungle creepers as big as cables. Across from us a black slit like a giant, toothless mouth showed in the white limestone. Vines overhung it like a straggly mustache. The older guide pointed. "This is the vampire grotto."

Leaving the horse to graze, we climbed through the opening into the great entrance hall, 70 feet high. The younger guide picked up some animal bones. "Sometimes animals are foolish enough to spend the night in the cave entrance," he remarked. "They never see daylight again."

As it would be extremely unlikely that any number of the little vampires could kill a large animal in a single night, the bones probably belonged to sick animals that had wandered into the cave to die, but they gave an uncanny touch to the place nonetheless.

We lighted our lamps in our miners' helmets and started downward into the cave. The entrance hall was filled with boulders, piled together like children's marbles. We stepped from one to another, descending deeper and deeper into the earth. The vast mouth of the cave diminished behind us until it looked no bigger than a rathole. Then it vanished completely. We began feeling our way down a great slope in complete darkness except for the puddles of light from our headlamps. At intervals the guides lit candles and left them sticking to the rocks to mark our path back. They showed in the intense darkness like tiny fireflies.

Then the slope ended in a steep drop, falling away into a vast black hole so deep that not even our powerful flashlights could reach the bottom of it. The guides started climbing down the sheer wall, working their way from handhold to handhold. As each of us climbed down the rock, the others held their flashlights so we could see the handholds. Bats began to pour out of the hole like clouds of black confetti but they were the little, insect-eating kind and although I could feel the wind of their leathery wings, none of them touched us.

Below us, the guides had stopped on a ledge. I could see them playing their lights back and forth along an overhang which projected over nothingness. One after another we landed on the ledge and looked over into the abyss. "This is where we use the rope, señor," the old man explained.

They doubled the rope so we could use one strand as a

safety line and climb down the other length. I wrapped my feet around the climbing rope and, gripping the safety line, slowly inched backward over the edge. I began to let myself down seventy feet, and then the rope ended. I hung there, knowing I could never climb up hand over hand, especially with a knapsack on my back containing sixty pounds of scientific equipment.

"I've come to the end of the rope. What shall I do?" I yelled.

"Just let go," the guides shouted.

"What do you mean by that?"

"There's a ledge right under you. Let go and you'll drop on it."

I turned my headlamp down and saw the ledge. As soon as I was off the rope, the rest came down one after another. We climbed down to the floor of the cave and Charlie Mohr held up his hand. "Hear them?"

I listened and heard a noise that sounded like the chittering call of ordinary bats combined with the whistle of steam from a teakettle. "That's the cry of the vampires," said Charlie.

We moved forward slowly into a big room with passages branching off on all sides. They were separated from the main hall by fringes of stalactites[2] hanging like draperies around the openings. Getting down on our hands and knees we crawled under a strip of the stone teeth and ahead of us was a series of great, billowing terraces like monster fountains turned to stone.

We began to climb up the terraces. The rock was as smooth and as slippery as ice, but there were occasional hollows full of water where we could sit and rest. Suddenly on the wall ahead we saw little shapes running and leaping among the formations. The long shadows thrown by our lamps added to their height and looked exactly like little men rushing frantically about, trying to decide what to do. Every now and then one of them would crane himself up to peer down at us. They did not look in the least animal-like. They looked like goblins. An artist trying to illustrate a child's book of fairy stories could not have done better than to reproduce that scene.

These were the vampires. Running on their hind feet and the elbows of their wings, they could go as fast as a four-legged animal. They kept turning their enormous ears about as a rab-

---

[2] *stalactites:* mineral deposits hanging from the roof of a cave.

bit would to pick up the noise we made. As we came closer several ran to the edge of the ledges and sprang into the air. Others stood their ground, baring their teeth and chattering fiercely. I grabbed one old warrior whose fur was a deep reddish-brown and as soft as moleskin. He fought savagely in my gloved hand, screaming with rage. As we put him into the collection box, he spit out two slivers of a brown substance we could not identify but later we found that he had sliced out two small pieces of leather from my glove. They were not bitten out; they were slashed out with his scalpel-sharp incisors. A razor could not have dug out those gouges in my glove as neatly.

Charlie tried to catch some with a net. The vampires seemed to understand perfectly what he was doing. Several of them leaped straight up in the air to avoid his strokes. Others bounced along the ledges like rubber balls and vanished into holes. Some vampires ran up the walls, lifting themselves with two long fingers growing out of the elbows of their wings. These fingers are amazing instruments, each ending in a curved nail like a squirrel's claw. Turning up our lights, we could see dozens of vampires hanging head down on the walls above us. They looked like miniature bearskin rugs, hung upside down with the open mouths and grinning teeth pointing downward.

We found three young vampires in a pocket of the rock, all huddled together with their weird little bulldog faces peering out at us anxiously. Every time they saw the net coming near them, two of the little devils would grab the third and shove him forward while they hid behind him. The victim would stare at us for a moment and then dive under his friends, shoving them back over his shoulder. Jule pulled them apart and lined all three up on a stalagmite[3] but before I could get a picture one of them had kicked another and the fight started all over again.

When we got back to our hotel in Valles, the nearest town to Los Sabinos, and opened our collecting box we found our vampires in a state of shock. We had three adults—including the tough old fellow who'd bitten my glove—and two little ones. The old warrior was the only one who showed any animation, he was still willing to fight, but the others seemed paralyzed. Charlie added to our troubles by telling us that vampires have to eat their own weight in blood every twenty-four hours or they'll die. The Los Sabinos Indians had told us that the bats,

---

[3] *stalagmite:* mineral deposit projecting upward from the floor of a cave.

in addition to feeding on humans and cattle, will also drink blood from a chicken, biting the bird in the leg (they can't get through the feathers). We had invested in a couple of chickens, but these bats were obviously in no condition to feed on anything and we didn't know when they had last eaten.

"You may as well let me make skins of them," Charlie suggested callously and I felt the same way, but Jule wouldn't listen to either of us. "There must be some way to save them," she insisted. All they need to do is find out that we're their friends."

As usual, Jule went to work with her medicine dropper although now it was filled with fresh blood, contributed by the local butcher who frankly thought we were crazy. The only one she could work with was the old warrior who, we discovered, had only one eye. He had presumably lost the other in a fight with another vampire, possibly over a lady bat. The old fighter didn't take kindly to being force-fed. He bit, shrieked, whistled, and struggled in Jule's gloved hand. He positively refused to suck from the end of the dropper. The whole project seemed hopeless, but Jule refused to be discouraged. "Give him time; he'll have to quiet down a little first," she insisted. An hour later the old boy had quieted down enough so he'd sit crouched in Jule's palm, only snarling slightly when she scratched his head.

Then Jule tried the medicine dropper again. To make sure the blood was flowing easily, she pressed the bulb of the dropper slightly until a drop of blood appeared at the glass tip. An astonishing thing happened. The bat sat up, stretched out his neck, and with his curious pink, club-shaped tongue licked the drop off. Jule offered him another drop and he licked that away too. He was feeding.

The other bats were rigid from shock and Jule had to massage them gently until they came around. By two o'clock that morning, Jule had managed to feed them all. Her system was to put one of the bats next to the old warrior who was feeding readily. After a minute or so, the other bat would nudge over to get some and a fight would start. Then I'd decoy the old fellow away with another medicine dropper while Jule continued feeding the other bat.

Our main problem was keeping the blood from coagulating.[4] Charlie Mohr solved that difficulty for us. By putting the

---

[4] *coagulating:* becoming a semisolid or solid mass.

fresh blood in a bottle with some marbles and shaking it up, the corpuscles of the blood were broken down and it would remain liquid for some time.

By the time we got back to Taxco, our bats were so used to us that we could feed them from a burro we rented for the purpose. The burro didn't mind the business—in fact, he was far more afraid of us than of the bats—and they took comparatively little blood. Most of the time, the burro didn't even know he was being bitten.

I wanted to see how vampires would attack a human being, but here Jule unreasonably rebelled. "Dan, I've been willing to do almost anything with you in the animal line, but I won't be eaten by vampire bats," she declared. So I had to act as the subject while Jule took notes.

But the bats positively refused to bite me. They would crawl up and down my bare arm or over my legs and never offer to bite. Finally Jule broke down, but they wouldn't bite her either. It was very discouraging.

At last we decided that they were still nervous about us. I would have to pretend to be asleep while Jule hid in our bathroom and watched through the curtains.

In spite of all our precautions, the bats still stubbornly refused to cooperate. I finally did fall asleep and Jule reported what happened.

As usual, it was the old fellow who proved the boldest. He

was hanging with the others from the cornice of our bedroom. He woke up, licked his lips, and then stretched his wings, one after the other. Then he began to turn his little bulldog head from side to side, his nose twitching as though he were scenting the air.

Instead of flying over to the bed, he climbed down the wall using his hooks, hopping across the floor like a toad, and then bounded onto the bed covers. He sat there some time watching me and listening to my breathing. Then he quietly reared up on the tips of his wings and crawled up the covers toward my face, every motion elaborately cautious.

When he reached my face, he moved back and forth around the pillow, looking for a good place to bite. We later found that a vampire tries to get a spot with few nerves and plenty of blood so he seldom chooses the throat—not as dramatic as sinking his fangs into the jugular vein but far more practical. When he finally decided on a good spot, he approached cautiously and nipped the side of my neck gently. I tossed and he scuttled back hurriedly and waited until I was quiet again. Then he tried the lobe of my ear.

Here Jule interfered. "I just couldn't stand there and watch him drink your blood," she told me later. I must say that I was just as happy.

We did, however, watch the bats drink from the burro. When a vampire bites, he stretches his mouth open to the fullest extent and makes a single quick slash with his two long incisors. He does not stab but slashes out two small gouges and then instantly jumps back to watch the quarry's reaction. If he has hit an insensitive spot, he then hurries in and begins to lap, not suck, the flowing blood. If the animal starts or shakes himself, the bat waits until he quiets down and then tries another spot. Once he has found a good spot, he will always return to that same place again. Each of our bats had a different spot where he fed on the burro. Indians told us that they can kill the bats by seeing where they've bitten an animal and then smearing poison on the scab. The bat will surely return to exactly the same spot.

A bite made by a vampire will continue to bleed long after the bat has left it, and more blood is lost this way than from the actual bite. Scientists have argued that the saliva of the bats must contain some chemical that prevents the blood from coagulating but apparently this is not so. The action of the tongue helps to keep the wound open while the bat is lapping but it seemed to us that the bats know enough to cut into a vein. The action of the victim's heart keeps pumping the blood out and this is why the wound continues to bleed. Our young vampires hadn't developed the approved technique and would bite the burro anywhere, but often they couldn't draw enough blood to satisfy them. Then they'd have to try somewhere else. But once they learned where a vein was, they never forgot the location.

I can't say the vampires made particularly good pets. They seemed to be highly specialized. Apart from their biting technique, they never showed any intelligence. They did learn to recognize Jule and would come to her for blood from the medicine dropper while they avoided me. Some even learned to lap from a saucer. Even when they became so tame that Jule could pick them up, stroke them, feed them, and then hang them up on the wall as though she were hanging up a scarf, they never responded to affection as did Reddy, our red-bellied squirrel, and never showed any interest in what was going on about them.

When it was time to leave Mexico, we let them go. As bats have an astonishing homing instinct, I've no doubt that they found their way back to their cave in Los Sabinos. They were interesting but hardly lovable.

**DISCUSSION**

1.   Mannix ends this account with the observation that bats are "interesting but hardly lovable." What statements in the selection make you agree or disagree with his statement?

2.   With bats in the room the author allows himself to fall asleep. What does the fact that he *can* fall asleep with vampires hanging from the ceiling tell you about him?

3.   **Fiction/Nonfiction.**   Fiction is prose writing that tells a story the author has created from her or his imagination. "Rikki-tikki-tavi" and "Old Ben" are works of fiction. Nonfiction, like "Bat Quest," is a factual account of an actual experience. Why do you think little fiction is written about bats?

For further activities, see page 108.

# Animals' Tails

ALAN DEVOE

What do animals use their tails for? For just about every purpose imaginable. A squirrel's bushy tail, for instance, is a steering rudder when the squirrel is making its big arboreal jumps and a balancing parasol when the squirrel is picking its way along fine twigs. When a squirrel misses its footing and falls (they sometimes do), the plumy tail acts as a parachute so effectively that squirrels often plunge 50 or 60 feet to earth without suffering any injury. A bushy tail is a warm wrap-around in cold weather—a winter fox, for instance, sleeps with his tail curled around over the tip of his nose—and a tail is also of incalculable help in making a predatory enemy misjudge a pounce. A predator, rushing after its victim, is likely to jump at the waving tail. It gets a mouthful of tail fur and the tail-owner gets away.

Is it true that mice use their tails to get food out of inaccessible places, such as out of bottles? Unschooled animalizers have always believed that, but some others have dismissed it as folk myth. It is no myth. It is true. If a mouse finds an unstoppered jug of, say, molasses, it will sit itself atop the neck, lower its tail into the jug in a mouse version of the gesture of a man lowering a bucket into a well, and haul up the sweet stuff tailful by tailful.

To what use does a kangaroo put its great heavy tail? It leans back and props itself on it, as a man does on a shooting stick. Many lizards use their tails that way too. The original monster lizards, almost certainly, swung their tails as weapons, in a carry-over from the tail-swinging technique of fish. And today? Is it true that a crocodile uses its tail as a weapon? Yes. It can knock a man over with one wallop. Do any warm-blooded animals do the same sort of thing? Yes again. Take an ant bear. It thwacks with its tail as powerfully as a bear with its forepaw.

Tails serve animals as flyswatters, as signals, as instruments of communication, as extra hands and tools of many uses. A woolly monkey curls the tip of his tail into a circle, plants this loop on the ground, stiffens the rest of the tail into a supporting column, and has a portable chair. A honey bear, raiding a nest of bees, hangs head downward and then, when it wants to make its getaway, climbs its own tail. Pangolins, which are scaly anteaters living in West Africa, block their burrow entrances with their armored tails.

There are almost as many tail uses as there are animals. There are also, however, some popular notions about animals' tails that aren't true.

Is it a fact that if you pick up a skunk by the tail the skunk can't discharge its malodorous spray? As a good many outdoors-explorers have learned the hard way, it isn't. It is true that sometimes a skunk, captured by the tail-grabbing technique, fails to loose its stench. This may be either because the particular skunk is exceptionally affable (*all* skunks, by the way, are placid, friendly animals, and don't ordinarily discharge their sulphide unless extremely frightened or harassed), or it may be because stench-loosing ability varies from skunk to skunk. The fact to be remembered is that a great many skunks can and do function just as effectively when hoisted by their tails as under any other circumstances.

How about squirrels using their tails as sails? The story goes that when numbers of migrating squirrels come to a river, each squirrel takes off from shore on a bit of bark or a big leaf, hoists its tail as a sail, and the whole squirrel horde goes whisking adrift in a great flotilla. True? No.

This brings up the matter of beavers' tails, and so of beavers in general. Few of our furred brothers are the subject of more frequent animal questions, the list of them being headed by:

Do beavers use their tails as trowels?

In the animal books of our childhoods, and particularly of our fathers'and grandfathers' childhoods, there used sometimes to be wonderful engravings showing beavers piling heaps of mud on their broad flat tails, toting the mud to their lodge, and then slapping and smoothing the mud into place like plasterers. They were enthralling pictures. They weren't, however, reliable. Do beavers use their tails as mortarboards and trowels? They never do. What do they use them for? Three things: They use them for swimming-rudders. They use them for props, to sit back on when they are gnawing at a tree. They use them to sound alarm signals. They slap them against the water with a resounding "whomp," and every beaver within earshot dives to safety.

DISCUSSION    1.   Animals' tails are used for many purposes. Which uses did you find most interesting and/or unusual?

2.   Find in the story one or two false notions about the uses of animals' tails. Were there any animals mentioned in this story that you had never heard of before? If so, which ones?

3.   Would you classify this selection as **fiction** or **nonfiction** (see page 103)? Why?

For further activities, see page 108.

# WHO IS SAD ?

ELIZABETH COATSWORTH

Who is sad and who is sorry?
Not the seagull flying high,
not the wren, brown as earth is,
not the bumblebee buzzing by,
not the cat upon the doorstep,
not the dog beside the gate—
they are neither sad nor sorry,
proud, ashamed, on
time, nor
late.

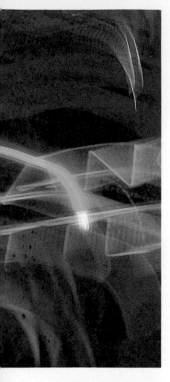

## VOCABULARY

### Rikki-tikki-tavi (page 72)

On separate paper, match the number of the word with the letter of the definition at the right.

| | | | |
|---|---|---|---|
| 1. | veranda | a. | rapid series of speechlike sounds |
| 2. | fibers | b. | porch, often partially enclosed |
| 3. | chattered | c. | recklessly or hopelessly |
| 4. | desperately | d. | comfort, cheer |
| 5. | consolation | e. | chirping or whistling |
| 6. | piping | f. | long slender structures; threads or strands |

### Bat Quest (page 95)

On separate paper, write the word closest in meaning to the word in bold type in the left column.

1. their *nocturnal* raids — secret nightly deadly
2. show intelligence in plotting his *forays* — raids plans endeavors
3. carefully filled in every *chink* — circle crack blank
4. no *polluted* wells — fresh contaminated drained

5. *slit* like a giant, toothless mouth — painted carved open
6. the vampire *grotto* — cavern prey flight
7. climbing the *sheer* wall — sloping uneven steep
8. the *chittering* call of ordinary bats — frantic yodeling twittering
9. *miniature* bearskin rugs — old small large
10. their *weird* faces — grotesque tiny revengeful

## COMPOSITION

### Lone Dog (page 70)

If you were going to make a TV commercial for a dog food, how would you do it using the lone dog? Write a plan and include a detailed description of the setting and people you would use. Describe the plot, humor, music, and wording. What kind of mood would you try to create?

## Rikki-tikki-tavi (page 72)

Suppose that you are Teddy, the boy in the story. Write a letter to a friend telling about the incident on the veranda when Rikki-tikki saved you from being killed by Nagaina, the cobra. You might begin the letter, "You will never guess what happened at our house today."

## READING

## Bat Quest (page 95)

On separate paper, list the numbers of those items below which are characteristic of vampire bats.

1. carry rabies
2. awake people from sleep when biting
3. are comparatively small
4. have bodies about six inches long
5. have wing spread of little more than a foot
6. can drink only about a tablespoon of blood
7. have small ears
8. run on their hind feet and elbows
9. have no fur
10. have razor-sharp teeth
11. hang upside down
12. have fingers growing out of their elbows
13. choose the throat to bite only rarely
14. sink their teeth deep into the skin
15. make good pets

## Animals' Tails (page 104)

Following are several uses for animals' tails. On separate paper, write which animal uses its tail for which purpose.

as a warm wrap-around     as a prop, a support
as a weapon               as a chair
         as a block to an entrance

# THE VENTRILOQUIST AND

Into a restaurant once upon a time strolled a ventriloquist with his handsome and very clever dog. The gentleman sat down at a table, called the waiter over, and said:

"Bring me a beefsteak."

As he started off to fill the order, the waiter suddenly stopped, surprised. He had distinctly heard the dog say:

"Bring *me* a beefsteak too."

Now opposite the dog's owner at the same table sat a man who was very rich but not all that bright. The rich man promptly dropped the knife he was holding and began gaping at the marvelous dog. In time the waiter returned and set one beefsteak on the table in front of the dog's owner, then put another down on the floor beside the dog. Then man and dog, ignoring stares and comments, fell to eating with hearty appetites. Afterward the owner of the dog said:

"Waiter, bring me a glass of wine."

"Bring *me* a glass of water," the dog threw in.

With that, everybody in the room stopped eating in order to watch this extraordinary scene.

"Hey, you wouldn't want to sell your dog?" the rich man

# HIS TALKING DOG

asked the gentleman after a moment. "I've never seen so intelligent an animal."

But the owner replied, "Ah, I'm afraid this fellow isn't for sale. He's the best friend I have in the world. We couldn't live without each other."

And hardly had he finished when the dog piped up: "That's the truth. I don't want to be sold, thank you!"

Whereupon the rich man pulled out his wallet, and spreading two thousand pesetas on the table without a word, gave the owner a questioning glance.

The ventriloquist hesitated. "Hmm," he mused aloud. "Now that does change things. I see money can talk too. The dog's all yours."

The rich man finished his meal at once and, ecstatic about his purchase, rose and started out the door with the animal, who at the moment of parting called back these words in a voice almost choking with rage and disgust:

"Some friend you are, you louse! You've sold me to a stranger! But just for that I swear by all the saints I'll never speak another word to a human being again!"

# CHOLMONDELY, THE CHIMPANZEE

GERALD DURRELL

When Cholmondely, the chimpanzee, joined the collection, he immediately became the uncrowned king of it, not only because of his size, but also because he was so remarkably intelligent. Cholmondely had been the pet of a District Officer who, wanting to send the ape to the London zoo and hearing that I was collecting wild animals in that region and would shortly be returning to England, wrote and asked me if I would mind taking Cholmondely with me and handing him over to the zoo authorities. I wrote back to say that, as I already had a large collection of monkeys, another chimpanzee would not make any difference, so I would gladly escort Cholmondely back to England. I imagined that he would be quite a young chimp, perhaps two years old, and standing about two feet high. When he arrived I got a considerable shock.

A small van drew up outside the camp one morning and in the back of it was an enormous wooden crate. It was big enough, I thought, to house an elephant. I wondered what on earth could be inside, and when the driver told me that it contained Cholmondely I remember thinking how silly his owner was to send such a small chimpanzee in such a huge crate. I opened the door and looked inside and there sat Cholmondely. One glance at him and I realized that this was no baby chimpanzee but a fully grown one about eight or nine years old. Sitting hunched up in the dark crate, he looked as though he were about twice as big as me, and from the expression on his face I gathered that the trip had not been to his liking. Before I could shut the door of the box, however, Cholmondely had extended a long, hairy arm, clasped my hand in his, and shaken it warmly. Then he turned round and gathered up a great length of chain (one end of which was fastened to a collar round his neck), draped it carefully over his arm, and stepped down out of the box. He stood there for a moment and, after surveying me carefully, examined the camp with great interest, whereupon he

*Cholmondely:* pronounced chŭm'lē.

held out his hand, looking at me inquiringly. I took it in mine and we walked into the marquee together.

Cholmondely immediately seated himself on one of the chairs by the camp table, dropped his chain on the floor, and sat back and crossed his legs. He gazed around the tent for a few minutes with a rather supercilious expression on his face, and evidently deciding that it would do he turned and looked at me inquiringly again. Obviously, he wanted me to offer him something after his tiring journey. I had been warned before he arrived that he was a hardened tea drinker, and so I called out to the cook and told him to make a pot of tea. Then I went out and had a look in Cholmondely's crate, and in the bottom I found an enormous and very battered tin mug. When I returned to the tent with this, Cholmondely was quite overjoyed and even praised me for my cleverness in finding it, by uttering a few cheerful "hoo hoo" noises.

While we were waiting for the tea to arrive, I sat down opposite Cholmondely and lit a cigarette. To my surprise, he became very excited and held out his hand across the table to me. Wondering what he would do, I handed him the cigarette packet. He opened it, took out a cigarette and put it between his lips. He then reached out his hand again and I gave him the matches; to my astonishment, he took one out of the box, struck it, lit his cigarette and threw the box down on the table. Lying back in his chair he blew out clouds of smoke in the most professional manner. No one had told me that Cholmondely smoked. I wondered rather anxiously what other bad habits he might have which his master had not warned me about.

Just as that moment, the tea was brought in and Cholmondely greeted its appearance with loud and expressive hoots of joy. He watched me carefully while I half filled his mug with milk and then added the tea. I had been told that he had a very sweet tooth, so I put in six large spoons of sugar, an action which he greeted with grunts of satisfaction. He placed his cigarette on the table and seized the mug with both hands; then he stuck out his lower lip very carefully and dipped it into the tea to make sure it was not too hot. As it was a trifle warm, he sat there blowing on it vigorously until it was cool enough, and then he drank it all down without stopping once. When he had drained the last drops, he peered into the mug and scooped out all the sugar he could with his forefinger. After that, he tipped the mug up on his nose and sat with it like that for about five minutes until the very last of the sugar had trickled down into his mouth.

I had Cholmondely's big box placed some distance away from the marquee, and fixed the end of his chain to a large tree stump. He was too far away, I thought, to make a nuisance of himself but near enough to be able to watch everything that went on and to conduct long conversations with me in his "hoo hoo" language. But on the day of his arrival he caused trouble almost as soon as I had fixed him to his tree stump. Outside the marquee were a lot of small, tame monkeys tied on long strings attached to stakes driven into the ground. They were about ten in number, and over them I had constructed a palm leaf roof as a shelter from the sun. As Cholmondely was examining his surroundings, he noticed these monkeys, some eating fruit and others lying asleep in the sun, and decided he would have a little underarm pitching practice. I was working inside the marquee when all at once I heard the most terrific uproar going on outside. The monkeys were screaming and chattering with rage, and I rushed out to see what had happened. Cholmondely, apparently, had picked up a rock the size of a cabbage and hurled it at the smaller monkeys, luckily missing them all, but frightening them out of their wits. If one of them had been hit by such a big rock, it would have been killed instantly.

Just as I arrived on the scene, Cholmondely had picked up another stone and was swinging it backwards and forwards like a professional ball player, taking better aim. He was annoyed at having missed all the monkeys with his first shot. I grabbed a stick and hurried towards him, shouting, and, to my surprise, Cholmondely dropped the rock and put his arms over his head, and started to roll on the ground and scream. In my haste, I had picked up a very small twig and this made no impression on him at all, for his back was as broad and as hard as a table.

I gave him two sharp cuts with this silly little twig and followed it up with a serious scolding. He sat there picking bits of leaf off his fur and looking very guilty. With the aid of the Africans, I set to work and cleared away all the rocks and stones near his box, and, giving him another scolding, went back to my work. I hoped that this telling-off might have some effect on him, but when I looked out of the marquee some time later, I saw him digging in the earth, presumably in search of more ammunition.

Not long after his arrival at the camp, Cholmondely, to my

alarm, fell ill. For nearly two weeks he went off his food, refusing even the most tempting fruit and other delicacies, and even rejecting his daily ration of tea, a most unheard-of occurrence. All he had was a few sips of water every day, and gradually he grew thinner and thinner, his eyes sank into their sockets, and I really thought he was going to die. He lost all interest in life and sat hunched up in his box all day with his eyes closed. It was very bad for him to spend all day moping in this fashion, so in the evenings, just before the sun went down, when it was cool, I used to make him come out for walks with me. These walks were only short, and we had to rest every few yards, for Cholmondely was weak with lack of food.

One evening, just before I took him out for a walk, I filled my pockets with a special kind of biscuit that he had been very fond of. We went slowly up to the top of a small hill just beyond the camp and then sat there to admire the view. As we rested, I took a biscuit out of my pocket and ate it, smacking my lips with enjoyment, but not offering any to Cholmondely. He looked very surprised, for he knew that I always shared my food with him when we were out together. I ate a second biscuit and he watched me closely to see if I enjoyed it as much as the first. When he saw that I did, he dipped his hand into my pocket, pulled out a biscuit, smelled it suspiciously, and then, to my delight, ate it up and started looking for another. I knew then that he was going to get better. The next morning he drank a mugful of sweet tea and ate seventeen biscuits, and for three days lived entirely on this diet. After this his appetite returned with a rush, and for the next fortnight he ate twice as much as he had ever done before, and cost me a small fortune in bananas.

Cholmondely was so quick at learning tricks and so willing to show off that when he returned to England, he became quite famous and even made several appearance on television, delighting the audiences by sitting on a chair, with a hat on, taking a cigarette and lighting it for himself; pouring out and drinking a glass of beer, and many other things. I think he must have become rather swollen-headed with his success, for not long after this he managed to escape from the zoo and went wandering off by himself through Regent's Park, much to the horror of everyone he met. On reaching the main road, he found a bus standing there and promptly climbed aboard, for he loved being taken for a ride. The passengers, however, decided they would

rather not travel by that particular bus if Cholmondely was
going to use it as well, and they were all struggling to get out
when some keepers arrived from the zoo and took Cholmondely
in charge. He was marched back to his cage in disgrace, but if I
know Cholmondely, he must have thought it worth any amount
of scoldings just for the sight of all those people trying to get off
the bus together and getting stuck in the door. Cholmondely
had a great sense of humor.

**DISCUSSION**    1.   Durrell says Cholmondely has a sense of humor. If you agree, find
examples in the story to show his humor. Find examples also of some of
Cholmondely's bad habits.

2.   Communication without the use of words is called nonverbal communication. Durrell and Cholmondely don't speak the same language, yet
they understand each other well. Find two or three examples of their
nonverbal communication.

3.   Would the English bus passengers like Cholmondely better if they
knew him better? Why or why not?

4.   What seem to be Durrell's feelings for Cholmondely? How can you
tell?

For further activities, see page 150.

# CATALOGUE

### ROSALIE MOORE

Cats sleep fat and walk thin.
Cats, when they sleep, slump;
When they wake, stretch and begin
Over, pulling their ribs in.
Cats walk thin.                                    5

Cats wait in a lump,
Jump in a streak.
Cats, when they jump, are sleek
As a grape slipping its skin—
They have technique.                          10
Oh, cats don't creak.
They sneak.

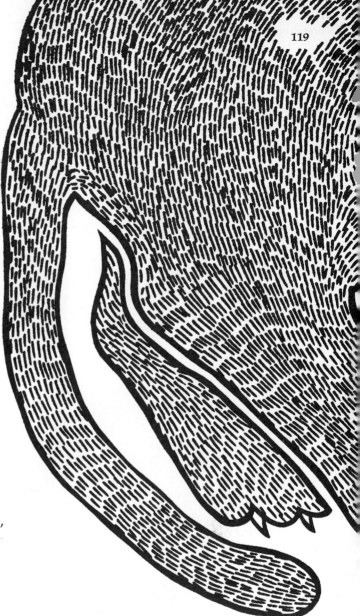

Cats sleep fat.
They spread out comfort underneath them
Like a good mat,                                      15
As if they picked the place
And then sat;
You walk around one
As if he were the City Hall
After that.                                           20

If male,
A cat is apt to sing on a major scale;
This concert is for everybody, this
Is wholesale.
For a baton, he wields a tail.                        25
(He is also found,
When happy, to resound
With an enclosed and private sound.)

A cat condenses.
He pulls in his tail to go under bridges,   30
And himself to go under fences.
Cats fit
In any size box or kit,
And if a large pumpkin grew under one,
He could arch over it.                                35

When everyone else is just ready to go out,
The cat is just ready to come in.
He's not where he's been.
Cats sleep fat and walk thin.

DISCUSSION        1.    The poet is playing with words when she calls this poem "Catalogue." How is this poem a catalogue?

2.    **Comparisons.**    A comparison points out what is similar about two
things that may otherwise be completely different. Writers often use comparisons to make a point clear or to help us visualize what they see.
There are many comparisons in this poem, like "Cats sleep fat," they
"jump in a streak," and they are sleek "as a grape slipping its skin."
Point out several others that help you to visualize cats and their movements.

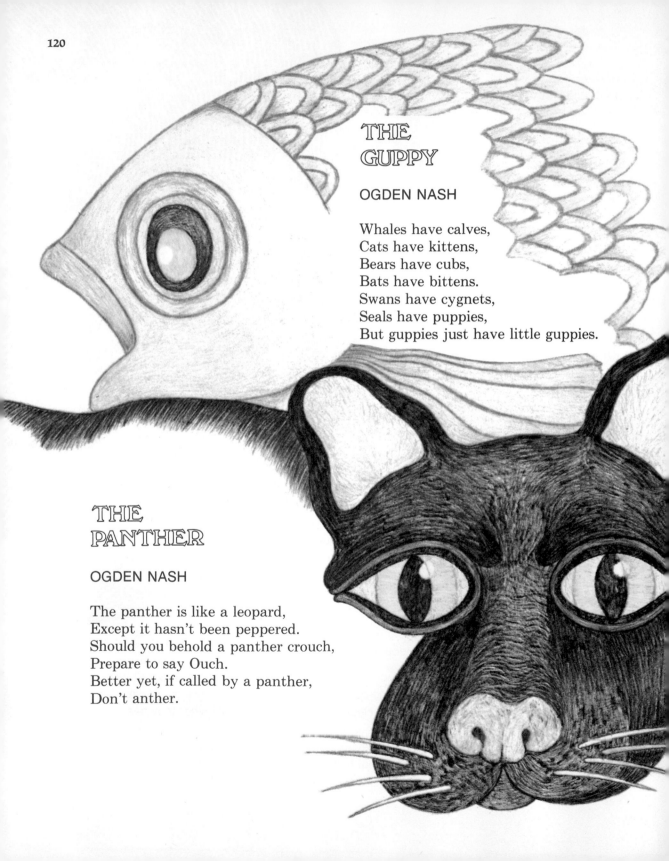

# THE GUPPY

**OGDEN NASH**

Whales have calves,
Cats have kittens,
Bears have cubs,
Bats have bittens.
Swans have cygnets,
Seals have puppies,
But guppies just have little guppies.

# THE PANTHER

**OGDEN NASH**

The panther is like a leopard,
Except it hasn't been peppered.
Should you behold a panther crouch,
Prepare to say Ouch.
Better yet, if called by a panther,
Don't anther.

# POLAR NIGHT

## NORAH BURKE

As the hot arctic summer drew to a close, till the magenta sun only slid along the horizon to sink again at once, the polar bear knew that a hard time lay ahead for her.

During the months of night, fifty degrees below zero, her cubs would be born. The great task of motherhood was already begun, the time soon coming when she would bury herself deep down under the snow to give birth. From then until the day when she and the cubs burrowed up into daylight again, she would not eat. She and they must live on what she had stored in her body during the summer, and on what she could catch and eat now. She must finish fattening herself up for the ordeal, and there was not much time left.

At the moment she was hunting along the edge of the ice, because where there was water there were seals, also fish, and the chance of a porpoise or walrus. As winter closed the roots and berries and lichen and seaweed of the polar islands into glass, the bears moved to the ice-edge for their food.

This was the arctic region, the area north of the limit of tree growth. The shores of Greenland, Siberia, Alaska, Canada bordered upon this spectral sea. It was a landscape of snow and old ice and new ice, of drifting pack ice, and berg ice from the glaciers, all in constant motion, lanes and pools of pure cobalt looking glass, opening and closing all the time in the pack. Where the old ice had been pushed up together in terraces, ice-eaves burned green and lilac underneath. In summer the skuas and ivory gulls and other birds made the air raucous with quarrels, but now all that the bear could hear was the wash of blue water against grinding ice.

Under the dark sky, on the white land, in the desolation of the arctic landscape, she was part of its white power, moving with a long swinging walk and huge fat yellow hairy snowman footfalls. Strong and dangerous, the largest of bears, able to swim forty miles out to sea if need be, she stalked her kingdom in which no natural enemy challenged her reign. Her feet, bristled underneath to give grip on the ice, carried her huge weight with a light and silent tread; while the low swinging head searched the ice all the time for food.

She was not clearly aware of what was happening in her body, but the instinct was there to love the unborn cubs, to prepare for them and protect them; she did not risk her body in careless adventures as she would at other times.

But food? Food——

Already the iron of winter was in the clean cold air, though she felt the cold only with her eyes and black nose and black lips, where the air stung her, and on the long pinkish gray tongue, moving all the time to prevent freezing, that slung in and out of her mouth among the large cruel teeth.

Suddenly, away down the ice field, where a dark blue lead showed in the pack, she saw a blackish slug on the ice—a seal. It was essential to catch him. In a moment she had decided on her approach, and slipped silently into the water to cut off his line of retreat. The ice rocked as her great weight left it.

The bear was as much at home in the water as on land—buoyant, swimming like a dog, but on top or submerged—and the water much warmer than the air on her face. Not wet, either. Inside the layer of fat and the shaggy oily watertight coat, she felt as dry as on land.

By a series of cunning dives and approaches, and keeping under the shoulder of ice, she got near to the seal. Breathing carefully, every nerve keyed to the task of silent approach, ready to spring—to dive—to slaughter, she slid nearer—nearer—

Suddenly the seal saw her. Terror convulsed his face. A moment of awful indecision—whether to plunge into the sea, his

natural line of escape, and perhaps fall straight into her jaws, or to struggle across the ice to that other hole—

He swung away from her, humping madly along. The bear lunged up out of the water, onto the ice, onto the terrified seal.

The water slushed off her everywhere like a tidal wave. There was a flurry of snow and water and fighting seal. His quick struggling body flapped under her as she slew him. Blood spurted onto the snow.

When the seal was dead, the bear attended first to herself, getting rid of the wet from her coat before it could freeze, although oil had kept off the frost so far. She shook, and the drops flew off in rainbows in all directions. She rolled and nosed along in the snow, wiping her flanks, her chin, and soon all was dry. A few hairs crisped up and stuck to each other with frost.

Now for the seal. She ripped up the body, turning back the skin and blubber, letting out a cloud of steam, and ate greedily of the hot crimson meat. Seal meat was her favorite, full of flavor, a hot meal, not like the white icy flakes of cod.

Then, although the bear had no natural enemies, she stopped suddenly as she ate, lifted her head, looked, listened, scented. Blood dripped from her chin on to the snow.

There was nothing.

All the same she trusted her instinct and, leaving the rest of the meal, slipped into the water, where she could keep her cubs safe, where it was warmer, and easier to move.

Presently she saw upright seals coming along the shore. They

were rather rare creatures, these, and dangerous for all they were
so weak. The places where they lived had light and noise, and
smelled full of good food. The she-bear often drew near the
places, attracted by those smells. She hunted these land-seals too,
and ate them when she could. They were not like the sea-seals,
though. They wore seal fur, and their skins were rubbed with seal
blubber, but there was a different taste inside.

They in their turn hunted bear, as the she-bear knew well.
She had sometimes found the place of the kill, and seen the white
empty skins hanging up by the camps, smelled the dark red gamy
flesh cooking.

Now as she watched the approaching men, she considered
whether to kill them, but the unborn life in her said get away. So
she dived and swam and melted out of their radius.

In the next few days the bear gorged on fish and seal. No
longer the hot rocks and scree of summer gave forth good-tasting
moss and lichens or the sharp-fleshed berries and sweet roots. She
dived into the cold blue ocean for her food.

But now the arctic day was over. In the pink twilight a snowy
owl was flitting silently across the waste, moving south and south
as life was squeezed out of the arctic desert by the polar night.

Then came the freezing of the sea. Crystals formed below the
surface and rose, and needles of ice shot across from one to another, joining them together, thickening, hardening, adding more
ice to the floes already many years old. The ice talked, grinding its
teeth, sending out every now and then a singing crack. Curtains of
colored flame rippled in the sky. The polar night began.

Now the real cold came. Now the food disappeared, and old
male bears grew lean and savage.

The she-bear chose her den.

There was a great raw range of decayed ice that had been
pushed up into mountains whose hollows were packed with snow.
Icicles yards long hung on the south side from the summer, and
behind this curtain of ice she found a great purple cave, carved in
diamond and full of snow.

This was the place.

Her body was ready now for the ordeal. Thick fat, gathered
from seal and halibut, lined her skin.

She burrowed down into the violet snow on the floor of the
cave. It was so light that the wind of moving blew it about like
feathers, and she could breathe in it. She burrowed deeper and
deeper, while the snow sifted and fell in soundlessly behind her,

till presently she was deep enough.

She curled and rolled herself round and round, pushing the snow, packing it, shaping the den. All the sides of it melted with her heat, then froze again into slippery walls. And the hot breath passed up through the way she had dug, melting the sides of the channel which also froze again and left a tube which would supply her with air until she came up in the spring.

Inside the snow and ice—inside her thick oily fur and the layer of blubber, she was warm, full fed, and sleepy. She slept and waited.

In the fullness of time, the first familiar pang of birth trembled in her stomach. Pain fluttered like a butterfly and was gone.

She stirred, lifted her head, rearranged herself.

It came again, stronger, longer.

She moved uneasily.

Then in long strong accomplishing strokes it was there—hard, forcing, contracting, out of her control. Moving to a crescendo.[1] She grunted, tensed all her muscles, pressed, and gasped. Another spasm, and on the smooth strong river of pain, she felt the first cub come out.

A wave of relief relaxed her.

There he lay mewing, so wet and tiny, hardly alive, and she nuzzled him delightedly, starting to clean him up.

But now another spasm—the same long final one as before, though easier—and the second cub was born.

It was over now. She felt the diminishing contractions, the subsidence of pain, pulsing quieter.

Now to clean them up. She licked and licked them, turning them over, rolling and caressing them; then life strengthened in them as they dried, as they fed. She lay in bliss, feeling her own life flowing from her heart.

Meanwhile in the world above, the sun had returned, first a green glow, then a rosy one, then touching the top-most peaks, days before the first sunrise.

Deep in the snow cave, the bear knew it as the snow grew luminous with the light pressing through.

One day she heard voices. The snow vibrated with footsteps, the ice ceiling cracked.

She rose, shook herself free of the cubs and stood ready in case the land-seals saw the warm yellow air hole that marked her den—in case one of them walked over her and fell in. . . .

[1] *crescendo* (krə-shĕn′dō): an increase in intensity.

She stood fierce, lean, ready, to defend her cubs, her heart pounding hot and loud as fever in her thin body.

Gradually the voices and the footsteps died away.

Presently it was time to come out into the world again. The cubs' eyes were open, their coats grown; they were walking, getting stronger every day. Now they must come out and face the world and swim and fight and catch seals. There was everything to teach them, and while they were still learning—still babies, they had got to be kept safe and fed. All this she had to do alone. Other years she'd had a mate to help her, but this time he was gone—lost— Those white skins hanging by the camps——

She began to tear her way out, the giant paws and black nails breaking open the ice walls of their den. The ice gave, snow fell in.

They climbed out.

Clean frozen air, dazzling with sun, hit them like the stroke of an axe. Light entered the brain in needles through the eyes. Only gradually, as the pupils contracted, did it become possible to see.

Under an iridescent sun-halo, the arctic landscape blazed white and navy blue. Everything hit them at once—light, noise, wind—the blast of a new world.

Down there was the water——

The mother bear plunged joyfully into the buoyant cleanness. All the dirt and staleness of winter were washed away. It was like flight. She plunged and rose and shook and plunged again in sheer joy. So fresh, so clean, the salt cold water running through her teeth——

Then she resumed the heavy duties of parenthood, turned to the cubs. They were sitting on the edge, squeaking with fright, and she began urging them to come in. They kept feeling forward, then scrambling back. Suddenly one ventured too far down the ice, and slithered, shrieking, into the sea, where he bobbed up again like a cork.

His brother, seeing this, plucked up courage and plunged in too, in one desperate baby-jump, landing with a painful *smack!* and blinking in the spray.

They found they could swim.

Presently she pushed them up on to the ice again where they shook and dried, and the next thing was food. She left them while she killed a seal, and the three of them ate it.

After that there were lessons, how to fish, how to kill. Living was thin at first, for three hunters cannot move as silently as one, but they got along.

Until the day when the land-seals approached them unseen from behind an ice ridge. The first they knew of it was an explosion, and one cub gasped and doubled up as he was hit. The bears dived for the water, even the wounded little one. He managed to keep up with them, and his mother and brother would die rather than desert him.

They all swam on, but slowly—slowly. Both cubs were still so small and *slow*, and they must hurry——

Blood ran in the sapphire water.

Other shots spattered beside them.

Anxiety roared in the she-bear's blood. Her heart was bursting. She pushed the cubs on, and turned to meet her enemies. Reared up on to the ice and galloped towards them, a charge that nothing could stop—not even death—if they'd stayed to face it, but they broke and ran.

The bear returned to her cubs.

The wounded one was sinking lower and lower in the water, breathing waves, and she managed to push him out at last onto distant ice. Then she licked him as he lay suffering in the snow, and his brother licked him too, whimpering with distress as he worked.

So that presently the blood stopped, and after a long time the suffering too. The cub sniffed the air. In the first real moment of recovery he consented to take food.

Pain went away from her heart.

Before them lay all the arctic lands, the snow in retreat. The floes, soft and friable[2] from solar radiation, were being broken up by the waves. Plant life teemed in the water, the more open sea colored bright green by diatoms.[3] Millions of wild flowers studded the rocky scree. There was everything to eat at once—lichen and moss and roots and halibut and seals. Salmon swam the green water, and cod. Seaweed washed round the rocks. On the land there were hares and young birds.

The summer gathered to almost tropical heat. Snow water dribbled into pools. Icicles glistened with wet, dropped and broke like glass.

And the mother bear, in the snow, with her cubs did not know why she behaved as she did. There was pain and there was happiness, and these two things drove her according to unfathomable laws. When the summer ended, and the polar night began, she would do the same things over again, and her children after her.

[2] *friable:* easily crumbled.
[3] *diatoms:* extremely tiny one-celled plants.

**DISCUSSION**

1.  According to the last paragraph, the mother bear is driven by two things. What are they? Give examples of each of them determining her actions.

2.  Near the beginning of the story, the bear thinks of men as ''rare creatures, and dangerous for all they were so weak'' (page 124). Why does she decide not to kill them?

3.  The bear's body is perfectly adapted to the arctic. Over the course of a year, how does it change?

4.  From what **point of view** (see page 52) is the story told? How does that point of view affect your feelings toward the bear? The seals? The hunter?

For further activities, see page 150.

When I was once in Baltimore,
  A man came up to me and cried,
"Come, I have eighteen hundred sheep,
  And we will sail on Tuesday's tide.

"If you will sail with me, young man,    5
  I'll pay you fifty shillings down;
These eighteen hundred sheep I take
  From Baltimore to Glasgow town."

# Sheep

### W. H. DAVIES

He paid me fifty shillings down,
  I sailed with eighteen hundred sheep;    10
We soon had cleared the harbor's mouth,
  We soon were in the salt sea deep.

The first night we were out at sea
  Those sheep were quiet in their mind;
The second night they cried with fear—    15
  They smelt no pastures in the wind.

They sniffed, poor things, for their green fields,
  They cried so loud I could not sleep;
For fifty thousand shillings down
  I would not sail again with sheep.    20

**DISCUSSION**

1. Why would the speaker not sail again with sheep, even for a large sum of money?

2. Which of the five senses tells the sheep they are away from home?

3. Do you feel more sorry for the sheep who miss their green pastures or the sailor who can't sleep? Or both?

4. What two meanings does "cried" have in the poem?

5. In each **stanza** (see page 70) the second and fourth lines rhyme. Which one of the stanzas does not have a perfect rhyme?

# The Buck in the Snow

EDNA ST. VINCENT MILLAY

White sky, over the hemlocks bowed with snow,
Saw you not at the beginning of evening the antlered buck and his
    doe
Standing in the apple-orchard? I saw them. I saw them suddenly
    go,
Tails up, with long leaps lovely and slow,
Over the stone-wall into the wood of hemlocks bowed with
    snow.        5

Now lies he here, his wild blood scalding the snow.

How strange a thing is death, bringing to his knees, bringing to his
    antlers
The buck in the snow.
How strange a thing,—a mile away by now, it may be,
Under the heavy hemlocks that as the moments pass    10
Shift their loads a little, letting fall a feather of snow—
Life, looking out attentive from the eyes of the doe.

**DISCUSSION**

1.  What happens to the buck in the course of the poem? What happens to the doe?

2.  "How strange a thing is death" the poet writes in line 7. And again, in line 9, "How strange a thing,—" What word later in the poem completes this thought?

3.  A poet often uses contrast to make an experience vivid. Where does Millay use contrast in this poem?

# MY FRIEND FLICKA

MARY O'HARA

Report cards for the second semester were sent out soon after school closed in mid-June.

Kennie's was a shock to the whole family.

"If I could have a colt all for my own," said Kennie, "I might do better."

Rob McLaughlin glared at his son. "Just as a matter of curiosity," he said, "how do you go about it to get a *zero* in an examination? Forty in arithmetic; seventeen in history! But a *zero? Just as one man to another, what goes on in your head?"

"Yes, tell us how you do it, Ken," chirped Howard.

"Eat your breakfast, Howard," snapped his mother.

Kennie's blond head bent over his plate until his face was almost hidden. His cheeks burned.

McLaughlin finished his coffee and pushed his chair back. "You'll do an hour a day on your lessons all through the summer."

Nell McLaughlin saw Kennie wince as if something had actually hurt him.

Lessons and study in the summertime, when the long winter was just over and there weren't hours enough in the day for all the things he wanted to do!

Kennie took things hard. His eyes turned to the wide-open window with a look almost of despair.

The hill opposite the house, covered with arrow-straight jack pines, was sharply etched in the thin air of the eight-thousand-foot altitude. Where it fell away, vivid green grass ran up to meet it; and over range and upland poured the strong Wyoming sunlight that stung everything into burning color. A big jack rabbit sat under one of the pines, waving his long ears back and forth.

Ken had to look at his plate and blink back tears before he could turn to his father and say carelessly, "Can I help you in the corral with the horses this morning, Dad?"

"You'll do your study every morning before you do anything else." And McLaughlin's scarred boots and heavy spurs clattered across the kitchen floor. "I'm disgusted with you. Come, Howard."

Howard strode after his father, nobly refraining from looking at Kennie.

"Help me with the dishes, Kennie," said Nell McLaughlin as she rose, tied on a big apron, and began to clear the table.

Kennie looked at her in despair. She poured steaming water into the dishpan and sent him for the soap powder.

"If I could have a colt," he muttered again.

"Now get busy with that dish towel, Ken. It's eight o'clock. You can study till nine and then go up to the corral. They'll still be there."

At supper that night, Kennie said, "But Dad, Howard had a colt all of his own when he was only eight. And he trained it and schooled it all himself; and now he's eleven and Highboy is three, and he's riding him. I'm nine now, and even if you did give me a colt now, I couldn't catch up to Howard because I couldn't ride it till it was a three-year-old and then I'd be twelve."

Nell laughed. "Nothing wrong with that arithmetic."

But Rob said, "Howard never gets less than a seventy-five average at school; and hasn't disgraced himself and his family by getting more demerits than any other boy in his class."

Kennie didn't answer. He couldn't figure it out. He tried hard, he spent hours poring over his books. That was supposed to get you good marks, but it never did. Everyone said he was bright; why was it that when he studied he didn't learn? He had a vague feeling that perhaps he looked out the window too much; or looked through the walls to see clouds and sky and hills, and wonder what was happening out there. Sometimes it wasn't even a wonder, but just a pleasant drifting feeling of nothing at all, as if nothing mattered, as if there was always plenty of time, as if the lessons would get done of themselves. And then the bell would ring and study period was over.

If he had a colt——

When the boys had gone to bed that night Nell McLaughlin sat down with her overflowing mending basket and glanced at her husband.

He was at his desk as usual, working on account books and inventories.

Nell threaded a darning needle and thought, "It's either that whacking big bill from the vet for the mare that died, or the last half of the tax bill."

It didn't seem just the auspicious moment to plead Kennie's cause. But then, these days, there was always a line between Rob's eyes and a harsh note in his voice.

"Rob," she began.

He flung down his pencil and turned around.

"That law!" he exclaimed.

"What law?"

"The state law that puts high taxes on pedigreed stock. I'll have to do as the rest of 'em do—drop the papers."

"Drop the papers! But you'll never get decent prices if you don't have registered horses."

"I don't get decent prices now."

"But you will someday, if you don't drop the papers."

"Maybe." He bent again over the desk.

Rob, thought Nell, was a lot like Kennie himself. He set his heart. Oh, how stubbornly he set his heart on just some one thing he wanted above everything else. He had set his heart on horses and ranching way back when he had been a crack rider at West Point; and he had resigned and thrown away his army career just for the horses. Well, he'd got what he wanted——

She drew a deep breath, snipped her thread, laid down the sock and again looked across at her husband as she unrolled another length of darning cotton.

To get what you want is one thing, she was thinking. The three-thousand-acre ranch and the hundred head of horses. But to make it pay—for a dozen or more years they had been trying to make it pay. People said ranching hadn't paid since the beef barons ran their herds on public land; people said the only prosperous ranchers in Wyoming were the dude ranchers; people said——

But suddenly she gave her head a little rebellious, gallant shake. Rob would always be fighting and struggling against something, like Kennie; perhaps like herself too. Even those first years when there was no water piped into the house, when every day brought a new difficulty or danger, how she had loved it! How she still loved it!

She ran the darning ball into the toe of a sock. Kennie's sock. The length of it gave her a shock. Yes, the boys were growing up fast, and now Kennie—Kennie and the colt—

After a while she said, "Give Kennie a colt, Rob."

"He doesn't deserve it." The answer was short. Rob pushed away his papers and took out his pipe.

"Howard's too far ahead of him; older and bigger and quicker and his wits about him, and ——"

"Ken doesn't half try; doesn't stick at anything."

She put down her sewing. "He's crazy for a colt of his own. He hasn't had another idea in his head since you gave Highboy to Howard."

"I don't believe in bribing children to do their duty."

"Not a bribe." She hesitated.

"No? What would you call it?"

She tried to think it out. "I just have the feeling Ken isn't going to pull anything off, and —" her eyes sought Rob's, "it's time he did. It isn't the school marks alone, but I just don't want things to go on any longer with Ken never coming out at the right end of anything."

"I'm beginning to think he's just dumb."

"He's not dumb. Maybe a little thing like this—if he had a colt of his own, trained him, rode him—"

Rob interrupted. "But it isn't a little thing, nor an easy thing to break and school a colt the way Howard has schooled Highboy. I'm not going to have a good horse spoiled by Ken's careless ways. He goes woolgathering. He never knows what he's doing."

"But he'd *love* a colt of his own, Rob. If he could do it, it might make a big difference in him."

"*If* he could do it! But that's a big if."

At breakfast next morning Kennie's father said to him, "When you've done your study come out to the barn. I'm going in the car up to section twenty-one this morning to look over the brood mares. You can go with me."

"Can I go too, Dad?" cried Howard.

McLaughlin frowned at Howard. "You turned Highboy out last evening with dirty legs."

Howard wriggled. "I groomed him——"

"Yes, down to his knees."

"He kicks."

"And whose fault is that? You don't get on his back again until I see his legs clean."

The two boys eyed each other, Kennie secretly triumphant and Howard chagrined. McLaughlin turned at the door, "And, Ken, a week from today I'll give you a colt. Between now and then you can decide what one you want."

Kennie shot out of his chair and stared at his father. "A—a—spring colt, Dad, or a yearling?"

McLaughlin was somewhat taken aback, but his wife concealed a smile. If Kennie got a yearling colt, he would be even up with Howard.

"A yearling colt, your father means, Ken," she said smoothly. "Now hurry with your lessons. Howard will wipe."

Kennie found himself the most important personage on the ranch.

Prestige lifted his head, gave him an inch more of height and a bold stare, and made him feel different all the way through. Even Gus and Tim Murphy, the ranch hands, were more interested in Kennie's choice of a colt than anything else.

Howard was fidgety with suspense. "Who'll you pick, Ken? Say—pick Doughboy, why don't you? Then when he grows up he'll be sort of twins with mine, in his name anyway. Doughboy, Highboy, see?"

The boys were sitting on the worn wooden step of the door which led from the tack room into the corral, busy with rags and polish, shining their bridles.

Ken looked at his brother with scorn. Doughboy would never have half of Highboy's speed.

"Lassie, then," suggested Howard. "She's black as ink, like mine. And she'll be fast——"

"Dad says Lassie'll never go over fifteen hands."

Nell McLaughlin saw the change in Kennie and her hopes rose. He went to his books in the morning with determination and really studied. A new alertness took the place of the daydreaming. Examples in arithmetic were neatly written out and, as she passed his door before breakfast, she often heard the monotonous drone of his voice as he read his American history aloud.

Each night, when he kissed her, he flung his arms around her and held her fiercely for a moment, then, with a winsome and blissful smile into her eyes, turned away to bed.

He spent days inspecting the different bands of horses and colts. He sat for hours on the corral fence, very important, chewing straws. He rode off on one of the ponies for half the day, wandering through the mile square pastures that ran down toward the Colorado border.

And when the week was up, he announced his decision. "I'll take that yearling filly of Rocket's. The sorrel with the cream tail and mane."

His father looked at him in surprise. "The one that got tangled in the barbed wire? that's never been named?"

In a second all Kennie's new pride was gone. He hung his head defensively. "Yes."

"You've made a bad choice, son. You couldn't have picked a worse."

"She's fast, Dad. And Rocket's fast——"

"It's the worst line of horses I've got. There's never one amongst them with real sense. The mares are hellions and the stallions outlaws; they're untamable."

"I'll tame her."

Rob guffawed. "Not I, nor anyone, has ever been able to really tame any one of them."

Kennie's chest heaved.

"Better change your mind, Ken. You want a horse that'll be a real friend to you, don't you?"

"Yes—" Kennie's voice was unsteady.

"Well, you'll never make a friend of that filly. She's all cut and scarred up already with tearing through barbed wire after that mother of hers. No fence'll hold 'em——"

"I know," said Kennie, still more faintly.

"Change your mind?" asked Howard briskly.

"No."

Rob was grim and put out. He couldn't go back on his word. The boy had to have a reasonable amount of help in breaking and taming the filly, and he could envision precious hours, whole days, wasted in the struggle.

Nell McLaughlin despaired. Once again Ken seemed to have taken the wrong turn and was back where he had begun—stoical, silent, defensive.

But there was a difference that only Ken could know. The way he felt about his colt. The way his heart sang. The pride and joy that filled him so full that sometimes he hung his head so they wouldn't see it shining out of his eyes.

He had known from the very first that he would choose that particular yearling because he was in love with her.

The year before, he had been out working with Gus, the big Swedish ranch hand, on the irrigation ditch,

when they had noticed Rocket standing in a gully on the hillside, quiet for
once, and eyeing them cautiously.

"Ay bet she got a colt," said Gus,
and they walked carefully up the
draw. Rocket gave a wild snort,
thrust her feet out, shook her head
wickedly, then fled away. And as they
reached the spot, they saw standing
there the wavering, pinkish colt, barely able to keep its feet. It gave a little
squeak and started after its mother
on crooked, wobbling legs.

"Yee whiz! Luk at de little
*flicka!*" said Gus.

"What does *flicka* mean, Gus?"

"Swedish for little gurl, Ken—"

Ken announced at supper, "You
said she'd never been named. I've
named her. Her name is Flicka."

The first thing to do was to get
her in. She was running with a band
of yearlings on the saddleback, cut
with ravines and gullies, on section
twenty.

They all went out after her, Ken,
as owner, on old Rob Roy, the wisest
horse on the ranch.

Ken was entranced to watch
Flicka when the wild band of youngsters discovered that they were being
pursued and took off across the
mountain. Footing made no difference
to her. She floated across the ravines,
always two lengths ahead of the others. Her pink mane and tail whipped
in the wind. Her long delicate legs
had only to aim, it seemed, at a particular spot, for her to reach it and
sail on. She seemed to Ken a fairy
horse.

He sat motionless, just watching
and holding Rob Roy in, when his father thundered past on Sultan and
shouted, "Well, what's the matter?
Why didn't you turn 'em?"

Kennie woke up and galloped
after.

Rob Roy brought in the whole
band. The corral gates were closed,
and an hour was spent shunting the
ponies in and out and through the
chutes, until Flicka was left alone in
the small round corral in which the
baby colts were branded. Gus drove
the others away, out the gate, and up
the saddleback.

But Flicka did not intend to be
left. She hurled herself against the
poles which walled the corral. She
tried to jump them. They were seven
feet high. She caught her front feet
over the top rung, clung, scrambled,
while Kennie held his breath for fear
the slender legs would be caught between the bars and snapped. Her hold
broke, she fell backward, rolled,
screamed, tore around the corral.
Kennie had a sick feeling in the pit of
his stomach and his father looked disgusted.

One of the bars broke. She hurled
herself again. Another went. She saw
the opening and as neatly as a dog
crawls through a fence, inserted her
head and forefeet, scrambled through
and fled away, bleeding in a dozen
places.

As Gus was coming back, just about to close the gate to the upper range, the sorrel whipped through it, sailed across the road and ditch with her inimitable floating leap, and went up the side of the saddleback like a jack rabbit.

From way up the mountain, Gus heard excited whinnies, as she joined the band he had just driven up, and the last he saw of them they were strung out along the crest running like deer.

"Yee whiz!" said Gus, and stood motionless and staring until the ponies had disappeared over the ridge. Then he closed the gate, remounted Rob Roy, and rode back to the corral.

Rob McLaughlin gave Kennie one more chance to change his mind. "Last chance, son. Better pick a horse that you have some hope of riding one day. I'd have got rid of this whole line of stock if they weren't so fast that I've had the fool idea that someday there might turn out one gentle one in the lot—and I'd have a race horse. But there's never been one so far, and it's not going to be Flicka."

"It's not going to be Flicka," chanted Howard.

"Perhaps she *might* be gentled," said Kennie; and Nell, watching, saw that although his lips quivered, there was fanatical determination in his eye.

"Ken," said Rob, "it's up to you. If you say you want her, we'll get her.

But she wouldn't be the first of that line to die rather than give in. They're beautiful and they're fast, but let me tell you this, young man, they're *loco!*"

Kennie flinched under his father's direct glance.

"If I go after her again, I'll not give up whatever comes, understand what I mean by that?"

"Yes."

"What do you say?"

"I want her."

They brought her in again. They had better luck this time. She jumped over the Dutch half door of the stable and crashed inside. The men slammed the upper half of the door shut and she was caught.

The rest of the band were driven away, and Kennie stood outside of the stable, listening to the wild hoofs beating, the screams, the crashes. His Flicka inside there! He was drenched with perspiration.

"We'll leave her to think it over," said Rob, when dinnertime came. "Afterward, we'll go up and feed and water her."

But when they went afterward, there was no Flicka in the barn. One of the windows, higher than the mangers, was broken.

The window opened into a pasture an eighth of a mile square, fenced in barbed wire six feet high. Near the stable stood a wagon load of hay. When they went around the back of the stable to see where Flicka had hidden herself, they found her between the stable and the hay wagon, eating.

At their approach she leaped away, then headed east across the pasture.

"If she's like her mother," said Rob, "she'll go right through the wire."

"Ay bet she'll go over," said Gus. "She yumps like a deer."

"No horse can jump that," said McLaughlin.

Kennie said nothing because he could not speak. It was, perhaps, the most terrible moment of his life. He watched Flicka racing toward the eastern wire.

A few yards from it, she swerved, turned, and raced diagonally south.

"It turned her! It turned her!" cried Kennie, almost sobbing. It was the first sign of hope for Flicka. "Oh, Dad! She has got sense. She has! She has!"

Flicka turned again as she met the southern boundary of the pasture; again at the northern; she avoided the barn. Without abating anything of her whirlwind speed, following a precise, accurate calculation and turning each time on a dime, she investigated every possibility. Then, seeing that there was no hope, she raced south toward the range where she had spent her life, gathered herself, and shot into the air.

Each of the three men watching had the impulse to cover his eyes, and Kennie gave a sort of a howl of despair.

Twenty yards of fence came down with her as she hurled herself through. Caught on the upper strands, she turned a complete somersault, landing on her back, her four legs dragging the wires down on top of her, and tangling herself in them beyond hope of escape.

Kennie followed the men miserably as they walked to the filly. They stood in a circle watching, while she kicked and fought and thrashed until the wire was tightly wound and knotted about her cutting, piercing and tearing great three-cornered pieces of flesh and hide. At last she was unconscious, streams of blood running on her golden coat, and pools of crimson widening and spreading on the grass beneath her.

With the wire cutter, which Gus always carried in the hip pocket of his overalls, he cut all the wire away, and they drew her into the pasture, repaired the fence, placed hay, a box of oats and a tub of water near her, and called it a day.

"I don't think she'll pull out of it," said McLaughlin.

Next norning Kennie was up at five, doing his lessons. At six he went out to Flicka.

She had not moved. Food and water were untouched. She was no longer bleeding, but the wounds were swollen and caked over.

Kennie got a bucket of fresh water and poured it over her mouth. Then he leaped away, for Flicka came to life, scrambled up, got her balance, and stood swaying.

Kennie went a few feet away and sat down to watch her. When he went in to breakfast, she had drunk deeply of the water and was mouthing the oats.

There began then, a sort of recovery. She ate, drank, limped about the pasture; stood for hours with hanging head and weakly splayed-out legs, under the clump of cottonwood trees. The swollen wounds scabbed and began to heal.

Kennie lived in the pasture too. He followed her around; he talked to her. He too lay snoozing or sat under the cottonwoods; and often, coaxing her with hand outstretched, he walked very quietly toward her. But she would not let him come near her.

Often she stood with her head at the south fence, looking off to the mountain. It made the tears come to Kennie's eyes to see the way she longed to get away.

Still Rob said she wouldn't pull out of it. There was no use putting a halter on her. She had no strength.

One morning, as Ken came out of the house, Gus met him and said, "De filly's down."

Kennie ran to the pasture, Howard close behind him. The right hind leg which had been badly swollen at the knee joint had opened in a festering wound, and Flicka lay flat and motionless, with staring eyes.

"Don't you wish now, you'd chosen Doughboy?" asked Howard.

"Go away!" shouted Ken.

Howard stood watching while Kennie sat down on the ground and took Flicka's head on his lap. Though she was conscious and moved a little, she did not struggle nor seem frightened. Tears rolled down Kennie's cheeks as he talked to her and petted her. After a few moments, Howard walked away.

"Mother, what do you do for an infection when it's a horse?" asked Kennie.

"Just what you'd do if it was a person. Wet dressings. I'll help you, Ken. We mustn't let those wounds close or scab over until they're clean. I'll make a poultice for that hind leg, and help you put it on. Now that she'll let us get close to her, we can help her a lot."

"The thing to do is see that she eats," said Rob. "Keep up her strength."

But he himself would not go near her. "She won't pull out of it," he said. "I don't want to see her or think about her."

Kennie and his mother nursed the filly. The big poultice was bandaged on the hind leg. It drew out much poisoned matter and Flicka felt better and was able to stand again.

She watched Kennie now, and followed him like a dog, hopping on three legs, holding up the right hind leg with its huge knob of a bandage in comical fashion.

"Dad, Flicka's my friend now; she likes me," said Ken.

His father looked at him. "I'm glad of that, son. It's a fine thing to have a horse for a friend."

Kennie found a nicer place for her. In the lower pasture the brook ran over cool stones. There was a grassy bank, the size of a corral, almost on a level with the water. Here she could lie softly, eat grass, drink fresh running water. From the grass, a twenty-foot hill sloped up, crested with overhanging trees. She was enclosed, as it were, in a green, open-air nursery.

Kennie carried her oats morning and evening. She would watch for him to come, eyes and ears pointed to the hill. And one evening Ken, still some distance off, came to a stop and a wide grin spread over his face. He had heard her nicker. She had caught sight of him coming and was calling to him!

He placed the box of oats under her nose and she ate while he stood beside her, his hand smoothing the satin-soft skin under her mane. It had a nap as deep as plush. He played with her long, cream-colored tresses; arranged her forelock neatly between her eyes. She was a bit dish-faced, like an Arab, with eyes set far apart. He lightly groomed and brushed her while she stood turning her head to him whichever way he went.

He spoiled her. Soon she would not step to the stream to drink but he must hold a bucket for her. And she would drink, then lift her dripping muzzle, rest it on the shoulder of his blue chambray shirt, her golden eyes dreaming off into the distance; then daintily dip her mouth and drink again.

When she turned her head to the south, and pricked her ears, and stood tense and listening, Ken knew she heard the other colts galloping on the upland.

"You'll go back there someday, Flicka," he whispered. "You'll be three and I'll be eleven. You'll be so strong you won't know I'm on your back, and we'll fly like the wind. We'll stand on the very top where we can look over the whole world, and smell the snow from the Neversummer Range. Maybe we'll see antelope——"

This was the happiest month of Kennie's life.

With the morning, Flicka always had new strength and would hop three-legged up the hill to stand broadside to the early sun, as horses love to do.

The moment Ken woke, he'd go to the window, and see her there; and when he was dressed and at his table studying, he sat so that he could raise his head and see Flicka.

After breakfast, she would be waiting for him and the box of oats at the gate; and for Nell McLaughlin with fresh bandages and buckets of disinfectant; and all three would go together to the brook, Flicka hopping along ahead of them, as if she was leading the way.

But Rob McLaughlin would not look at her.

One day all the wounds were swollen again. Presently they opened, one by one; and Kennie and his mother made more poultices.

Still the little filly climbed the hill in the early morning and ran about on three legs. Then she began to go down in flesh and almost overnight wasted away to nothing. Every rib showed; the glossy hide was dull and brittle, and was pulled over the skeleton as if she was a dead horse.

Gus said, "It's de fever. It burns up her flesh. If you could stop de fever she might get vell."

McLaughlin was standing in his window one morning and saw the little skeleton hopping about three-legged in the sunshine, and he said, "That's the end. I won't have a thing like that on my place."

Kennie had to understand that Flicka had not been getting well all this time; she had been slowly dying.

"She still eats her oats," he said mechanically.

They were all sorry for Ken. Nell McLaughlin stopped disinfecting and dressing the wounds. "It's no use, Ken," she said gently, "you know Flicka's going to die, don't you?"

"Yes, Mother."

Ken stopped eating, Howard said, "Ken doesn't eat anything any more. Don't he have to eat his dinner, Mother?"

But Nell answered, "Leave him alone."

Because the shooting of wounded animals is all in the day's work on the western plains, and sickening to everyone, Rob's voice, when he gave the order to have Flicka shot, was as flat as if he had been telling Gus to kill a chicken for dinner.

"Here's the Marlin, Gus. Pick out a time when Ken's not around and put the filly out of her misery."

Gus took the rifle. "*Ja,* Boss—"

Ever since Ken had known that Flicka was to be shot, he had kept his eye on the rack which held the firearms. His father allowed no firearms in the bunkhouse. The gun rack was in the dining room of the ranch house; and, going through it to the kitchen three times a day for meals, Ken's eye scanned the weapons to make sure that they were all there.

That night they were not all there. The Marlin rifle was missing.

When Kennie saw that, he stopped walking. He felt dizzy. He kept staring at the gun rack, telling himself that it surely was there—he counted again and again—he couldn't see clearly—

Then he felt an arm across his shoulders and heard his father's voice.

"I know, son. Some things are awful hard to take. We just have to take 'em. I have to, too."

Kennie got hold of his father's hand and held on. It helped steady him.

Finally he looked up. Rob looked down and smiled at him and gave him a little shake and squeeze. Ken managed a smile too.

"All right now?"

"All right, Dad."

They walked in to supper together.

Ken even ate a little. But Nell looked thoughtfully at the ashen color of his face; and at the little pulse that was beating in the side of his neck.

After supper he carried Flicka her oats, but he had to coax her and she would only eat a little. She stood with her head hanging, but when he stroked it and talked to her, she pressed her face into his chest and was content. He could feel the burning heat of her body. It didn't seem possible that anything so thin could be alive.

Presently Kennie saw Gus come into the pasture carrying the Marlin. When he saw Ken, he changed his direction and sauntered along as if he was out to shoot some cottontails.

Ken ran to him. "When are you going to do it, Gus?"

"Ay was goin' down soon now, before it got dark—"

"Gus, don't do it tonight. Wait till morning. Just one more night, Gus."

"Vell, in de morning den, but it got to be done, Ken. Yer fader gives de order."

"I know. I won't say anything more."

An hour after the family had gone to bed, Ken got up and put on his clothes. It was a warm moonlight night. He ran down to the brook, calling softly. "Flicka! Flicka!"

But Flicka did not answer with a little nicker; and she was not in the nursery, nor hopping about the pasture. Ken hunted for an hour.

At last he found her down the creek, lying in the water. Her head had been on the bank, but as she lay there, the current of the stream had sucked and pulled at her, and she had had no strength to resist; and little by little her head had slipped down until when Ken got there only the muzzle was resting on the bank, and the body and legs were swinging in the stream.

Kennie slid into the water, sitting on the bank, and he hauled at her head. But she was heavy and the current dragged like a weight; and he began to sob because he had no strength to draw her out.

Then he found a leverage for his heels against some rocks in the bed of the stream, and he braced himself against these, and pulled with all his might; and her head came up onto his knees, and he held it cradled in his arms.

He was glad that she had died of her own accord, in the cool water, under the moon, instead of being shot by Gus. Then, putting his face close to hers, and looking searchingly into her eyes, he saw that she was alive and looking back at him.

And then he burst out crying, and hugged her, and said, "Oh, my little Flicka, my little Flicka."

The long night passed.

The moon slid slowly across the heavens.

The water rippled over Kennie's legs, and over Flicka's body. And gradually the heat and fever went out of her. And the cool running water washed and washed her wounds.

When Gus went down in the morning with the rifle, they hadn't moved. There they were, Kennie sitting in water over his thighs and hips, with Flicka's head in his arms.

Gus seized Flicka by the head, and hauled her out on the grassy bank, and then, seeing that Kennie couldn't move, cold and stiff and half-paralyzed as he was, lifted him in his arms and carried him to the house.

"Gus," said Ken through chattering teeth, "don't shoot her, Gus."

"It ain't fur me to say, Ken. You know dat."

"But the fever's left her, Gus."

"Ay wait a little, Ken——"

Rob McLaughlin drove to Laramie to get the doctor, for Ken was in violent chills that would not stop. His mother had him in bed wrapped in hot blankets when they got back.

He looked at his father imploringly as the doctor shook down the thermometer.

"She might get well now, Dad. The fever's left her. It went out of her when the moon went down."

"All right, son. Don't worry. Gus'll feed her, morning and night, as long as she's——"

"As long as I can't do it," finished Kennie happily.

The doctor put the thermometer in his mouth and told him to keep it shut.

All day Gus went about his work, thinking of Flicka. He had not been back to look at her. He had been given no more orders. If she was alive, the order to shoot her was still in effect. But Kennie was ill, McLaughlin making his second trip to town taking the doctor home, and would not be back till long after dark.

After their supper in the bunkhouse, Gus and Tim walked down to the brook. They did not speak as they approached the filly, lying stretched out flat on the grassy bank, but their eyes were straining at her to see if she was dead or alive.

She raised her head as they reached her.

"By the powers!" exclaimed Tim, "there she is!"

She dropped her head, raised it again, and moved her legs and became tense as if struggling to rise. But to do so she must use her right hind leg to brace herself against the earth. That was the damaged leg, and at the first bit of pressure with it, she gave up and fell back.

"We'll swing her on to the other side," said Tim. "Then she can help herself."

"*Ja*——"

Standing behind her, they leaned over, grabbed hold of her left legs, front and back, and gently hauled her over. Flicka was as lax and willing as a puppy. But the moment she found herself lying on her right side, she began to scramble, braced herself with her good left leg, and tried to rise.

"Yee whiz!" said Gus. "She got plenty strength yet."

"Hi!" cheered Tim. "She's up!"

But Flicka wavered, slid down again, and lay flat. This time she gave notice that she would not try again by heaving a deep sigh and closing her eyes.

Gus took his pipe out of his mouth and thought it over. Orders or no orders, he would try to save the filly. Ken had gone too far to be let down.

"Ay'm goin' to rig a blanket sling fur her, Tim, and get her on her feet and keep her up."

There was bright moonlight to work by. They brought down the posthole digger and set two aspen poles deep into the ground either side of the filly, then, with ropes attached to the blanket, hoisted her by a pulley.

Not at all disconcerted, she rested comfortably in the blanket under her belly, touched her feet on the ground, and reached for the bucket of water Gus held for her.

Kennie was sick a long time. He nearly died. But Flicka picked up. Every day Gus passed the word to Nell, who carried it to Ken. "She's cleaning up her oats." "She's out of the sling." "She bears a little weight on the bad leg."

Tim declared it was a real miracle. They argued about it, eating their supper.

"Na," said Gus. "It was de cold water, washin' de fever outa her. And more dan dot—it was Ken—you tink it don't count? All night dot boy sits dere, and says, 'Hold on, Flicka, Ay'm here wid you. Ay'm standin' by, two of us togedder'——"

Tim stared at Gus without answering, while he thought it over. In the silence, a coyote yapped far off on the plains; and the wind made a rushing sound high up in the jack pines on the hill.

Gus filled his pipe.

"Sure," said Tim finally. "Sure, that's it."

Then came the day when Rob McLaughlin stood smiling at the foot of Kennie's bed and said, "Listen! Hear your friend?"

Ken listened and heard Flicka's high, eager whinny.

"She don't spend much time by the brook any more. She's up at the gate of the corral half the time, nickering for you."

"For me!"

Rob wrapped a blanket around the boy and carried him out to the corral gate.

Kennie gazed at Flicka. There was a look of marveling in his eyes. He felt as if he had been living in a world where everything was dreadful and hurting but awfully real; and *this* couldn't be real; this was all soft and happy, nothing to struggle over or

worry about or fight for any more.
Even his father was proud of him! He
could feel it in the way Rob's big
arms held him. It was all like a dream
and far away. He couldn't, yet, get
close to anything.

But Flicka—Flicka—alive, well,
pressing up to him, recognizing him,
nickering—

Kennie put out a hand—weak
and white—and laid it on her face.
His thin little fingers straightened her
forelock the way he used to do, while
Rob looked at the two with a strange
expression about his mouth, and a
glow in his eyes that was not often
there.

"She's still poor, Dad, but she's
on four legs now."

"She's picking up."

Ken turned his face up, suddenly
remembering. "Dad! She did get
gentled, didn't she?"

"Gentle—as—a kitten—"

They put a cot down by the
brook for Ken, and boy and filly got
well together.

**DISCUSSION**    1.   "Ken doesn't half try; doesn't stick at anything," Rob McLaughlin
says during a discussion with his wife (page 135). Yet the boy saves his
colt's life. How? What qualities do his actions on that occasion reveal?

2.   Kennie's mother pleads with her husband to give their younger son
a colt. Do you feel that she was right? In what ways does Kennie change
after his father allows him to choose a colt?

3.   Why does Kennie pick Flicka for his colt? Why does his father think
the choice is a poor one?

4.   In what ways are Kennie and his father alike?

5.   **Dialogue.**   In short stories and novels authors frequently use dialogue, conversations among characters. Dialogue gives life to a story and
tells you what characters are like. Look closely at this passage from
page 132. "Yes, tell us how you do it, Ken." Through this comment
Howard reveals that he is mocking Ken, who has made a zero on an
examination. Pick two or three other examples of dialogue from the story
and tell what they show about the characters who speak them.

For further activities, see page 150.

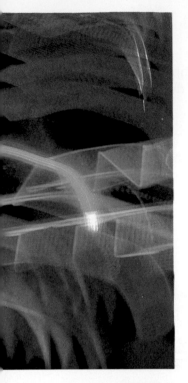

## VOCABULARY

### Polar Night (page 121)

On separate paper, write the word that is closest in meaning to the word in bold type in the left column.

1. the *magenta* sun      purplish red, dying, rising
2. bordered upon this *spectral* sea      vacant, frozen, ghostly
3. a *cobalt* looking glass      greenish blue, black, bronzed
4. the *subsidence* of pain      increasing, decreasing, ending
5. snow grew *luminous*      cold, light, dark
6. an *iridescent* sun-halo      large, fading, rainbowlike
7. the *sapphire* water      murky, sparkling, blue
8. life *teemed* in the water      abounded, remained, decreased

### My Friend Flicka (page 132)

English has borrowed words from many other languages. *Corral* and *loco* come from Spanish, as do many other words found in writing about the American West. The following five words are Spanish in origin. Use each in a sentence that will show you know the meaning of the word. Check in a dictionary if you need to.

canyon    mesa    arroyo    paloverde    ranch

## COMPOSITION

### Cholmondely, the Chimpanzee (page 112)

Suppose that you are one of the English bus riders and Cholmondely has just hopped on the bus. Describe in some detail what happens next. Since Durrell's story is nonfiction, you might want to create fiction (your own story) about a chimp. Change the name if you want. Make sure you include specific communication between the chimp and the passengers. You could easily use both nonverbal communication and dialogue.

### Polar Night (page 121)

Imagine you are one of the hunters that the bear frightened away. That night, around the fire, you tell what happened. Write the story that gives your version of the encounter.

## My Friend Flicka (page 132)

Writers often have their characters reveal themselves through the words they say. In this story, for example, we learn much about Kennie's mother through the words she speaks to her husband and young sons. In order to write good dialogue, we must first become good observers/listeners. Try to capture the dialogue of someone you know—friend, classmate, parent, or teacher. First, try to record accurately what the person says; then, see if you can remember a line or phrase used that catches something of the personality of the speaker.

## READING

### Polar Night (page 121)

On separate paper, write the number of the item that best completes each statement.

1. "Polar Night" describes the events (a) as the mother bear sees them (b) as the seal sees them (c) as the hunters see them.
2. An animal's *natural* enemy is one who (a) lives in the same dwelling (b) needs to eat that animal to survive (c) is the same size and kind.
3. The setting of the story—the arctic region, north of the limit of tree growth—is very important because (a) it is the polar bear's natural home (b) the arctic cold is almost like a character that influences the actions of the animals (c) both of the above.
4. Men are described in the story as (a) giant seals (b) land seals (c) playful seals.

### My Friend Flicka (page 132)

On separate paper, put the following events into the order in which they happened in the story.

1. Nell McLaughlin tells Kennie that Flicka is going to die.
2. Kennie stops daydreaming and begins to study harder.
3. Kennie stays up all night holding Flicka's head out of the water.
4. Kennie receives his report card for the second semester.
5. Kennie is sick for a long time and nearly dies.
6. Flicka badly hurts herself on the barbed-wire fence.
7. Rob McLaughlin tells Kennie he can have a yearling colt.
8. Flicka's fever is broken.

# COMPOSITION

**CHOOSING
WORDS**

When we speak or write, we try to choose—from the thousands of English words we know—those that come closest to expressing our thoughts and experiences and feelings. And all of us must write as well as speak. We write notes, reports, tests, school themes, letters, requests, instructions, applications, explanations. Here are a couple of hints that may help you, when you write, to choose words that express your opinions and experiences and thoughts effectively.

1. *Choose from words you know.*

If you know what *bamboozle* means, or *sesquipedalian,* or *brouhaha*—and *know* you know, and know that the sentence you want to write offers the perfect opportunity to use such a word—then do so. Otherwise, stay away from fancy words or words half-understood. "Cats," Rosalie Moore writes on page 119, "sleep fat and walk thin." Her words are simple, direct, familiar. But they express her meaning perfectly. You will express your meaning more clearly, more naturally, with words that you know well.

2. *Choose words that are specific.*

Jesse Stuart writes not about a "thing," or a "creature," or even a "reptile." He writes specifically about a "big bull blacksnake" (page 87). Daniel Mannix might have written vaguely about "somebody" or "some villager" furnishing the scientist with blood to feed his bats; instead, he writes more specifically that the blood was contributed "by the local butcher" (page 100). Alan Devoe might have asked in a general way, "Is it true that mice use their tails to get food out of inaccessible places?" But the sentence is vaguer, less specific than the one he did write (page 104): "Is it true that mice use their tails to get food out of inaccessible places, *such as out of bottles?"*

By writing more specifically, you too will let us see better, understand better. Instead of showing us vague "places" and "people" and "things," you will let us see bottles and butchers and blacksnakes. To repeat: the more specifically you write, the more vividly you will let your readers know what you have in mind.

ABOUT THE SELECTIONS

1. In a paragraph describe the animal from this section that you remember most clearly. Choose words that tell specifically how the animal looked and acted. When you have finished, compare your description with the description in the selection. Has the author used words that would make your description even clearer?

2. Some animals in the section are appealing. Others are terrifying. Write a paragraph that contrasts an appealing animal (Rikki-tikki-tavi, Old Ben, Cholmondely) with one that might frighten you if you met it in the wilds (the cobra Nag, the stinging jellyfish, a vampire bat). Choose words that show why one is likable, the other not.

3. Consider these two sentences:
    a. Rikki-tikki looked down between the boy's collar and neck, snuffed at his ear, and climbed down to the floor, where he sat rubbing his nose.

    b. I've had a lot of pets—ground hogs, crows, and hawks—but Old Ben's the best yet.
In a paragraph explain how each author's choice of words helps us understand his meaning exactly. Remember: the more specific the word, the clearer the picture or meaning.

4. Here are two pairs of sentences:

    Suddenly one of the cubs got too near the edge and fell into the water, then came up again. / Suddenly one ventured too far down the ice, and slithered, shrieking, into the sea, where he bobbed up again like a cork (page 127).

The next morning the chimpanzee drank and ate a lot. / The next morning he drank a mugful of sweet tea and ate seventeen biscuits (page 116).

Explain in a paragraph why the second sentence in each pair is more effective than the first.


ON YOUR OWN

1. Imagine animals from two different selections in this unit meeting each other. What would happen? What would happen if Flicka met Old Ben? Suppose the lone dog met Cholmondely. What would each of them do? Briefly describe such a meeting, using as specific words as possible.

2. The story "Old Ben" (page 87) brings a rather unusual pet clearly before us. Write a portrait in words of a pet you know, making it stand out distinctly as does Old Ben.

3. What qualities should a pet have? Pick the two or three that seem most important (loyalty? affection? intelligence? cleanliness? beauty?) and write a paragraph, with examples, that tells your reader what those qualities are.

4. Rewrite the following paragraph, substituting more specific words for all the general ones:

    The thing came off, then in a moment was down on the floor. The man tried to get it, but it got away and ended up in a place across the room. The man went toward it, and for a while he tried to get it back. Then he quit and walked away.

ACTION & BRAVERY

# The Day the Sun Came Out

DOROTHY M. JOHNSON

We left the home place behind, mile by slow mile. We were heading for the mountains, across the prairie where the wind blew forever.

At first there were four of us with the one-horse wagon and its skimpy load. Pa and I walked because I was a big boy of eleven. My two little sisters walked until they got tired. Then they had to be boosted up in the wagon bed.

That was no covered Conestoga, like Pa's folks came West in. It was just an old farm wagon, drawn by one tired horse. It creaked and rumbled westward to the mountains, toward the little woods town where Pa thought he had an old uncle who owned a little two-bit sawmill.

Two weeks we had been moving when we picked up Mary. She had run away from somewhere that she wouldn't tell. Pa didn't want her along. But she stood up to him with no fear in her voice.

"I'd rather go with a family and look after kids," she said, "but I ain't going back. If you won't take me, I'll travel with any wagon that will."

Pa scowled at her, and wide blue eyes stared back.

"How old are you?" he demanded.

"Twenty," she said. "There's teamsters come this way sometimes. I'd rather go with you folks. But I won't go back."

"We're prid'near out of food," my father told her. "We're clean out of money. I got all I can handle without taking anybody else." He turned away as if he hated the sight of her. "You'll have to walk," he said.

So she went along with us. She looked after the little girls, but Pa wouldn't talk to her.

On the prairie, the wind blew. But in the mountains, there was rain. When we stopped at little timber claims along the way, the homesteaders said it had rained all summer. Crops among the blackened stumps were rotted and spoiled. There was no cheer anywhere. The people we talked to were past worrying. They were scared and desperate.

So was Pa. He traveled twice as far each day as the wagon. He ranged through the woods with his rifle. But he never saw game. He had been depending on killing a deer. But we never got any deer meat except as a grudging gift from the homesteaders.

He brought in a porcupine once. And that was fat meat and good. Mary roasted it in chunks over the fire, half crying with the smoke. Pa and I rigged up the tarp sheet for a shelter to keep the rain from putting the fire clean out.

The porcupine was long gone, except for some of the tried-out fat that Mary had saved, when we came to an old, empty cabin. Pa said we'd have to stop. The horse was wore out. It couldn't pull any more up those hills in the mountains.

At the cabin, at least there was a place to stay. We had a few potatoes left and some cornmeal. There was a creek that probably had fish in it, if a person could catch them. Pa tried it for half a day before he gave up. To this day I don't care for fishing. I remember my father's sunken eyes in his sad face.

He took Mary and me outside the cabin to talk. Rain dripped on us from branches overhead.

"I think I know where we are," he said. "I figure to get to old John's and back in about four days. There'll be food in the town. They'll let me have some whether old John's still there or not."

He looked at me. "You do like she tells you," he warned. It was the first time he had admitted Mary was on earth since we picked her up two weeks before.

"You're my pardner," he said to me, "but it might be she's got more brains. You mind what she says."

He burst out with bitterness. "There ain't anything good left in the world. Or people to care if you live or die. But I'll get food in the town and come back with it."

He took a deep breath and added, "If you get too all-fired hungry, butcher the horse. It'll be better than starvin'."

He kissed the little girls good-bye. Then he plodded off through the woods with one blanket and the rifle.

The cabin was moldy and had no floor. We kept a fire going under a hole in the roof, so it was full of blinding smoke, but we had to keep the fire so as to dry out the wood.

The third night, we lost the horse. A bear scared him. We heard the racket. Mary and I ran out. But we couldn't see anything in the pitch-dark.

In gray daylight I went looking for him. I must have walked fifteen miles. It seemed like I had to have that horse at the cabin when Pa came or he'd whip me. I got plumb lost two or three times. I thought maybe I was going to die there alone and nobody would ever know it. But I found the way back to the clearing.

That was the fourth day. And Pa didn't come. That was the day we ate up the last of the grub.

The fifth day, Mary went looking for the horse. My sisters cried. They huddled in a blanket by the fire, because they were scared and hungry.

I never did get dried out, always having to bring in more damp wood and going out to yell to see if Mary would hear me and not get lost. But I couldn't cry like the little girls did, because I was a big boy, eleven years old.

It was near dark when there was an answer to my yelling. Mary came into the clearing.

Mary didn't have the horse. We never saw hide nor hair of that old horse again. But she was carrying something big and white that looked like a pumpkin with no color to it.

She didn't say anything, just looked around and saw Pa wasn't there yet, at the end of the fifth day.

"What's that thing?" my sister Elizabeth demanded.

"Mushroom," Mary answered. "I bet it hefts ten pounds."

"What are you going to do with it now?" I said. "Play football here?"

"Eat it—maybe," she said, putting it in a corner. Her wet hair hung over her shoulders. She huddled by the fire.

My sister Sarah began to cry again. "I'm hungry!" she kept saying.

"Mushrooms ain't good eating," I said. "They can kill you."

"Maybe," Mary answered. "Maybe they can, I don't set up to know all about everything, like some people."

"What's that mark on your shoulder?" I asked her. "You tore your dress on the brush."

"What do you think it is?" she said. Her head was bowed in the smoke.

"Looks like scars," I guessed.

" 'Tis scars. They whipped me, them I used to live with. Now mind your own business. I want to think."

Elizabeth cried, "Why don't Pa come back?"

"He's coming," Mary promised. "Can't come in the dark. Your pa'll take care of you soon's he can."

She got up and looked around in the grub box.

"Nothing there but empty dishes," I growled. "If there was anything, we'd know it."

Mary stood up. She was holding the can with the porcupine grease.

"I'm going to have something to eat," she said coolly. "You kids can't have any yet. And I don't want any crying, mind."

It was a cruel thing, what she did then. She sliced that big, solid mushroom and heated grease in a pan.

The smell of it brought the little girls out of their bed. But she told them to go back in so fierce a voice that they obeyed. They cried to break your heart.

I didn't cry. I watched, hating her.

I endured the smell of the mushroom frying as long as I could. Then I said, "Give me some."

"Tomorrow," Mary answered "Tomorrow, maybe. But not to-night." She turned to me with a sharp command: "Don't bother me! Just leave me be."

She knelt there by the fire and finished frying the slice of mushroom.

If I'd had Pa's rifle, I'd have been willing to kill her right then and there.

She didn't eat right away. She looked at the brown, fried slice for a while and said, "By tomorrow morning, I guess you can tell whether you want any."

The girls stared at her as she ate. Sarah was chewing on an old leather glove.

When Mary crawled into the quilts with them, they moved away as far as they could get.

I was so scared that my stomach heaved, empty as it was.

Mary didn't stay in the quilts long. She took a drink out of the water bucket and sat down by the fire and looked through the smoke at me.

She said in a low voice, "I don't know how it will be if it's poison. Just do the best you can with the girls. Because your pa will come back, you know. . . . You better go to bed. I'm going to sit up."

And so would you sit up. If it might be your last night on earth and the pain of death might seize you at any moment, you would sit up by the smoky fire, wide-awake, remembering what-ever you had to remember, savoring life.

We sat in silence after the girls had gone to sleep. Once I asked, "How long does it take?"

"I never heard," she answered. "Don't think about it."

I slept after a while, with my chin on my chest.

Mary's moving around brought me wide-awake. The black of night was fading.

"I guess it's all right," Mary said. "I'd be able to tell by now, wouldn't I?"

I answered gruffly, "I don't know."

Mary stood in the doorway for a while, looking out at the dripping world as if she found it beautiful. Then she fried slices of the mushroom while the little girls danced with anxiety.

We feasted, we three, my sisters and I, until Mary ruled, "That'll hold you," and would not cook any more. She didn't touch any of the mushroom herself.

That was a strange day in the moldy cabin. Mary laughed and was gay. She told stories. And we played "Who's Got the Thimble?" with a pine cone.

In the afternoon we heard a shout. My sisters screamed and I ran ahead of them across the clearing.

The rain had stopped. My father came plunging out of the woods leading a pack horse—and well I remember the treasures of food in that pack.

He glanced at us anxiously as he tore at the ropes that bound the pack.

"Where's the other one?" he demanded.

Mary came out of the cabin then, walking sedately. As she came toward us, the sun began to shine.

My stepmother was a wonderful woman.

DISCUSSION

1. What does the last line of the story tell you?

2. Mary's not sharing the mushroom is a "cruel thing," the narrator thinks. Why does he think this? Does he still think Mary is cruel at the end of the story? Explain.

3. **Conflict.**  Conflict is a struggle between opposing forces—between one person and another, between a person and a group, between a person and nature, between different things that a person wants or feels. In this story there is a conflict between Pa and Mary. Find one other conflict in the story and tell what it is.

For further activities, see page 194.

# The Christmas Hunt

BORDEN DEAL

It should have been the best Christmas of them all, that year at Dog Run. It started out to be, anyway. I was so excited, watching my father talking on the telephone, that I couldn't stand still. For I was thirteen years old and I had never been on a quail shoot in my whole life. I wanted to go on the big Christmas Day hunt even more than I wanted that bicycle I was supposed to get. And I really needed the bicycle to cover with speed and ease the two miles I had to walk to school.

The Christmas Day hunt was always the biggest and best of the season. It was almost like a field trial; only the best hunters and the finest dogs were invited by my father. All my life I had been hearing great tales of past Christmas Day hunts. And now I knew with a great thirteen-year-old certainty that I was old enough to go.

My father hung up the phone and turned around, grinning. "That was Walter," he said. "There'll be ten of them this year. And Walter is bringing his new dog. If all he claims for that dog is true——"

"Papa," I said.

"Goodness," my mother said. "That'll be a houseful to feed."

My father put his arm around her shoulders, hugging her. "Oh, you know you like it," he said. "They come as much for your cooking as they do for the hunting, I think."

My mother pursed her lips in the way she had, and then smiled. "Wild turkey," she said. "You think you could shoot me four or five nice fat wild turkeys?"

I wanted to jump up and down to attract attention. But that was kid stuff, all right for the five-year-olds, though I had to admit it was effective. But I was thirteen.

So I said, "Papa."

My father laughed. "I think I can," he said. "I'll put in a couple of mornings trying."

"Papa," I said desperately.

"Wild turkey stuffed with wild rice," my mother said quickly, thoughtfully, in her planning voice. "Giblet gravy, mashed potatoes, maybe a nice potato salad——"

"If I don't fail on the turkeys," my father said.

"Papa!" I said.

My father turned to me. "Come on, Tom," he said. "We got to feed those dogs."

That's the way parents are, even when you're thirteen years old. They can talk right on and never hear a word you say. I ran after my father as he left the kitchen, hoping for a

chance to get my words in edgewise. But my father was walking fast, and already the clamor of the bird dogs was rising up to cover any speech I might want to make.

The dogs were standing on the wire fence in long dappled rows, their voices lifted in greeting. Even in my great need I had to stop and admire them. There's nothing prettier in the whole world than a good bird dog. There's a nobleness to its head, an intelligence in its eyes, that no other animal has. Just looking at them sent a shiver down my backbone; and the thought of shooting birds over them—well, the shiver wasn't just in my backbone now, I was shaking all over.

All of the dogs except one were in the same big run. But my father kept Calypso Baby in her own regal pen. I went to her and looked into her soft brown eyes. She stood up tall on the fence, her strong, lithe body stretched to its full height, as tall as I was.

"Hello, Baby," I whispered, and she wagged her tail. "You gonna find me some birds this Christmas, Baby? You gonna hunt for me like you do for Papa?"

She lolled her tongue, laughing at me. We were old friends. Calypso Baby was the finest bird dog in that part of the country. My father owned a number of dogs and kept and trained others for his town friends. But Calypso Baby was his personal dog, the one that he took to the field trials, the one he shot over in the big Christmas Day hunt held at Dog Run.

My father was bringing the sack of feed from the shed. I put out my hand, holding it against the wire so Calypso Baby could lick my fingers.

"This year," I whispered to her. "This year I'm going." I left Calypso Baby, went with determination toward my father.

"Papa," I said, in a voice not to be denied this time.

My father was busy opening the sack of dog food.

"Papa," I said firmly. "I want to talk to you."

It was the tone and the words my father used often toward me, so much so that my father looked down at me in surprise, at last giving me his attention.

"What is it?" he said. "What do you want?"

"Papa, I'm thirteen years old," I said.

My father laughed. "Well, what of it?" he said. "Next year you'll be fourteen. And the next year fifteen."

"I'm old enough to go on the Christmas hunt," I said.

My father laughed. "At thirteen?" he said. "I'm afraid not."

I stood, stricken. "But—" I said.

"No," my father said, in the voice that meant No, and no more talking about it. He hoisted the sack of feed and took it into the wire dog-pen, the bird dogs crowding around him, rearing up on him in their eagerness.

"Well, come on and help me,"

my father said impatiently. "I've got a lot of things to do."

Usually I enjoyed the daily feeding of the dogs. But not today; I went through the motions dumbly, silently, not paying any attention to the fine bird dogs crowding around me. I cleaned the watering troughs with my usual care, but my heart was not in it.

After the feeding was over, I scuffed stubbornly about my other tasks and then went up to my room, not even coming down when my father came home at dusk excited with the two wild turkeys he had shot. I could hear him talking to my mother in the kitchen, and the ring of their voices had already the feel of Christmas, a hunting cheer that made them brighter, livelier than usual. But none of the cheer and the pleasure came into me, even though Christmas was almost upon us and yesterday had been the last day of school.

That night I hunted. In my dreams I was out ahead of all the other men and dogs, Calypso Baby quartering the field in her busy way, doing it so beautifully I ached inside to watch her. All the men and dogs stopped their own hunting to watch us, as though it were a field trial. When Calypso Baby pointed, I raised the twelve-gauge shotgun, moved in on her on the ready, and Calypso Baby flushed the birds in her fine, steady way. They came up in an explosive whir, and I had the gun to my shoulder, squeezing off the shot just the way I'd been told to do. Three

quail dropped like stones out of the covey and I swung the gun, following a single. I brought down the single with the second barrel, and Calypso Baby was already bringing the first bird to me in her soft, unbruising mouth. I knelt to pat her for a moment, and Baby whipped her tail to tell me how fine a shot I was, how much she liked my being the one shooting over her today.

Soon there was another covey, and I did even better on this one, and then another and another, and nobody was hunting at all, not even my father, who was laughing and grinning at the other men, knowing this was his boy, Tom, and his dog, Calypso Baby, and just full of pride with it all. When it was over, the men crowded around and patted me on the shoulder, hefting the full game bag in admiration, and then there was my father's face close before me, saying, "I was wrong, son, when I said a thirteen-year-old boy isn't old enough to go bird hunting with the best of us."

Then I was awake and my father, dressed in his hunting clothes, was shaking me, and it was morning. I looked up dazedly into his face, unable to shake off the dream, and I knew what it was I had to do. I had to show my father. Only then would he believe.

"Are you awake?" my father said. "You'll have to change the water for the dogs. I'm going to see if I can get some more turkeys this morning."

"All right," I said. "I'm awake now."

My father left. I got up and ate breakfast in the kitchen, close to the warm stove. I didn't say anything to my mother about my plans. I went out and watered the dogs as soon as the sun was up, but I didn't take the time, as I usually did, to play with them.

"Me and you are going hunting," I told Calypso Baby as I changed her water. She jumped and quivered all over, knowing the word as well as I did.

I went back into the house, listening for my mother. She was upstairs, making the beds. I went into the spare room where my father kept all the hunting gear. I was trembling, remembering the dream, as I went to the gun rack and touched the cold steel of the double-barreled twelve-gauge. But I knew it would be very heavy for me. I took the single-barreled gun instead, though I knew that pretty near ruined my chances for a second shot unless I could reload very quickly.

I picked up a full shell bag and hung it under my left arm. I found a game bag and hung it under my right arm. The strap was too long and the bag dangled emptily to my knees, banging against me as I walked. I tied a knot in the strap so the bag would rest comfortably on my right hip. The gun was heavy in my hands as I walked into the hallway, listening for my mother. She was still upstairs.

"Mamma, I'm gone," I shouted up to her. "I'll be back in a little while." That was so she wouldn't be looking for me.

"All right," she called. "Don't wander far off. Your father will be back in an hour or two and might have something for you to do."

I hurried out of the house, straight to Calypso Baby's pen. I did not look up, afraid that my mother might be watching out of the window. That was a danger I could do nothing about, so I just ignored it. I opened the gate to Baby's pen and she came out, circling and cavorting.

"Come on, Baby," I whispered. "Find me some birds now. Find me a whole lot of birds."

We started off, circling the barn so we would not be seen from the house, and going straight away in its shadow as far as we could. Beyond the pasture we crossed a cornfield, Calypso Baby arrowing straight for the patch of sedgegrass beyond. Her tail was whiplike in its thrash, her head high as she plunged toward her work, and I had to hurry to keep up. The gun was clumsy in my hands and the two bags banged against my hips. But I remembered not to run with the gun, remembered to keep the breech open until I was ready to shoot. I knew all about hunting; I just hadn't had a chance to practice what I knew. When I came home with a bag full of fine birds my father would have to admit that I knew how to hunt, that I was old enough for the big Christmas Day hunt when all the great hunters came out from town for the biggest day of the season.

When I ducked through the barbed-wire fence Calypso Baby was waiting for me, standing a few steps into the sedgegrass, her head up watching me alertly. Her whole body quivered with her eagerness to be off. I swept my arm in the gesture I had seen my father use so many times, and Calypso Baby plunged instantly into the grass. She was a fast worker, quartering back and forth with an economical use of her energy. She could cover a field in half the time it took any other dog. The first field was empty, and we passed on to the second one. Somehow Calypso Baby knew that birds were here. She steadied down, hunting slowly, more thoroughly.

Then, startling me though I had been expecting it, she froze into a point, one foot up, her tail straight back, her head flat with the line of her backbone. I froze too. I couldn't move, I couldn't even remember to breech the gun and raise it to my shoulder. I stood as still as the dog, all of my knowledge flown out of my head, and yet far back under the panic I knew that the birds weren't going to hold, they were going to rise in just a moment. Calypso Baby, surprised at my inaction, broke her point

to look at me in inquiry. Her head turned toward me and she asked the question as plain as my father's voice: *Well, what are you going to do about these fine birds I found for you?*

I could move then. I took a step or two, fumblingly breeched the gun, raised it to my shoulder. The birds rose of their own accord in a sudden wild drum of sound. I yanked at the trigger, unconsciously bracing myself against the blast and the recoil. Nothing happened. Nothing at all happened. I tugged at the trigger wildly, furiously, but it was too late and the birds were gone.

I lowered the gun, looking down at it in bewilderment. I had forgotten to release the safety. I wanted to cry at my own stupidity. This was not at all like my dream of last night, when I and the dog and the birds had all been so perfect.

Calypso Baby walked back to me and looked up into my face. I could read the puzzled contempt in her eyes. She lay down at my feet, putting her muzzle on her paws. I looked down at her, ashamed of myself and knowing that she was ashamed. She demanded perfection, just as my father did.

"It was my fault, Baby," I told her. I leaned over and patted her on the head. "You didn't do anything wrong. It was me."

I started off then, looking back at the bird dog. She did not follow me. "Come on," I told her. "Hunt."

She got up slowly and went out ahead of me again. But she worked in a puzzled manner, checking back to me frequently. She no longer had the joy, the confidence, with which she had started out.

"Come on, Baby," I coaxed her. "Hunt, Baby. Hunt."

We crossed into another field, low grass this time, and when we found the covey there was very little time for setting myself. Calypso Baby pointed suddenly; I jerked the gun to my shoulder, remembering the safety this time, and then Calypso Baby flushed the birds. They rose up before me and I pulled the trigger, hearing the blast of the gun, feeling the shock of it into my shoulder knocking me back a step.

But not even one bird dropped like a fateful stone out of the covey. The covey had gone off low and hard on an angle to the left, and I had completely missed the shot, aiming straight ahead instead of swinging with the birds. Calypso Baby did not even attempt to point singles. She dropped her head and her tail and started away from me, going back toward the house.

I ran after her, calling her. Baby would never like me again. She would hold me in the indifference she felt toward any person who was not a bird hunter. She would tolerate me as she tolerated my mother, and the men who came out with shiny new hunting clothes and walked all over the land talking about how the dogs didn't hold the birds properly so you could get a decent shot.

I couldn't be one of those! I ran after the dog, calling her, until at last she allowed me to come near. I knelt,

fondling her head, talking to her, begging her for another chance.

"I'll get some birds next time," I told her. "You just watch. You hear?"

At last, reluctantly, she consented to hunt again. I followed her, my hands gripping the heavy gun, determined this time. I knew it was my last chance; she would not give me another. I could not miss this time.

We hunted for an hour before we found another covey of birds. I was tired; the gun was heavier with every step. But, holding only last night's dream in my mind, I refused to quit. At last Calypso Baby froze into a beautiful point. I could feel myself sweating, my teeth gritted hard. I had to bring down a bird this time.

It seemed to be perfect. I had plenty of time but I hurried anyway, just to be sure. Then the birds were rising in a tight cluster and I was pulling the trigger before I had the heavy gun lined up—and in the midst of the thundering blast I heard Calypso Baby yell with pain as the random shot tore into her hip.

I threw down the gun and ran toward her, seeing the blood streaking down her leg as she staggered away from me, whimpering. I knelt, trying to coax her to me, but she was afraid. I was crying, feeling the full weight of the disaster. I had committed the worst crime of any bird hunter; I had shot my own dog.

Calypso Baby was trying to hide in a clump of bushes. She snapped at me in her fear when I reached in after her, but I did not feel the pain in my hand. I knelt over her, looking at the shredded hip. It was a terrible wound. I could see only blood and raw flesh. I snatched off the empty hunting bag I had put on so optimistically, the shell bag, and took off my coat. I wrapped her in the coat and picked her up in my arms. She was very heavy, hurting, whining with each jolting step as I ran toward the house.

I came into the yard doubled over with the catch in my side from the running, and my legs were trembling. My father was sitting on the back porch with three wild turkeys beside him, cleaning his gun. He jumped to his feet when he saw the wounded dog.

"What happened?" he said. "Did some fool hunter shoot her?"

I stopped, standing before my father and holding the wounded dog; I looked into his angry face. They were the most terrible words I ever had to say. "I shot her, Papa," I said.

My father stood very still. I did not know what would happen. I had never done anything so bad in my whole life and I could not even guess how my father would react. The only thing right would be to wipe me off the face of the earth with one angry gesture of his hand.

I gulped, trying to move the pain in my throat out of the way of the words. "I took her out bird hunting," I said. "I wanted to show you—if I got a full bag of birds, I thought you'd let me go on the Christmas Day hunt——"

"I'll talk to you later," my father said grimly, taking the dog from me and starting into the kitchen. "I've got to try to save this dog's life now."

I started into the kitchen behind my father. He turned. "Where's the gun you shot her with?" he said.

"I—left it."

"Don't leave it lying out there in the field," my father said in a stern voice.

I wanted very badly to go into the kitchen, find out that Calypso Baby would live. But I turned, instead, and went back the way I had come, walking with my head down, feeling shrunken inside myself. I had overreached; I had risen up today full of pride beyond my ability, and in the stubbornness of the pride I had been blind until the terrible accident had opened my eyes so that I could see myself clearly—too clearly. I found the gun, the two bags, where I had dropped them. I picked them up without looking at the smear of blood where Calypso had lain. I went back to the house slowly, not wanting to face it, reluctant to see the damage I had wrought.

When I came into the kitchen, my father had the dog stretched out on the kitchen table. My mother stood by his side with bandages and ointment in her hands. The wound was cleaned of the bird shot and dirt and blood. Calypso Baby whined when she saw me and I felt my heart cringe with the rejection.

My father looked at me across the dog. The anger was gone out of him, his voice was slow and searching and not to be denied.

"Now I want to know why you took my gun and my dog without permission," he said.

"David," my mother said to him.

My father ignored her, kept his eyes hard on my face. I knew it wouldn't do any good to look toward my mother. This was between me and my father, and there was no refuge for me anywhere in the world. I didn't want a refuge; I knew I had to face not only my father, but myself.

"I—I wanted to go on the Christmas Day hunt," I said again. "I thought if I. . . ." I stopped. It was all that I had to say; it seemed pretty flimsy to me now.

My father looked down at the dog. I was surprised at the lack of anger in him. I could read only sadness in his voice. "She may be ruined for hunting," he said. "Even if the wound heals good, if she doesn't lose the use of her leg, she may be gun-shy for the rest of her life. At best, I'll never be able to show her in field trials again. You understand what you've done?"

"Yes, sir," I said. I wanted to cry. But that would not help, any more than anger from my father would help.

"You see now why I said you weren't old enough?" my father said. "You've got to be trained for hunting,

just as a dog is trained. Suppose other men had been out there, suppose you had shot a human being?"

"David!" my mother said.

My father turned angrily toward her. "He's got to learn!" he said. "There are too many people in this world trying to do things without learning how to do them first. I don't want my boy to be one of them."

"Papa," I said. "I'm—I'm sorry. I wouldn't have hurt Calypso Baby for anything in the world."

"I'm not going to punish you," my father said. He looked down at the dog. "This is too bad for a whipping to settle. But I want you to think about today. I don't want you to put it out of your mind. You knew that when the time came ripe for it, I intended to teach you, take you out like I'd take a puppy, and hunt with you. After a while, you could hunt by yourself. Then if you were good enough—and *only* if you were good enough—you could go on the Christmas Day hunt. The Christmas Day hunt is the place you come to, not the place you start out from. Do you understand?"

"Yes, sir," I said. I would have been glad to settle for a whipping.

"You've got to take special care of Calypso Baby," my father said. "Maybe if you take care of her yourself while she's hurt, she'll decide to be your friend again."

I looked at the dog and I could feel the need of her confidence and trust. "Yes, sir," I said. Then I said humbly, "I hope she will be friends with me again."

I went toward the hall, needing to be alone in my room. I stopped at the kitchen doorway, looked back at my father and mother watching me. I had to say it in a hurry if I was going to say it at all.

"Papa," I said, the words rushing softly in my throat, threatening to gag there before I could get them out. "I—I don't think I deserve that bicycle this Christmas. I don't deserve it at all."

My father nodded his head. "All right, son," he said gravely. "This is your own punishment for yourself."

"Yes," I said, forcing the word, the loss making me empty inside and yet feeling better too. I turned and ran out of the room and up the stairs.

Christmas came, but without any help from me at all. I went to bed on Christmas Eve heavy with the knowledge that tomorrow morning there would be no shiny new bicycle under the tree, there would be no Christmas Day hunt for me. I couldn't prevent myself from waking up at the usual excited time, but I made myself turn over and go back to sleep. When I did, reluctantly, go downstairs, the Christmas tree did not excite me, nor the usual gifts I received every year: the heavy sweater, the gloves, the scarf, the two new pairs of blue jeans. I just wouldn't let myself think about the bicycle.

After my father had gone outside, my mother hugged me to her in a sudden rush of affection. "He would have given you the bicycle anyway," she said. "If you hadn't told him you didn't want it."

I looked up at her. "I didn't deserve it," I said. "Maybe next year I will."

She surprised me then by holding me and crying. I heard the first car arrive outside, the voices of the men excited with the promise of hunting. My mother stood up and said briskly, "Well, this is not getting that big dinner cooked," and went into the kitchen without looking back.

I went out on the front porch. It was perfect quail-hunting weather, cold but not too cold, with a smoky haze lying over the earth. The dogs knew that today was for hunting; I could hear them from around behind the house, standing on the wire fence in broad-shouldered rows, their voices yelping and calling. All except Calypso Baby. All except me.

I stood aside, watching the men arrive in their cars, my father greeting them. Their breaths hung cloudy in the air and they moved with a sharp movement to their bodies. These were the best hunters in the whole countryside, and today would be a great comradeship and competition. Any man invited on this hunt could be proud of the invitation alone.

I felt almost remote as I watched, as I went with them around the side of the house to the dogs. They all went to examine Calypso Baby, and I felt a freezing inside; but my father only said, "She got shot by accident," and did not tell the whole terrible story.

Then my father looked at his watch and said, "Let's wait a few more minutes. Walter ought to be here soon. Hate to start without him."

One of the men called, "Here he comes now," and Walter drove up in his battered car.

"Come here, son," my father said, speaking to me for the first time this morning, and I went reluctantly to his side. I was afraid it was coming now, the whole story, and all the men would look at me in the same way that Calypso Baby had after I had shot her.

My father drew me to the side of Walter's car, reached in, and brought out a basket. "You wanted a bicycle," he said. "Then you decided yourself you should wait. Because you made the decision yourself, I decided you were old enough for this."

I looked at the bird-dog puppy in the basket. All of a sudden Christmas burst inside me like a skyrocket, out of the place where I had kept it suppressed all this time.

"Papa," I said. "Papa——"

"Take him," my father said.

I reached into the basket and took out the puppy. The puppy licked my chin with his harsh warm tongue. He was long, gangly—his feet and head too big for his body—but absolutely beautiful.

My father knelt beside me, one hand on the puppy. "I told Walter to bring me the finest bird-dog puppy he could find," he said. "He's kin to Calypso Baby; he's got good blood."

"Thank you, Papa," I said in a choking voice. "I—I'd rather have him than the bicycle. I'll name him Calypso Boy. I'll——"

"When this puppy is ready for birds, we'll train him," my father said. "While we train the puppy, we'll train you too. When the time comes, you can both go on the Christmas Day hunt—if you're good enough."

"We'll be good enough," I said. "*Both* of us will be good enough."

"I hope so," my father said. He stood up and looked at the men standing around us, all of them smiling down at me and Calypso Boy.

"Let's go," he said. "Those birds are going to get tired of waiting on us."

They laughed and hollered, and the dogs moiled and sounded in the excitement as they were let out of the pen. They fanned out across the pasture, each man or two men taking a dog. I stood watching, holding the puppy warm in my arms. I looked at Calypso Baby, standing crippled in her pen looking longingly after the hunters. I went over and spoke to her. She whined; then for the first time since the accident she wagged her tail at me.

I looked down at the puppy in my arms. "We'll be going," I told him, as he licked at my chin. "One of these days, when you're a dog and I'm a man, we'll be right out there with the best of them."

It was three years more before I went on my first Christmas hunt. Papa had been right, of course. In the time between, I had learned a great deal myself while training Calypso Boy to hunt. With the good blood in him he turned out to be a great bird dog—second only, I guess, to Calypso Baby, who recovered well from her wound and was Papa's dog the day Calypso Boy and I made our first Christmas Day hunt.

But of all the Christmases, before and since, I guess I remember best the one when Calypso Baby was hurt—and Calypso Boy first came to me.

**DISCUSSION**

1.   "I don't think I deserve that bicycle this Christmas," Tom says to his father. Why does Tom decide he doesn't deserve the bicycle? Why does Tom's father decide to give him a bird-dog puppy?

2.   Tom wants to go on the Christmas hunt so badly that he dreams about it. The hunt in the dream turns out beautifully. The attempt to enact the dream turns into a disaster. What are some of the differences between the events in the dream and the next-day reality?

3.   While Tom's father is very upset about the shooting of Calypso Baby, he chooses not to whip Tom. Why does Tom's father make this decision? Do you think this was a good or a poor decision? Why?

For further activities, see page 194.

# Grandmother and the Workmen

ANTHONY QUINN

Grandmother had been watching the men digging out on the street for five days. At first there had been an army of engineers surveying with their transits and levels. The neighborhood had been excited by the rumor that we would finally get a sewer pipe. The men had marked the street with red and yellow chalk marks, put pegs down, and then had disappeared.

Then one day three trucks arrived, unloaded men and equipment, and the digging began. Grandmother kept close check on their progress. They dug about a cubic foot and a half per man in one week. According to my grandmother, she dug more than that an hour in the vegetable garden.

Every night as she prepared our frijoles and mustard greens, she cursed the injustice that we should be starving while those men out in the street were getting the enormous wage of three dollars a day, enough money to feed our family for a month.

One morning she couldn't stand it any longer and went out and accosted the fat foreman.

"I want a job!"

"Doing what, lady?"

"Digging like these men."

"Are you kidding, lady? That's man's work."

"Look, mister, I can lean on a shovel as good as they can. I've been watching them all week. A dog can dig faster."

"Look, you got any complaints, go to City Hall."

"I just want a job. I've got two hungry kids to feed."

"Go and do some sewing or washing."

Feeling challenged, my grandmother pulled a pick from the hands of a stunned workman and began to tear up the street.

The foreman tried to wrest the pick out of her hand, but she threatened him with it.

"I'm going to dig here all day. If you don't think I've earned my money at the end of the day you won't have to pay me."

The foreman shrugged and walked away. All the men, who had gathered around to watch the spectacle, laughed uproariously at her. An hour later, when she was still furiously swinging the pick, the men started to gather off to one side and mutter about going on strike. Meanwhile, various spectators had gathered on the side, cheering.

The men finally went back to their work, at the insistence of the foreman, who seemed to hope the old lady would disappear and that it was all just a bad dream—a nightmare. After a while, the superintendent showed up and was amazed at the sight that greeted him. The foreman rushed up to him and explained. The superintendent looked at the other workers and said, "From what I can see, this is the first time these bums have done any work. Maybe she's right. Maybe we should let her work."

He walked over to Grandmother and said, "Lady, stop a minute. I want to talk to you."

She went on digging.

"Lady, listen to me. You can't work like a common laborer."

"Why not?"

"I don't know," he said, "but it don't look right. Besides," he smiled, "you're making them all look bad. You're right, they are bums, but this would start a revolution, lady. My business is to get this street done. I don't want to be involved in any crazy revolution by women picking and shoveling like ordinary laborers."

The old lady stopped for a second and considered.

"All you want is this street done, right? I promise you, with me among them, you will get it done in half the time."

"I don't doubt it, lady, but there'd be an awful lot of explaining to do. I beg you to leave the men alone. Look, tell you what I'll do. I understand you've worked three hours already. I'll pay you for the whole day. We'll be around for some time and you can bring the men water. I'll pay you for a full day's work."

For the rest of the month, the men had the best water carrier of their lives. My grandmother took her job very seriously. In the morning she would make ice-cold lemonade for the men working out on the street. Sometimes she would vary it and put in strawberry. No group of pick-and-shovel workers ever drank such nectar as she made. I think they were a little sad when they finished the job and had to move to another neighborhood. But that month my grandmother made a grand total of sixty dollars, which kept us in three square meals a day for a long time.

**DISCUSSION**

1. The superintendent told Grandmother that if she kept working, "this would start a revolution." What changed when Grandmother started digging? Why did the superintendent want her to stop?

2. How do you think the writer feels about his grandmother? Explain your answer.

# The Most Important Day

HELEN KELLER

When Helen Keller (1880–1968) was just under two years old, she was left blind and deaf
after an illness. The next four years she spent
in what she later described as "a dense fog."
When Annie Sullivan arrived at the Keller
household she found her six-year-old pupil a
"deaf, mute, blind bundle of fierce flesh." But
within a month Annie Sullivan had worked a
miracle. It is this miracle that Helen Keller describes in the story you are about to read.

Annie Sullivan continued to teach Helen
Keller, devoting her life to her pupil. The pho-
tograph on page 182 shows Helen "listening"
as Annie helps her to prepare for college.
When Helen entered Radcliffe in 1900, Annie
was at her side, tapping words into her hand.
Helen earned her degree with honors in the
normal four-year period. Later she became a
world-famous writer and lecturer.

The most important day I remember in all my
life is the one on which my teacher, Anne
Mansfield Sullivan, came to me. I am filled
with wonder when I consider the immeasurable
contrasts between the two lives which it con-
nects. It was the third of March, 1887, three
months before I was seven years old.

On the afternoon of that eventful day I
stood on the porch—dumb, expectant. I
guessed vaguely from my mother's signs and
from the hurrying to and fro in the house that
something unusual was about to happen, so I
went to the door and waited on the steps. The
afternoon sun penetrated the mass of honeysuckle that covered the porch, and fell on my
upturned face. My fingers lingered almost unconsciously on the familiar leaves and blossoms
which had just come forth to greet the sweet

Southern spring. I did not know what the future held of marvel or surprise for me. Anger and bitterness had preyed upon me continually for weeks, and a deep languor had succeeded this passionate struggle.

Have you ever been at sea in a dense fog when it seemed as if a tangible, white darkness shut you in, and the great ship, tense and anxious, groped her way toward the shore with plummet[1] and sounding line, and you waited with beating heart for something to happen? I was like that ship before my education began, only I was without compass or sounding line and had no way of knowing how near the harbor was. "Light! Give me light!" was the wordless cry of my soul, and the light of love shone on me in that very hour.

I felt approaching footsteps. I stretched out my hand, as I supposed, to my mother. Someone took it, and I was caught up and held close in the arms of her who had come to reveal all things to me and, more than all things else, to love me.

The morning after my teacher came she led me into her room and gave me a doll. The little blind children at the Perkins Institution had sent it, and Laura Bridgman had dressed it, but I did not know this until afterward. When I had played with it a little while, Miss Sullivan slowly spelled into my hand the word "d-o-l-l." I was at once interested in this finger play and tried to imitate it. When I finally succeeded in making the letters correctly, I was flushed with childish pleasure and pride. Running downstairs to my mother, I held up my hand and made the letters for *doll*. I did not know that I was spelling a word or even that words existed; I was simply making my fingers go in monkey-like imitation. In the days that

---

[1] *plummet:* weight at the end of a sounding line, dropped into the water to measure its depth.

followed I learned to spell in this uncomprehending way a great many words, among them *pin, hat, cup* and a few verbs like *sit, stand,* and *walk*. But my teacher had been with me several weeks before I understood that everything has a name.

One day while I was playing with my new doll, Miss Sullivan put my big rag doll into my lap also, spelled "d-o-l-l," and tried to make me understand that "d-o-l-l" applied to both. Earlier in the day we had had a tussle over the words "m-u-g" and "w-a-t-e-r." Miss Sullivan had tried to impress it upon me that "m-u-g" is *mug* and that "w-a-t-e-r" is *water,* but I persisted in confounding the two. In despair, she had dropped the subject for the time, only to renew it at the first opportunity. I became impatient at her repeated attempts, and seizing the new doll, I dashed it upon the floor. I was keenly delighted when I felt the fragments of the broken doll at my feet. Neither sorrow nor regret followed my passionate outburst. I had not loved the doll. In the still, dark world in which I lived, there was no strong sentiment or tenderness. I felt my teacher sweep the fragments to one side of the hearth, and I had a sense of satisfaction that the cause of my discomfort was removed. She brought me my hat, and I knew I was going out into the warm sunshine. This thought, if a wordless sensation may be called a thought, made me hop and skip with pleasure.

We walked down the path to the well house, attracted by the fragrance of the honeysuckle with which it was covered. Someone was drawing water, and my teacher placed my hand under the spout. As the cool stream gushed over one hand, she spelled into the other the word *water,* first slowly, then rapidly. I stood still, my whole attention fixed upon the motions of her fingers. Suddenly I felt a misty consciousness as of something forgotten—a

thrill of returning thought—and somehow the mystery of language was revealed to me. I knew then that "w-a-t-e-r" meant the wonderful cool something that was flowing over my hand. That living word awakened my soul, gave it light, hope, joy, set it free! There were barriers still, it is true, but barriers that could in time be swept away.

I left the well house eager to learn. Everything had a name, and each name gave birth to a new thought. As we returned to the house, every object which I touched seemed to quiver with life. That was because I saw everything with the strange, new sight that had come to me. On entering the door, I remembered the doll I had broken. I felt my way to the hearth and picked up the pieces. I tried vainly to put them together. Then my eyes filled with tears, for I realized what I had done, and for the first time I felt repentance and sorrow.

**DISCUSSION**

1.  What has happened to Helen that makes her sorry she broke the doll?

2.  What senses does the writer draw on to let you know what she experienced? Find examples in the story.

3.  **Biography and autobiography.** Biography is an account of a person's life, written by someone else. Because it is true, it is called nonfiction. When the account is written by the person herself or himself, it is called autobiography. Is this story biography or autobiography? How would it be different if the teacher, Annie Sullivan, had written it from *her* point of view?

# FOUL SHOT

**EDWIN A. HOEY**

With two 60's stuck on the scoreboard
And two seconds hanging on the clock,
The solemn boy in the center of eyes,
Squeezed by silence,
Seeks out the line with his feet,                     5
Soothes his hands along his uniform,
Gently drums the ball against the floor,
Then measures the waiting net,
Raises the ball on his right hand,
Balances it with his left,                            10
Calms it with fingertips,
Breathes,
Crouches,
Waits,
And then through a stretching of stillness,           15
Nudges it upward.

The ball
Slides up and out,
Lands,
Leans,                                                20
Wobbles,
Wavers,
Hesitates,
Exasperates,
Plays it coy                                          25
Until every face begs with unsounding screams—

And then

        And then

              And then,

Right before ROAR-UP,                                 30
Dives down and through.

## DISCUSSION

1.  "Foul Shot" presents a vivid picture of a boy preparing and finally shooting a foul shot. What are the first and last things the boy does?

2.  How are the movements of the ball, in the second part of the poem, like the movements of the boy, in the first part of the poem?

3.  The words of a poem are chosen very carefully for their meaning, and also for their sound. The boy "nudges" the ball (line 16). Why do you think the writer chose "nudges" instead of "throws"? In the last line, why do you think the writer chose "dives" instead of "falls"?

# Casey at the Bat

ERNEST LAWRENCE THAYER

The outlook wasn't brilliant for the Mudville nine that day:
The score stood four to two, with but one inning more to play,
And then when Cooney died at first, and Barrows did the same,
A pall-like silence fell upon the patrons of the game.

A straggling few got up to go in deep despair. The rest    5
Clung to that hope which springs eternal in the human breast;
They thought, "If only Casey could but get a whack at that—
We'd put up even money now, with Casey at the bat."

But Flynn preceded Casey, as did also Jimmy Blake,
And the former was a hoodoo, while the latter was a cake;    10
So upon that stricken multitude grim melancholy sat,
For there seemed but little chance of Casey getting to the bat.

But Flynn let drive a single, to the wonderment of all,
And Blake, the much-despisèd, tore the cover off the ball;
And when the dust had lifted, and men saw what had occurred,    15
There was Jimmy safe at second and Flynn a-hugging third.

Then from five thousand throats and more there rose a lusty yell;
It rumbled through the valley, it rattled in the dell;
It pounded on the mountain and recoiled upon the flat,
For Casey, mighty Casey, was advancing to the bat.    20

There was ease in Casey's manner as he stepped into his place;
There was pride in Casey's bearing and a smile lit Casey's face.
And when, responding to the cheers, he lightly doffed his hat,
No stranger in the crowd could doubt 'twas Casey at the bat.

Ten thousand eyes were on him as he rubbed his hands with dirt;    25
Five thousand tongues applauded when he wiped them on his shirt;
Then while the writhing pitcher ground the ball into his hip,
Defiance flashed in Casey's eye, a sneer curled Casey's lip.

And now the leather-covered sphere came hurtling through the air,
And Casey stood a-watching it in haughty grandeur there.    30

Close by the sturdy batsman the ball unheeded sped—
"That ain't my style," said Casey. "Strike one!" the umpire said.

From the benches, black with people, there went up a muffled roar,
Like the beating of the storm-waves on a stern and distant shore;
"Kill him! Kill the umpire!" shouted some one on the stand;    35
And it's likely they'd have killed him had not Casey raised his hand.

With a smile of Christian charity great Casey's visage shone;
He stilled the rising tumult; he bade the game go on;
He signaled to the pitcher, and once more the dun sphere flew;
But Casey still ignored it, and the umpire said, "Strike two!"    40

"Fraud!" cried the maddened thousands, and echo answered "Fraud!"
But one scornful look from Casey and the audience was awed.
They saw his face grow stern and cold, they saw his muscles strain,
And they knew that Casey wouldn't let that ball go by again.

The sneer has fled from Casey's lip, his teeth are clenched in hate;    45
He pounds with cruel violence his bat upon the plate.
And now the pitcher holds the ball, and now he lets it go,
And now the air is shattered by the force of Casey's blow.

Oh, somewhere in this favored land the sun is shining bright;
The band is playing somewhere, and somewhere hearts are light,    50
And somewhere men are laughing, and little children shout;
But there is no joy in Mudville—great Casey has struck out.

**DISCUSSION**    1.  Were you surprised at the way the poem ended? Explain.

2.  "There is no joy in Mudville." What do you think makes the crowd sadder—that a player has struck out or that the player who struck out was Casey? What lines in the poem back up your answer?

# Good Sportsmanship

RICHARD ARMOUR

Good sportsmanship we hail, we sing;
   It's always pleasant when you spot it.
There's only one unhappy thing:
   You have to lose to prove you've got it.

# HOCKEY

SCOTT BLAINE

The ice is smooth, smooth, smooth.
The air bites to the center
Of warmth and flesh, and I whirl.
It begins in a game . . .
The puck swims, skims, veers,                        5
Goes leading my vision
Beyond the chasing reach of my stick.

The air is sharp, steel-sharp.
I suck needles of breathing,
And feel the players converge.                       10
It grows to a science . . .
We clot, break, drive,
Electrons in motion
In the magnetic pull of the puck.

The play is fast, fierce, tense.                     15
Sticks click and snap like teeth
Of wolves on the scent of a prey.
It ends in the kill . . .
I am one of the pack in a mad,
Taut leap of desperation                             20
In the wild, slashing drive for the goal.

DISCUSSION

1. The writer wants the reader to feel exactly what it is like to be in a hockey game. Which parts of the poem do this best?

2. What does the writer compare the game with in the last stanza? Do you think the poem would be as good if this were the first stanza? Explain.

# To James

FRANK HORNE

Do you remember
How you won
That last race . . . ?
How you flung your body
At the start . . .                          5
How your spikes
Ripped the cinders
In the stretch . . .
How you catapulted
Through the tape . . .                      10
Do you remember . . . ?
Don't you think
I lurched with you
Out of those starting holes . . . ?
Don't you think                             15
My sinews tightened
At those first
Few strides . . .
And when you flew into the stretch
Was not all my thrill                       20
Of a thousand races
In your blood . . . ?
At your final drive
Through the finish line
Did not my shout                            25
Tell of the
Triumphant ecstasy
Of victory . . . ?
Live
As I have taught you                        30
To run, Boy—
It's a short dash
Dig your starting holes
Deep and firm
Lurch out of them                           35
Into the straightaway
With all the power

That is in you
Look straight ahead
To the finish line                          40
Think only of the goal
Run straight
Run high
Run hard
Save nothing                                45

And finish
With an ecstatic burst
That carries you
Hurtling
Through the tape                            50
To victory. . . .

## DISCUSSION

1.  Put into your own words the advice the speaker gives James.

2.  The poem is in two parts. Since all the speaker's advice is in the second part, why is the first part needed? How does the first part of the poem affect the advice the speaker gives James?

For further activities, see page 195.

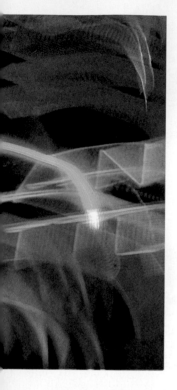

## VOCABULARY

### The Christmas Hunt (page 162)

On separate paper, match the letter of the definition in the right column with the number of the word in the left column.

1. random
2. gangly
3. fondle
4. covey
5. flimsy

a. flock
b. stroke lovingly
c. haphazard
d. ungraceful or awkward
e. weak

### The Most Important Day (page 178)

On separate paper, write the word closest in meaning to the word in bold type.

1. consider the *immeasurable* contrasts
      comic   unimportant   vast
2. a *tangible* white darkness
      thick   real   aromatic
3. tried to *imitate* it
      explain   ridicule   copy
4. had a *tussle* over the words
      disagreement   laugh   game
5. there were *barriers* still
      jokes   obstacles   cynics

## COMPOSITION

### The Day the Sun Came Out (page 156)

Pa is very bitter about the way people do not care about each other. On page 158 he says, "There ain't anything good left in the world. Or people to care if you live or die." Because Mary proves that she is caring, Pa marries her. Write a brief dialogue between Pa and Mary which shows Pa asking Mary to marry him.

### The Most Important Day (page 178)

Anne Sullivan must have found her job very challenging. Write a letter you think she might have written to a friend in which she describes her experiences. Base your letter on the incidents Helen Keller described in the story.

## To James (page 192)

What advice would you give to an athlete? Think of a young athlete you know, not necessarily a runner. In a brief composition or poem, give your advice, using sports images and terms.

## READING

### The Day the Sun Came Out (page 156)

On separate paper, match the number of the character to the letter of the action or detail that pertains to that character.

1. the father
2. the girls
3. the boy
4. Mary

a. lived with cruel people
b. wife has died
c. whimper and cry with hunger
d. eats mushroom to see if it is poison
e. searches for help
f. has scars from cruel treatment
g. hates Mary for eating the mushroom
h. tells the story

### The Most Important Day (page 178)

On separate paper, write the numbers of the events in the story in the order in which they happened.

1. Miss Sullivan and Helen sit in the sunshine by the well house.

2. Helen feels approaching footsteps which she supposes are her mothor'c.

3. Miss Sullivan gives Helen a doll.

4. For the first time, Helen understands that everything has a name.

5. Helen feels repentance and sorrow for the first time and regrets breaking the doll.

6. Helen learns to finger-spell *doll*.

7. Anne Sullivan pours water over one of Helen's hands and taps the word *water* into her other hand.

8. Helen throws the doll onto the floor and breaks it.

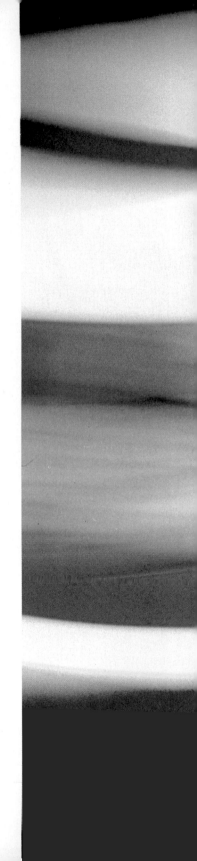

| FLIGHT | DEPARTURE | ARRIVE | GATE | REM. |
|--------|-----------|--------|------|------|
| 7 1 4 | 9 : 1 5 | | 3 | VANC |
| 9 0 1 | 8 : 3 0 | 10 : 45 | 5 | arriva |
| 505 | 5 : 20 | ON TIME | 7 | arriva |
| 6 | 7 : 30 | 9 : 00 | 2 | |

# Flight into Danger

A TELEVISION PLAY

**ARTHUR HAILEY**

CHARACTERS

Aboard Flight 714:
The Passengers:
GEORGE SPENCER
DR. FRANK BAIRD
SEVEN MALE PASSENGERS
TWO WOMEN PASSENGERS
The Crew:
CAPTAIN
FIRST OFFICER
STEWARDESS

At Vancouver Airport:
CAPTAIN MARTIN TRELEAVEN
AIRPORT CONTROLLER
HARRY BURDICK
SWITCHBOARD OPERATOR
RADIO OPERATOR
TOWER CONTROLLER
TELETYPE OPERATOR
At Winnipeg Airport:
FIRST PASSENGER AGENT
SECOND PASSENGER AGENT

## Act I

Fade In: The passenger lobby of Winnipeg Air Terminal at night. At the departure counter of Cross-Canada Airlines, a male passenger agent in uniform (First Agent) is checking a manifest.[1] He reaches for P.A. mike.

[1] *manifest:* here, a passenger list.

FIRST AGENT: Flight 98, direct fleetliner service to Vancouver, with connections for Victoria, Seattle, and Honolulu, leaving immediately through gate four. No smoking. All aboard, please.

During the announcement George Spencer enters through the main lobby doorway. About thirty-five, he is a senior factory salesman for a motor-truck manufacturer. Spencer pauses to look for the Cross-Canada counter, then hastens toward it, arriving as the announcement concludes.

SPENCER: Is there space on Flight 98 for Vancouver?

FIRST AGENT: Sorry, sir, that flight is full. Did you check with reservations?

SPENCER: Didn't have time. I came straight out on the chance you might have a "no show" seat.

FIRST AGENT: With the big football game on tomorrow in Vancouver, I don't think you'll have much chance of getting out before tomorrow afternoon.

SPENCER: That's no good. I've got to be in Vancouver tomorrow by midday.

FIRST AGENT [hesitates]: Look, I'm not supposed to tell you this, but there's a charter flight in from Toronto. They're going out to the coast for the game. I did hear they were a few seats light.

SPENCER: Who's in charge? Where do I find him?

FIRST AGENT: Ask at the desk over there. They call themselves Maple Leaf Air Charter. But mind, I didn't send you.

SPENCER [smiles]: Okay, thanks.

Spencer crosses to another departure counter which has a cardboard sign hanging behind it—Maple Leaf Air Charter. Behind the desk is an agent in a lounge suit. He is checking a manifest.

SPENCER: Excuse me.

SECOND AGENT: Yes?

SPENCER: I was told you might have space on a flight to Vancouver.

SECOND AGENT: Yes, there's one seat left. The flight's leaving right away, though.

SPENCER: That's what I want.

SECOND AGENT: Very well, sir. Your name, please?

SPENCER: Spencer—George Spencer.

SECOND AGENT: That'll be fifty-five dollars for the one-way trip.

SPENCER: Will you take my air travel card?

SECOND AGENT: No, sir. Just old-fashioned cash.

SPENCER: All right. [Produces wallet and counts out bills.]

SECOND AGENT [handing over ticket]: Do you have any bags?

SPENCER: One. Right here.

SECOND AGENT: All the baggage is aboard. Would you mind keeping that with you?

SPENCER: Be glad to.

SECOND AGENT: Okay, Mr. Spencer. Your ticket is your boarding pass. Go through gate three and ask the commissionaire for Flight 714. Better hurry.

SPENCER: Thanks a lot. Good night.

SECOND AGENT: Good night.

Exit Spencer. Enter Stewardess.

SECOND AGENT: Hi, Janet. Did the meals get aboard?

STEWARDESS: Yes, they've just put them on. What was the trouble?

SECOND AGENT: Couldn't get service from the regular caterers here. We had to go to some outfit the other side of town. That's what held us up.

STEWARDESS: Are we all clear now?

SECOND AGENT: Yes, here's everything you'll need. [Hands over papers.] There's one more passenger. He's just gone aboard. So that's fifty-six souls in your lovely little hands.

STEWARDESS: I'll try not to drop any.

SECOND AGENT [reaching for coat]: Well, I'm off home.

STEWARDESS [as she leaves]: 'Night.

SECOND AGENT [pulling on coat]: 'Night, Janet. [Calls after her.] Don't forget to cheer for the Blue Bombers tomorrow.

The Stewardess waves and smiles.

Dissolve To: The passenger cabin of a DC-4 airliner. There is one empty aisle seat. Seated next to it is Dr. Frank Baird, 55. George Spencer enters, sees the unoccupied seat, and comes toward it.

SPENCER: Pardon me, is this anyone's seat?

BAIRD: No.

SPENCER: Thanks.

Spencer sheds his topcoat and puts it on the rack above the seats. Meanwhile the plane's motors can be heard starting.

Cut To: Film insert of four-engined airplane exterior. Night, the motors starting.

Cut To: The passenger cabin.

BAIRD: I presume you're going to the big game like the rest of us.

SPENCER: I'm ashamed to admit it, but I'd forgotten about the game.

BAIRD: I wouldn't say that too loudly if I were you. Some of the more exuberant fans might tear you limb from limb.

SPENCER: I'll keep my voice down. [Pleasantly] Matter of fact, I'm making a sales trip to the coast.

BAIRD: What do you sell?

SPENCER: Trucks.

BAIRD: Trucks?

SPENCER: That's right. I'm what the local salesmen call the son-of-a-gun from head office with the special prices. . . . Need any trucks? How about forty? Give you a real good discount today.

BAIRD [laughs]: I couldn't use that many, I'm afraid. Not in my line of country.

SPENCER: Which is?

BAIRD: Medicine.

SPENCER: You mean you're a doctor?

BAIRD: That's right. Can't buy one truck, leave alone forty. Football is the one extravagance I allow myself.

SPENCER: Delighted to hear it, Doctor. Now I can relax.

As he speaks, the run-up of the aircraft engines begins, increasing to a heavy roar.

BAIRD [raising his voice]: Do you think you can in this racket? I never can figure out why they make all this noise before take-off.

SPENCER [shouting, as noise increases]: It's the normal run-up of the engines. Airplane engines don't use battery ignition like you have in your car. They run on magneto ignition, and each of the magnetos is tested separately. If they're okay and the motors are giving all the power they should—away you go!

BAIRD: You sound as if you know something about it.

SPENCER: I'm pretty rusty now. I used to fly fighters in the air force. But that was ten years ago. Reckon I've forgotten most of it. . . . Well, there we go.

The tempo of the motors increases. Baird and Spencer lean toward the window to watch the take off, although it is dark outside.

Cut To: Film insert of airplane taking off, night.

Cut To: The passenger cabin. The noise of the motors is reduced slightly, and the two men relax in their seats. Spencer reaches for cigarettes.

SPENCER: Smoke?

BAIRD: Thank you.

They light up. The Stewardess enters from aft [2] of airplane and reaches for two pillows from the rack above.

STEWARDESS: We were held up at Winnipeg, sir, and we haven't served dinner yet. Would you care for some?

SPENCER: Yes, please.

The Stewardess puts a pillow on his lap.

STEWARDESS [to Baird]: And you, sir?

BAIRD: Thank you, yes. [To Spencer] It's a bit late for dinner, but it'll pass the time away.

STEWARDESS: There's lamb chop or grilled halibut.

[2] *aft:* the back.

BAIRD: I'll take the lamb.

SPENCER: Yes, I'll have that, too.

STEWARDESS: Thank you, sir.

BAIRD [to Spencer]: Tell me . . . By the way, my name is Baird.

SPENCER: Spencer, George Spencer.

They shake hands.

BAIRD: How'd 'do. Tell me, when you make a sales trip like this, do you. . . .

Fade voices and pan with the Stewardess, returning aft. Entering the airplane's tiny galley, she picks up a telephone and presses a call button.

VOICE OF FIRST OFFICER: Flight deck.

STEWARDESS: I'm finally serving the dinners. What'll "you all" have—lamb chops or grilled halibut?

VOICE OF FIRST OFFICER: Just a minute. [Pause] Skipper says he'll have the lamb . . . Oh, hold it! . . . No, he's changed his mind. Says he'll take the halibut. Make it two fish, Janet.

STEWARDESS: Okay. [The Stewardess hangs up the phone and begins to arrange meal trays.]

Cut To: Spencer and Baird.

SPENCER: No, I hadn't expected to go west again this quickly.

BAIRD: You have my sympathy. I prescribe my travel in small doses.

The Stewardess enters and puts meal tray on pillow.

BAIRD: Oh, thank you.

STEWARDESS: Will you have coffee, tea, or milk, sir?

BAIRD: Coffee, please.

STEWARDESS: I'll bring it later.

BAIRD: That'll be fine. [To Spencer] Tell me do you follow football at all?

SPENCER: A little. Hockey's my game, though. Who are you for tomorrow?

BAIRD: The Argos, naturally. [As the Stewardess brings second tray] Thank you, dear.

STEWARDESS: Will you have coffee, tea, or——

SPENCER: I'll have coffee, too. No cream.

The Stewardess nods and exits.

SPENCER [to Baird]: Must be a calm night outside. No trouble in keeping the dinner steady.

BAIRD [looking out of window]: It is calm. Not a cloud in sight. Must be a monotonous business flying these things, once they're off the ground.

SPENCER: It varies, I guess.

Audio: Fade up the roar of motors.

Dissolve To: Film insert of airplane in level flight, night.

Dissolve To: The aircraft flight deck. The Captain is seated on left, the First Officer on right. Neither is touching the controls.

FIRST OFFICER [into radio mike]: Height 16,000 feet. Course 285 true. ETA[3] Vancouver 0505 Pacific Standard. Over.

VOICE ON RADIO: Flight 714. This is Winnipeg Control. Roger. Out.

The First Officer reaches for a log sheet and makes a notation, then relaxes in his seat.

[3] *ETA:* abbreviation for estimated time of arrival.

FIRST OFFICER: Got any plans for Vancouver?

CAPTAIN: Yes, I'm going to sleep for two whole days.

The Stewardess enters with a meal tray.

STEWARDESS: Who's first?

CAPTAIN: You take yours, Harry.

The Stewardess produces a pillow and the First Officer slides back his seat, well clear of the control column. He places the pillow on his knees and accepts the tray.

FIRST OFFICER: Thanks, honey.

CAPTAIN: Everything all right at the back, Janet? How are the football fans?

STEWARDESS: They tired themselves out on the way from Toronto. Looks like a peaceful, placid night.

FIRST OFFICER [with mouth full of food, raising fork for emphasis]: Aha! Those are the sort of nights to beware of. It's in the quiet times that trouble brews. I'll bet you right now that somebody's getting ready to be sick.

STEWARDESS: That'll be when you're doing the flying. Or have you finally learned how to hold this thing steady? [To Captain] How's the weather?

CAPTAIN: General fog east of the mountains, extending pretty well as far as Manitoba. But it's clear to the west. Should be rockaby smooth the whole way.

STEWARDESS: Good. Well, keep junior here off the controls while I serve coffee. [Exits.]

FIRST OFFICER [calling after her]: Mark my

words, woman! Stay close to that mop and pail.

CAPTAIN: How's the fish?

FIRST OFFICER [hungrily]: Not bad. Not bad at all. If there were about three times as much it might be a square meal.

Audio: Fade voices into roar of motors.

Dissolve To: The passenger cabin. Spencer and Baird are concluding their meal. Baird puts down a coffee cup and wipes his mouth with a napkin. Then he reaches up and presses a call button above his head. There is a soft "ping," and the Stewardess enters.

STEWARDESS: Yes, sir?

BAIRD: That was very enjoyable. Now, if you'll take the tray I think I'll try to sleep.

STEWARDESS: Surely. [To Spencer] Will you have more coffee, sir?

SPENCER: No, thanks.

The Stewardess picks up the second tray and goes aft. Spencer yawns.

SPENCER: Let me know if the noise keeps you awake. If it does, I'll have the engines stopped.

BAIRD [chuckles]: Well, at least there won't be any night calls—I hope.

Baird reaches up and switches off the overhead reading lights so that both seats are in semi-darkness. The two men prepare to sleep.

Dissolve To: Film insert of airplane in level flight, night.

Dissolve To: The passenger cabin. The Captain emerges from the flight deck and strolls aft, saying "Good evening" to one or two people who glance up as he goes by. He passes Spencer and Baird, who are sleeping. As the Captain progresses, the Stewardess can be seen at the

rear of the cabin. She is bending solicitously over a woman passenger, her hand on the woman's forehead. The Captain approaches.

CAPTAIN: Something wrong, Miss Burns?

STEWARDESS: This lady is feeling a little unwell. I was going to get her some aspirin. [To the Woman Passenger] I'll be back in a moment.

CAPTAIN: Sorry to hear that. What seems to be the trouble?

The Woman Passenger has her head back and her mouth open. A strand of hair has fallen across her face, and she is obviously in pain.

FIRST WOMAN PASSENGER [speaking with effort]: I'm sorry to be such a nuisance, but it hit me all of a sudden . . . just a few minutes ago . . . dizziness and nausea and a sharp pain . . . [Indicating abdomen] down here.

CAPTAIN: Well, I think the Stewardess will be able to help you.

Stewardess returns.

STEWARDESS: Now, here you are; try these. [She hands over two aspirins and a cup of water. The passenger takes them, then puts her head back on the seat rest.]

FIRST WOMAN PASSENGER: Thank you very much. [She smiles faintly at the Captain.]

CAPTAIN [quietly, taking the Stewardess aside]: If she gets any worse you'd better let me know and I'll radio ahead. But we've still five hours' flying to the coast. Is there a doctor on board, do you know?

STEWARDESS: There was no one listed as a doctor on the manifest. But I can go round and ask.

CAPTAIN [looks around]: Well, most everybody's sleeping now. We'd better not disturb them unless we have to. See how she is in the next half hour or so. [He bends down and puts a hand on the woman's shoulder.] Try to rest, madam, if you can. Miss Burns will take good care of you.

The Captain nods to the Stewardess and begins his return to the flight deck. The Stewardess arranges a blanket around the Woman Passenger. Spencer and Baird are still sleeping as the Captain passes.

Dissolve To: Film insert of airplane in level flight, night.

Dissolve To: The passenger cabin. Spencer stirs and wakes. Then he glances forward to where the Stewardess is leaning over another section of seats, and her voice can be heard softly.

STEWARDESS: I'm sorry to disturb you, but we're trying to find out if there's a doctor on board.
FIRST MALE PASSENGER: Not me, I'm afraid. Is something wrong?
STEWARDESS: One of the passengers is feeling unwell. It's nothing too serious. [Moving on to the next pair of seats] I'm sorry to disturb you, but we're trying to find out if there's a doctor on board.

There is an indistinct answer from the two people just questioned, then Spencer sits forward and calls the Stewardess.

SPENCER: Stewardess! [Indicating Baird, who is still sleeping] This gentleman is a doctor.
STEWARDESS: Thank you. I think we'd better wake him. I have two passengers who are quite sick.
SPENCER: All right. [Shaking Baird's arm]

Doctor! Doctor! Wake up!
BAIRD: Um . . . Um . . . What is it?
STEWARDESS: Doctor. I'm sorry to disturb you. But we have two passengers who seem quite sick. I wonder if you'd take a look at them.
BAIRD [sleepily]: Yes . . . yes . . . of course.

Spencer moves out of seat to permit Baird to reach the aisle. Baird then follows the Stewardess aft to the First Woman Passenger. Although a blanket is around her, the woman is shivering and gasping, with her head back and eyes closed. The doctor places a hand on her forehead, and she opens her eyes.

STEWARDESS: This gentleman is a doctor. He's going to help us.
FIRST WOMAN PASSENGER: Oh, Doctor! . . .
BAIRD: Now, just relax.

He makes a quick external examination, first checking pulse, then taking a small pen-type flashlight from his pocket and looking into her eyes. He then loosens the blanket and the woman's coat beneath the blanket. As he places a hand on her abdomen, she gasps with pain.

BAIRD: Hurt you there? [With an effort she nods.] There?
FIRST WOMAN PASSENGER: Oh, yes! Yes!

Baird replaces the coat and blanket, then turns to the Stewardess.

BAIRD [with authority]: Please tell the captain we must land at once. This woman has to be gotten to a hospital immediately.
STEWARDESS: Do you know what's wrong, Doctor?
BAIRD: I can't tell. I've no means of making a proper diagnosis. But

it's serious enough to land at the nearest city with hospital facilities. You can tell your captain that.

STEWARDESS: Very well, Doctor. [Moving across the aisle and forward] While I'm gone will you take a look at this gentleman here? He's also complained of sickness and stomach pains.

Baird goes to a male passenger indicated by the Stewardess. The man is sitting forward and resting his head on the back of the seat ahead of him. He is retching.

BAIRD: I'm a doctor. Will you put your head back, please?

The man groans, but follows the doctor's instruction. He is obviously weak. Baird makes another quick examination, then pauses thoughtfully.

BAIRD: What have you had to eat in the last twenty-four hours?

SECOND MALE PASSENGER [with effort]: Just the usual meals . . . breakfast . . . bacon and eggs . . . salad for lunch . . . couple of sandwiches at the airport . . . then dinner here.

The Stewardess enters, followed by the Captain.

BAIRD [to the Stewardess]: Keep him warm. Get blankets around him. [To the Captain] How quickly can we land, Captain?

CAPTAIN: That's the trouble. I've just been talking to Calgary. There was light fog over the prairies earlier, but now it's thickened and everything is closed in this side of the mountains. It's clear at the coast, and we'll have to go through.

BAIRD: Is that faster than turning back?

CAPTAIN: It would take us longer to go back now than to go on.

BAIRD: Then, how soon do you expect to land?

CAPTAIN: At about 5 A.M. Pacific time. [As Baird glances at his watch] You need to put your watch on two hours because of the change of time. We'll be landing in three hours forty-five minutes from now.

BAIRD: Then, I'll have to do what I can for these people. Can my bag be reached? I checked it at Toronto.

CAPTAIN: We can get it. Let me have your tags, Doctor.

Baird takes out a wallet and selects two baggage tags which he hands to the Captain.

BAIRD: There are two tags. It's the small overnight case I want.

As he finishes speaking, the airplane lurches violently. Baird and the Stewardess and the Captain are thrown sharply to one side. Simultaneously the telephone in the galley buzzes several times. As the three recover their balance the Stewardess answers the phone quickly.

STEWARDESS: Yes?

FIRST OFFICER'S VOICE [under strain]: Come forward quickly. I'm sick!

STEWARDESS: The First Officer is sick. He says come quickly.

CAPTAIN [to Baird]: You'd better come too.

The Captain and Baird move quickly forward, passing through the flight deck door.

Cut To: The flight deck. The First Officer is at the controls on the right-hand side. He is retching and shuddering, flying the airplane by will power and nothing else. The Captain promptly slides into the lefthand seat and takes the controls.

CAPTAIN: Get him out of there!

Together Baird and the Stewardess lift the First Officer from his seat, and, as they do, he collapses. They lower him to the floor, and the Stewardess reaches for a pillow and blankets. Baird makes the same quick examination he used in the two previous cases. Meanwhile the Captain has steadied the aircraft, and now he snaps over a button to engage the automatic pilot. He releases the controls and turns to the others, though without leaving his seat.

CAPTAIN: He must have been changing course when it happened. We're back on auto pilot now. Now, Doctor; what is it? What's happening?

BAIRD: There's a common denominator in these attacks. There has to be. And the most likely thing is food. [To the Stewardess] How long is it since we had dinner?

STEWARDESS: Two and a half to three hours.

BAIRD: Now, then, what did you serve?

STEWARDESS: Well, the main course was a choice of fish or meat.

BAIRD: I remember that, I ate meat. [Indicating the First Officer] What did he have?

STEWARDESS [faintly, with dawning alarm]: Fish.

BAIRD: Do you remember what the other two passengers had?

STEWARDESS: No.

BAIRD: Then, go back quickly, and find out, please.

As the Stewardess exits Baird kneels beside the First Officer, who is moaning.

BAIRD: Try to relax. I'll give you something in a few minutes to help the pain. You'll feel better if you stay warm.

Baird arranges the blanket around the First Officer. Now the Stewardess reappears.

STEWARDESS [alarmed]: Doctor, both those passengers had fish. And there are three more cases now. And they ate fish too. Can you come?

BAIRD: Yes, but I need that bag of mine.

CAPTAIN: Janet, take these tags and get one of the passengers to help you. [Hands over Baird's luggage tags.] Doctor, I'm going to get on the radio and report what's happening to Vancouver. Is there anything you want to add?

BAIRD: Yes. Tell them we have three serious cases of suspected food poisoning, and there appear to be others. When we land we'll want ambulances and medical help waiting, and the hospitals should be warned. Tell them we're not sure, but we suspect the poisoning may have been caused by fish served on board. You'd better suggest they put a ban on serving all food which originated wherever ours came from until we've established the source for sure.

CAPTAIN: Right. [He reaches for the radio

mike, and Baird turns to go aft. But suddenly a thought strikes the Captain.]
Doctor, I've just remembered. . . .

BAIRD: Yes.

CAPTAIN [quietly]: I ate fish.

BAIRD: When?

CAPTAIN: I'd say about half an hour after he did. [Pointing to the First Officer] Maybe a little longer. Is there anything I can do?

BAIRD: It doesn't follow that everyone will be affected. There's often no logic to these things. You feel all right now?

CAPTAIN: Yes.

BAIRD: You'd better not take any chances. Your food can't be completely digested yet. As soon as I get my bag I'll give you something to help you get rid of it.

CAPTAIN: Then, hurry, Doctor. Hurry! [Into mike] Vancouver control. This is Maple Leaf Charter Flight 714. I have an emergency message. Do you read? Over.

VOICE ON RADIO [Vancouver Operator]: Go ahead, 714.

CAPTAIN: We have serious food poisoning on board. Several passengers and the First Officer are seriously ill. . . .

Dissolve To: The luggage compartment below the flight deck. A passenger is hurriedly passing up bags to the Stewardess. Baird is looking down from above.

BAIRD: That's it! That's it down there! Let me have it!

Fade Out.

END OF ACT ONE

# Act II

Fade In: The control room, Vancouver Airport. At a radio panel an operator, wearing headphones, is transcribing a message on a typewriter. Partway through the message he presses a button on the panel and a bell rings stridently, signaling an emergency. At once an Airport Controller appears behind the operator and reads the message as it continues to come in. Nearby is a telephone switchboard manned by an Operator, and a battery of teletypes clattering noisily.

CONTROLLER [over his shoulder, to the Switchboard Operator]: Get me Area Traffic Control, then clear the teletype circuit to Winnipeg. Priority message. [Stepping back to take phone] Vancouver Controller here. I've an emergency report from Maple Leaf Charter Flight 714, ex-Winnipeg for Vancouver. There's serious food poisoning among the passengers, and the First Officer is down too. They're asking for all levels below them to be cleared, and priority approach and landing. ETA is 0505 . . . Roger. We'll keep you posted. [To a Teletype Operator who has appeared] Got Winnipeg? [As the Teletype Operator nods] Send this message. Controller Winnipeg. Urgent. Maple Leaf Charter Flight 714 reports serious food poisoning among passengers believed due to fish dinner served on flight. Imperative check source and suspend all other food service originating same place. That's all. [To the Switchboard Operator] Get me the local agent for Maple Leaf Charter. Burdick's his name—call his home. And after that, I want the city police—the senior officer on

duty. [Controller crosses to radio control panel and reads message which is just being completed. To the Radio Operator] Acknowledge. Say that all altitudes below them are being cleared, and they'll be advised of landing instructions here. Ask them to keep us posted on condition of the passengers.

SWITCHBOARD OPERATOR: Mr. Burdick is here at the airport. I have him on the line now.

CONTROLLER: Good. Controller here. Burdick, we've got an emergency on one of your flights—714, ex-Toronto and Winnipeg. [Pause] No, the aircraft is all right. There's food poisoning among the passengers, and the First Officer has it too. You'd better come over. [Replaces phone. Then to the Switchboard Operator] Have you got the police yet? [As the Operator nods] Right, put it on this line. Hullo, this is the Controller, Vancouver Airport. Who am I speaking to, please? [Pause] Inspector, we have an emergency on an incoming flight. Several of the passengers are seriously ill, and we need ambulances and doctors out here at the airport. [Pause] Six people for sure, maybe more. The flight will be landing at five minutes past five local time—that's about three and a half hours. Now, will you get the ambulances, set up traffic control, and alert the hospitals? Right. We'll call you again as soon as there's anything definite.

During the above, Harry Burdick, local manager of Maple Leaf Air Charter, has entered.

BURDICK: Where's the message?

The Radio Operator hands him a copy which Burdick reads.

BURDICK [to Radio Operator]: How's the weather at Calgary? It might be quicker to go in there.
CONTROLLER: No dice! There's fog down to the deck everywhere east of the Rockies. They'll have to come through.
BURDICK: Let me see the last position report. [As Controller passes a clipboard] You say you've got medical help coming?
CONTROLLER: The city police are working on it now.
BURDICK: That message! They say the First Officer is down. What about the Captain? Ask if he's affected, and ask if there's a doctor on board. Tell them we're getting medical advice here in case they need it.
CONTROLLER: I'll take care of that.
BURDICK [to the Switchboard Operator]: Will you get me Doctor Knudsen, please? You'll find his home number on the emergency list.
CONTROLLER [into radio mike]: Flight 714, this is Vancouver.

Dissolve To: The airplane passenger cabin. Baird is leaning over another prostrate passenger. The main lighting is on in the cabin, and other passengers, so far not affected, are watching, with varying degrees of concern and anxiety. Some have remained in their seats, others have clustered in the aisle. The doctor has obtained his bag and it is open beside him. The Stewardess is attending to another passenger nearby.

BAIRD [to the Stewardess]: I think I'd better talk to everyone and tell them the story. [Moving to center of cabin, he raises his voice.] Ladies and gentlemen, may I have your attention, please? If you can't hear me, perhaps you would come a little closer. [Pause, as passengers move in] My name is Baird, and I am a doctor. I think it's time that everyone knows what is happening. So far as I can tell, we have several cases of food poisoning, and we believe that the cause of it was the fish which was served for dinner.
SECOND WOMAN PASSENGER [with alarm, to man beside her]: Hector! We both had fish!
BAIRD: Now, there is no immediate cause for alarm or panic, and even if you did eat fish for dinner, it doesn't follow that you are going to be affected too. There's seldom any logic to these things. However, we *are* going to take some precautions, and the Stewardess and I are coming around to everyone, and I want you to tell us if you ate fish. If you did we'll tell you what to do to help yourselves. Now, if you'll go back

to your seats we'll begin right away. [To the Stewardess, as passengers move back to their seats] All we can do now is to give immediate first aid.

STEWARDESS: What should that be, Doctor?

BAIRD: Two things. First, everyone who ate fish must drink several glasses of water. That will help dilute the poison. After that we'll give an emetic. I have some emetic pills in my bag, and if there aren't enough we'll have to rely on salt. Do you have salt in the galley?

STEWARDESS: A few small packets which go with the lunches, but we can break them open.

BAIRD: All right. We'll see how far the pills will go first. I'll start at the back here. Meanwhile you begin giving drinking water to the passengers already affected and get some to the First Officer too. I'll ask someone to help you.

FIRST MALE PASSENGER: Can I help, Doc?

BAIRD: What did you eat for dinner—fish or meat?

FIRST MALE PASSENGER: Meat.

BAIRD: All right. Will you help the Stewardesses bring glasses of water to the people who are sick? I want them to drink at least three glasses each—more if they can.

STEWARDESS [going to galley]: We'll use these cups. There's drinking water here and at the rear.

FIRST MALE PASSENGER: All right, let's get started.

BAIRD [to the Stewardess]: The Captain! Before you do anything else

you'd better get him on to drinking water, and give him two emetic pills. Here. [Takes bottle from his bag and shakes out the pills.] Tell him they'll make him feel sick, and the sooner he is, the better.

STEWARDESS: Very well, Doctor.

SECOND WOMAN PASSENGER [frightened]: Doctor! Doctor! I heard you say the pilots are ill. What will happen to us if they can't fly the plane? [To husband] Hector, I'm frightened.

THIRD MALE PASSENGER: Take it easy, my dear. Nothing has happened so far, and the doctor is doing all he can.

BAIRD: I don't think you'll have any reason to worry, madam. It's quite true that both of the pilots had the fish which we believe may have caused the trouble. But only the first officer is affected. Now, did you and your husband eat fish or meat?

THIRD MALE PASSENGER: Fish. We both ate fish.

BAIRD: Then, will you both drink at least three—better make it four—of those cups of water which the other gentleman is bringing around. After that, take one of these pills each. [Smiling] I think you'll find there are little containers under your seat. Use those. [Goes to rear of plane.]

FOURTH MALE PASSENGER [in broad English Yorkshire accent]: How's it commin', Doc? Everything under control?

BAIRD: I think we're holding our own. What did you have for dinner?

FOURTH MALE PASSENGER: Ah had the

bloomin' fish. Didn't like it neither. Fine how d'you do this is. Coom all this way t'see our team win, and now it looks like ah'm headed for a mortuary slab.

BAIRD: It really isn't as bad as that, you know. But just as a precaution, drink four cups of water—it's being brought around now—and after that take this pill. It'll make you feel sick.

FOURTH MALE PASSENGER [pulls carton from under seat and holds it up]: It's the last time I ride on a bloomin' airplane! What service! They give you your dinner and then coom round and ask for it back.

BAIRD: What did you have for dinner, please—meat or fish?

SECOND MALE PASSENGER: Meat, Doctor.

FIFTH MALE PASSENGER: Yes, I had meat too.

BAIRD: All right, we won't worry about you.

SIXTH MALE PASSENGER: I had meat, Doctor.

SEVENTH MALE PASSENGER: I had fish.

DOCTOR: Very well, will you drink at least four cups of water, please? It'll be brought round to you. Then take this pill.

SIXTH MALE PASSENGER [slow speaking]: What's caused this food poisoning, Doctor?

BAIRD: Well, it can either be caused through spoilage of the food, or some kind of bacteria—the medical word is staphylococcus poisoning.

SIXTH MALE PASSENGER [nodding knowledge-

ably]: Oh yes . . . staphylo . . . I see.

BAIRD: Either that, or some toxic substance may have gotten into the food during its preparation.

SEVENTH MALE PASSENGER: What kind do you think this is, Doctor?

BAIRD: From the effect I suspect a toxic substance.

SEVENTH MALE PASSENGER: And you don't know what it is?

BAIRD: We won't know until we make laboratory tests. Actually, with modern food-handling methods—the chances of this happening are probably a million to one against.

STEWARDESS [entering]: I couldn't get the First Officer to take more than a little water, Doctor. He seems pretty bad.

BAIRD: I'll go to him now. Have you checked all the passengers in the front portion?

STEWARDESS: Yes, and there are two more new cases—the same symptoms as the others.

BAIRD: I'll attend to them—after I've looked at the First Officer.

STEWARDESS: Do you think. . . .

Before the sentence is completed the galley telephone buzzes insistently. Baird and the Stewardess exchange glances quickly, then, without waiting to answer the phone, race to the flight deck door.

Cut To: The flight deck. The Captain is in the left-hand seat. Sweat pouring down his face, he is racked by retching, and his right hand is on his stomach. Yet he is fighting against the pain and attempting to reach the radio transmitter mike. But he doesn't make it, and as Baird and the Stewardess reach him, he falls back in his seat.

CAPTAIN [weakly]: I did what you said . . . guess it was too late. . . . You've got to give me something, Doctor . . . so I can hold out . . . till I get this airplane on the ground. . . . You understand? . . . It'll fly itself on this course . . . but I've got to take it in . . . Get on the radio . . . Tell control. . . .

During the above Baird and the Stewardess have been helping the Captain from his seat. Now he collapses into unconsciousness, and Baird goes down beside him. The Doctor has a stethoscope now and uses it.

BAIRD: Get blankets over him. Keep him warm. There's probably a reaction because he tried to fight it off so long.

STEWARDESS [alarmed]: Can you do what he said? Can you bring him round long enough to land?

BAIRD [bluntly]: You're part of this crew, so I'll tell you how things are. Unless I can get him to a hospital quickly, I'm not even sure I can save his life. And that goes for the others too.

STEWARDESS: But—

BAIRD: I know what you're thinking, and I've thought of it too. How many passengers are there on board?

STEWARDESS: Fifty-six.

BAIRD: And how many fish dinners did you serve?

STEWARDESS [composing herself]: Probably about fifteen. More people ate meat than fish, and some didn't eat at all because it was so late.

BAIRD: And you?

STEWARDESS: I had meat.

BAIRD [quietly]: My dear, did you ever hear the term "long odds"?

STEWARDESS: Yes, but I'm not sure what it means.

BAIRD: I'll give you an example. Out of a total field of fifty-five, our chances of safety depends on there being one person back there who not only is qualified to land this airplane, but who didn't choose fish for dinner tonight.

After her initial alarm the Stewardess is calm now, and competent. She looks Baird in the eye and even manages a slight smile.

STEWARDESS: Then, I suppose I should begin asking.

BAIRD [thoughtfully]: Yes, but there's no sense in starting a panic. [Decisively] You'd better do it this way. Say that the First Officer is sick and the Captain wondered if there's someone with flying experience who could help him with the radio.

STEWARDESS: Very well, Doctor. [She turns to go.]

BAIRD: Wait! The man who was sitting beside me! He said something about flying in the war. And we both ate meat. Get him first! But still go round to the others. There may be someone else with more experience.

The Stewardess exits and Baird busies himself with the First Officer and the Captain. After a moment, George Spencer enters.

SPENCER: The Stewardess said—[Then, as he sees the two pilots] . . . No! Not both pilots!

BAIRD: Can *you* fly this airplane—and land it?

SPENCER: No! No! Not a chance! Of course not!

BAIRD: But you told me you flew in the war.

SPENCER: So I did. But that was fighters—little combat airplanes, not a great ship like this. I flew airplanes which had one engine. This has four. Flying characteristics are different. Controls don't react the same way. It's another kind of flying altogether. And besides that, I haven't touched an airplane for over ten years.

BAIRD [grimly]: Then, let's hope there's someone else on board who can do the job . . . because neither of these men can.

The Stewardess enters and pauses.

STEWARDESS [quietly]: There's no one else.

BAIRD: Mr. Spencer, I know nothing of flying. I have no means of evaluating what you tell me. All I know is this: that among the people on this airplane who are physically able to fly it, you are the only one with any kind of qualification to do so. What do you suggest?

SPENCER [desperately]: Isn't there a chance—of either pilot recovering?

BAIRD: I'll tell you what I just told the Stewardess here. Unless I can get them to a hospital quickly, I can't even be sure of saving their lives.

There is a pause.

SPENCER: Well—I guess I just got drafted. If either of you are any good at praying, you can start any time. [He slips into the left-hand seat.] Let's take a look. Altitude 16,000. Course 290. The ship's on automatic pilot—we can be thankful for that. Air speed 210 knots. [Touching the various controls] Throttles, pitch, mixture, landing gear, flaps, and the flap indicator. We'll need a check list for landing, but we'll get that on the radio. . . . Well, maybe we'd better tell the world about our problems. [To the Stewardess] Do you know how to work this radio? They've added a lot of gismos since my flying days.

STEWARDESS [pointing]: It's this panel up here they use to talk to the ground, but I'm not sure which switches you have to set.

SPENCER: Ah, yes, here's the channel selector. Maybe we'd better leave it where it is. Oh, and here we are—"transmit." [He flicks a switch, and a small light glows on the radio control panel.] Now we're in business. [He picks up the mike and headset beside him, then turns to the other two.] Look, whatever happens I'm going to need another pair of hands here. Doc, I guess you'll be needed back with the others, so I think the best choice is Miss Canada here. How about it?

STEWARDESS: But I know nothing about all this!

SPENCER: Then, that'll make us a real

good pair. But I'll tell you what to do ahead of time. Better get in that other seat and strap yourself in. That all right with you, Doc?

BAIRD: Yes, do that. I'll take care of things in the back. And I'd better go there now. Good luck!

SPENCER: Good luck to *you*. We're all going to need it.

Baird exits.

SPENCER: What's your first name?

STEWARDESS: Janet.

SPENCER: Okay, Janet. Let's see if I can remember how to send out a distress message. . . . Better put on that headset beside you. [Into mike] May Day! May Day! May Day! [To the Stewardess] What's our flight number?

STEWARDESS: 714.

SPENCER [into mike]: This is Flight 714, Maple Leaf Air Charter, in distress. Come in anyone. Over.

VOICE ON RADIO [immediately, crisply]: This is Calgary, 714. Go ahead!

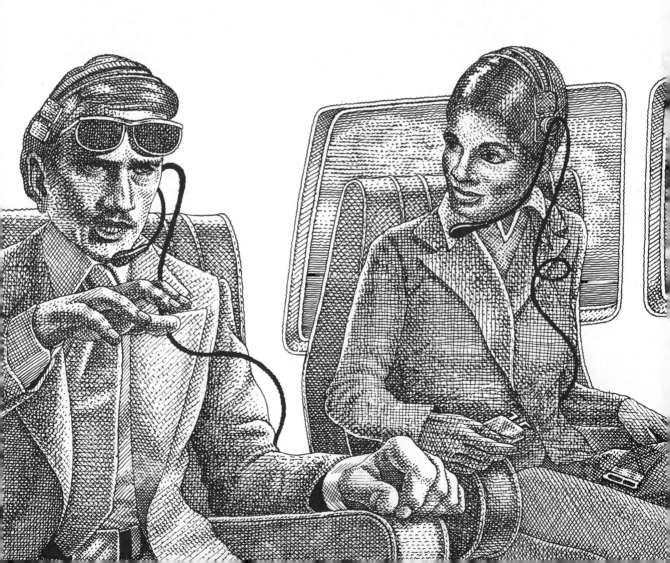

VOICE ON RADIO [Vancouver Operator]: Vancouver here, 714. All other aircraft stay off the air. Over.

SPENCER: Thank you, Calgary and Vancouver. This message is for Vancouver. This aircraft is in distress. Both pilots and some passengers—[To the Stewardess] How many passengers?

STEWARDESS: It was seven a few minutes ago. It may be more now.

SPENCER: Correction. At least seven passengers are suffering from food poisoning. Both pilots are unconscious and in serious condition. We have a doctor on board who says that neither pilot can be revived. Did you get that, Vancouver? [Pause] Now we come to the interesting bit. My name is Spencer, George Spencer. I am a passenger on this airplane. Correction: I was a passenger. I have about a thousand hours' total flying time, but all of it was on single-engine fighters. And also, I haven't flown an airplane for ten years. Now, then, Vancouver, you'd better get someone on this radio who can give me some instructions about flying this machine. Our altitude is 16,000, course 290 magnetic, air speed 210 knots. We are on automatic pilot. Your move, Vancouver. Over. [To the Stewardess] You want to make a bet that that stirred up a little flurry down below?

The Stewardess shakes her head, but does not reply.

Dissolve To: The control room, Vancouver. The Controller is putting down a phone as the Radio Operator brings a message to him. He reads the message.

CONTROLLER: Oh, no! [To the Radio Operator] Ask if—No, let me talk to them.

The Controller goes to panel and takes the transmitter mike. The Radio Operator turns a switch and nods.

CONTROLLER [tensely]: Flight 714. This is Vancouver control. Please check with your doctor on board for any possibility of either pilot recovering. Ask him to do everything possible to revive one of the pilots, even if it means neglecting other people. Over.

SPENCER'S VOICE ON RADIO: Vancouver, this is 714, Spencer speaking. I understand your message. But the doctor says there is no possibility whatever of either pilot recovering to make the landing. He says they are critically ill and may die unless they get hospital treatment soon. Over.

CONTROLLER: All right, 714. Stand by, please. [He pauses momentarily to consider the next course of action. Then briskly to the Switchboard Operator] Get me Area Traffic Control—fast. [Into phone] Vancouver controller. The emergency we had! . . . Right now it looks like its shaping up for a disaster.

Fade Out

END OF ACT TWO

# Act III

Fade In: The control room, Vancouver. The atmosphere is one of restrained pandemonium. The Radio Operator is typing a message. The teletypes are busy. The Controller is on one telephone, and Harry Burdick on another. During what follows, cut back and forth from one to the other.

CONTROLLER [into phone]: As of right now, hold everything taking off for the East. You've got forty-five minutes to clear any traffic for South, West, or North. After that, hold everything that's scheduled outward. On incoming traffic, accept anything you can get on the deck within the next forty-five minutes. Anything you can't get down by then for sure, divert away from this area. Hold it. [A messenger hands him a message which he scans. Then to messenger] Tell the security officer. [Into phone] If you've any flights coming in from the Pacific, divert them to Seattle. And any traffic inland is to stay well away from the east-west lane between Calgary and Vancouver. Got that? Right.

BURDICK [into phone]: Is that Cross-Canada Airlines? . . . Who's on duty in operations? . . . Let me talk to him. [Pause] Mr. Gardner, it's Harry Burdick of Maple Leaf Charter. We have an incoming flight that's in bad trouble, and we need an experienced pilot to talk on the radio. Someone who's flown DC-4's. Can you help us? [Pause] Captain Treleaven? Yes, I know him well. [Pause] You mean he's with you now? [Pause] Can he come over to control right away? [Pause] Thank you. Thank you very much. [To the Switchboard Operator] Get me Montreal. I want to talk with Mr. Barney Whitmore. You may have to try Maple Leaf Air Charter office first, and someone there'll have his home number. Tell them the call is urgent.

SWITCHBOARD OPERATOR: Right. [To the Controller] I've got the fire chief.

CONTROLLER [into phone]: Chief, we have an emergency. It's Flight 714, due here at 0505. It may be a crash landing. Have everything you've got stand by. If you have men off duty, call them in. Take your instructions from the tower. They'll tell you which runway we're using. And notify the city fire department. They may want to move equipment into this area. Right. [To the Switchboard Operator] Now get me the city police again—Inspector Moyse.

SWITCHBOARD OPERATOR: I have Seattle and Calgary waiting. They both received the message from Flight 714 and want to know if we got it clearly.

CONTROLLER: Tell them thank you, yes,

and we're working the aircraft direct. But ask them to keep a listening watch in case we run into any reception trouble. [Another message is handed him. After reading, he passes it to Burdick.] There's bad weather moving in. That's all we need. [To the Switchboard Operator] Have you got the police? Right! [Into phone] It's the Airport Controller again, Inspector. We're in bad trouble, and we may have a crash landing. We'll need every spare ambulance in the city out here—and doctors and nurses too. Will you arrange it? [Pause] Yes, we do—fifty-six passengers and a crew of three. [Pause] Yes, the same time—0505. That's less than three hours.

BURDICK [to the Switchboard Operator]: Is Montreal on the line yet? . . . Yes, give it to me. . . . Hullo. Hullo. Is that you, Barney? . . . It's Harry Burdick in Vancouver. I'll give you this fast, Barney. Our flight from Toronto is in bad trouble. They have food poisoning on board, and both pilots and a lot of the passengers have passed out. There's a doctor on board, and he says there's no chance of recovery before they get to a hospital. [Pause] It's a passenger doing the flying. He's just been on the radio. [Pause] No, he isn't qualified. He flew single-engine fighters in the war, nothing since. [Pause] I've asked him that. This doctor on board says there isn't a chance. [Pause] What else can we do? We've got to talk him down.

Cross-Canada is lending us a pilot. It's Captain Treleaven, one of their senior men. He's here now, just arrived. We'll get on the radio with a check list and try to bring him in. [Pause] We'll do the best we can. [Pause. Then impatiently] Of course it's a terrible risk, but can you think of something better? [Pause] No, the papers aren't on to it yet, but don't worry, they will be soon. We can't help that now. [Pause. Anxious to get off phone] That's all we know, Barney. It only just happened. I called you right away. ETA is 0505 Pacific time; that's just under three hours. I've got a lot to do, Barney. I'll have to get on with it. [Pause. Nodding impatiently] I'll call you. I'll call you as soon as I know anything more . . . G'bye.

During the foregoing Captain Martin Treleaven, forty-five, has entered. He is wearing an airline uniform. As Burdick sees Treleaven, he beckons him, indicating that he should listen.

BURDICK [to Treleaven]: Did you get that?
TRELEAVEN [calmly]: Is that the whole story?
BURDICK: That's everything we know. Now, what I want you to do is get on the horn and talk this pilot down. You'll have to help him get the feel of the airplane on the way. You'll have to talk him round the circuit. You'll have to give him the cockpit check for landing, and—so help me—you'll have to talk him onto the ground.

Captain Treleaven is a calm man, not easily

perturbed. While Burdick has been talking, the Captain has been filling his pipe. Now, with methodical movements, he puts away his tobacco pouch and begins to light the pipe.

TRELEAVEN [quietly]: You realize, of course, that the chances of a man who has only flown fighter airplanes, landing a four-engine passenger ship safely are about nine to one against.

BURDICK [rattled]: Of course I know it! You heard what I told Whitmore. But do *you* have any other ideas?

TRELEAVEN: No. I just wanted to be sure you knew what we were getting into, Harry . . . All right. Let's get started. Where do I go?

CONTROLLER: Over here.

They cross to the radio panel, and the Operator hands him the last message from the aircraft. When he has read it, he takes the transmitter mike.

TRELEAVEN: How does this thing work?

RADIO OPERATOR [turning a switch]: You're on the air now.

TRELEAVEN [calmly]: Hullo, Flight 714. This is Vancouver, and my name is Martin Treleaven. I am a Cross-Canada Airlines captain, and my job right now is to help fly this airplane in. First of all, are you hearing me okay? Over.

VOICE OF SPENCER: Yes, Captain, loud and clear. Go ahead, please.

TRELEAVEN: Where's that message? [As Operator passes it, into mike] I see that I'm talking to George Spencer. Well, George, I don't think you're going to have much trouble. These DC-4's handle easily, and we'll give you the drill for land-ing. But first of all, please tell me what your flying experience is. The message says you have flown single-engine fighters. What kind of airplanes were these, and did you fly multi-engine airplanes at all? Let's hear from you, George. Over.

Cut To: The flight deck.

SPENCER [into mike]: Hullo, Vancouver, this is 714. Glad to have you along, Captain. But let's not kid each other, please. We both know we need a lot of luck. About my flying. It was mostly on Spitfires and Mustangs. And I have around a thousand hours' total. And all of that was ten years ago. Over.

Cut To: The control room.

TRELEAVEN [into mike]: Don't worry about that, George. It's like riding a bicycle. You never forget it. Stand by.

CONTROLLER [to Treleaven]: The air force has picked up the airplane on radar, and they'll be giving us courses to bring him in. Here's the first one. See if you can get him on that heading.

TRELEAVEN [nods. Then into mike]: 714, are you still on automatic pilot? If so, look for the auto pilot release switch. It's a push button on the control yoke and is plainly marked. Over.

Cut To: The flight deck.

SPENCER [into mike]: Yes, Vancouver. I see the auto pilot switch. Over.

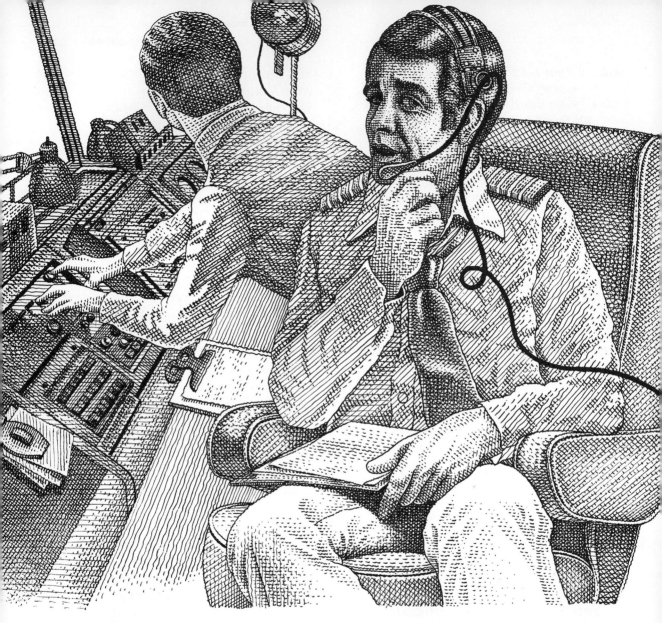

Cut To: The control room.

TRELEAVEN [into mike]: Now, George, in a minute you can unlock the automatic pilot and get the feel of the controls, and we're going to change your course a little. But first, listen carefully. When you use the controls they will seem very heavy and sluggish compared with a fighter airplane. But don't worry, that's quite normal. You must take care, though, to watch your air speed carefully, and do not let it fall below 120 knots while your wheels and flaps are up. Otherwise you will stall. Now, do you have someone up there who can work the radio to leave you free for flying? Over.

Cut To: The flight deck.

SPENCER [into mike]: Yes, Vancouver. I have the Stewardess here with me, and she will take over the radio now. I am now going to unlock the automatic pilot. Over. [To the Stewardess as he depresses the auto pilot release] Well, here we go. [Feeling the controls, Spencer eases into a left turn. Then, straightening out, he eases the control column slightly forward and back.]

Cut To: The control room.

TRELEAVEN'S VOICE: Hullo, 714. How are you making out, George? Have you got the feel of her yet?

Cut To: The flight deck.

SPENCER: Tell him I'm on manual now and trying out some gentle turns.
STEWARDESS [into mike]: Hullo, Vancouver. We are on manual now and trying out some gentle turns.

Cut To: The control room.

TRELEAVEN [into mike]: Hullo, George Spencer. Try the effect on fore-and-aft control on your air speed. To begin with, close your throttles slightly and bring your air speed back to 160. Adjust the trim as you go along. But watch that air speed closely. Remember to keep it well above 120. Over.

Cut To: The flight deck.

SPENCER [tensely. Still feeling out the controls]: Tell him okay.
STEWARDESS [into mike]: Okay, Vancouver. We are doing as you say.

TRELEAVEN'S VOICE [after a pause]: Hullo, 714. How does she handle, George?
SPENCER [disgustedly]: Tell him sluggish like a wet sponge.
STEWARDESS: Sluggish like a wet sponge, Vancouver.

Cut To: The control room. There is a momentary relaxing of tension as Captain Treleaven and the group around him exchange grins.

TRELEAVEN [into mike]: Hullo, George Spencer. That would be a natural feeling, because you were used to handling smaller airplanes. The thing you have got to remember is that there is a bigger lag in the effect of control movements on air speed, compared with what you were used to before. Do you understand that? Over.

Cut To: The flight deck.

SPENCER: Tell him I understand.
STEWARDESS [into mike]: Hullo, Vancouver. Yes, he understands. Over.

Cut To: The control room.

TRELEAVEN [into mike]: Hullo, George Spencer. Because of that lag in air speed you must avoid any violent movements of the controls, such as you used to make in your fighter airplanes. If you *do* move the controls violently, you will over-correct and be in trouble. Is that understood?

Cut To: The flight deck.

SPENCER [nodding, beginning to perspire]: Tell him—yes, I understand.
STEWARDESS [into mike]: Yes, Vancouver.

Your message is understood. Over.

Cut To: The control room.

TRELEAVEN [into mike]: Hullo, George Spencer. Now I want you to feel how the ship handles at lower speeds when the flaps and wheels are down. But don't do anything until I give you the instructions. Is that clear? Over.

Cut To: The flight deck.

SPENCER: Tell him okay; let's have the instructions.

STEWARDESS [into mike]: Hullo, Vancouver. Yes, we understand. Go ahead with the instructions. Over.

TRELEAVEN'S VOICE: First of all, throttle back slightly, get your air speed steady at 160 knots, and adjust your trim to maintain level flight. Then tell me when you're ready. Over.

SPENCER: Watch that air speed, Janet. You'll have to call it off to me when we land, so you may as well start practicing.

STEWARDESS: It's 200 now . . . 190 . . . 185 . . . 180 . . . 175 . . . 175 . . . 165 . . . 155 . . . 150 . . . [Alarmed] That's too low! He said 160!

SPENCER [tensely]: I know. I know. Watch it! It's that lag on the air speed I can't get used to.

STEWARDESS: 150 . . . 150 . . . 155 . . . 160 . . . 160 . . . It's steady on 160.

SPENCER: Tell them.

STEWARDESS [into mike]: Hullo, Vancouver. This is 714. Our speed is steady at 160. Over.

Cut To: The control room.

TRELEAVEN [into mike]: Okay, 714. Now, George, I want you to put down twenty degrees of flap. But be careful not to make it any more. The flap lever is at the base of the control pedestal and is plainly marked. Twenty degrees will mean moving the lever down to the second notch. Over.

Cut To: The flight deck.

SPENCER: Janet, *you'll* have to put the flaps down. [Pointing] There's the lever.

TRELEAVEN'S VOICE: Can you see the flap indicator, George? It's near the center of the main panel.

SPENCER: Here's the indicator he's talking about. When I tell you, push the lever down to the second notch and watch the dial. Okay?

STEWARDESS: Okay. [Then with alarm] Oh, look at the air speed! It's down to 125!

Spencer grimaces[4] and pushes the control column forward.

SPENCER [urgently]: Call off the speed! Call off the speed!

STEWARDESS: 140 . . . 150 . . . 160 . . . 170 . . . 175 . . . Can't you get it back to 160?

SPENCER [straining]: I'm trying! I'm trying! [Pause] There it is.

Cut To: The passenger cabin.

SECOND WOMAN PASSENGER [frightened]: Hector! We're going to crash! I know

---

[4] *grimace:* (grĭ-mās'): facial expression showing pain or fear.

it! Oh, do something! Do something!

BAIRD [appears at her elbow]: Have her take
this. It'll help calm her down.
[Gives pill and cup to the Third Male Passenger.] Try not to worry. That
young man at the front is a very
experienced pilot. He's just what
they call "getting the feel" of the
airplane. [He moves aft in the cabin.]

FIRST MALE PASSENGER: Doctor!

BAIRD: Yes.

FIRST MALE PASSENGER: Tell us the truth,
Doctor. Have we got a chance?
Does this fellow know how to fly
this thing?

BAIRD: We've got all kinds of chances.
He's a very experienced pilot, but
it's just that he's not used to
flying this particular type and
he's getting the feel of it.

FOURTH MALE PASSENGER: You didn't need
none of them pills to make me
sick. Never mind me dinner.
Now ah'm workin' on yesterday's
breakfast.

Cut To: The flight deck.

STEWARDESS [into mike]: Hullo, Vancouver.
Air speed is 160, and we are
ready to put down the flaps.
Over.

Cut To: The control room.

TRELEAVEN [into mike]: Okay, 714. Go
ahead with your flaps. But be
careful—only twenty degrees.
Then, when you have twenty degrees down, bring back the air
speed to 140, adjust your trim,
and call me again. Over.

Cut To: The flight deck.

SPENCER: Okay, Janet—flaps down!
Twenty degrees.

The Stewardess pushes down the flap lever to
its second notch.

SPENCER: Tell them we've got the flaps
down, and the air speed's coming to 140.

STEWARDESS [into mike]: Hullo, Vancouver.
This is 714. The flaps are down,
and our air speed is 140.

Cut To: The control room.

TRELEAVEN: All right, 714. Now, the next
thing is to put the wheels down.
Are you still maintaining level
flight?

Cut To: The flight deck.

SPENCER: Tell him—more or less.

STEWARDESS [into mike]: Hullo, Vancouver.
More or less.

Cut To: The control room.

RADIO OPERATOR: This guy's got a sense
of humor.

BURDICK: That's a *real* help.

TRELEAVEN [into mike]: Okay, 714. Try to
keep your altitude steady and
your speed at 140. Then, when
you *are* ready, put down the
landing gear and let your speed
come back to 120. You will have
to advance your throttle setting
to maintain that air speed, and
also adjust your trim. Is that understood? Over.

Cut To: The flight deck.

SPENCER: Ask him—what about the

propeller controls and mixture?

STEWARDESS [into mike]: Hullo, Vancouver. What about the propeller controls and mixture? Over.

Cut To: The control room.

CONTROLLER: He's thinking, anyway.

TRELEAVEN [into mike]: Leave them alone for the time being. Just concentrate on holding that air speed steady with the wheels and flaps down. Over.

Cut To: The flight deck.

SPENCER: Wheels down, Janet, and call off the air speed.

STEWARDESS [selects landing gear down]: 140. . . 145 . . . 140 . . . 135 . . . 130 . . . 125 . . . 120 . . . 115 . . . The speed's too low!

SPENCER: Keep calling it!

STEWARDESS: 115 . . . 120 . . . 120 . . . Steady on 120.

Cut To: The control room.

TRELEAVEN [into mike]: Hullo, George Spencer. Your wheels should be down by now, and look for three green lights to show that they're locked. Over.

Cut To: The flight deck.

SPENCER: Are they on?

STEWARDESS: Yes—all three lights are green.

SPENCER: Tell them.

STEWARDESS [into mike]: Hullo, Vancouver. Yes, there are three green lights.

Cut To: The control room.

TRELEAVEN: Okay, 714, now let's put down full flap so that you can feel how the airplane will handle when you're landing. As soon as full flap is down, bring your air speed back to 110 knots and trim to hold it steady. Adjust your throttle setting to hold your altitude. Is that understood? Over.

Cut To: The flight deck.

SPENCER: Tell him yes.

STEWARDESS [into mike]: Yes, Vancouver. That is understood.

SPENCER: Full flap, Janet! Push the lever all the way down, and call off the air speed.

STEWARDESS: 120 . . . 115 . . . 115 . . . 110 . . . 110. . . .

SPENCER: Okay, tell 'em we've got full flap and air speed 110, and she still handles like a sponge, only more so.

STEWARDESS [into mike]: Hullo, Vancouver. We have full flap, and air speed is 110. And the pilot says she still handles like a sponge, only more so.

Cut To: The control room. Again there is a momentary sense of relief.

TRELEAVEN [into mike]: That's nice going, George. Now I'm going to give you instructions for holding your height and air speed while you raise the flaps and landing gear. Then we'll run through the whole procedure again.

Cut To: The flight deck.

SPENCER: Again! I don't know if my nerves'll stand it. [Pause] All right. Tell him okay.

Dissolve To: Control room clock showing 2:55.

Dissolve To: Control room clock showing 5:20.

Dissolve To: The control room. Captain Treleaven is still seated in front of the transmitter, but has obviously been under strain. He now has his coat off and his tie loosened, and there is an empty carton of coffee beside him. Burdick and the Controller are in the background, watching tensely. A phone rings and the Controller answers it. He makes a note and passes it to Treleaven.

TRELEAVEN [into mike]: Hullo, Flight 714. Our flying practice has slowed you down, and you are later than we expected. You are now twelve minutes flying time from Vancouver Airport, but it's getting light, so your landing will be in daylight. You should be able to see us at any minute. Do you see the airport beacon? Over.

STEWARDESS'S VOICE: Yes, we see the airport beacon. Over.

TRELEAVEN: Okay, George, now you've practiced everything we need for a landing. You've flown the ship with wheels and flaps down, and you know how she handles. Your fuel feeds are checked, and you're all set to come in. You won't hear from me again for a few minutes because I'm moving to the control tower so I'll be able to see you on the circuit and approach. Is that clear? Over.

STEWARDESS'S VOICE: Yes, Vancouver, that is understood. Over.

TRELEAVEN: All right, George. Continue to approach at two thousand feet on your present heading and wait for instructions. We'll let you know the runway to use at the last minute, because the wind is shifting. Don't forget, we want you to do at least one dummy run, and then go round again so you'll have practice in making the landing approach. Over. [He mops his forehead with a crumpled handkerchief.]

Cut To: The flight deck. Spencer, too, has his coat off and tie loosened. His hair is ruffled, and the strain is plainly beginning to tell on him. The Stewardess is still in the copilot's seat, and Baird is standing behind them both. The Stewardess is about to acknowledge the last radio message, but Spencer stops her.

SPENCER: I'll take it, Janet. [Into mike] No dice, Vancouver. We're coming straight in and the first time is "it." Dr. Baird is here beside me. He reports two of the passengers and the First Officer are in critical condition, and we must land in the next few minutes. The doctor asks that you have stomach pumps and oxygen equipment ready. Over.

Cut To: The control room.

BURDICK: He mustn't! We need time!

TRELEAVEN: It's his decision. By all the rules he's in command of the airplane. [Into mike] 714, your message is understood. Good luck to us all. Listening out. [To Burdick and the Controller] Let's go!

Dissolve To: The flight deck.

SPENCER: This is it, Doctor. You'd better go back now and make sure everybody's strapped in tight. Are both the pilots in seats?

BAIRD: Yes.

SPENCER: How about the passengers who aren't sick? Are they worried?

BAIRD: A little, but there's no panic. I exaggerated your qualifications. I'd better go. Good luck.

SPENCER [with ironic grin]: Thanks.

Dissolve To: The control tower, Vancouver Airport. It is a glass-enclosed area, with radio panels and other equipment, and access is by a stairway from below. It is now daylight and the Tower Controller is looking skyward, using binoculars. There is the sound of hurried feet on the stairway and Treleaven, the Controller, and Burdick emerge in that order.

TOWER CONTROLLER: There he is!

Treleaven picks up a second pair of binoculars, looks through them quickly, then puts them down.

TRELEAVEN: All right—let's make our decision on the runway. What's it to be?

TOWER CONTROLLER: Zero eight. It's pretty well into wind now, though there'll be a slight crosswind from the left. It's also the longest.

TRELEAVEN [into mike]: Hullo, Flight 714. This is Martin Treleaven in Vancouver tower. Do you read me? Over.

Cut To: The flight deck.

STEWARDESS [into mike]: Yes, Vancouver Tower. Loud and clear. Over.

Cut To: The tower.

TRELEAVEN [crisply, authoritatively, yet calmly]: From here on, do not acknowledge any further transmissions unless you wish to ask a ques-

tion. You are now ready to join the airport circuit. The runway for landing is zero eight. That means you are now crosswind and will shortly make a left turn on to the downwind leg. Begin now to lose height to one thousand feet. Throttle back slightly and make your descent at 400 feet a minute. Let your air speed come back to 160 knots and hold it steady there. . . . Air speed 160.

CONTROLLER [reaching for phone]: Runway is zero eight. All vehicles stand by near the extreme south end. Do not, repeat not, go down the runway until the aircraft has passed by you, because it may swing off. Is that clear? [Pause] Right.

Cut To: Film insert of fire trucks and ambulances. They are manned and move away with sirens wailing.

Cut To: The flight deck. Spencer is pushing the throttles forward, and the tempo of the motors increases.

SPENCER: Tell them we're at one thousand feet and leveling off.

STEWARDESS [into mike]: Vancouver Tower. We are now at one thousand feet and leveling off. Over.

TRELEAVEN'S VOICE: Now let's have twenty degrees of flap. Do not acknowledge this message.

SPENCER: Twenty degrees of flap, Janet.

The Stewardess reaches for flap lever and pushes it down while she watches the flap indicator.

TRELEAVEN'S VOICE: When you have your flaps down, bring your air speed

back slowly to 140 knots, adjust your trim, and begin to make a left turn onto the downwind leg. When you have turned, fly parallel with the runway you see on your left. I repeat—air speed 140 and begin a left turn.

Cut To: Close-up of an instrument panel showing artificial horizon and air-speed indicator. The air speed first comes back to 130, goes slightly below it, then returns to 130. The artificial horizon tilts so that the airplane symbol is banked to the left.

Cut To: The flight deck. Spencer has control yoke turned to the left and is adjusting the throttles.

Cut To: The tower.

TRELEAVEN: Watch your height! Don't make that turn so steep! Watch your height! More throttle! Keep the air speed on 140 and the nose up! Get back that height! You need a thousand feet!

Cut To: The flight deck. Spencer eases the throttles open, and the tempo of the motors increases. He eases the control column forward, then pulls back again.

Cut To: Close-up of climb and descent indicator. The instrument first shows a descent of 500 feet per minute, then a climb of 600 feet, and then gradually begins to level off.

Cut To: The control tower. Captain Treleaven is looking out through binoculars, the others anxiously behind him.

TRELEAVEN [angrily]: He can't fly the bloody thing! Of course he can't fly it! You're watching fifty people going to their deaths!
BURDICK [shouting]: Keep talking to him!

Keep talking! Tell him what to do!
TRELEAVEN [urgently, into mike]: Spencer, you can't come straight in! You've got to do some circuits, and practice that approach. You've enough fuel left for three hours' flying. Stay up, man! Stay up!

Cut To: The flight deck.

SPENCER: Give it to me! [Taking the mike. Then tensely] Listen, down there! I'm coming in! Do you hear me? . . . I'm coming in. There are people up here who'll die in less than an hour, never mind three. I may bend your precious airplane a bit, but I'll get it down. Now, get on with the landing check. I'm putting the gear down now. [To the Stewardess] Wheels down, Janet!

The Stewardess selects landing gear "down," and Spencer reaches for the throttles.

Cut To: Film insert of airplane in flight, day. Its landing wheels come down.

Cut To: The flight deck.

STEWARDESS [looks out of window, then back to Spencer]: Wheels down and three green lights.

Cut To: The tower.

BURDICK: He may not be able to fly, but he's sure got guts.
TRELEAVEN [into mike]: Increase your throttle slightly to hold your air speed now that the wheels are down. Adjust your trim and keep that height at a thousand feet.

Now check your propeller setting and your mixture—propellers to fully fine; mixture to full rich. I'll repeat that. Propellers to fully fine; mixture to full rich.

Cut To: The flight deck.

SPENCER [to himself, as he moves controls]: Propellers fully fine. Mixture full rich. [To the Stewardess] Janet, let me hear the air speed.
STEWARDESS: 130 . . . 125 . . . 120 . . . 125 . . . 130 . . .

Cut To: The tower.

TRELEAVEN [into mike]: You are well downwind now. You can begin to make a left turn on the cross-wind leg. As you turn, begin losing height to 800 feet and let your air speed come back to 120. I'll repeat that. Start a left turn. Lose height to 800. Air speed 120. [He picks up binoculars, then puts them down hurriedly, and takes mike again.] You are losing height too fast! You are losing height too fast! Open up! Open! Hold your height, now! Keep your air speed at 120.

Cut To: The flight deck.

STEWARDESS: 110 . . . 110 . . . 105 . . . 110 . . . 110 . . . 120 . . . 120 . . . Steady at 120.
SPENCER: What a blasted insensitive wagon this is! It doesn't respond! It doesn't respond at all!
STEWARDESS: 125 . . . 130 . . . 130 . . . Steady on 130.

Cut To: The tower.

TRELEAVEN: Start your turn into wind now to line up with the runway. Make it a gentle turn—you've plenty of time. As you turn, begin losing height, about 400 feet a minute. But be ready to correct if you lose height too fast. Adjust your trim as you go . . . That's right! . . . Keep turning! As soon as you've completed the turn, put down full flap and bring your air speed to 115. I'll repeat that. Let down 400 feet a minute. Full flap. Then air speed 115. [To the others] Is everything ready on the field?
CONTROLLER: As ready as we'll ever be.
TRELEAVEN: Then, this is it. In sixty seconds we'll know.

Cut To: The flight deck.

SPENCER [muttering]: Not quite yet . . . a little more . . . that should do it. [As he straightens out of the turn] Janet, give me full flap!

The Stewardess reaches for the flap control, pushes it down, and leaves it down.

SPENCER: Height and air speed!
STEWARDESS: 700 feet, speed 130 . . . 600 feet, speed 120 . . . 500 feet, speed 105 . . . We're going down too quickly!
SPENCER: I know! I know! [He pushes throttles forward, and the tempo of the motors increases.] Keep watching it!
STEWARDESS: 450 feet, speed 100 . . . 400 feet, speed 100 . . .

Cut To: Film insert of airplane (DC-4) with wheels and flaps down, on a landing approach.

Cut To: The tower.

TRELEAVEN [urgently into mike]: Open up! Open up! You're losing height too fast! [Pause] Watch the air speed! Your nose is too high! Open up quickly or she'll stall! Open up, man! Open up!

BURDICK: He heard you. He's recovering.

TRELEAVEN [into mike]: Maintain that height until you get closer into the runway. But be ready to ease off gently . . . You can start now . . . Let down again . . . That looks about right . . . But watch the air speed. Your nose is creeping up . . . [More steadily] Now, listen carefully, George. There's a slight crosswind on the runway, and your drift is to the right. Straighten up just before you touch down, and be ready with your right rudder as soon as you *are* down. And remember to cut the switches if you land too fast. [Pause] All right, your approach is good . . . Get ready to round out—now! [Pause. Then urgently] You're coming in too fast! Lift the nose up!

Cut To: The flight deck.

TRELEAVEN'S VOICE: Lift the nose up! Back on the throttles! Throttles right back! Hold her off! Not too much! Not too much! Be ready for that crosswind! Ease her down, *now!* Ease her down!

Cut To: Film insert of a landing wheel skimming over a runway and about to touch down. As it makes contact, rock picture to show instability.

Cut To: The flight deck. There is a heavy thud,

and Spencer and the Stewardess are jolted in their seats. There is another, another, and another. Everything shakes.

SPENCER [shouting]: Cut the switches! Cut the switches!

The Stewardess reaches upward and pulls down the cage of the master switches. Instantly the heavy roar of motors stops, but there is still a whistling because the airplane is traveling fast. Spencer stretches out his legs as he puts his full strength into applying the airplane toe brakes, at the same time pulling back on the control column. There is a screaming of rubber on pavement, and Spencer and the Stewardess are thrown violently to the left. Then, except for the hum of the radio and gyros, there is a silence as the airplane stops.

SPENCER [disgustedly]: I ground looped! I did a lousy stinking ground loop! We're turned right around the way we came!

STEWARDESS: But we're all right! We're all right! You did it! You did it!

She leans over and kisses him. Spencer pulls off his radio headset. Outside there is a rising note of approaching sirens. Then, from the headset we hear Captain Treleaven's voice.

TRELEAVEN'S VOICE [exuberantly]: Hullo, George Spencer. That was probably the lousiest landing in the history of this airport. So don't ever ask us for a job as a pilot. But there are some people here who'd like to shake you by the hand, and later on we'll buy you a drink. Stay right where you are, George! We're coming over.

Fade Out.

THE END

DISCUSSION

1.   Although you probably guessed that Spencer would be able to land the plane, the play is full of suspense. Find the places in the play where the situation is the most tense. Begin at the point where you first realized that everyone in the plane was in danger—not just the people who had eaten the fish.

2.   A play is made up almost completely of **dialogue** (see page 149). This is how we find out about the characters, and this is how the plot unfolds. In this play the writer does not tell us directly what is happening—we listen while the characters tell each other. Find the section of dialogue where you first find out that a passenger is ill. What characters are talking? Find the section of dialogue where you find that neither pilot can land the plane. What characters are talking?

3.   **Foreshadowing.**   Sometimes a writer gives hints or clues in the beginning of a play or story about what the problem is going to be or how it will turn out. This is called foreshadowing. If you go back and look at the beginning of this play you can see that the writer has given you little bits of information that all fit together later. Where is food first mentioned? What do you find out about the food? When do you find out that Spencer knows about planes? How does the conversation between Spencer and Baird affect the way the play turns out?

For further activities, see page 260.

# Interview with a Crow Chief

FRANK B. LINDERMAN

Plenty-coups[1] seated himself in the shade of the tall cottonwood trees that surrounded his cabin on Arrow Creek. "I am glad you have come, Sign-talker," he said, his nearly sightless eyes turned upon me. "Many men, both of my people and yours, have asked me to tell you the story of my life. This I have promised to do, and have sent for you; but why do you wish to write down my words, Sign-talker?"

"Because," I said, "if you tell me what I wish to know, and I write it down, my people will better understand your people. A better understanding between your people and mine will be good for both."

Magpies[2] jabbered above the racks of red meat hung to cure in the dry air, and the Chief's dogs, jealous and noisy, raced below them. By gift, the dogs would get very little of the meat they guarded; the magpies, more by theft.

"You are my friend, Sign-talker. I know your heart is good. I will tell you what you wish to know, and you may write it down," said Plenty-coups, at last.

The Chief's face, upturned to the speaker, was in profile to me. The broad-brimmed hat, with its fluttering eagle feather, hid the contour of his head. His gray hair fell in braids upon his broad shoulders. He had been a powerful man, not over-tall, and was now bent a little by the years. His deep chest and long arms told me that in his prime Plenty-coups had known few physical equals among his people.

He removed the hat from his head, laid it upon the grass beside him, and gripping the arms of the chair to steady himself, stood up. He turned as though his nearly sightless eyes could see the land he so much loves. "On this beautiful day, with its flowers, its sunshine, and green grass, a man in his right mind should speak straight to his friends. I will begin at the beginning," he said, and sat down again.

A score of questions came to my mind, but I banished them in the interest of order. "Where were you born?" I asked.

[1] *Plenty-coups* (plĕn'-tē-ko͞oz): Many Achievements.
[2] *magpies:* birds related to crows or jays.

"I was born eighty snows ago this summer [1848] at the place we call The-cliff-that-has-no-pass," said Plenty-coups slowly. "It is not far from the present site of Billings. My mother's name was Otter-woman. My father was Medicine-bird. I have forgotten the name of one of my grandmothers, but I remember her man's name, my grandfather's. It was Coyote-appears. My other grandmother, a Crow woman, married a man of the Shoshone. Her name was It-might-have-happened. She was my mother's mother."

"What are your earliest remembrances?" I asked, feeling that I had interrupted him with my question.

He smiled, his pipe ready to light. "Play," he said happily. "All boys are much alike. Their hearts are young, and they let them sing. We moved camp very often, and this to me, and the other boys of my age, was great fun. As soon as the crier rode through the village telling the people to get ready to travel, I would find my young friends and we would catch up our horses as fast as the herders brought them in. Lodges would come down quickly, horses would be packed, travois[3] loaded, and then away we would go to some new place we boys had never seen before. The long line of pack-horses and travois reaching farther than we could see, the dogs and bands of loose horses, all sweeping across the rolling plains or up a mountain trail to some mysterious destination, made our hearts sing with joy.

"More and more we gathered by ourselves to talk and play. Often our talking was of warriors and war, and always in our playing there was the object of training ourselves to become warriors. We had our leaders just as our fathers had, and they became our chiefs in the same manner that men become chiefs, by distinguishing themselves."

The pleasure which thoughts of boyhood had brought to his face vanished now. His mind wandered from his story. "My people were wise," he said thoughtfully. "They never neglected the young or failed to keep before them deeds done by illustrious men of the tribe. Our teachers were willing and thorough. They were our grandfathers, fathers, or uncles. All were quick to praise excellence without speaking a word that might break the spirit of a boy who might be less capable than others. The boy who failed at any lesson got only more lessons, more care, until he was as far as he could go."

---

[3] *travois* (trə-voiz′): sledlike construction attached to horses to carry goods.

"Your first lessons were with the bow and arrow?" I asked, to give him another start on his boyhood.

"Oh no. Our first task was learning to run," he replied, his face lighting up again. "How well I remember my first lesson, and how proud I felt because my grandfather noticed me.

"The day was in summer, the world green and very beautiful. I was playing with some other boys when my grandfather stopped to watch. 'Take off your shirt and leggings,' he said to me.

"I tore them from my back and legs, and naked except for my moccasins, stood before him.

" 'Now catch me that yellow butterfly,' he ordered. 'Be quick!'

"Away I went after the yellow butterfly. How fast these creatures are, and how cunning! In and out among the trees and bushes, across streams, over grassy places, now low near the ground, then just above my head, the dodging butterfly led me far before I caught and held it in my hand. Panting, but concealing my shortness of breath as best I could, I offered it to Grandfather, who whispered, as though he told me a secret, 'Rub its wings over your heart, my son, and ask the butterflies to lend you their grace and swiftness.'

" 'O Butterflies, lend me your grace and swiftness!' I repeated, rubbing the broken wings over my pounding heart. If this would give me grace and speed I should catch many butterflies, I knew. But instead of keeping the secret I told my friends, as my grandfather knew I would," Plenty-coups chuckled, "and how many, many we boys caught after that to rub over our hearts. We chased butterflies to give us endurance in running, always rubbing our breasts with their wings, asking the butterflies to give us a portion of their power. We worked very hard at this, because running is necessary both in hunting and in war. I was never the swiftest among my friends, but not many could run farther than I."

"Is running a greater accomplishment than swimming?" I asked.

"Yes," he answered, "but swimming is more fun. In all seasons of the year most men were in the rivers before sunrise. Boys had plenty of teachers here. Sometimes they were hard on us, too. They would often send us into the water to swim among cakes of floating ice, and the ice taught us to take care of our bodies. Cold toughens a man. The buffalo-runners, in winter, rubbed their hands with sand and snow to prevent their fingers from stiffening in using the bow and arrow.

"Perhaps we would all be in our fathers' lodges by the fire when some teacher would call, 'Follow me, and do as I do!' Then we would run outside to follow him, racing behind him to the bank of a river. On the very edge he would turn a flip-flop into the water. Every boy who failed at the flip-flop was thrown in and ducked. The flip-flop was difficult for me. I was ducked many times before I learned it.

"We were eager to learn from both the men and the beasts who excelled in anything, and so never got through learning. But swimming was most fun, and therefore we worked harder at this than at other tasks. Whenever a boy's father caught a beaver, the boy got the tail and brought it to us. We would take turns slapping our joints and muscles with the flat beaver's tail until they burned under our blows. 'Teach us your power in the water, O Beaver!' we said, making our skins smart with the tail.

"I remember the day my father gave me a bow and four arrows. The bow was light and small, the arrows blunt and short. But my pride in possessing them was great, since in spite of its smallness the bow was like my father's. It was made of cedar and was neatly backed with sinew[4] to make it strong.

"Nobody could tell where an arrow would go," he said. "We always straightened our arrows with a bone straightener or with our teeth, before using them. First we shot for distance. No particular care was given to accuracy until the required distance was reached. Then we were taught to shoot with precision. This requires even more work than shooting for distance.

"All arrow shafts were marked. Each boy knew his own arrows, and those of the other boys as well. Even the men of the tribe knew each other's arrows by their marks.

"Speed in shooting was very necessary, since both in war and hunting a man must be quick to send a second arrow after his first. We were taught to hold one, and sometimes more arrows in the left hand with the bow. They were held points down, feathers up, so that when the right hand reached and drew them, the left would not be wounded by their sharp heads. Sometimes men carried an extra arrow in their mouths. This was quicker than pulling them from a quiver over the shoulder, but was a method used only in fighting, or dangerous situations.

---

[4] *sinew* (sĭn'-yōō): tendon (muscle fibers).

"The bow was the best of weapons for running the buffalo," he said, turning to me. "Even the old-time white men, who had only the muzzle-loading guns, were quick to adopt the bow and arrow in running buffalo. But a powerful arm and a strong wrist are necessary to send an arrow deep into a buffalo. I have often seen them driven *through*."

"How old were you when you were given a genuine bow?" I asked.

"Seven," he answered. "When I was seven, my arrows had good iron points which my father got from the white trader on Elk River. This trader's name was Lumpy-neck."

"But your bow was not very strong when you were seven years old," I said.

"No, of course not," he laughed. "But I thought it was strong. It was much stronger than my first one, and we hunted deer in the river bottoms and antelope on the plains. But our teachers were still our masters, and each day we had work to do.

"One morning after I was eight years old we were called together by my grandfather. He had killed a grizzly bear the day before, and when we gathered near him I saw that he held the grizzly's heart in his hand. We all knew well what was expected of us, since every Crow warrior has eaten some of the heart of a grizzly bear, so that he may truthfully say, 'I have the heart of a grizzly!' I say this, even to this day, when there is trouble to face, and the words help me to keep my head. They clear my mind, make me suddenly calm.

"I felt myself growing stronger, more self-reliant, and cool from the day I ate a piece of that bear's heart. I believed I might soon be taken on war-parties, and with my friends began to play war.

"One day when the chokecherries were black and the plums red on the trees, my grandfather rode through the village, calling twenty of us older boys by name. The buffalo-runners had been out since daybreak, and we guessed what was before us. 'Get on your horses and follow me,' said my grandfather, riding out on the plains.

"We rode fast. Nothing was in sight until Grandfather led us over a hill. There we saw a circle of horsemen about one hundred yards across, and in its center a huge buffalo bull. We knew he had been wounded and tormented until he was very dangerous, and when we saw him there defying the men on

horseback we began to dread the ordeal that was at hand.

"The circle parted as we rode through it, and the bull, angered by the stir we made, charged and sent us flying. The men were laughing at us when we returned, and this made me feel very small. They had again surrounded the bull, and I now saw an arrow sticking deep in his side. Only its feathers were sticking out of a wound that dripped blood on the ground.

" 'Get down from your horses, young men,' said my grandfather. 'A cool head, with quick feet, may strike this bull on the root of his tail with a bow. Be lively, and take care of yourselves. The young man who strikes, and is himself not hurt, may count coup.' [5]

"I was first off my horse. Watching the bull, I slipped out of shirt and leggings, letting them fall where I stood. Naked, with only my bow in my right hand, I stepped away from my clothes, feeling that I might never see them again. I was not quite nine years old.

"The bull saw me, a human being afoot! He seemed to know that now he might kill, and he began to paw the ground and bellow as I walked carefully toward him.

"Suddenly he stopped pawing, and his voice was still. He came to meet me, his eyes green with anger and pain. I saw blood dropping from his side, not red blood now, but mixed with yellow.

"I stopped walking and stood still. This seemed to puzzle the bull, and he too stopped in his tracks. We looked at each other, the sun hot on my naked back. Heat from the plains danced on the bull's horns and head; his sides were panting, and his mouth was bloody.

"I knew that the men were watching me. I could feel their eyes on my back. I must go on. One step, two steps. The grass was soft and thick under my feet. Three steps. 'I am a Crow. I have the heart of a grizzly bear,' I said to myself. Three more steps. And then he charged!

"A cheer went up out of a cloud of dust. I had struck the bull on the root of his tail! But I was in even greater danger than before.

"Two other boys were after the bull now, but in spite of them he turned and came at me. To run was foolish. I stood still, waiting. The bull stopped very near me and bellowed,

[5] *coup* (ko͞o): achievement or victory.

blowing bloody froth from his nose. The other boys, seeing my danger, did not move. The bull was not more than four bows' lengths from me, and I could feel my heart beating like a war-drum.

"Two large gray wolves crossed the circle just behind him, but the bull did not notice them, did not move an eye. He saw only me, and I was growing tired from the strain of watching him. I must get relief, must tempt him to come on. I stepped to my right. Instantly he charged—but I had dodged back to my left, across his way, and I struck him when he passed. This time I ran among the horsemen, with a lump of bloody froth on my breast. I had had enough."

DISCUSSION

1. The grandfather took twenty boys with him to where the wounded buffalo was. Why did he do this?

2. The boys catch butterflies and rub themselves with their wings. They slap themselves with beaver tails. They eat of the heart of a grizzly bear. Do these actions actually help them become faster and stronger? Explain.

3. The boys do not go to school; yet they learn all the time. Who are the teachers? What are the lessons? Why are things done this way?

4. Plenty-coups tells many other stories about his life in the book *Plenty-coups: Chief of the Crows,* by Frank B. Linderman. If you read it, you might want to tell the class some of the other stories from it.

For further activities, see page 260.

# Paul Revere's Ride

HENRY WADSWORTH LONGFELLOW

Listen, my children, and you shall hear
Of the midnight ride of Paul Revere,
On the eighteenth of April in seventy-five;
Hardly a man is now alive
Who remembers that famous day and year.                5

He said to his friend, "If the British march
By land or sea from the town tonight,
Hang a lantern aloft in the belfry arch
Of the North Church tower as a signal light—
One, if by land, and two, if by sea;                10
And I on the opposite shore will be,
Ready to ride and spread the alarm
Through every Middlesex village and farm
For the country folk to be up and to arm."
Then he said, "Good night!" and with muffled oar        15
Silently rowed to the Charlestown shore
Just as the moon rose over the bay,
Where swinging wide at her moorings lay
The *Somerset,* British man-of-war,
A phantom ship, with each mast and spar            20
Across the moon like a prison bar,
And a huge black hulk that was magnified
By its own reflection in the tide.
Meanwhile, his friend through alley and street
Wanders and watches with eager ears,                25
Till in the silence around him he hears
The muster of men at the barrack door,
The sound of arms, and the tramp of feet,
And the measured tread of the grenadiers
Marching down to their boats on the shore.            30

Then he climbed the tower of the Old North Church,
By the wooden stairs, with stealthy tread,
To the belfry chamber overhead,
And startled the pigeons from their perch

On the somber rafters, that round him made          35
Masses and moving shapes of shade—
By the trembling ladder, steep and tall,
To the highest window in the wall,
Where he paused to listen and look down
A moment on the roofs of the town,               40
And the moonlight flowing over all.

Beneath, in the churchyard, lay the dead
In their night-encampment on the hill,
Wrapped in silence so deep and still
That he could hear, like a sentinel's tread,       45
The watchful night-wind as it went
Creeping along from tent to tent
And seeming to whisper, "All is well!"
A moment only he feels the spell
Of the place and the hour, and the secret dread    50
Of the lonely belfry and the dead;
For suddenly all his thoughts are bent
On a shadowy something far away
Where the river widens to meet the bay—
A line of black that bends and floats              55
On the rising tide, like a bridge of boats.

Meanwhile, impatient to mount and ride,
Booted and spurred, with a heavy stride
On the opposite shore walked Paul Revere.
Now he patted his horse's side,                    60
Now gazed at the landscape far and near,
Then, impetuous, stamped the earth,
And turned and tightened his saddle girth;
But mostly he watched with eager search
The belfry tower of the Old North Church           65
As it rose above the graves on the hill,
Lonely and spectral and somber and still.
And lo! as he looks, on the belfry's height
A glimmer, and then a gleam of light!
He springs to the saddle, the bridle he turns,     70
But lingers and gazes, till full on his sight
A second lamp in the belfry burns!

A hurry of hoofs in a village street,
A shape in the moonlight, a bulk in the dark,

And beneath, from the pebbles, in passing, a spark                    75
Struck out by a steed flying fearless and fleet:
That was all! And yet, through the gloom and the light
The fate of a nation was riding that night,
And the spark struck out by that steed in his flight
Kindled the land into flame with its heat.                            80

He has left the village and mounted the steep,
And beneath him, tranquil and broad and deep,
Is the Mystic, meeting the ocean tides;
And under the alders that skirt its edge,
Now soft on the sand, now loud on the ledge,                          85
Is heard the tramp of his steed as he rides.

It was twelve by the village clock
When he crossed the bridge into Medford town.
He heard the crowing of the cock
And the barking of the farmer's dog,                                  90
And felt the damp of the river fog
That rises after the sun goes down.

It was one by the village clock
When he galloped into Lexington.
He saw the gilded weathercock                                         95
Swim in the moonlight as he passed,
And the meeting-house windows, blank and bare,
Gaze at him with a spectral glare,
As if they already stood aghast
At the bloody work they would look upon.                              100

It was two by the village clock
When he came to the bridge in Concord town.
He heard the bleating of the flock
And the twitter of birds among the trees,
And felt the breath of the morning breeze                            105
Blowing over the meadows brown.
And one was safe and asleep in his bed
Who at the bridge would be first to fall,
Who that day would be lying dead,
Pierced by a British musket-ball.                                     110

83. *Mystic:* river flowing into Boston Harbor.

You know the rest. In the books you have read
How the British regulars fired and fled;
How the farmers gave them ball for ball
From behind each fence and farmyard wall,
Chasing the redcoats down the lane,                          115
Then crossing the fields to emerge again
Under the trees at the turn of the road,
And only pausing to fire and load.

So through the night rode Paul Revere,
And so through the night went his cry of alarm          120
To every Middlesex village and farm—
A cry of defiance and not of fear,
A voice in the darkness, a knock at the door,
And a word that shall echo forevermore!
For, borne on the night wind of the past,                   125
Through all our history, to the last,
In the hour of darkness and peril and need
The people will waken and listen to hear
The hurrying hoofbeats of that steed
And the midnight message of Paul Revere.                 130

DISCUSSION    1.  Paul Revere's message was that the British soldiers were coming. What does the writer mean, then,
in the last stanza, when he says that in the future in
times of need people will awaken in the night and
hear Paul Revere's horse and his message?

2.  The poem helps us experience what Paul Revere
and his friend felt on that night. Start with the second
stanza and find the lines that best help you *see* what
they saw and *hear* what they heard.

3.  **Alliteration.**  Look at lines 73–76. Read them out
loud to yourself, being careful to pronounce the first
sounds of the words. When a first sound is repeated,
like the *h*'s in line 73, the *p*'s in line 75, and the *s*'s
and *f*'s in line 76, the writer is using alliteration. Here
the writer wants you to hear the horse hurrying along.
Read the lines faster and see how the sound works.

For further activities, see page 260.

# Lochinvar

### Sir Walter Scott

Oh, young Lochinvar is come out of the west;
Through all the wide border his steed was the best,
And save his good broadsword, he weapons had none;
He rode all unarmed, and he rode all alone.
So faithful in love, and so dauntless in war,                    5
There never was knight like the young Lochinvar.

He stayed not for brake, and he stopped not for stone,
He swam the Eske River where ford there was none;
But ere he alighted at Netherby gate
The bride had consented, the gallant came late:                  10
For a laggard in love and a dastard in war
Was to wed the fair Ellen of brave Lochinvar.

So boldly he entered the Netherby hall,
Among bridesmen and kinsmen and brothers and all;
Then spoke the bride's father, his hand on his sword            15
(For the poor craven bridegroom said never a word),
"O come ye in peace here, or come ye in war,
Or to dance at our bridal, young Lord Lochinvar?"

"I long wooed your daughter, my suit you denied;
Love swells like the Solway, but ebbs like its tide;           20
And now am I come, with this lost love of mine,
To lead but one measure, drink one cup of wine.
There are maidens in Scotland, more lovely by far,
That would gladly be bride to the young Lochinvar."

The bride kissed the goblet; the knight took it up,            25
He quaffed off the wine, and he threw down the cup.
She looked down to blush, and she looked up to sigh,

---

Lochinvar: pronounced lŏk′ ĭn-vär.    7. brake: very thick shrubbery.    8. ford: shallow place, for crossing.    10. gallant: suitor (Lochinvar).    11. laggard: slow, hesitant person; dastard: coward. 16. craven: cowardly.    20. Solway: inlet south of Scotland, noted for its high tides.    22. lead . . . measure: dance only one dance.

With a smile on her lips, and a tear in her eye.
He took her soft hand ere her mother could bar—
"Now tread we a measure!" said young Lochinvar.          30

So stately his form, and so lovely her face,
That never a hall such a galliard did grace;
While her mother did fret, and her father did fume,
And the bridegroom stood dangling his bonnet and plume,
And the bride-maidens whispered, "Twere better by far          35
To have matched our fair cousin with young Lochinvar."

One touch to her hand, and one word in her ear;
When they reached the hall door, and the charger stood near,
So light to the croup the fair lady he swung,
So light to the saddle before her he sprung!          40
"She is won! we are gone, over bank, bush, and scaur;
They'll have fleet steeds that follow," quoth young Lochinvar.

There was mounting 'mong Graemes of the Netherby clan;
Forsters, Fenwicks, and Musgraves, they rode and they ran:
There was racing and chasing on Cannobie Lee,          45
But the lost bride of Netherby ne'er did they see.
So daring in love, and so dauntless in war,
Have ye e'er heard of gallant like young Lochinvar?

32. *galliard* (găl'yərd): type of spirited dance.   39. *croup:* place behind the saddle.   41. *scaur* (skär): rock.

DISCUSSION

1. "Lochinvar" tells a story about a knight and the girl he loves. Where does the story take place? Who is Ellen? What happens at the end of the story?

2. When the bride and Lochinvar dance together, the people watching them react in different ways. How do the girl's parents react? What do the bridesmaids whisper? How do you suppose they feel about the way Lochinvar brings the dance to an end?

3. **Rhythm.** "Lochinvar" is the kind of poem that is made to be read aloud. The lines have a strong beat that you could tap out on your desk. This rhythmic sound carries the poem along. Why does the strong beat fit what this poem is about?

For further activities, see page 260.

In the spring of 1940 during the war with Germany, thousands of British and French troops were trapped on the coast near a town called Dunkirk. People sailed across the English channel in every kind of small boat and picked up and brought back more than 330,000 soldiers.

# DUNKIRK

ROBERT NATHAN

Will came back from school that day,
And he had little to say.
But he stood a long time looking down
To where the gray-green Channel water
Slapped at the foot of the little town,                          5

And to where his boat, the *Sarah P,*
Bobbed at the tide on an even keel,
With her one old sail, patched at the leech,
Furled like a slattern down at heel.

He stood for a while above the beach;                       10
He saw how the wind and current caught her;
He looked a long time out to sea.
There was steady wind—and the sky was pale—
And a haze in the east that looked like smoke.

Will went back to the house to dress.                        15
He was halfway through, when his sister Bess,
Who was near fourteen and younger than he
By just two years, came home from play.
She asked him, "Where are you going, Will?"
He said, "For a good long sail."                             20
"Can I come along?" "No, Bess," he spoke.
"I may be gone for a night and a day."
Bess looked at him. She kept very still.
She had heard the news of the Flanders rout,

8. *leech:* edge.    9. *slattern:* untidy woman.

How the English were trapped above Dun-
   kirk,                                                 25
And the fleet had gone to get them out—
But everyone thought that it wouldn't work.
There was too much fear, there was too much
   doubt.

She looked at him, and he looked at her.
They were English children, born and bred.      30
He frowned her down, but she wouldn't stir.
She shook her proud young head.
"You'll need a crew," she said.

They raised the sail on the *Sarah P*,
Like a penoncel on a young knight's lance,      35
And headed the *Sarah* out to sea,
To bring their soldiers home from France.

There was no command; there was no set plan,
But six hundred boats went out with them
On the gray-green waters, sailing fast—         40
River excursion and fisherman,
Tug and schooner and racing M—
And the little boats came following last.
From every harbor and town they went
Who had sailed their craft in the sun and
   rain,                                                45
From the South Downs, from the cliffs of Kent,
From the village street, from the country lane.
There are twenty miles of rolling sea
From coast to coast, by the seagull's flight,
But the tides were fair and the wind was
   free,                                                50
And they raised Dunkirk by the fall of night.

They raised Dunkirk, with its harbor torn
By the blasted stern and the sunken prow.
They had raced for fun on an English tide;
They were English children bred and born,       55

---

35. *penoncel* (pĕn'ən-sĕl): small, narrow flag.
42. *racing M:* class of sailboat.    51. *raised:* came
within sight of.

And whether they lived or whether they died,
They raced for England now.

Bess was as white as the *Sarah's* sail;
She set her teeth and smiled at Will.
He held his course for the smoky veil          60
Where the harbor narrowed thin and long.
The British ships were firing strong.

He took the *Sarah* into his hands;
He drove her in through fire and death
To the wet men waiting on the sands.           65
He got his load and he got his breath,
And she came about, and the wind fought her.

He shut his eyes and he tried to pray.
He saw his England where she lay,
The wind's green home, the sea's proud
      daughter,                                 70
Still in the moonlight, dreaming deep,
The English cliffs and the English loam—
He had fourteen men to get away,
And the moon was clear, and the night like day
For planes to see where the white sails
      creep                                     75
Over the black water.

He closed his eyes and he prayed for her,
For England's hope and for England's fate;
He prayed to the men who had made her great,
Who had built her land of forest and park,     80
Who had made the seas an English lake;
He prayed for a fog to bring the dark;
He prayed to get home for England's sake.
And the fog came down on the rolling sea
And covered the ships with English mist,       85
And diving planes were baffled and blind.

For Nelson was there in the *Victory*,
With his one good eye and his sullen twist,

87. *Nelson:* famous British admiral, of the late 1700s.

And guns were out on the *Golden Hind,*
Their shot flashed over the *Sarah P.*                    90
He could hear them cheer as he came about.

By burning wharves, by battered slips—
Galleon, frigate, and brigantine—
The old dead captains fought their ships,
And the great dead admirals led the line.         95
It was England's night, it was England's sea.

The fog rolled over the harbor key.
Bess held to the stays and conned him out.

And all through the dark, while the *Sarah's* wake
Hissed behind him and vanished in foam,            100
There at his side sat Francis Drake,
And held him true, and steered him home.

89. *guns were out:* guns were in position to fire (to
provide protection for the English ships);     *Golden
Hind:* ship of Sir Francis Drake, naval hero of the late
1500s.     94. *fought . . . ships:* had combat with the
enemy.     98. *stays:* ropes supporting the mast;
*conned him out:* directed his steering.

## DISCUSSION

1. Why does Will want fog? What gives the brother
and sister the courage to make this dangerous trip?

2. This poem is based on an actual historical event.
Find out the details of this World War II battle. Does
this poem help you "experience" what happened at
Dunkirk better than reading a description of the
event? Explain.

For further activities, see page 261.

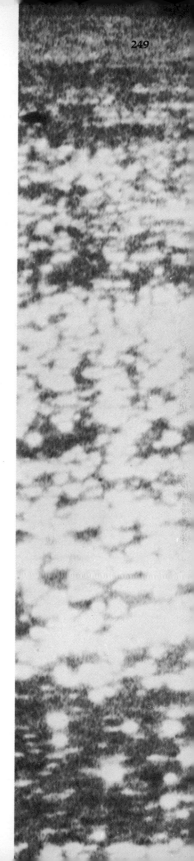

Harriet Tubman was a slave on a plantation in Maryland.

# A Glory over Everything

ANN PETRY

One day, in 1849, when Harriet was working in the fields, near the edge of the road, a white woman wearing a faded sunbonnet went past, driving a wagon. She stopped the wagon, and watched Harriet for a few minutes. Then she spoke to her, asked her what her name was, and how she had acquired the deep scar on her forehead.

Harriet told her the story of the blow she had received when she was a girl.[1] After that, whenever the woman saw her in the fields, she stopped to talk to her. She told Harriet that she lived on a farm, near Bucktown. Then one day she said, not looking at Harriet, but looking instead at the overseer, far off at the edge of the fields, "If you ever need any help, Harriet, ever need any help, why you let me know."

That same year the young heir to the Brodas estate died. Harriet mentioned the fact of his death to the white woman in the faded sunbonnet, the next time she saw her. She told her of the panic-stricken talk in the quarter,[2] told her that the slaves were afraid that the master, Dr. Thompson, would start selling them. She said that Doc Thompson no longer permitted any of them to hire their time.[3] The woman nodded her head, clucked to the horse, and drove off, murmuring, "If you ever need any help—"

The slaves were right about Dr. Thompson's intention. He began selling slaves almost immediately. Among the first ones sold were two of Harriet Tubman's sisters. They went South with the chain gang on a Saturday.

When Harriet heard of the sale of her sisters, she knew that the time had finally come when she must leave the plantation.

---

[1] blow . . . girl: a head injury, that caused her to fall asleep at inconvenient times.
[2] *quarter:* area where slaves lived.
[3] *hire their time:* earn money on their own.

She was reluctant to attempt the long trip North alone, not because of John Tubman's[4] threat to betray her, but because she was afraid she might fall asleep somewhere along the way and so would be caught immediately.

She persuaded three of her brothers to go with her. Having made certain that John was asleep, she left the cabin quietly, and met her brothers at the edge of the plantation. They agreed that she was to lead the way, for she was more familiar with the woods than the others.

The three men followed her, crashing through the underbrush, frightening themselves, stopping constantly to say, "What was that?" or "Someone's coming."

She thought of Ben[5] and how he had said, "Any old body can go through a woods crashing and mashing things down like a cow." She said sharply, "Can't you boys go quieter? Watch where you're going!"

One of them grumbled, "Can't see in the dark. Ain't got cat's eyes like you."

"You don't need cat's eyes," she retorted. "On a night like this, with all the stars out, it's not black dark. Use your own eyes."

She supposed they were doing the best they could but they moved very slowly. She kept getting so far ahead of them that she had to stop and wait for them to catch up with her, lest they lose their way. Their progress was slow, uncertain. Their feet got tangled in every vine. They tripped over fallen logs, and once one of them fell flat on his face. They jumped, startled, at the most ordinary sounds: the murmur of the wind in the branches of the trees, the twittering of a bird. They kept turning around, looking back.

They had not gone more than a mile when she became aware that they had stopped. She turned and went back to them. She could hear them whispering. One of them called out, "Halt!"

"What's the matter? We haven't got time to keep stopping like this."

"We're going back."

---

[4] *John Tubman:* Harriet's husband.
[5] *Ben:* Harriet's father.

"No," she said firmly. "We've got a good start. If we move fast and move quiet—"

Then all three spoke at once. They said the same thing, over and over, in frantic hurried whispers, all talking at once:

They told her that they had changed their minds. Running away was too dangerous. Someone would surely see them and recognize them. By morning the master would know they had "took off." Then the handbills advertising them would be posted all over Dorchester County. The patterollers[6] would search for them. Even if they were lucky enough to elude the patrol, they could not possibly hide from the bloodhounds. The hounds would be baying after them, snuffing through the swamps and the underbrush, zigzagging through the deepest woods. The bloodhounds would surely find them. And everyone knew what happened to a runaway who was caught and brought back alive.

She argued with them. Didn't they know that if they went back they would be sold, if not tomorrow, then the next day, or the next? Sold South. They had seen the chain gangs. Was that what they wanted? Were they going to be slaves for the rest of their lives? Didn't freedom mean anything to them?

"You're afraid," she said, trying to shame them into action. "Go on back. I'm going North alone."

Instead of being ashamed, they became angry. They shouted at her, telling her that she was a fool and they would make her go back to the plantation with them. Suddenly they surrounded her, three men, her own brothers, jostling her, pushing her along, pinioning her arms behind her. She fought against them, wasting her strength, exhausting herself in a furious struggle.

She was no match for three strong men. She said, panting, "All right. We'll go back. I'll go with you."

She led the way, moving slowly. Her thoughts were bitter. Not one of them was willing to take a small risk in order to be free. It had all seemed so perfect, so simple, to have her brothers go with her, sharing the dangers of the trip together, just as a family should. Now if she ever went North, she would have to go alone.

---

[6] *patterollers:* slave catchers.

Two days later, a slave working beside Harriet in the fields motioned to her. She bent toward him, listening. He said the water boy had just brought news to the field hands, and it had been passed from one to the other until it reached him. The news was that Harriet and her brothers had been sold to the Georgia trader, and that they were to be sent South with the chain gang that very night.

Harriet went on working but she knew a moment of panic. She would have to go North alone. She would have to start as soon as it was dark. She could not go with the chain gang. She might die on the way, because of those inexplicable sleeping seizures. But then she—how could she run away? She might fall asleep in plain view along the road.

But even if she fell asleep, she thought, the Lord would take care of her. She murmured a prayer, "Lord, I'm going to hold steady on to You and You've got to see me through."

Afterward, she explained her decision to run the risk of going North alone, in these words: "I had reasoned this out in my mind; there was one of two things I had a *right* to, liberty or death; if I could not have one, I would have the other; for no man should take me alive; I should fight for my liberty as long as my strength lasted, and when the time came for me to go, the Lord would let them take me."

At dusk, when the work in the fields was over, she started toward the Big House. She had to let someone know that she was going North, someone she could trust. She no longer trusted John Tubman and it gave her a lost, lonesome feeling. Her sister Mary worked in the Big House, and she planned to tell Mary that she was going to run away, so someone would know.

As she went toward the house, she saw the master, Doc Thompson, riding up the drive on his horse. She turned aside and went toward the quarter. A field hand had no legitimate reason for entering the kitchen of the Big House—and yet— there must be some way she could leave word so that afterward someone would think about it and know that she had left a message.

As she went toward the quarter she began to sing. Dr. Thompson reined in his horse, turned around and looked at her. It was not the beauty of her voice that made him turn and watch her, frowning, it was the words of the song that she was singing, and something defiant in her manner, that disturbed and puzzled him.

*When that old chariot comes,*
  *I'm going to leave you,*
*I'm bound for the promised land,*
  *Friends, I'm going to leave you.*

*I'm sorry, friends, to leave you,*
  *Farewell! Oh, farewell!*

*I'll meet you in the morning,*
  *When I reach the promised land;*
*On the other side of Jordan,*
  *For I'm bound for the promised land.*

That night when John Tubman was asleep, and the fire had died down in the cabin, she took the ashcake that had been baked for their breakfast, and a good-sized piece of salt herring, and tied them together in an old bandanna. By hoarding this small stock of food, she could make it last a long time, and with the berries and edible roots she could find in the woods, she wouldn't starve.

She decided that she would take the quilt with her, too. Her hands lingered over it. It felt soft and warm to her touch. Even in the dark, she thought she could tell one color from another, because she knew its pattern and design so well.

Then John stirred in his sleep, and she left the cabin quickly, carrying the quilt carefully folded under her arm.

Once she was off the plantation, she took to the woods, not following the North Star, not even looking for it, going instead toward Bucktown. She needed help. She was going to ask the white woman who had stopped to talk to her so often if she would help her. Perhaps she wouldn't. But she would soon find out.

When she came to the farmhouse where the woman lived, she approached it cautiously, circling around it. It was so quiet. There was no sound at all, not even a dog barking, or the sound of voices. Nothing.

She tapped on the door, gently. A voice said, "Who's there?" She answered, "Harriet, from Dr. Thompson's place."

When the woman opened the door she did not seem at all surprised to see her. She glanced at the little bundle that Harriet was carrying, at the quilt, and invited her in. Then she sat down at the kitchen table, and wrote two names on a slip of paper, and handed the paper to Harriet.

She said that those were the next places where it was safe for Harriet to stop. The first place was a farm where there was a gate with big white posts and round knobs on top of them. The people there would feed her, and when they thought it was safe for her to go on, they would tell her how to get to the next house, or take her there. For these were the first two stops on the Underground Railroad—going North, from the Eastern Shore of Maryland.

Thus Harriet learned that the Underground Railroad that ran straight to the North was not a railroad at all. Neither did it run underground. It was composed of a loosely organized group of people who offered food and shelter, or a place of concealment, to fugitives who had set out on the long road to the North and freedom.

Harriet wanted to pay this woman who had befriended her. But she had no money. She gave her the patchwork quilt, the only beautiful object she had ever owned.

That night she made her way through the woods, crouching in the underbrush whenever she heard the sound of horses' hoofs, staying there until the riders passed. Each time she wondered if they were already hunting for her. It would be so easy to describe her, the deep scar on her forehead like a dent, the old scars on the back of her neck, the husky speaking voice, the lack of height, scarcely five feet tall. The master would say she was wearing rough clothes when she ran away, that she had a bandanna on her head, that she was muscular and strong.

She knew how accurately he would describe her. One of the slaves who could read used to tell the others what it said on those handbills that were nailed up on the trees, along the edge of the roads. It was easy to recognize the handbills that advertised runaways, because there was always a picture in one corner, a picture of a black man, a little running figure with a stick over his shoulder, and a bundle tied on the end of the stick.

Whenever she thought of the handbills, she walked faster. Sometimes she stumbled over old grapevines, gnarled and twisted, thick as a man's wrist, or became entangled in the rough, sinewy vine of the honeysuckle. But she kept going.

In the morning, she came to the house where her friend had said she was to stop. She showed the slip of paper that she carried to the woman who answered her knock at the back door of the farmhouse. The woman fed her, and then handed her a broom and told her to sweep the yard.

Harriet hesitated, suddenly suspicious. Then she decided that with a broom in her hand, working in the yard, she would look as though she belonged on the place, certainly no one would suspect that she was a runaway.

That night the woman's husband, a farmer, loaded a wagon with produce. Harriet climbed in. He threw some blankets over her, and the wagon started.

It was dark under the blankets, and not exactly comfortable. But Harriet decided that riding was better than walking. She was surprised at her own lack of fear, wondered how it was that she so readily trusted these strangers who might betray her. For all she knew, the man driving the wagon might be taking her straight back to the master.

She thought of those other rides in wagons, when she was a child, the same clop-clop of the horses' feet, creak of the wagon, and the feeling of being lost because she did not know where she was going. She did not know her destination this time either, but she was not alarmed. She thought of John Tubman. By this time he must have told the master that she was gone. Then she thought of the plantation and how the land rolled gently down toward the river, thought of Ben and Old Rit, and that Old Rit would be inconsolable because her favorite daughter was missing. "Lord," she prayed, "I'm going to hold steady onto You. You've got to see me through." Then she went to sleep.

The next morning when the stars were still visible in the sky, the farmer stopped the wagon. Harriet was instantly awake.

He told her to follow the river, to keep following it to reach the next place where people would take her in and feed her. He said that she must travel only at night, and she must stay off the roads because the patrol would be hunting for her. Harriet climbed out of the wagon. "Thank you," she said simply, thinking how amazing it was that there should be white people who were willing to go to such lengths to help a slave get to the North.

When she finally arrived in Pennsylvania, she had traveled roughly ninety miles from Dorchester County. She had slept on the ground outdoors at night. She had been rowed for miles up the Choptank River by a man she had never seen before. She had been concealed in a haycock, and had, at one point, spent a week hidden in a potato hole in a cabin which belonged to a family of free Negroes. She had been hidden in the attic of the home of a Quaker. She had been befriended by stout German farmers, whose guttural speech surprised her and whose well-kept farms astonished her. She had never before seen barns and fences, farmhouses and outbuildings, so carefully painted. The cattle and horses were so clean they looked as though they had been scrubbed.

When she crossed the line into the free state of Pennsylvania, the sun was coming up. She said, "I looked at my hands to see if I was the same person now I was free. There was such a glory over everything, the sun came like gold through the trees, and over the fields, and I felt like I was in heaven."

DISCUSSION

1. The first thing Harriet did when she realized she was free was to look at her own hands. Explain in your own words why she did this.

2. One of the ways the slaves communicated with each other was by singing. Sometimes they added people's names, to make the message even clearer. What was Harriet's message when she sang "When that old chariot comes"?

3. Harriet did not stay in Pennsylvania. She went back to the South eighteen or nineteen times and helped hundreds of slaves to escape. If they tried to turn back, as her brothers had, Harriet pulled a pistol on them and said, "You *will* go on—or you'll die." If you would like to read about some of her narrow escapes, read the book this story is taken from *Harriet Tubman*—or the shorter piece, "Harriet Tubman: The Moses of Her People," in *Famous American Negroes*, by Langston Hughes.

For further activities, see page 261.

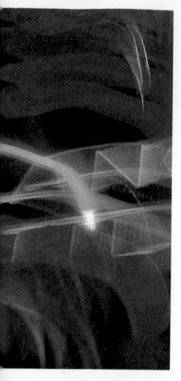

FOCUS

## VOCABULARY

### Paul Revere's Ride (page 239)

On separate paper, match the letter of the definition in the right column with the number of the word in the left column.

1. belfry        a. ghostly-looking
2. muffled       b. deadened
3. tranquil      c. bell tower
4. spectral      d. quiet
5. stealthy      e. unwieldy ship
6. hulk          f. calm

### Lochinvar (page 244)

The three words in the left column have two correct definitions. Select the letter of the definition which best defines the word as used in the poem.

1. brake     a. thick shrubbery
             b. way to stop motion
2. croup     a. childhood illness
             b. place behind the saddle
3. gallant   a. suitor
             b. stately

## COMPOSITION

### Flight into Danger (page 196)

Write a character sketch of at least two of the following characters: (a) Dr. Frank Baird   (b) the Stewardess   (c) George Spencer   (d) Captain Treleaven

### Interview with a Crow Chief (page 230)

As a young boy, Plenty-coups proved his speed, his grace, his strength, and his bravery. Imagine that you are Plenty-coups as a youngster. Write how you might feel and what you might do when you faced the bull for the first time.

## Dunkirk (page 246)

The poem is written from the point of view of young Bess and Will. Suppose you had been one of the soldiers stranded at Dunkirk and you were rescued by Bess and Will. Tell the story from your point of view, in the form of a letter to a friend.


## READING

### Dunkirk (page 246)

Select those items you think the poet is using to show that he admires and respects the boy's actions.

1. The boy and his sister rescue fourteen men from certain death.
2. Great war heroes from the past are mentioned frequently.
3. The boy wept with fear when he got close to the beach.
4. England was fighting an unjust war.
5. Many other Englishmen not in military service made similar trips.

### A Glory over Everything (page 251)

Indicate on separate paper which of the following statements are true and which are false. Correct the false statements.

1. We know how Harriet felt during her escape.
2. Harriet's preparations for leaving the plantation are carefully described.
3. We find out what happened to her brothers after she left.
4. We know the people who Harriet stayed with on the Underground Railroad very well.
5. We know how Harriet felt when she found out that she was "sold South."

# COMPOSITION

You are reading a sentence. Some sentences are short. Others, like this one, are longer, because they have several related ideas to express through different, related parts. The short sentence above has four words in it. The longer one has eighteen. But, long or short, every sentence contains at least one subject and one verb: a subject that tells what the sentence is about, and a verb that tells what the subject is or does.

We may have a lot of subjects and only one verb:

The Graemes and the Forsters and the Fenwicks and the Musgraves rode after Lochinvar.

Or we may have a single subject and several verbs:

The basketball lands, leans, wobbles, wavers, hesitates, then falls.

Some sentences are general:

There's nothing prettier in the world than a good bird dog.

Some are specific, about one dog, one moment:

In the midst of the thundering blast I heard Calypso Baby yell with pain as the random shot tore into her hip.

Some sentences exclaim:

Don't come back here!

Others state:

I stretched out my hand, as I supposed, to my mother.

Most sentences put the subject before the verb:

She persuaded three of her brothers to go with her.

Others put the verb before the subject:

Among the first slaves sold were two of Harriet's sisters.

In short, sentences can be written in many different ways. Make use of those differences. Avoid choppy writing like this:

I stopped walking. The bull was puzzled. He stopped too. We looked at each other. I felt the sun on my back. It was hot. The bull looked hot.

Instead, vary your sentences:

I stopped walking and stood still. This seemed to puzzle the bull, and he too stopped in his tracks. We looked at each other, the sun hot on my naked back. Heat from the plains danced on the bull's horns and head.

But whatever kind of sentences you write, the most important point to remember is this—make sure that each one of them is clear.

## ABOUT THE SELECTIONS

1. What single moment in these selections seems to have called for the most courage to live through? Was it when Spencer started to land the DC-4 at Vancouver in "Flight into Danger"? Was it when Tom in "The Christmas Hunt" admitted to his father that he had shot their favorite bird dog? Write a paragraph explaining specifically why the moment you chose demanded the most courage.

2. Do you think Helen Keller and her teacher Anne Sullivan show courage in "The Most Important Day"? Why, or why not? Is Mary courageous in "The Day the Sun Came Out"? Write a paragraph defining courage, using examples from these selections to make your definition clear.

3. Many of these selections present some kind of crisis—a plane with no pilot, the rescue of over 330,000 soldiers trapped at Dunkirk, foreign troops attacking your country. Which of the crises in this unit would you have found most challenging to live through? Imagine what you might have done, specifically, if you had been living through that crisis. Write a description of the situation and your reactions.

4. Several selections in this unit describe a sport: hunting, hockey, track, basketball, baseball. Pick the selection that you think describes the feel of the sport most vividly. In a paragraph examine some of the words the author has chosen to describe the sport. Why do these words work well? What are some other words that might describe the sport? Can you think of more effective words? Explain.

## ON YOUR OWN

1. Rewrite the following paragraph to make the sentences more interesting.

It was the middle of the morning. It was cold and bright. A girl jumped off the bus. She was fourteen. The bus was in front of the old people's home. The home was on the outskirts of town. The girl wore a red coat. She had straight yellow hair. Her hair hung down loose. She had a red beret on her head. All the girls wore that kind of hat that year.

Compare your rewriting with what others in the class have written. Which revised paragraph seems most effective?

2. Several selections in this section describe journeys—on an airliner, on a horse, in a boat. Briefly describe a journey you have taken by car, bus, motorcycle, diving gear, or any other means. Try to find just the right words to give us the feel of the experience. How did it look, smell, sound?

3. Who is the most courageous person you have known? (The bravery of that person may have been simply the courage to admit a mistake.) Describe the person you have chosen in a way that lets your reader come to admire that person too.

4. Describe a specific action that you have experienced: riding a bicycle in rain, climbing along a cliff or over the roof of a building, hiding from someone. Try to vary your sentences as you write, and choose words that let the reader feel what you were feeling at that time.

# CONFLICTS

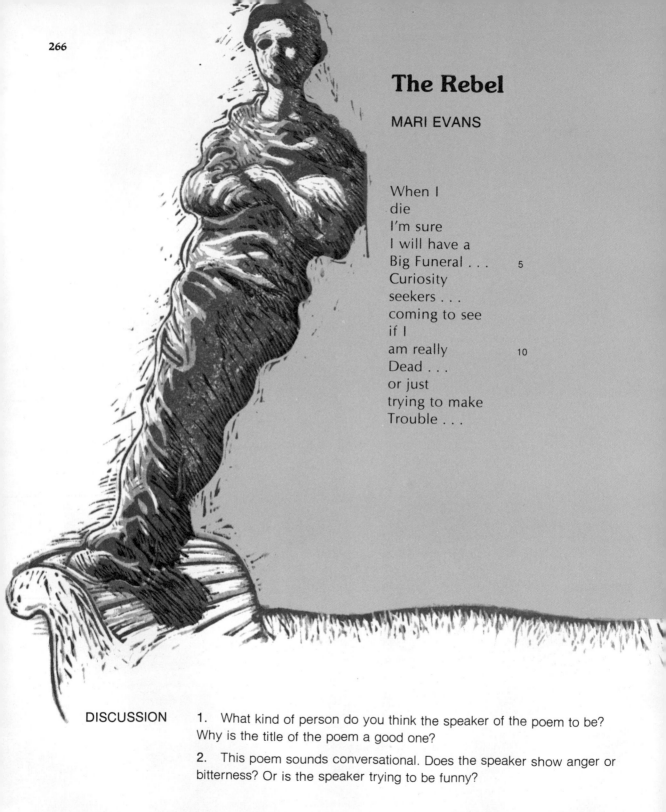

# The Rebel

MARI EVANS

When I
die
I'm sure
I will have a
Big Funeral . . .        5
Curiosity
seekers . . .
coming to see
if I
am really        10
Dead . . .
or just
trying to make
Trouble . . .

DISCUSSION

1. What kind of person do you think the speaker of the poem to be? Why is the title of the poem a good one?

2. This poem sounds conversational. Does the speaker show anger or bitterness? Or is the speaker trying to be funny?

The day my son Laurie started kindergarten he renounced corduroy overalls with bibs and began wearing blue jeans with a belt; I watched him go off the first morning with the older girl next door, seeing clearly that an era of my life was ended, my sweet-voiced nursery-school tot replaced by a long-trousered, swaggering character who forgot to stop at the corner and wave good-bye to me.

# CHARLES

## SHIRLEY JACKSON

He came home the same way, the front door slamming open, his cap on the floor, and the voice suddenly become raucous, shouting, "Isn't anybody *here?*"

At lunch he spoke insolently to his father, spilled his baby sister's milk, and remarked that his teacher said we were not to take the name of the Lord in vain.

"How *was* school today?" I asked, elaborately casual.

"All right," he said.

"Did you learn anything?" his father asked.

Laurie regarded his father coldly. "I didn't learn nothing," he said.

"Anything," I said. "Didn't learn anything."

"The teacher spanked a boy, though," Laurie said, addressing his bread and butter. "For being fresh," he added, with his mouth full.

"What did he do?" I asked. "Who was it?"

Laurie thought. "It was Charles," he said. "He was fresh. The teacher spanked him and made him stand in a corner. He was awfully fresh."

"What did he do?" I asked again, but Laurie slid off his chair, took a cookie, and left, while his father was still saying, "See here, young man."

The next day Laurie remarked at lunch, as soon as he sat down, "Well, Charles was bad again today." He grinned enormously and said, "Today Charles hit the teacher."

"Good heavens," I said, mindful of the Lord's name, "I suppose he got spanked again?"

"He sure did," Laurie said. "Look up," he said to his father.

"What?" his father said, looking up.

"Look down," Laurie said. "Look at my thumb. Gee, you're dumb." He began to laugh insanely.

"Why did Charles hit the teacher?" I asked quickly.

"Because she tried to make him color with red crayons," Laurie said. "Charles wanted to color with green crayons so he hit the teacher and she spanked him and said nobody play with Charles but everybody did."

The third day—it was Wednesday of the first week—Charles bounced a see-saw onto the head of a little girl and made her bleed, and the teacher made him stay inside all during recess. Thursday Charles had to stand in a corner during story time because he kept pounding his feet on the floor. Friday Charles was deprived of blackboard privileges because he threw chalk.

On Saturday I remarked to my husband, "Do you think kindergarten is too unsettling for Laurie? All this toughness, and bad grammar, and this Charles boy sounds like such a bad influence."

"It'll be all right," my husband said reasuringly. "Bound to be people like Charles in the world. Might as well meet them now as later."

On Monday Laurie came home late, full of news. "Charles," he shouted as he came up the hill; I was waiting anxiously on the front steps. "Charles," Laurie yelled all the way up the hill, "Charles was bad again."

"Come right in," I said, as soon as he came close enough. "Lunch is waiting."

"You know what Charles did?" he demanded, following me through the door. "Charles yelled so in school they sent a boy in from first grade to tell the teacher she had to make Charles keep quiet, and so Charles had to stay after school. And so all the children stayed to watch him."

"What did he do?" I asked.

"He just sat there," Laurie said, climbing into his chair at the table. "Hi, Pop, y'old dust mop."

"Charles had to stay after school today," I told my husband. "Everybody stayed with him."

"What does this Charles look like?" my husband asked Laurie. "What's his other name?"

"He's bigger than me," Laurie said. "And he doesn't have any rubbers and he doesn't ever wear a jacket."

Monday night was the first Parent-Teachers meeting, and only the fact that the baby had a cold kept me from going; I wanted passionately to meet Charles's mother. On Tuesday Laurie remarked suddenly, "Our teacher had a friend come to see her in school today."

"Charles's mother?" my husband and I asked simultaneously.

"Naah," Laurie said scornfully. "It was a man who came and made us do exercises; we had to touch our toes. Look." He climbed down from his chair and squatted down and touched his toes. "Like this," he said. He got solemnly back into his chair and said, picking up his fork, "Charles didn't even *do* exercises."

"That's fine," I said heartily. "Didn't Charles want to do exercises?"

"Naaah," Laurie said. "Charles was so fresh to the teacher's friend he wasn't *let* do exercises."

"Fresh again?" I said.

"He kicked the teacher's friend," Laurie

said. "The teacher's friend told Charles to touch his toes like I just did and Charles kicked him."

"What are they going to do about Charles, do you suppose?" Laurie's father asked him.

Laurie shrugged elaborately. "Throw him out of school, I guess," he said.

Wednesday and Thursday were routine; Charles yelled during story hour and hit a boy in the stomach and made him cry. On Friday Charles stayed after school again and so did all the other children.

With the third week of kindergarten Charles was an institution in our family—the baby was being a Charles when she cried all afternoon; Laurie did a Charles when he filled his wagon full of mud and pulled it through the kitchen; even my husband, when he caught his elbow in the telephone cord and pulled telephone, ashtray, and a bowl of flowers off the table, said, after the first minute, "Looks like Charles."

During the third and fourth weeks it looked like a reformation in Charles; Laurie reported grimly at lunch on Thursday of the third week, "Charles was so good today the teacher gave him an apple."

"What?" I said, and my husband added warily, "You mean Charles?"

"Charles," Laurie said. "He gave the crayons around and he picked up the books afterward and the teacher said he was her helper."

"What happened?" I asked incredulously.

"He was her helper, that's all," Laurie said, and shrugged.

"Can this be true, about Charles?" I asked my husband that night. "Can something like this happen?"

"Wait and see," my husband said cynically. "When you've got a Charles to deal with, this may mean he's only plotting."

He seemed to be wrong. For over a week Charles was the teacher's helper; each day he handed things out and he picked things up; no one had to stay after school.

"The P.T.A. meeting's next week again," I told my husband one evening. "I'm going to find Charles's mother there."

"Ask her what happened to Charles," my husband said. "I'd like to know."

"I'd like to know myself," I said.

On Friday of that week things were back to normal. "You know what Charles did today?" Laurie demanded at the lunch table, in a voice slightly awed. "He told a little girl to say a word and she said it and the teacher washed her mouth out with soap and Charles laughed."

"What word?" his father asked unwisely, and Laurie said, "I'll have to whisper it to you, it's so bad." He got down off his chair and went around to his father. His father bent his head down and Laurie whispered joyfully. His father's eyes widened.

"Did Charles tell the little girl to say *that?*" he asked respectfully.

"She said it *twice*," Laurie said: "Charles told her to say it *twice*."

"What happened to Charles?" my husband asked.

"Nothing," Laurie said. "He was passing out the crayons."

Monday morning Charles abandoned the little girl and said the evil word himself three or four times, getting his mouth washed out with soap each time. He also threw chalk.

My husband came to the door with me that evening as I set out for the P.T.A. meeting. "Invite her over for a cup of tea after the meeting," he said. "I want to get a look at her."

"If only she's there," I said prayerfully.

"She'll be there," my husband said. "I don't see how they could hold a P.T.A. meeting without Charles's mother."

At the meeting I sat restlessly, scanning each comfortable matronly face, trying to determine which one hid the secret of Charles. None of them looked to me haggard enough. No one stood up in the meeting and apologized for the way her son had been acting. No one mentioned Charles.

After the meeting I identified and sought out Laurie's kindergarten teacher. She had a plate with a cup of tea and a piece of chocolate cake; I had a plate with a cup of tea and a piece of marshmallow cake. We maneuvered up to one another cautiously, and smiled.

"I've been so anxious to meet you," I said. "I'm Laurie's mother."

"We're all so interested in Laurie," she said.

"Well, he certainly likes kindergarten," I said. "He talks about it all the time."

"We had a little trouble adjusting, the first week or so," she said primly, "but now he's a fine little helper. With occasional lapses, of course."

"Laurie usually adjusts very quickly," I said. "I suppose this time it's Charles's influence."

"Charles?"

"Yes," I said laughing, "you must have your hands full in that kindergarten, with Charles."

"Charles?" she said. "We don't have any Charles in the kindergarten."

DISCUSSION

1. Laurie and Charles are the same little boy. Why does Laurie invent Charles? What do you think his parents' reactions would have been if Laurie had told them that he was actually doing the things he said Charles did?

2. The mother in the beginning of the story describes Laurie as "my sweet-voiced nursery-school tot" (page 267). How do you see Laurie? What things does Laurie do at home that remind you of Charles?

3. **Characterization.**   The way a writer helps you to see and know the characters in a story is called characterization. One way writers show how a character feels is by expressing the tone of voice that is used in conversation. Another is to describe the character's actions. For example, on page 267 Laurie comes home "slamming open" the door, throwing his cap on the floor and shouting in a "raucous" voice. He is feeling reckless and a little wild.

In the story there are other clues to help you know what the character is feeling. When Laurie "grinned enormously" (p. 268), how is he feeling? When the mother wanted "passionately" (p. 269) to meet Charles's mother, how was she feeling?

4. The end of the story may surprise you. What clues did the author give that **foreshadowed** (see page 229) the ending?

For further activities, see page 308.

# MY SISTER JANE

## TED HUGHES

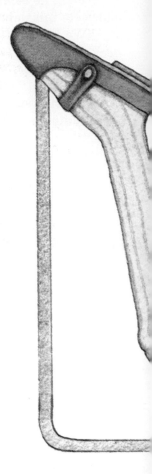

And I say nothing—no, not a word
About our Jane. Haven't you heard
She's a bird, a bird, a bird, a bird.
Oh it never would do to let folks know
My sister's nothing but a great big crow.                    5


Each day (we daren't send her to school)
She pulls on stockings of thick blue wool
To make her pin crow legs look right,
Then fits a wig of curls on tight,
And dark spectacles—a huge pair                              10
To cover her very crowy stare.
Oh it never would do to let folks know
My sister's nothing but a great big crow.


When visitors come she sits upright
(With her wings and her tail tucked out of sight.)           15
They think her queer but extremely polite.
Then when the visitors have gone
She whips out her wings and with her wig on
Whirls through the house at the height of your head—
Duck, duck, or she'll knock you dead.                        20
Oh it never would do to let folks know
My sister's nothing but a great big crow.


At meals whatever she sees she'll stab it—
Because she's a crow and that's a crow habit.
My mother says, 'Jane! Your manners! Please!'               25
Then she'll sit quietly on the cheese,
Or play the piano nicely by dancing on the keys—
Oh it never would do to let folks know
My sister's nothing but a great big crow.

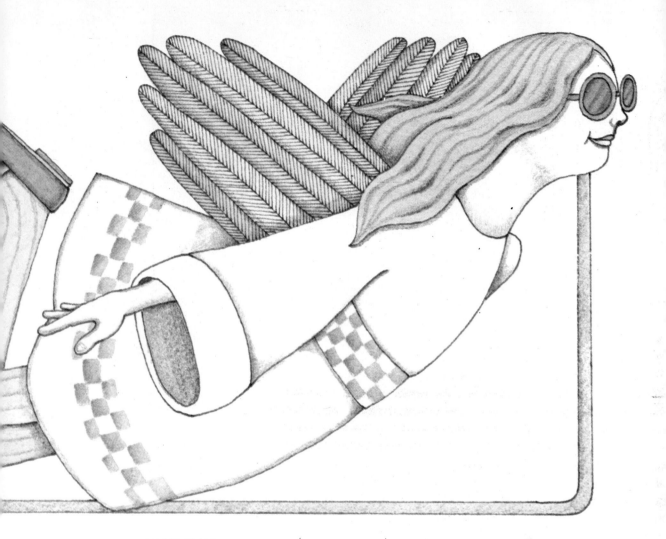

**DISCUSSION**

1. Who is the person describing Jane as "nothing but a great big crow" (line 5)? What does Jane do that makes her like a crow to the person describing her in the poem?

2. Crows, as birds, are not particularly well liked. Does the person in this poem like or dislike Jane? Why do you think so?

3. Poetry often relies on repeating certain words or sounds for its effect. What is repeated in this poem? How many times? What effect does it have on you as you read?

For further activities, see page 308.

# IRONMAN GREGORY

## DICK GREGORY

"You run before?"

"Sure, coach, I do a lot of running."

"Where?"

"Around the neighborhood."

He shook his head. "We've given out all the lockers and uniforms for this year."

"All I want to do is take a shower in the afternoon."

He looked me over and kind of smiled. "All right. But you'll have to bring your own sweat suit. And stay off the track and out of my boys' way."

That's how I started in sports. Sumner had a fine athletic field. While the team ran inside the field, around the track, I ran outside, around a city block.

Every day when school let out at three o'clock, I'd get into an old pair of sneakers and a T-shirt and gym shorts and run around that block. In the beginning, I'd just run for an hour, then go and take a hot shower. And then one day two girls walked by and one of them said: "What's he think he's doing?" And the other one said: "Oh, he must be training for the big races." I just kept running that day, around and around the block, until every time I hit the pavement pain shot up my leg and a needle went into my side, and I kept going around and around until I was numb and I didn't feel anything any more. Suddenly, it was dark and the track team had all left. I could hardly walk home my feet hurt so much, but I couldn't wait until the next day to get out there again. Maybe I couldn't run as fast as the other guys, but I could run longer, longer than anybody in all of the city of St. Louis. And then everybody would know who I was.

I kept running all that fall and all that winter, sometimes through the snow, until everybody in school knew who I was, the guy who never took a rest from three o'clock until six o'clock. I don't think I ever would have finished high school without running. It was something that kept me going from day to day, a reason to get up in the morning, to sit through classes with the Helene Tuckers and the doctors' sons who knew all the answers and read books at home, to look forward to going a little faster and a little longer at three o'clock. And I felt so good when I ran, all by myself like a room of my own. I could think anything I wanted while I ran and talked to myself and sometimes I'd write stories on "My Favorite Daddy" and "What I'd Buy with a Million Dollars," and I could figure out why people did certain things and why certain things happened. Nobody would point to me and say I was poor or crazy; they'd just look at me with admiration and say: "He's training." I never got hungry while I was running even though we never ate breakfast at home and I didn't always have money for lunch. I never was cold or hot or ashamed of my clothes. I was proud of my body that kept going around and around and never had to take a rest.

After six o'clock I'd go to White's Eat Shop and wash dishes in return for dinner. Sometimes I'd go downtown and sneak into a white hotel and put on a busboy's uniform and get a good meal in the kitchen. The Man never knew the difference. And then I'd go home and go to sleep because I was tired and I needed a rest. I'd be running again tomorrow.

When spring came, the coach called me over one day and asked me if I'd like to run on the track. I ran against the guys on the team, and they were still faster than me, but I could keep going long after they were pooped out. Every so often the coach would walk by and tell me I was holding my arms wrong, or that my body was at the wrong angle, or my knees weren't coming up high enough. But I was on the inside now and I was getting a little faster every day. By the time school closed in June I was beating the boys on the track team. The coach told me to report for track first thing in September. There would be a locker for me and a uniform.

That summer was the roughest I ever spent. The Korean War was on, and good jobs were opening up at ammunition plants. I lied four years, told them I was twenty-one, and went to work for a company manufacturing 105-millimeter howitzer shells. The unfinished shells weighed forty-five pounds each, and I had to pick up 243 every twenty minutes. I always had stomach trouble, never could wear a belt, and every time I bent over and picked up a shell my insides tore a little. But with overtime I could pull down as much as $200 some weeks. When the other workers found out how old I was, there was a lot of resentment. They'd slip up behind me with crowbars and shove the casings down the belt faster than I could pick them up. I'd be so tired when I came home it was a real effort to get out and practice my running.

Then they put me on the night shift, eleven o'clock to seven in the morning. Now I did my running in the mornings after work, when the other folks were just going to their jobs. I kind of liked that, but it hurt not being able to be with Boo and my friends in the evening.

And then the foreman told another boss to put me down in the furnace pit. Well, the system wasn't going to beat me. I stood up next to that furnace, and I ate their salt tablets and just refused to pass out. They weren't going to make me quit, and I wasn't going to give them cause to fire me. I'd lean into that blazing pit until my face would sting, and when the lunch whistle blew I'd fall on the floor and vomit and I'd clean it up myself.

It was all worth it. I could walk home at the end of the week and put money in Momma's hand. We could go shopping with cash instead of the green tablet; we could walk into a supermarket instead of Mister Ben's. I could stand at the checkout counter and listen to the cash register and my heart didn't jump with every ring. Momma could pay some back bills and buy some new secondhand furniture and some clothes, and not have to go to the white folks' every day. We had a little money around the house now.

I kept my job when school started. The band had a special music class at eight o'clock in the morning, one hour before regular classes started, and I worked out a deal with the bandmaster, Mr. Wilson, to let me take it. That way I could come to school right from the plant, and finish up classes and track practice early enough to grab a few hours' sleep before leaving for the eleven o'clock shift. In return, I cleaned up the band room every morning, set the music out on the stands for the musicians, and kept out of their way. I liked sitting on the side and watching the band play, everybody working together to make a good sound, the bandmaster, a real sophisticated conductor with his baton, telling everybody when to come in, when to stop. I started watching the drummer. He seemed to be having the most fun, sitting there so cool, beating on that big kettledrum. When he brought those sticks down everybody heard him. He played all by himself, but he kept the whole thing going. I started tapping my hands on my knees along with him, and sometimes I'd get there a little earlier and take some licks on the drum myself. And after a while, when I was home, I'd keep time to the radio, beating a fork on one of Momma's pots.

After school I'd be out on the track, inside the fence with my own uniform. There was a new coach, Warren St. James. And he started spending a lot of time with me, teaching me how to start, how to pace myself, when to make that closing kick. I learned fast because I was hungry to learn, and when the season opened I was running in dual meets, in the mile and the half-mile. I was doing well, finishing third and second, and once in a while I'd win a little race. But I was always tired, sometimes too tired to sleep before I went to work at the plant.

Momma came into the bedroom one evening, about eight o'clock. I was sitting up in bed, thinking about last week's race and the mistakes I made, how I just didn't have it at the end, how I couldn't get those knees up high enough for the stretch sprint.

"Can't you sleep, Richard?"

"No, Momma."

"I don't know why you don't quit that old sport, Richard." She sat down on the bed. She always sighed when she sat down. "I worry about you, Richard, you got so much trouble with your stomach and your mind drifts so."

"Momma?"

"Yes, honey."

"Remember when you took me to that old woman, I was a real little kid, and she said I'd be a great man some day."

Momma took my head in her lap and rocked back and forth. "She saw a star right in the center of your head, and I knew it, oh, how I knew it. You're gonna be a great man, Richard."

"Momma, I'm gonna be a great runner, the coach said I could be a great runner. Momma?"

"Yes, honey?"

"I want to quit my job."

And my Momma rocked me in her arms and she said: "Okay, honey. And don't you worry, my special little man, we're gonna be all right."

That was my last night at work. The next morning I got to the band room and the bandmaster was staring out the window looking mad. There was a concert the next week, and the drummer was in the hospital.

"You read music, Gregory?"

"No, sir."

"Well, I know you been fooling around with the drums. Now I want to try something. Whenever I tip my head toward you like this, see, I want you to hit the drum like this, hear, and when I. . . ."

The drummer never got his job back. We got through the concert, and the one after that, and then it was football season and I was banging the big bass drum in the marching band.

Life really began to open up for me. Everybody in school knew me now, the athletic crowd and the musical crowd, and the girls that hung around both. I didn't go out very much. I didn't have money, and I was pretty shy. I could make quick talk outside the corner drugstore, or at a party, but when it came to that big step of asking a girl to have a date with me, I just couldn't get those words out.

But I was all right, man. The band was taking big trips, to West Virginia and Illinois and Kansas, and we were playing Beethoven and Bach and Mozart, cats I never even heard of. Once, just once, I invited Momma to a concert. I sat on the stage of the school auditorium, and I got sick and ashamed when I saw her come in wearing that shabby old coat, her swollen ankles running over the edges of those dyed shoes, that dress the rich white folks gave her, a little too much lipstick, the cheap perfume. They asked her to go sit up in the balcony. I should have got up and thrown that kettledrum right into the faces of all those doctors and society people and light-complected snobs sitting in the orchestra. But I didn't. I just was glad she was up in the balcony where she couldn't be seen by too many people.

I never wanted her at track meets. That was mine, all mine. Flagpole Gregory, they called me, Ironman Gregory. I could run all day. I had style. I wore argyle socks in the races and a handkerchief wrapped around my head. I had a little trick. When I came down the stretch I'd look up at the flagpole and make a little salute. Then I'd go into my closing kick and win going away. They thought I was very patriotic, that the flag gave me extra strength. Once, in a meet against Vashon High, the other big Negro high school in St. Louis, some kids took the flag down, figuring that would beat me. I never even knew it.

Most of the meets were on Saturday, and I'd stay out until ten or eleven o'clock Friday night, talking with Mister Ben, or walking with Boo, or hanging around with the guys at the candy store and the poolroom. They'd tell me about a fight they were going to have with another gang, and maybe some of the boys would come by with some wine. I'd tell them I couldn't make it, I was in training. I didn't tell them I didn't need it, I had something bigger going for me. Then, about eleven o'clock, when I was sure I was so tired I'd fall right to sleep, I'd go home.

I'd wake up early on Saturday mornings with a smirk on my face. I'd walk around the house, look at the peeling linoleum floor, the dirty dishes in the sink, all the raggedy shoes under the bed. I'd punch Garland on the arm and tickle Ronald and maybe pinch the girls. I'd hug Momma. "We're all right, Momma, we're all right." And then I'd take that one big step out of the house, jump the stoop, and I was in another world.

I'd walk to the stadium through the early morning, my uniform bag swinging in my hand, and with each step my stomach would turn over again and the little hairs would start standing up on the back of my neck. When I got to the stadium I'd just wave at the guard and he'd open the gate for me. I didn't even have to show him my competitor's pass. "Good luck, Greg, as if you need it." He'd wink at me and I'd wink back.

And the sun would be coming up high and it would still be cold under my sweater. I could feel the sweat under my armpits and between my shoulder blades and behind my knees. "Hey, Greg, hey, Greg," and I'd never look around, just climb quietly up to the grandstand and sit on a wooden bench like any other spectator. They'd be running off the shot-put and high jump early and I'd just sit there and watch. Just another spectator at the track and field meet.

The loud-speaker would crackle and snap: "Will all entrants in the one-mile run please report to the official's table, will all. . . ."

I'd stand up real slow, and feel this thing start to take me over, this monster that started at my toes like hot water flowing upward through a cold body. By the time I got down the steps I'd be on fire. I dressed fast in the locker room under the stands, put on my bright argyles, wrapped a handkerchief

around my head. Then I'd walk out on the field and I knew I could crush the world.

"There you are, Gregory, I've been looking all over for you. Where you been?"

"I'm ready, coach."

St. James looked me over. "You better be. I want to talk to you. That big boy from Vashon, he's good, you have to watch his. . . ."

"Don't tell me about him, coach. You go on over and tell him about me."

I got to the line with the other runners, and now, for just a moment, I was scared. I'm bringing 118 pounds of bones to this line, been training right, going to bed every night, trying to keep the rules, now. . . .

Bang.

Let the pack get ahead of you for the first quarter, no need to get banged around and elbowed up there with the pace-setters burning themselves out. Take it easy, Greg baby, that's the way, that's the way. At the half they started falling back, the guys who don't know how to run, the guys who smoked, the guys who don't really have it. Take them now at the three-quarter, take one at the curve, get the other one coming off, and come around the straightaway and clean them all up. One by one. Don't play with them, Greg baby, don't play with them, just pass them by. Now you feel that thing, the monster, and you're going, man, you're going, ripping and running and here comes that bad dog. There's only two up front now and they're way over their heads, and here comes the flagpole, don't forget to look up and salute, Greg, that's your trademark. Somewhere Coach St. James is saying, "Look at that Gregory, look at that machine." And my knees are coming up higher and higher and I'm running faster and faster and I pass those two like the Greyhound Bus passes telephone poles and the tape snaps against my chest and then, slowly, I'm off the stride, slowly, my head goes down, and, slowly, the thing inside of me lets go. The monster slips out, and I'm left all alone there. Richard Gregory, not Dick, not Flagpole or Ironman, just Richard. I fall on my knees and then on my face, and the grass smells sweet and my stomach explodes. "That . . . that . . . my last race, coach . . . no . . . more."

"Come on, Gregory, on your feet. They're getting ready for the relays."

And I'm up again and waiting, and it starts all over, the hot water seeping up, the monster slipping back in. I can see our number three man hit the curve and slow down like I told him to and now I'm running and the stick hits my hand like an electric charge. I put my head down and I go and the charge stays with me because everyone else is ahead and they have to settle down and run a race, but I have to go out and catch them all. Now my knees are coming up again, higher and higher and higher than the flagpole, and I salute my knees and then I snap the tape again. This time, when I fall on the grass, I go right to sleep, into a dream world. I'm standing on the back of an open car riding up Fifth Avenue in New York City, ticker tape falling out of the buildings like a Christmas snow and everybody in the world is cheering me as I go by. I'm asleep in the middle of a stadium and I don't even hear them screaming my name.

DISCUSSION

1. Richard's mother wonders "what's inside her son," the coach marvels at "that machine," and Richard says of himself "I had style." What qualities does Richard have that make him outstanding?

2. The nicknames given him are Flagpole Gregory and Ironman Gregory. Where do these names come from? Are they appropriate?

3. "Life really began to open up for me," (page 281) Richard says. What does he mean? What was happening to him that he felt good about?

4. **Interpreting Emotions.** In this selection Dick Gregory tells about his experience as a runner. He tells also how he feels about running and about his life at that time. If he were talking, a listener could tell much just by Gregory's tone of voice. But the reader has only the written word to go by. On page 282 Richard says "We're all right, Momma, we're all right." Can you tell what his emotions are when he says that? If he were speaking, what tone of voice would he use? Why does he repeat "We're all right"?

5. Dick Gregory has written this story himself about his own life. What is this kind of writing called?

# Fifty-Fifty

## CARL SANDBURG

What is there for us two
to split fifty-fifty,
to go halvers on?
    A Bible, a deck of cards?
    a farm, a frying pan?      5
    a porch, front steps to sit on?
How can we be pals
    when you speak English
    and I speak English
    and you never understand me    10
    and I never understand you?

**DISCUSSION**

1. How do you split a frying pan? What happens if you "go halvers" (line 3) on a deck of cards?

2. The poem is suggesting that much that is valuable in life cannot be parceled out or divided up without destroying its value. We might divide a bag of marbles among friends, or a piece of candy, but with much else in life we must not demand our half, our share. What, according to the poem, must we learn to do instead in order to enjoy life? How does the suggestion apply to the way we speak to each other?

# The Long Way Around       JEAN McCORD

I hadn't spoken to my stepmother in three days. I was absorbed by an inner grief and anger because she had given away my mother's dresses to the Salvation Army.

I could still feel my mother around the house. Sometimes I'd come bursting in from school with some important piece of news that I wanted to share immediately, and coming through the door, I'd shout, "Mother, I'm home. Where are you?" and instantly, before the echo had died, I'd remember, too late.

My stepmother had answered once, the first time, coming out from her bedroom with a smile on her face, thinking I was calling her, saying "Yes, Patty, what is it?" But my face was set in a frozen scowl, and I was standing there rigid, unyielding and furious at myself for such a mistake. She understood and turning away without pressing me any further, she went back into her room and closed her door.

My mother had died two years before when I was twelve, and even though I knew better, sometimes in the middle of the night, I'd awake in a terrible fear and to comfort myself back to sleep I'd whisper into the pillow, "She's only gone away on a trip. And she'll be back." In the morning I had to face my own lie.

My father had married again last year and though my two little brothers, Jason and Scott, called this new woman "Mother," my father had told me I didn't have to do so. I called her Alice even though sometimes it felt strange to call a grown woman by her first name. This Alice wasn't anything at all like my own mother. For one thing, she couldn't cook. My mother had been the best cook in the whole neighborhood. Even the other mothers around us used to say that and would come over for coffee and butter scones and things that my mother would just whip up on a moment's notice. This Alice . . . well, sometimes our whole supper ended up in the garbage can, and my father would take us out to a restaurant. I thought it was pretty stupid and expensive, but of course Jason and Scott loved it.

To make things even worse, so it seemed to me, my father had taken a new job, and we had moved away from the town and the neighborhood where I'd spent my whole life with kids I knew and had grown up with and gone to school with and graduated with.

Now I was in junior high with a whole new batch of kids and I didn't like any of them. They didn't like me, either. I kept my distance and when school was over, I walked home alone, carrying my books with my head down and hurrying by the groups of girls laughing and giggling over some private joke. I could feel them looking at my back and the talk always hushed a little until I was by, then they'd break out into silly, stifled snickers when I was down the street a ways.

Actually I hated them all. I hated the teachers and the new school and my new stepmother and my father who seemed a new person too. Even my little brothers seemed to deserve a good slap for the way they had forgotten and called this Alice "Mother" as if they had never had a mother of their own.

The only one who hadn't changed, who was still the way he had always been, was Rufus, our old Samoyed. Rufus is as old as I am, and in his way he understood. After my mother died, he'd lain on his braided rag rug and refused to move for over two weeks. He wouldn't eat because he was used to my mother fixing him up a strange mixture of dog food with raw egg and bacon drippings, and nobody else seemed to know just how to do it. Finally I tried and after a while he ate while looking at me from the corner of his eyes and seeming to apologize for it. I sat down beside him and cried into his neck, and he stopped eating long enough to lick my face which only made me cry harder.

Now the only reason I had for getting up in the morning was to greet Rufus and give him an egg. After school the only reason I came home was to take Rufus for a walk and together we had covered most of this new town. The only trouble was that the town stayed new. Somehow no matter how often we walked down the same streets, the houses always seemed strange. Rufus would plod along at my side, his head just at the reach of my hand. He stumbled once in a while over a curb, but that was because his eyesight wasn't too good any more. My own eyesight seemed slightly affected too because there was a gray film between me and everything I looked at.

We walked all over town after school, my feet just leading the two of us. Finally I knew we had tromped over every square inch of all the streets, but still nothing looked familiar. Sometimes returning home, I wouldn't even know we had reached the end of the walk until Rufus turned off the sidewalk and went up our front steps.

One Saturday morning I woke up very early. This was about a month ago, I think, or maybe two months. I had lain awake a long time that night watching the shadow patterns change on the ceiling when the wind tossed the big snowball bush outside my window. It seemed like the night was trying to tell me something, but I couldn't quite make out what it was. Out in the kitchen I could hear that Rufus was awake too, because every time he left his rug and walked across the floor, his toenails clicked on the linoleum. He seemed to be pacing the floor as if he wanted to go out into the night. Maybe he sensed something waiting out there for him. If my mother had been here, she'd know . . . she would have known. . . .

Somewhere there in the middle of the night, I must have made up my mind what I was going to do. When the dawn came, I just rose and dressed and without even consciously thinking about it, I packed my small overnight case, putting in my parents' wedding picture which I had retrieved from a trunk in the attic, all the socks I had, two books from the library which were due in three days, one book of my own, and a little stuffed felt doll which I had given to Jason and then taken back from him. I rolled up my printed-rose quilt and tied it in several places with my belts. Then in blue jeans and a ski jacket I tiptoed out to the kitchen with my belongings and looked down at Rufus who thumped his tail hard against the floor and got up. He stood with his chin over his dish waiting for me to break his egg into it. I saw then that I couldn't leave him behind so while he slurped his egg I rolled his rug around the outside of my quilt. Now it was a big sloppy bundle but I didn't care.

Just as I was easing open the kitchen door I remembered I had no money, so I had to carefully put everything down and return to my bedroom. I had had a dollar put away for a long time because there was nothing I wanted to spend it on. Outside in the snowball bush the birds were beginning to cheep and call with a tremendous clatter. They were so noisy I wondered how anyone could sleep through that, and I knew I had to get away quickly.

Rufus was waiting with his head leaning against the kitchen door. He knew we were going for a walk. I wanted to take his dish, but didn't see how I could carry everything. We'd manage somehow. I stepped out into the cool grayness with those birds still clattering and the eastern sky beginning to flag out in streaks of red. It was going to be a warm day, and I knew I wouldn't need the ski jacket. Still, I thought . . . at night. . . .

Rufus and I headed toward what I hoped was south. This was vaguely the direction where our old town and old friends were. I had looked at it often enough on the map, but I wasn't sure of just what road to go along. And besides I wanted to stay off the roads. I could picture my father driving along looking for us soon enough, right about breakfast time, I thought, when they would first miss me. But they wouldn't know anything for sure, I told myself, until I remembered I was carrying Rufus' rug.

"That was very stupid of you," I told Rufus severely, "to let me take your old rug when you knew it would give us away."

I walked a few swift steps ahead of him.

"Just for that, I ought to make you go back alone. Without me. Serve you right."

I was very angry. Rufus was hanging his head. The tone of my voice told him he'd done something really bad, but I finally had to forgive him. After all, it had been my own idea.

We used the road only far enough to get us out of town, then I decided we'd better strike across country even though it would be harder traveling, and we would have to climb a lot of fences. It would be safer that way. I soon found out I was right about one thing; it was a lot harder going. We walked through pasture where the ground was spongy and wet and my shoes became water-logged. We fought our way through brush that kept trying to tear my bundles away from me, and by this time, they really felt heavy. I gave Rufus a sour look, wishing he could carry his own rug at least. We puffed up hills that gave me a stitch in the side, and I noticed that Rufus wasn't holding up too well. He was panting and beginning to lag behind.

By the time the sun was high, I was starving to death. Rufus, at least, had eaten an egg for breakfast, but I hadn't had a bite. And of course by now, I had lost my sense of direction completely. I had no idea which way was south although I had been keeping my eyes open looking for the moss that is supposed to grow on the north side of trees. I hadn't found any.

Every once in a while we would come close to a farmhouse and there was always trouble. Farmers must keep the meanest dogs in the world. At each place a big shrieking dog would come bounding out at us, and try to pick a fight with Rufus just because we were walking nearby. Rufus would say, "Urrgghh," and show all his teeth with his black lips drawn so far back he looked like a snarling wolf and the farm dogs would back off towards home, but never shut up. I was afraid the farmers might call the police, so we would hurry on.

It was a long time before I saw a country road which I figured was safe enough to walk on. In a couple of miles we came up to a crossroads and a store with one red gas pump squatting to one side and looking like it never had any customers.

I dropped my bundles outside and went into darkness and unfamiliar smells and there was this old farmer-type man dressed in striped overalls sitting on a sack of something. I didn't know what I wanted to buy, but anything would do. He had a small candy counter, so I bought three chocolate bars. I decided that canned dog food would keep the best for Rufus, so I got seven cans which took all the rest of my money.

"Stranger round here, aren't you, Miss?" the storekeeper said.

I mumbled something and waved backwards, because my mouth was full of stale-tasting candy. He put the cans in a sack and I left, but he followed me to the door and watched very slyly as I had to pick up my suitcase and rolled quilt which left me no way to carry the dog food. I struggled to force it under my arm, but the sack broke and the cans rolled all over the ground. In desperation I knelt and shoved them into my suitcase and Rufus and I marched down the road with the striped overalls watching us all the way.

I could just almost hear him on the telephone, if he had such a thing, saying, "Sheriff, there's a strange gal going down the road with a big old dog and a suitcase full of dog food. Looks mighty suspicious to me." So there was no choice; we had to leave the road and go back to the pastures and farmhouses.

In the middle of the day I knew I couldn't carry that terribly heavy suitcase any further, so I said to Rufus, "You are going to carry some of your own food inside of you."

We sat down in the shade of some bushes, and I opened the suitcase to get out a couple of the cans. Then I broke into tears from sheer rage. I had forgotten to bring along a can opener.

I cried a long time while Rufus looked at me sadly, laying his heavy head on my knee, and banging his tail, which was full of burrs and briars, against the stony ground.

My vaguely formed idea when we first started out was that we'd make our way back to our old town and maybe one of the old neighbors or even my favorite teacher, Miss Virginia Townsend, would take us in and keep us both if I worked for our board and room. Now I saw clearly that we weren't going to make it. It was over two hundred miles back there, and without even a can opener, well. . . .

We rested for an hour or so while I talked it over with Rufus who was a good listener and always agreed with me.

"You knew it was a long ways when you started out with me, didn't you?"

He thumped his tail once. I guess he was too tired to argue.

"I always understood that dogs knew their own way back to their old homes. Why didn't you lead?"

He looked away down the hill as if he was searching for the right direction.

"If we go back, you know what it means, don't you? They'll all be against us, and you'll certainly have to mind your P's and Q's from here on in!"

He hung his head in shame, but how can you ask a fourteen-year-old dog to walk two hundred miles when he was all worn out from doing about ten?

We stood up and looked out over a valley that faded into a blue haze in the far distance. I picked up the luggage, and we went back down the hill toward the country store. By the time we got there Rufus was limping.

I went into that dim interior again, and the man was back on his sack, just resting and waiting with his legs crossed.

"Thought you'd be back," he said with a snort of choked laughter.

"Could I please use your telephone?" I asked with great dignity.

"In the back there. Ask the Missus." He jerked his head.

I had to go into their living quarters. It seems they lived right there surrounded by all those groceries and hardware and chicken feed and medicine for cows and horses. His Missus was a pleasant, stumpy woman with square glasses, and after I'd called home, she gave me a glass of lemonade. I had to ask her where we were, and she took the telephone to give my father directions. He was really boiling mad and hollored over the phone at me, "Swanson's Corner! Where is that?"

I went outside to call Rufus, and she let him come into the kitchen for a drink of cold water. While we waited for my father, I tried to think how to explain all those cans of dog food and the quilt and Rufus' rug, but there didn't seem to be any way. When my father drove up we climbed in and rode all the way home in guilty silence. My stepmother, Alice, must have told him not to say a word.

When we got home my little brothers looked at me fearfully and my father said with a glint in his eye, "Go to your room and stay there. I'll deal with you later."

Nothing more ever came of it which surprised me no end because I waited all week for punishment.

So now it was a month later, or maybe more.

I still kept to myself at school and if a person talked to me, I just turned away because I had nothing to say to any of them.

On the 5th of November it was my birthday. I woke up with poison in my heart and an ache in my throat that I had to keep swallowing because I was remembering my twelfth birthday when my mother had made a dress for me and also bought me *Tales of Robin Hood* which I don't read anymore, but it was the book I had

taken with me when Rufus and I ran away.

Breakfast seemed strangely quiet, all the more so because nobody said a thing, not even "Happy Birthday." I knew they had forgotten.

At school, like always, I answered if I was called on, but not otherwise. I ate my lunch by myself and passed most of the day thinking of how many birthdays I would have to live through before Rufus and I could leave again for good. About four more, I decided, then knew with a deep sorrow that Rufus wouldn't last to be eighteen.

When school was out, I turned in the wrong direction from home and headed for a park up on a high bluff. It was pleasant and empty. The trees were dropping their leaves in little piles and a couple of squirrels chased each other around tree trunks like they were on a merry-go-round. I wanted to stay there forever. I wanted the leaves to cover me like little Hansel and Gretel when they were lost in the woods. I wondered if they had had a stepmother who drove them off, and then I said aloud, "No, that isn't fair. You know it isn't Alice's fault. I don't know whose fault it is for feeling so left out of things."

I looked again at the fallen leaves and thought that my family was like the strong tree that would survive the winter, but I was probably one of the lost leaves.

"I didn't expect them to give me any presents," I kicked at the leaves. I propped my chin on my knees and sat for a long time, thinking, and because it was getting late, I read my next day's history lesson. Finally it was too hard to read, and looking up, I saw it was almost dark and it was a long way home.

I walked home like I always walked, neither slow nor hurrying. It was just too bad if I was late for supper. I didn't want any anyhow.

When I opened the door the house felt strange. My father was sitting in the front room behind his paper which he put aside for a moment, looked at me and said, "Humph!"

Jason came dancing up to me and grabbed me by the hand, pulling me into the dining room.

"Where you been, Patty?" he said. "Everybody waited and waited."

Rufus rushed out from the kitchen to greet me as always, but he was wearing a silly little paper hat tied under his chin. I stood in the brightly lighted room and looked around confused. There had obviously been a party. Used paper plates lay all over and the remains of a big frosted cake was crumpled in the center of the table which had a good linen cloth on it. A pile of wrapped presents lay on the sideboard. In the kitchen I could hear Scott chattering to Alice like a little parakeet and Jason, still clutching my hand, was trying to tell me something.

"All your classmates, Patty," he was saying. "All of them. When you dint come home, we had to have the party without you. Your presents are here."

He tried to drag me towards them, but I shucked him off and rushed to my room.

I was pretty shamefaced when Alice came in to see if I wanted supper. She sat beside me on the bed and patted me on the back.

"It was my fault," she said. "I shouldn't have tried to surprise you. Anyway, come on out and feed Rufus. I think he's going to be sick from all that cake he was given."

So that's how matters stand now.

Nothing is going to change very much. I don't feel quite so mad at the whole world, and I notice my actions toward Alice are a lot friendlier. It doesn't bother me any when the boys call her "Mother." Maybe, sometime, a long time from now, I might start calling her that myself. Maybe, by spring or so, I might start growing myself back on that family tree.

**DISCUSSION**

1.   Patty leaves on her journey one morning with the birds "clattering and the eastern sky beginning to flag out in streaks of red" (page 290). Why does she leave? What did she take with her?

2.   Patty had not planned her trip well and did not take with her all the things she would need. What is the turning point that makes her decide to go back?

3.   Toward the end of the story Patty describes her family as "the strong tree that would survive the winter" (p. 295). What does she see herself as? What has happened in the family that has caused Patty to feel lost and alone?

4.   Is the **conflict** (see page 161) in this story between Patty and her stepmother or is it within Patty? How has Patty changed by the end of the story?

For further activities, see page 308.

# A Choice of Weapons

PHYLLIS McGINLEY

Sticks and stones are hard on bones.
Aimed with angry art,
Words can sting like anything.
But silence breaks the heart.

# An Unpredictable Japanese Lady

## MONICA SONE

One of Mother's many consuming desires was to learn to speak the English language. Mother's younger sister, Kikue[1], had the opportunity to attend high school and in a short time, Kikue was able to speak fluently. Mother had been married too soon and missed out on this chance, but she was determined to master the language with whatever facilities she had. If her four children could learn to speak it, there was no reason why she couldn't. Still, we felt something was amiss whenever we were welcomed home by Mother with a beaming smile, "Well, did you guys have a good time?"

Mother was really too busy and we were too impatient to sit down and teach her in a systematic way. It was mostly a trial and error method . . . a great trial to us while she made the errors. She drove us frantic by asking us the meaning of odd phrases to which she was invariably attracted. She liked the lilt of a phrase in a song which she had heard over the radio, "nothing but a nothing." She repeated it over and over to master the difficult "th" sound. We told her it meant nothing at all and that no one ever talked that way, really, so there was no sense in memorizing it.

Father had no practical need to learn a polite version of the English language because his contacts were with Skidrow men and it was better for him to speak to his rambunctious

Sone: pronounced sō-nĕ.
[1] *Kikue:* pronounced kē-kōō-ĕ.

guests on equal earthy terms. But Mother simply could not get away with a similar dialect. She had to attend teas, P.T.A. meetings, and festivals at school and carry on conversation with our teachers. Many Japanese mothers never appeared at these functions because it was such an excruciating experience. Some who did attend stayed close to their children, smiled tirelessly, and said, "yes," "no," "thank you," and laughed at the wrong time. But Mother was not satisfied with just a spiritual evening of good will. Although I was secretly proud that Mother showed spunk in wading into a full-sized conversation, I often wished that she was not quite so spirited with her words. As she chatted with my teacher, I listened in agony, for it was always a mangled dialogue in which the two parties never seemed to be talking about the same thing at the same time. Miss Powers would smile at Mother, "So you are KaZOOko's[2] mother." Miss Powers could never remember that there is no accent on any syllable in pronouncing my Japanese name. "You seem so young, Mrs. Itoi,[3] you look more like her big sister."

"Yes, I am, thank you." Mother smiled back, more intent on being gracious at the moment than on the subject matter. Miss Powers remained unruffled.

[2] *KaZOOko's:* this spelling is used to show how the name was mispronounced. The correct spelling is Kazuko.
[3] *Itoi:* pronounced ē-tō-ē.

"Did KaZOOko tell you we're having a special program for the May Festival soon?"

"Oh yes, it was very nice. I enjoyed program so much." Mother nodded her head enthusiastically. I curled inside. I had not yet told Mother about May Festival and I knew she had become lost after the words, "special program." Mother was speaking about the Christmas program. Miss Powers's blue eyes fluttered, but she quickly figured that Mother was thinking about last year's May Festival.

"Oh yes, we had a nice time all right, but KaZOOko wasn't in my class then. This year she's going to be one of the crocuses and we want her to dress in a real pretty costume . . . a lavender skirt and purple petal hat made from crepe paper. Do you think you could help us make the dress if I sent the instructions home with KaZOOko?"

"Oh yes, I make them all the time," Mother smiled with great assurance. It was a bare-faced lie. Mother had never made a single crocus costume for me nor had she ever seen one; but Mother did make lots of pretty dresses for me for which she thought Miss Powers was complimenting her. I had to bolster this crippled dialogue.

"Mother can help with the costume, Miss Powers. She made this for me," I said, holding out the skirt of my new dress. It was a flaming, candy-red taffeta dress, crawling with dainty ruffles, according to my tyrannical specifications. Miss Powers was

back on the track and she gushed politely, "Did she really? My what a wonderful seamstress you are, Mrs. Itoi. And I love that color! It's as lovely as can be."

"Oh, no, it's not so good," Mother said modestly. She could have said "thank you" at this moment, but I was content that Mother was talking about the same thing as Miss Powers. All of a sudden Mother burst out, "It's too red, but my daughter, she likes red. I think it's *lousy!*"

A tense silence followed. Miss Powers was struggling to keep a straight face. I felt as if I were standing inside a furnace. I managed to tug at Mother's elbow and whisper, "*Kaero,*[4] Mama, let's go home."

I thought, miserably, as I walked home with Mother, how much the other teachers would laugh when Miss Powers told them about Mother's *faux pas.*[5] I pointed out to Mother in a tearful, disgraced-for-life voice that she had made a terrible mistake. Mama, you should have said, loud, loud! not lousy! Lousy is a vulgar word, a bad word.

"Soh? I didn't know. I heard you children using it all the time so I thought it was perfectly all right." Mother didn't sound at all sorry. I fell into a morose silence the rest of the way home, wondering how I was ever going back to school and face my teacher. But when I saw her next

---

[4] *Kaero* (kä-ĕ-rō): Let's go home.
[5] *faux pas* (fō pä'): French expression meaning social blunder.

she seemed to have forgotten all about the episode.

Mother's haphazard way with the language did not always work against her. I remember once she became involved in a switch of identity and lived for a day like royalty, suddenly swept into high society. It happened when Sumiko[6] and I were rabid fans of Mickey Mouse and members of the Mickey Mouse Club at the Coliseum Theater which met every Saturday morning. We sang Mickey Mouse songs, we saw Mickey Mouse pictures, we wore Mickey Mouse sweaters, we owned Mickey Mouse wrist watches. Because the club had the endorsement of the Parent-Teacher Association, Father and Mother raised no objections to our latest craze.

One Saturday there was to be a very special party to which we could invite our mothers. There would be a Mickey Mouse drawing contest for the members and refreshments for everyone. Mother said although she would like to be there, she was too busy Saturday morning. Sumiko and I wept.

"But, Mama, everybody else's mother will be there. We'll be the *only* ones without a mother. People will think we're orphans."

Fortunately, a few days before the event, Mother went to a P.T.A. meeting at Bailey Gatzert School at which time Miss Mahon, our school principal, pleaded with the Japanese mothers to go to this particular party with their children. Women of differ-

ent nationalities would be there and Miss Mahon wanted to see the Japanese represented. Miss Mahon stirred Mother's conscience. Mother decided to go. Sumiko and I knew it was going to be one of the biggest, happiest parties we would ever attend.

That bright Saturday morning Sumiko and I put on our best red coats and matching red berets. We bounded down the long flight of stairs, clutching our Mickey Mouse sketches and ran all the way downtown. Mother had promised that she would follow later, as soon as she had finished the hotel chores. We had drilled Mother on the location of the theater building. With a thick red crayon, we printed the name of the theater, its address and the name "Pike Street," the block where she was supposed to get off the streetcar, on a big sheet of paper so Mother could not lose it or herself.

Having taken these precautions, Sumiko and I relaxed. At the Coliseum Theater, we pushed our dimes through the box-office window, deposited our drawings in a large chest in the foyer and slid into our seats, breathless with hope that one of us would win a prize. The meeting started off as usual. The same, double-chinned master of ceremonies greeted us, shook with laughter at his jokes and raved a great deal about what a wonderful time we were going to have. He introduced a bouncy, Dutch-bobbed five-year-old girl named Patsy who tap danced and sang for us. Later the lights were dimmed, the words of songs were

---

[6] *Sumiko* (sōō-mē-kō): Kazuko's sister.

flashed on the screen and Patsy led us in singing our Mickey Mouse songs. Soon it was time for the judging of the picture contest. Sumiko and I also thought it was time for Mother's appearance. We went to the lounge where we had agreed to meet her. No one was there. Little Sumiko's lips started to tremble. I said, hastily, "She'll be here soon. Let's wait."

We sank deep into the luxurious low sofa and waited silently. Hours seemed to pass and still there was no Mother. We hurried back to our seats to see what was going on, but it was hard to keep our attention focused on the stage. We learned that the pictures were still being judged upstairs. Everyone was getting restless, and two boys started wrestling in the aisle. Soon a team of usherettes swooped down the aisles, distributing ice cream in Dixie cups, and cookies. While we thoughtfully ate our refreshment, the master of ceremonies suddenly appeared and announced the names of three contest winners. Our spirits sagged when neither of our names was mentioned; and, worse than that, Mother was lost.

The party over, the auditorium, hallway, and lounge soon filled with chattering boys and girls and their smiling, bright-eyed mothers. We made one last inspection of the theater without success. Maybe Mother was wandering downtown, lost and bewildered. Or maybe she had just decided not to attend.

We headed back home with an ache lodged deep in our throats.

How could Mother have failed us, after she had promised us a dozen times. We climbed heavily up the hotel stairs, made our way to our living quarters with a solemn expression on our faces, all set to reprove Mother. The rooms were empty. We scurried through the dim labyrinth of halls until we found Father in the last room at the other end of the hotel. He was busily making the bed. Indignantly I asked, "Papa, where is Mama? Why didn't she come to the party?"

"*Nani?*[7] Why, Mama left about half an hour after you both had gone. I was afraid she would be late so I told her to take a taxi. Where could she have gone?"

We were thoroughly alarmed. Sumiko burst out crying. Father, looking harried, put the finishing touches on the bed, picked Sumiko up and led me out of the room.

"Now, now, don't start that. Mama's all right, wherever she is. She's been downtown before by herself. Maybe she just walked into the wrong place. If Mama isn't home in an hour, I'll call the police."

At the word "police," I started to cry, too. Father sighed and took us into the kitchen where he tried to stifle our sobs with cookies. "Now, why don't you two go back to the parlor and play a while. I have a little more work to do."

No, we didn't feel like it. We wanted to be with him. We trailed after him with wet faces and damp

cookies, really feeling like orphans now. As Father pushed the carpet sweeper carefully over the frayed edges of the rug, he asked questions about the party. Between sniffles and bites, we managed to give Father all the boring details. Then all of a sudden behind us, we heard the sweetest voice in the world. It was Mother.

"Ka-chan, Sumi-chan,"[8] she said happily, "wasn't that a lovely party?"

Father stopped sweeping. Sumiko and I stared at her, wondering what party she had attended. Mother was still glowing with excitement. She looked exquisite and beautiful, in her best gown of pale lavender silk velvet. Delicate floral patterns were traced in velvet, woven over a background of sheer voile. A huge butterfly rhinestone pin held the drape on the side of the skirt. Mother also wore a close-fitting, beige helmet over her freshly marcelled black hair. The long length of hair was coiled into a low, thick bun at the nape of her neck. She looked pretty and out of place, standing in the doorway near the mop and the laundry pile. She turned brightly to Father, "By the way, what does 'consul's wife' mean?"

"Consul's wife? What in the world . . . why, that's the wife of a *ryoji.*[9] Why do you ask?"

"Arrra!" Mother shrieked in horror. "A *ryoji's* wife! *Doshima sho!*"[10]

[7] *Nani* (nä-nē): what.

[8] *Ka-chan, Sumi-chan:* chan (chän) used as part of a person's name to show affection.
[9] ryoji (rē-yō-jē): consul.
[10] *Doshima sho* (dō-shē-mä-shō): What shall I do.

Mother clapped her hand to her mouth, then to her head as if she didn't know what to do next. Sumiko and I jumped all over her, trying to get her attention.

"Mama, Mama, what happened? Where were you anyway? We waited for you all morning."

Mother then burst into hysterical laughter and the only words we could get out of her were, *"Mah, iyayo!*[11] What shall I do? *Tondemo nai kotoyo."*[12]

We went back to the parlor and waited impatiently for Mother to subside. Father scolded her, "Where were you all this time? The children have been crying all morning."

With tears of laughter in her eyes, Mother told us the whole story. She had gone to our Mickey Mouse party. The taxi driver had delivered her to the front of the Coliseum Theater. Just as soon as she had stepped out of the cab, a suave, beautifully groomed woman pounced on Mother and escorted her into the theater. "We're so glad you could come, Mrs. Saito. We're having quite a party this morning."

Mother felt slightly overpowered with this warm reception, but she smiled politely back at the nice lady as if she were quite used to such cordiality.

"Thank you. I'm late little bit. I'm so sorry."

"It doesn't matter in the least, Mrs. Saito.[13] You're in time for the important part of the program."

Mother didn't completely understand what the woman was saying, but she realized she was being addressed as Mrs. Saito. She corrected her new friend, "I'm Mrs. Itoi."

"Oh? Er . . . you're the Japanese consul's wife, aren't you?"

Mother didn't know what she meant, but she knew very well she should be agreeable at all times. She said, "Yes, thank you."

Obviously, the hostess had been assigned the special task of taking charge of the Japanese consul's wife, Mrs. Saito. The eager hostess had stepped out of the theater door several times and when at last a beautifully gowned Oriental woman had stepped out of a cab she thought the quarry was safe in her hands. The woman trilled to Mother, "Oh, Mrs. Saito, I wonder if you would do us the honor of acting as one of the judges for our Mickey Mouse drawing contest?"

"Yes, yes," Mother answered absent-mindedly, wondering why the woman kept calling her Mrs. Saito. "I'm Mrs. Itoi."

"I beg your pardon, Mrs. Itoi." The hostess paused for a moment and then began again, "You *are* the consul's wife?" This time she asked the question slowly and loudly. "Yes!" Mother replied, almost snapping. The woman was certainly asking a lot of

---

[11] *Mah, iyayo* (mä-e-yä-yō): Oh, what a mistake.
[12] *Tondemo nai kotoyo* (tōn-děm-ō-nä-ē-kō-tō-yō):
.  Nothing could be more absurd.

[13] *Saito:* pronounced sä-ē-tō.

questions. The hostess finally seemed satisfied with Mother's positive reply.

Just then, a woman walking in front of her stumbled. Her high heel had caught the edge of the carpet and both heel and shoe came off. Mother dove for the torn heel and shoe. She had fixed many a broken heel. The woman with the broken heel said, "Dear me, it would happen now."

"I fix for you," Mother assured her.

The hostess's eyes widened, "Please, Mrs. Saito, er, Mrs. Itoi, the maid will do that." She turned in desperation to the woman, "I'd like you to meet Mrs. Saito, the Japanese consul's wife."

The introductions were made, but Mother ignored them both, adjusted the heel into the nail holes, kneeled down, and pounded it back into place on the marble floor.

"Fixed now, I think." Mother returned the shoe to the pink-faced woman while the hostess made high-pitched sounds.

Mother was led upstairs to a luxuriously furnished room which glittered with mirrors and elegant crystal chandeliers, the like of which Mother had never seen. The room was filled with the subdued murmurs of distinguished-looking guests. The hostess introduced Mother to many gay, enchanting people. Mother caught words like "Swedish . . . English . . . German . . ." and heard the same mysterious expression, "consul's wife" over and over again. Soon

everyone was addressing Mother as Mrs. Saito and Mother let it pass good-naturedly. Far be it from her to keep correcting these lovely people. Nobody seemed to mind that Mother hardly said anything except, "I'm glad to meet you," and "Yes, thank you" whenever refreshments were offered to her, and "I think so" when she couldn't understand the topic of conversation.

Mother sipped delicious coffee from a tiny, doll-sized cup and nibbled at dainty sandwiches of all shapes and colors. On the tables were gleaming silver platters of bonbons, cookies, and assorted nuts. Mother felt as if she were part of a movie set.

Soon the hostess came up to Mother again and closeted her in a small, adjoining room with three other smartly dressed women who spoke English with heavy foreign accents. No one understood what the other was saying, but somehow they picked the prize pictures of Mickey Mouse. They went back to the reception room again for some more polite chatter and laughter. Half an hour later the party drew to a close. Mother bade farewell to her new acquaintances, the French consul's wife, the English consul's wife, the German consul's wife and a few more. They all shook her hand cordially, "Goot-bye, Mrs. Saito. It was just loavely meeting you. . . ."

What charming manners! What delightful ladies! The same attentive hostess escorted Mother out of the theater, hailed a taxi for her and waved farewell. Mother sank back in the rear seat, feeling positively giddy with the personal attention and hospitality that had surrounded her from the beginning to the end. The cab driver had to ask her, "Where to, lady?"

"Yes, please. Oh! . . . 217 Occidental Avenue."

The driver glanced back at her twice. Mother, looking like an Oriental princess of the court, sat fanning herself with her perfumed silk handkerchief and sighing . . . my, my what a grand party it had been and such cultured, gentle people. Miss Mahon will be certainly glad to know I took part and helped with the picture contest. The taxicab sped through the downtown shopping district and plunged into the fish and barnacle atmosphere of the waterfront where our hotel was located.

We have often wondered if the reception committee of the gala Mickey Mouse Club party ever discovered this error. We thanked God that Mrs. Saito, the Japanese consul's wife, had not appeared. Mother might have been hustled out of the theater as an impostor and criminal. Then we thought of something worse . . . maybe Mrs. Saito did attend, but nobody had met her at the door. She would have had to pay an admission fee at the box office to get in and been forced to find a seat for herself in the audience of screaming, squirming youngsters. I wondered if an usherette had handed her a Dixie cup of ice cream and a cookie, too. She probably would have resented such shabby treatment and reported it to her husband, the Japanese consul. We saw international complications arise and diplomatic relationships slip a notch between America and Japan. For days after, Mother was not quite herself as she wavered between sudden bursts of laughter and mortified mutterings.

DISCUSSION

1.  In her efforts to learn English, Mrs. Itoi shows great determination. What other characteristics does she show at other times?

2.  Mrs. Itoi learns English by trial and error—"a great trial for us while she made the errors," says her daughter (page 298). How does the daughter feel about her mother? How do the other members of the family feel about her?

3.  At the Coliseum party, Mrs. Itoi's mistaken identity leads to an adventure. How is the mangled dialogue between her and the hostess responsible for the mistake? What happens to her as a result of the misunderstanding?

4.  **Flashback.**   A flashback is a device writers use to interrupt the story to tell the reader about something that happened before. This story contains one flashback sequence. Do you recognize it? Where does it begin and where does it end?

For further activities, see page 308.

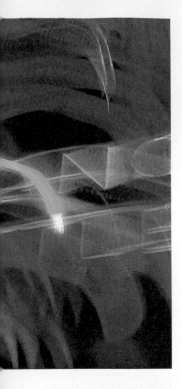

## VOCABULARY

### Charles (page 267)

Sometimes you can tell what an unfamiliar word means by looking at the words around it. Choose the correct definition for the words in bold type in these sentences. It you need more clues, turn back to the story.

1. . . . the voice suddenly became *raucous,* shouting ''Isn't anybody here?'' (p. 267)

harsh    shy    faint

2. ''Charles's mother?'' my husband and I asked *simultaneously.* (p. 269)

with fear    in loud tones    at the same time

3. ''Naaah,'' Laurie said *scornfully.* (p. 269)

with contempt    with a smile    with a shrug

4. ''What?'' I said, and my husband added *warily,* ''You mean Charles?'' (p. 270)

with laughter    with caution    with a wink

### An Unpredictable Japanese Lady (page 298)

There are many Japanese words that have become a part of English. Can you define these? Can you think of others?

kimono    tycoon    karate
judo    tempura    sukiyaki

## COMPOSITION

### My Sister Jane (page 274)

The speaker likes Jane, but nevertheless describes her as ''nothing but a great big crow.'' This is an unusual description. In a poem or short composition, describe in an unusual way someone you know and are fond of.

### The Long Way Around (page 287)

This story is told from Patty's point of view. Patty explains why she feels left out, why she doesn't belong. But in the story there is someone else who probably feels left out also: her stepmother. Write a letter to Patty from her stepmother, saying the things you think she would say.

# READING

## Charles (page 267)

Some of the statements below are facts and some are opinions. On separate paper, write only the numbers of those statements that are facts.

1. The teacher spanked a boy.
2. The boy was being fresh.
3. Laurie left while his father was still talking.
4. Charles hit the teacher.
5. The teacher made Charles stay inside during recess.
6. Charles didn't mind staying in.
7. Once, the teacher gave Charles an apple.
8. The boy Charles sounds like such a bad influence.
9. Charles yelled so in school they sent a boy in from first grade to tell the teacher to quiet him.
10. None of the women looked haggard enough to be Charles's mother.
11. The teacher really liked Laurie, even when he was naughty.
12. There was no boy named Charles in the kindergarten.

## The Long Way Around (page 287)

Here is a list of things that happened in the story. On separate paper, write them in the order in which they happened in the story.

1. Rufus got tired and couldn't keep up.
2. When school was out, Patty went to the park instead of going home.
3. Patty's father married a woman named Alice.
4. Patty went back to the store to make a telephone call.
5. Rufus, wearing a paper hat tied under his chin, ran to greet Patty.
6. When they were ready to eat, Patty discovered that she had no can opener.
7. Patty discovered there had been a surprise party for her.
8. Alice came to see if Patty wanted any supper.
9. When dawn came, Patty got up and packed a small overnight case.
10. She went back to her bedroom to get some money.
11. Patty bought chocolate bars for herself and canned dog food for Rufus.
12. Feeling ashamed, Patty ran off to her room.

# Song of a Man About to Die in a Strange Land

TRADITIONAL CHIPPEWA SONG

If I die here
In a strange land,
If I die
In a land I do not know,
Nevertheless, the thunder,                          5
The rolling thunder will take me home.

If I die here, the wind,
The wind rushing over the prairie,
The wind will take me home.

The wind and the thunder                            10
They are the same everywhere.
What does it matter then,
If I die here in a strange land.

DISCUSSION

1. What is the feeling of the speaker? Can you imagine where he might be?

2. In the last two lines the speaker asks "What does it matter then/ If I die here in a strange land." Does it matter to him or do you sense he would rather die somewhere else? Where?

# Nancy Hanks

ROSEMARY CARR BENÉT

If Nancy Hanks
Came back as a ghost,
Seeking news
Of what she loved most,
She'd ask first,                    5
"Where's my son?
What's happened to Abe?
What's he done?

"Poor little Abe,
Left all alone                      10
Except for Tom,
Who's a rolling stone;
He was only nine
The year I died.
I remember still                    15
How hard he cried.

"Scraping along
In a little shack,
With hardly a shirt
To cover his back,                  20
And a prairie wind
To blow him down,
Or pinching times
If he went to town.

"You wouldn't know                  25
About my son?
Did he grow tall?
Did he have fun?
Did he learn to read?
Did he get to town?                 30
Do you know his name?
Did he get on?"

## DISCUSSION

1.   What do you learn about Nancy Hanks's son? Did he grow tall? Learn to read? Get on?

2.   What kind of person was Lincoln's mother according to this poem? What worried her most about her son's future?

3.   A mother dying and leaving a young child is a sad situation. What words or phrases in this poem seem sad to you?

4.   **Allusion.**   An allusion is a reference to a person or place with which the reader is supposed to be familiar. This entire poem is an allusion to Abraham Lincoln. What line in the poem first tells you this?

# Florida Road Workers

### LANGSTON HUGHES

Hey, Buddy!
Look at me!

I'm makin' a road
For the cars to fly by on,
Makin' a road                                    5
Through the palmetto thicket
For light and civilization
To travel on.

I'm makin' a road
For the rich to sweep over              10
In their big cars
And leave me standin' here.

Sure,
A road helps everybody.
Rich folks ride—                                15
And I get to see 'em ride.
I ain't never seen nobody
Ride so fine before.

Hey, Buddy, look!
*I'm makin' a road!*

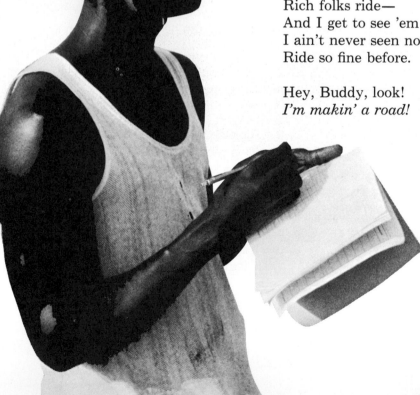

**DISCUSSION**  1.   What pictures did you see in your mind as you read this poem? Who is saying "Hey, Buddy/ Look at me"? To whom is he saying it?

2.   What are the worker's feelings about being a road worker? Does he like what he is doing? What phrases in the poem tell you that?

For further activities, see page 344.

# The Girl Who Hated Christmas

CELESTINE SIBLEY

Araminta Morley stood at the office window of the Open Door Mission and watched the December rain blow in against her grandfather's sign.

"Open Door Mission," read the sign. "Welcome All."

The mission sign was as plain and colorless as the life of a preacher's family, Araminta decided, looking at it. Black letters on white with a dim light (because electricity was something to save) burning over the sign. The wind blew the rain straight at the sign and made it swing drunkenly and clank with an eerie sound.

As Araminta watched, the bright gold and red and green beer sign across the street winked on and off, staining the mission's dull sign with cheerful reflected light.

Araminta grinned with lively twelve-year-old malice and gave her blond hair a little toss. Grandpa disapproved of drink. So many of the people who came to the Open Door were alcoholics. But even he had to admit the beer sign was the most cheerful thing on Dog Alley.

Dog Alley.

Araminta sighed. On city maps, and maybe a few street signs the residents had not knocked down and hauled off for purposes of their own, the street was called Dogwood Drive. And maybe years ago when the houses were new and proud back of snowy wood lace galleries, maybe then there had been dogwood trees.

Now it was called Dog Alley and, as Slick, the night clerk liked to say, only the dogs were left—whipped dogs, stray dogs, and dead dogs.

Slick meant human dogs and Araminta sighed again. It would be so much easier if he meant real dogs. With a real dog you might accomplish something. Food and warmth and kindness could be given in moderation. And that was all that was needed. You still had something left over for yourself.

But Grandpa's "dogs"! The term was Slick's and Araminta felt guilty even thinking of it. Grampa, being a preacher, didn't get angry often but he would be very angry if he heard belittling talk about The Folks of the mission. You couldn't beat

Grandpa, funny, stubborn old man. He believed in something called human dignity and worth. He really believed that everybody, even the alcoholics, the ex-convicts, and the beggars, had a divine spark inside.

Araminta brushed at her hair again but it wasn't a lively, complacent gesture. It was slow and dispirited.

Sometimes she got so *tired* of Grandpa and his goodness!

Sometimes, especially at Christmas, she longed to be gala, giddily selfish. She wanted warmth and comfort around her. She wanted to see her sweet, tired mother looking smart and stylish again as she used to before Daddy died and they came home to Grandpa and the mission.

"It can't be wicked," Araminta whispered fiercely to herself, "to want something just for *us*. I don't want to have to worry about The Folks all the time. The late-comers don't even sober up in time for Christmas. And most of the others just droop around, eating and sleeping and saying it's the saddest season of the year."

"Lord. . . ." Without intending to, Araminta found she was falling into Grandpa's habit of talking to Him. "Lord, look after The Folks, if You will. But give *us* something for a change. Let Grandpa and Mother and me have a happy Christmas."

Araminta may have added an "Amen." (Grandpa peppered his talks with his Friend with reverent "Amens.") But the hall door opened behind her, letting in a shaft of light.

It was Mother.

" 'Minta, honey," she said, her soft voice high with surprise, "what are you doing here in the dark? Is anything wrong?"

Mother was not any taller than Araminta and, considering that she was terribly old, practically thirty-five, she looked pretty neat. She was slim in a way that made even her skirts and sweaters from the old, prosperous days look good on her. Her hair was a deeper gold than Araminta's and although she wore it long in a smooth knot on her neck, capricious little tendrils slipped out and curled behind her face.

If she hurried, before she got too old, Mother might marry again—somebody nice and rich and distinguished. But if she stuck around the mission the best she could do would probably be Tom, which was all right, really. Araminta had no objection to his mooning over Mother, except that, like Grandpa, he was a dreamy minister who planned to do mission work and thought being poor was fine.

Araminta grinned at her mother.

"I was just admiring the beer sign," she said impishly.

Her mother put a hand on her shoulder and shook it in playful rebuke. "You need a spanking," she said, "but come and help The Folks decorate the chapel."

Araminta made a face of cheerful distaste.

"Oh, joy," she said. "Are we going to do it in something stunning this year like chartreuse and pink?"

"You're going to do it," said Mother firmly, looking a little tired again, "in just exactly what the Auxiliary Ladies brought."

Because she was twelve years old Araminta Morley was perhaps just the age to be cynical, even at Christmastime. Sometimes she suspected that the Open Door Auxiliary Ladies, the mission's main benefactors, used the mission and The Folks as a pious excuse for getting rid of unwanted junk in their closets.

She was positive that some of the clothes they sent hadn't been in use since the days of some silent old movie star named Theda Bara. And poor Miss Starry-Sky Higgins, although possibly the age, was not the type for voluptuous Theda Bara fashions.

From her stepladder, where she struggled to loop a garland of green over the chapel door, Araminta thoughtfully regarded Miss Starry-Sky, who was picking over the strings of burned-out Christmas tree lights the auxiliary sent. She looked, Araminta decided, like an old bone one of the real dogs of Dog Alley might have buried, dug up, found unpalatable, and buried again.

A beaded crepe dress in a strange shade of violet hung to her crooked, skinny little frame—too skimpy and too ruffled. On the whole, Araminta decided, it looks like the paper frill on a lamb chop after the chop has been eaten. And yet, because she reigned imperiously as queen of the Ladies Dorm at the Open Door Mission, Miss Starry-Sky had grabbed the dress when the auxiliary box came and nobody—especially nobody like Grandpa and Mother—had the heart to take it away from her. In spite of his being a minister and all wrapped up in running a mission for hungry and homeless people in a big city, in spite of having no raincoat or overcoat, Grandpa looked wonderful, Araminta decided. He was tall and thin and stooped now so his best blue suit, now threadbare, seemed too big for him. But there was something about him. . . . Araminta's heart swelled with love.

"Hi, Grand," she called from the stepladder.

Grandpa smiled at her. Grandpa was always pretty quiet in the chapel between services. He stood for a moment looking at the garlands of green and at the small Christmas tree in the corner with the lights which would not burn. There was a look of radiance on his face like he might be praying.

But it was quickly dimmed by The Folks.

"Oh, Mr. McIntosh," cried Miss Starry-Sky, hurrying over. "If any of these transient families in the private rooms get situated before Christmas, could I have a room to myself? When one has been accustomed to privacy it's so difficult. . . ."

Grandpa put down his bundles on one of the folding chairs and started to answer her in his gentle, patient way but before he could deal with Miss Starry-Sky's need for privacy, the others were crowding around him.

Old Mr. Hunt had slipped on the wet pavement with his crutches while looking for work and one of them broke. He demonstrated by hobbling back and forth before the minister how pitifully immobilized he was with only one crutch. Fat Mrs. Dumas, who made a pig of herself at every meal and hid any extras that came into the mission under her bedclothes and in her shoes, whispered to him that one of the cooks, probably the new one because he was just out of jail, must be stealing the coffee and diluting the sugar. The coffee was weak and the sugar wasn't as sweet as it should be.

And Charlie Puckett, one of the younger men who had come stumbling into the mission faint and feverish one night with a worried policeman to help him, just stood at Grandpa's elbow, looking gaunt and hungry-eyed, waiting.

"Any word, Reverunt?" he asked at last.

Grandpa shook his head and held out a hand to detain Charlie while he listened to somebody else. But the young man suddenly said a rude and shocking word, shook off the minister's hand, and strode from the room.

Araminta, seeing a look of pain cross Grandpa's face, was outraged. She climbed down from the stepladder with her blue eyes blazing. Selfish, demanding, ungrateful things . . . every one of them!

It was for these people that they gave up their own Christmas. For them Grandpa did without a winter coat and Mother worked too hard and was hidden away from fun and nice people in a dreary mission. For them Araminta herself had lost the memory of what "merry" meant in Merry Christmas.

Suddenly she felt that she could stand them no more.

"I think you're all horrid," she cried, looking from one to the other. "And I hate Christmas!"

And bursting into tears, she ran from the chapel.

Talk of spanking Araminta was not unusual around the Open Door Mission, where her grandfather, the Reverend Alex McIntosh, was superintendent. But it was all in fun. After all, she was twelve years old and supposedly knew how to behave.

And yet the night that she cried out she hated Christmas she wished somebody would spank her.

It was not that she wanted to take anything back. She did think the people who lived at the mission were selfish and she hated Christmas. But up in the room she shared with her mother in the superintendent's quarters on the third floor she felt so lonely and miserable she would have welcomed even somebody wanting to punish her.

Nobody came.

At least Mother didn't come until she had cried herself to sleep. And when she awakened it was morning and Mother had already dressed and gone downstairs. She had missed the night service, too, and Grandpa would not like that. She heard them singing down there, all The Folks, as they did every night after Scriptures and Grandpa's talk. Only now it was the songs of Christmas and they made her very sad up in her room alone.

Slick, the night clerk, was just coming up the stairs as Araminta went down to breakfast.

"Hi baby," said Slick, but his tone lacked its usual buoyancy. "You okay?"

"So far," said Araminta dismally. "I bet I catch it this morning though. Oh, Slick, wasn't it awful of me to act that way? Are Mother and Grandpa very mad at me?"

Slick shrugged and yawned. "I wouldn't know, baby. Your mother looks blue enough to dye a shirt these days anyhow. I thought it was because she was busting up with Tom."

"Oh . . . Tom," said Araminta scornfully. "Mother's smart to skip Tom. Another preacher, like Grandpa. Another mission, probably like this one. I wouldn't let my mother waste herself on such a marriage."

"So I hear." Slick sniffed. "Well, you know everything, Miss Fixit. Tell your mother not to hurt—and your grandpa too. He's somewhere now all cut up because Charlie Puckett tried to kill himself last night."

Araminta was shocked into silence.

She stood on the stairs looking at Slick, openmouthed. To throw away the gift of life . . . that was a sin. Charlie Puckett wouldn't dare. Grandpa wouldn't have it!

She started to speak but Slick had yawned again and gone on. She went down the stairs, slowly, troubled.

Grandpa was not in his office and Mother was not at her desk outside his door. Araminta looked in forlornly and wandered on back to the dining room. The breakfast dishes had been cleared away but some of The Folks continued to sit— complaining about the weak coffee, Araminta supposed. She got a bowl of cereal and a glass of milk and returned to the table, feeling shy about sitting with them after her outburst of the night before.

But they paid her scant attention. They were so busy talking.

"And Mrs. Dumas was so upset she went into the pantry and ate every last one of them fruitcakes the Reverunt was saving for Christmas," Mr. Hunt was finishing an account. "So this morning they had to take her to the Grady—she's that sick."

Miss Starry-Sky Higgins, still in her beaded violet crepe, was listening attentively and Araminta expected her to say something grand about the greedy ways of common people.

Instead she looked as if she were going to cry.

"I tell you, trouble's among us," she said softly. "That poor boy. All the time his heart hungering and us not knowing it. And now Mrs. Dumas, poor soul. People ought to help one another, Mr. Hunt. Mr. McIntosh and that dear, sad girl can't do everything for us all. Come with me to the chapel and let's talk to the others."

Miss Starry-Sky in her ridiculous hand-me-down finery led the way and Mr. Hunt, walking with difficulty with his one crutch, stumped along behind her.

Araminta watched them. What did they think they could do? There was plainly nothing anyone could do. Christmas in a mission was bound to be perfectly dreadful. Everybody's troubles came home to roost. She didn't know what Charlie

Puckett's heart was "hungering" for. She didn't know why anybody should feel sorry for Mrs. Dumas for being a pig. And if
her mother was a "poor, sad girl" it was no wonder—no money
to spend, no home of her own, no nice presents.

A feeling of sadness and self-pity gathered in her throat
and Araminta found she couldn't swallow any more cereal.
What about me? Christmas should have been her time—and
here she was, having no fun at all. The family didn't exchange
many presents and with all the trouble infecting The Folks . . .
if she just had some money she'd have some fun.

The solution to her problem came to Araminta so suddenly
she put her spoon down with a bang that caused her milk glass
to jump on the scrubbed tabletop.

The honor box.

Grandpa kept a few dollars in an old tin box on the office
desk for anyone who needed it. The idea was to take what you
needed and pay it back when you could.

Well, she needed the money. She needed some fun. What
was to prevent her taking the money and going downtown?

Araminta didn't once think about paying the money back.

Araminta never had taken any money from the Open Door Mission's honor box before, but she didn't really know why she
shouldn't. All The Folks under Grandpa's care had access to it.

Grandpa felt that it was humiliating for them to have to
ask for carfare when they went to look for work or to have to
beg a stamp when they had a letter to mail, which wasn't often.

He always told them the money was there for all and they
were to use it when they needed it and then replace it for others
when they could. Grandpa was proud that box had never been
really empty.

"And I won't empty it," Araminta promised herself right-
eously as she ran upstairs to get her coat. "I'll leave something
. . . for seed. But I just hope it's got a wad of paper money in it
today—lots of it."

Araminta stood before the mirror longer than she intended,
trying to decide if she should change her hairdo and if she
somehow could wear lipstick enough to make her feel made up
without Grandpa noticing that she was. When she finally left
the mirror and went downstairs she found the hall crowded with
people.

Charlie Puckett was being helped up the stairs by Grandpa. And Mrs. Dumas, looking weak and pale, was sitting on the bench by the door facing half a dozen of The Folks.

Araminta watched Grandpa and Charlie enter the men's dormitory and then she heard Mrs. Dumas say, "I just want to tell you all I'm mortally ashamed." She wiped her eyes. "I knowed them cakes I et wasn't mine. But looked like when I woke up in the night and heard about that young feller being nigh to dying, I felt so bad I plumb had to eat."

She started crying in earnest now and some of The Folks tried to soothe her by patting her plump shoulder.

"And the worst of it," she moaned piteously, burying her face in her hands, "I never did like the taste of fruitcake!"

Araminta turned away in disgust.

Grandpa was coming out of the men's dormitory and Araminta followed him slowly into the office. Maybe he was mad at her. Instead of sitting down at his desk he stood at the window, his hands locked behind him, his back to her.

"Grand," Araminta said, "I'm sorry I was ugly last night."

"Yes, child," Grand said without turning, "I knew you would be."

"Grand," Araminta's hand played with the honor box and surprisingly she saw it held bills—three or four or maybe as many as eight. Her heart beat faster as she eased out the money with one hand and crammed it into her pocket. It felt fine there, crisp and fine.

"Look, Grand," she went on. "I am sorry for saying it but what I said is true. These people are hopeless. You can't do anything for them. Look how good you've been to Charlie Puckett and Mrs. Dumas and look how they turned out—a coward and a glutton."

The old man at the window was quiet and Araminta went on urgently. "Grand, why do you waste yourself on poor dependent people? If you had a nice church where respectable people went, wouldn't that be just as good?"

Grand turned and for a moment Araminta thought he was angry. His blue eyes blazed. "Thou shalt not judge! Charlie is a troubled boy. He got in difficulties and lost his job and when he couldn't support his wife and baby he decided to run off and leave them. He loved them and he thought they'd do better without him.

"When he came here and got work I wrote to his wife for him and she hasn't answered—not yet. He's a sensitive boy and he is tortured by his guilt—more than I knew. What happened last night happened because I failed him. But thank the Lord," the minister's voice was fervent, "we've got another chance. He's going to live."

Araminta was silent and Grandpa went on.

"Mrs. Dumas eats because she is frightened. All her family is gone. She has nobody of her own and she has been close to starvation. When the police brought her to us it was because she had fainted on the street from hunger. You've never had that happen to you, have you, Araminta?"

The question was asked gently. Araminta shook her head mutely.

"You say I can't change The Folks." Grandpa's white eyebrows lifted humorously. "Of course, I can't. But with God's help they can change themselves. That was the first Christmas gift to all of us."

Araminta gulped.

"Well, g'bye, Grand," she said and turning, she walked toward the door. Looking back, her hand in her pocket, warm against the honor box money, she added, "Thanks for the Christmas Eve sermon."

Mother was in the hall as Araminta started out the Open Door Mission to buy herself a holiday treat with the honor box money. She was helping Miss Starry-Sky Higgins and crippled Mr. Hunt get into enough scarves and ill-fitting galoshes to make up for the fact that their thin coats were no protection against the damp cold.

"Oh, are you going out too, 'Minta?" Mother asked, taking in her coat. "Well, walk a way with Miss Starry-Sky and Mr. Hunt, won't you? The streets are slick and they need a strong arm to help them across Peachtree in the crowd."

The prospect of walking down the street with Mr. Hunt and his one crutch and Miss Starry-Sky with a man's old battered hat on her head and her violet dress flapping beneath an even shorter moth-chewed old fur coat, didn't invite Araminta. But she knew better than to refuse.

They left together and Mother stood at the door, smiling anxiously after them.

When they had gone a few yards Miss Starry-Sky looked back furtively and clutched Araminta's arm excitedly with one of her clawlike hands.

"Don't tell anybody yet but we think we know where Charlie Puckett's wife and baby are," she whispered.

"You do?" Araminta asked without much interest. "I thought he gave Grandpa their address."

"Yes, but we think they've come to Atlanta," Mr. Hunt put in. "Last night when Old Looey was trying to sell shoestrings and razor blades to the late shoppers he got so cold he went in Terminal Station to get warm. There was a young girl with a baby in there. The baby was asleep but Old Looey said when he thought about it a little it seemed to him the baby kind of favored Charlie Puckett."

Araminta smiled uncertainly. "Well, that's . . . nice."

Miss Starry-Sky and Mr. Hunt looked at each other, their spirits dampened a little by her lack of enthusiasm. They resumed their halting, hobbling progress toward town.

Araminta walked beside them. Old dreamers, she thought. Not making any more sense than usual. If Charlie Puckett's wife were in the station she must be running away from him. Otherwise she would have answered Grandpa's letter or come straight to the mission. Besides, what made them think it was Charlie Puckett's wife and baby? Just because a bleary-eyed old peddler thought he saw a resemblance between a sleeping baby and a man who tried to commit suicide?

Araminta dutifully saw the grotesque-looking pair across Peachtree Street and then she left them with a polite good-bye.

In spite of the damp and the cold the streets looked beautiful to her. Lights from the windows made a false sunshine in the gray morning and the music pouring from the loudspeakers sounded to her the way Christmas carols should sound. The majestic tones of an organ swelling with the trained voices of a big choir, instead of Mother's courageous fight to get music out of the old chapel piano and the quavering, tone-deaf voices of The Folks.

Araminta walked down Peachtree Street and looked in all the windows first and when she had looked her fill that way she ventured into the stores. She meant to have a milk-shake first but then she thought of Mrs. Dumas and she couldn't.

Even when lunchtime came and went she didn't eat.

She felt sad somehow and not very hungry. She thought to cheer herself by buying a lipstick and some nail polish to match. But when the saleswoman came to wait on her she shook her head.

"I don't want anything," she said. "I'm just looking."

The honor box money in her pocket no longer felt crisp and good. She had not even counted it and now she didn't want to. She thought of Miss Starry-Sky and Mr. Hunt walking in the cold and the damp on their pitiful, fruitless little errand. They could have borrowed carfare from the honor box. But they didn't. They had left the money for the others, which was more than she did.

"They're better than I am," she thought with sudden wonder. "They may not accomplish anything for Charlie Puckett, but at least they're trying. They care."

Grandpa and Mother cared too, she realized with a strange, growing sense of humility. They didn't care about Christmas presents and a bright comfortable way of life. They cared about The Folks.

Araminta found herself out on the sidewalk, her feet hurrying toward the mission.

"Lord," she prayed silently, "let me take back what I asked for. Give *them* something for Christmas, not *us*."

Darkness had not fallen, but because of the chill gray mist the mission sign had been lighted by the time Araminta turned in Dog Alley. Somehow the plain little sign looked warm and welcoming to her as she hurried along.

*Open Door Mission. Welcome All.*

Araminta didn't even look for its cheerful neighbor, the bright beer sign, but hurried straight for the front door.

There was such a hubbub in the hall nobody noticed her arrival at first.

Charlie Puckett and a pretty brown-eyed girl sat on the bottom stairstep holding hands. Mrs. Dumas was back at her old place on the bench by the door, looking strangely peaceful and happy over . . . a baby!

Araminta looked twice at the baby, who was not asleep now but making delighted crowing noises in response to delighted gibberish from Mrs. Dumas. The baby *did* look like Charlie Puckett.

Miss Starry-Sky, who had forgotten to take off her man's hat but had added a corsage of Christmas ornaments to her beaded dress, fluttered all about, telling over and over again how it happened.

"When I heard Mr. Lewis tell about seeing a girl and a baby in the station, I said to Mr. Hunt here, 'We must act at once.' "

"I can't get over it, Reverunt," Charlie Puckett said, lifting his eyes to Grandpa. "Polly was looking for me all the time. That's why she didn't get your letter. And if these folks hadn't taken an interest and gone looking for her, we'd still be separated."

Grandpa smiled at Miss Starry-Sky and Mr. Hunt.

"That's so," he said. "They tried, against considerable chances of failure. That takes faith and courage."

Mr. Hunt ducked his head modestly. Old Looey, wiping the dampness off his trays of precious shoelaces and razor blades, smiled with pleasure at his part of the affair. Araminta's mother, passing cookies and coffee, was quiet but a kind of light—Grandpa's kind of light—seemed to shine on her from somewhere.

She brushed Araminta's forehead with a kiss as she handed her cookies.

"Was it a good day for you, darling?" she asked.

A good day? Araminta thought. No . . . and then . . . *yes!*

"Yes, Mother," she said. "A lovely day. And this is so good. Isn't it wonderful to have them all so happy? Things are changing for some of them, aren't they?"

Mother nodded. "Yes. Charlie and Polly Puckett are getting jobs and Mrs. Dumas is going to live with them and keep house and look after the baby. She's so thrilled, 'Minta, to have a family to look after again."

"Mother. . . ." Araminta was hesitant. "If you married Tom we would have a mission somewhere, wouldn't we?"

Mother looked away, her face not so radiant now.

"That's right," she said. "Tom's going into mission work."

"Well, look, Mother. . . ." Araminta was shy. "I wish you'd marry him. He's nice and I *like* missions."

"'Minta"—Mother's voice was low and tender—"do you mean it? Would you be happy if Tom and I . . . oh, darling, I'd love to!"

When The Folks were all in the chapel, ready for the evening service, Araminta slipped into the office to return the wad of crumpled bills to the honor box.

It was dark in the office except for the light from the sign outside and at first Araminta thought her eyes were playing tricks. She had lifted the lid to the box and instead of coins she had left for "seed" there was a fifty dollar bill, the first Araminta ever saw.

"Grand!" she cried, running toward the chapel. Then she stopped. He would be beginning the service. But he wasn't. The day's events had made him late. He was just now coming down the stairs, his old blue suit freshly brushed, his white hair shining, his Bible in his hands.

"Look, Grand, what I found in the honor box!" Araminta cried, holding out the money. "Where did it come from?"

Grandpa looked at it, pleased but not excited. Money to Grandpa wasn't so awfully important.

"I think I know," he said casually. "Sometimes some of our folks go on from here to what you might call . . . success." He smiled whimsically. "A businessman who made a new start here a year or so ago paid us a call this afternoon. I didn't see him leave the money but I expect he did. It happens sometimes."

"Grand, does it?" asked Araminta, astonished.

"Oh, yes, I told you people can change," Grandpa said, smiling at her. "You never know who you are really helping when you do for 'the least of these.' Sometimes"—his tone was jaunty—"even capitalists turn up."

Grandpa hurried on to the chapel and Araminta followed. But The Folks began singing before she got there. It rang out, about as usual.

"O come, all ye faithful, joyful and triumphant," with the piano needing tuning and Miss Starry-Sky's cracked soprano rushing pell-mell ahead of everybody else.

But somehow it had a beautiful Christmasy sound.

**DISCUSSION**

1.   Grand's private Christmas Eve sermon to Araminta is about the possibility of people changing their lives. Speaking of The Folks, Araminta says that her grandfather can't change them. He replies, "Of course I can't. But . . . they can change themselves" (page 323). What does he mean? How does Araminta later prove that he's right?

2.   "I think you're all horrid," Araminta cried (p. 319). Who are these "horrid" people she despises? What do they do that she complains about?

3.   Later she sees "with a strange, growing sense of humility" (p. 325) that they are better than she is. What do they do that she hasn't learned to do yet? Which of the "horrid" people teach her this lesson?

4.   The beer sign across the street is bright gold and red and cheerful. It contrasts with the plain and colorless mission sign. Araminta wants a life away from the mission that would be colorful like the sign. What does she do in an attempt to get some color into her life? Why doesn't it work for her?

For further activities, see page 344.

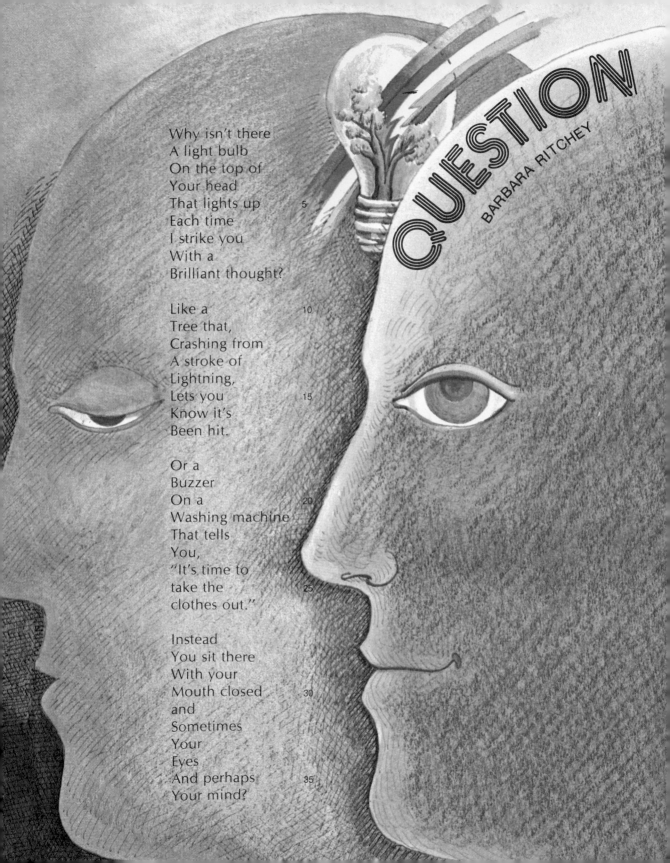

# QUESTION

BARBARA RITCHEY

Why isn't there
A light bulb
On the top of
Your head
That lights up          5
Each time
I strike you
With a
Brilliant thought?

Like a                   10
Tree that,
Crashing from
A stroke of
Lightning,
Lets you                 15
Know it's
Been hit.

Or a
Buzzer
On a                     20
Washing machine
That tells
You,
"It's time to
take the                 25
clothes out."

Instead
You sit there
With your
Mouth closed             30
and
Sometimes
Your
Eyes
And perhaps              35
Your mind?

# The Monsters Are Due on Maple Street

A Television Play    ROD SERLING

CHARACTERS

NARRATOR
DON MARTIN
STEVE BRAND
MRS. BRAND
PETE VAN HORN
CHARLIE
TOMMY
SALLY

LES GOODMAN
MAN
SECOND MAN
WOMAN
FIVE DIFFERENT VOICES
FIRST FIGURE
SECOND FIGURE

# Act One

Scene: It's a tree-lined, quiet, residential American street, very typical of the small town. The houses have front porches on which people sit and swing on gliders, conversing across from house to house. Steve Brand polishes his car parked in front of his house. His neighbor, Don Martin, leans against the fender watching him. A Good Humor man rides a bicycle and is just in the process of stopping to sell some ice cream to a couple of kids. Two women gossip on the front lawn. Another man waters his lawn.

NARRATOR: Maple Street, U.S.A., late summer. A tree-lined little world of front-porch gliders, hopscotch, the laughter of children, and the bell of an ice cream vendor. At the sound of the roar and the flash of the light, it will be precisely six forty-three P.M. on Maple Street.

At this moment one of the boys, Tommy, looks up to listen to a sound of a tremendous screeching roar from overhead. A flash of light plays on both their faces, and then it moves down the street past lawns and porches and rooftops and then disappears. Steve Brand, the man who's been polishing his car, stands there transfixed, staring upwards. He looks at Don Martin, his neighbor from across the street.

STEVE: What was that? A meteor?

DON [nods]: That's what it looked like. I didn't hear any crash, though, did you?

STEVE [shakes his head]: Nope, I didn't hear anything except a roar.

MRS. BRAND [from her porch]: Steve? What was that?

STEVE [raising his voice and looking toward the porch]: Guess it was a meteor, honey. Came awful close, didn't it?

MRS. BRAND: Too close for my money! Much too close.

On the various porches people stand watching and talking in low conversing tones.

NARRATOR: Maple Street. Six forty-four P.M., on a late September evening. [A pause.] Maple Street in the last calm and reflective moment . . . before the monsters came!

We see a man screwing a light bulb on a front porch, then getting down off the stool to flick the switch and find that nothing happens. A man working on an electric power mower plugs in the plug, flicks on the switch of the power mower, off and on, with nothing happening. Through the window of a front porch a woman is seen pushing her finger back and forth on the dial hook. Her voice is distant but repetitive.

WOMAN: Operator, operator, something's wrong on the phone, operator!

Mrs. Brand comes out on the porch and calls to Steve.

MRS. BRAND [calling]: Steve, the power's off. I had the soup on the stove, and the stove just stopped working.

WOMAN: Same thing over here. I can't get

anybody on the phone either. The phone seems to be dead.

FIRST VOICE: Electricity's off.

SECOND VOICE: Phone won't work.

THIRD VOICE: Can't get a thing on the radio.

FOURTH VOICE: My power mower won't move, won't work at all.

FIFTH VOICE: Radio's gone dead!

Pete Van Horn, a tall, thin man, is seen standing in front of his house.

VAN HORN: I'll cut through the back yard. . . . See if the power's still on on Floral Street. I'll be right back!

STEVE: Doesn't make sense. Why should the power go off all of a sudden *and* the phone line?

DON: Maybe some kind of an electrical storm or something.

CHARLIE: That don't seem likely. Sky's just as blue as anything. Not a cloud. No lightning. No thunder. No nothing. How could it be a storm?

WOMAN: I can't get a thing on the radio. Not even the portable.

CHARLIE: Well, why don't you go downtown and check with the police, though they'll probably think we're crazy or something. A little power failure and right away we get all flustered and everything—

STEVE: It isn't just the power failure, Charlie. If it was, we'd still be able to get a broadcast on the portable.

There's a murmur of reaction to this. Steve looks from face to face and then over to his car.

STEVE: I'll run downtown. We'll get this all straightened out.

Steve walks over to the car, gets into it, turns the key. Steve starts the engine. It turns over sluggishly and then just stops dead. He tries it again, and this time he can't get it to turn over. Then very slowly and reflectively he turns the key back to "off" and then slowly gets out of the car. He stands for a moment by the car and then walks toward the group.

STEVE: I don't understand it. It was working fine before——
DON: Out of gas?
STEVE [shakes his head]: I just had it filled up.
WOMAN: What's it mean?
CHARLIE: It's just as if . . . as if everything had stopped. [Then he turns toward Steve.] We'd better *walk* downtown.

Another murmur of assent to this.

STEVE: The two of us can go, Charlie. [He turns to look back at the car.] It couldn't be the meteor. A meteor couldn't do *this*.

He and Charlie exchange a look. Then they start to walk away from the group. Tommy, a serious-faced young boy in spectacles, stands a few feet away from the group, halfway between them and the two men who start to walk down the sidewalk.

TOMMY: Mr. Brand . . . you'd better not!
STEVE: Why not?
TOMMY: They don't want you to.

Steve and Charlie exchange a grin, and Steve looks back toward the boy.

STEVE: *Who* doesn't want us to?
TOMMY [jerks his head in the general direction of the distant horizon]: Them!
STEVE: Them?
CHARLIE: Who are them?

TOMMY [very intently]: Whoever was in that thing that came by overhead.
STEVE: What?
TOMMY: Whoever was in that thing that came over. I don't think they want us to leave here.

Steve leaves Charlie and walks over to the boy. He kneels down in front of him. He forces his voice to remain gentle. He reaches out and holds the boy.

STEVE: What do you mean? What are you talking about?
TOMMY: They don't want us to leave. That's why they shut everything off.
STEVE: What makes you say that? Whatever gave you *that* idea?
WOMAN [from the crowd]: Now isn't that the craziest thing you ever heard?
TOMMY [persistently]: It's always that way, in every story I ever read about a ship landing from outer space.
WOMAN [to the boy's mother, Sally, who stands on the fringe of the crowd]: From outer space yet! Sally, you better get that boy of yours up to bed. He's been reading too many comic books or seeing too many movies or something!
SALLY: Tommy, come over here and stop that kind of talk.
STEVE: Go ahead, Tommy. We'll be right back. And you'll see. That wasn't any ship or anything like it. That was just a . . . a meteor or something. Likely as not—[He turns to the group, now trying to weight his words with an optimism he obviously doesn't feel but is desperately trying to instill in himself as well as the others.] No doubt it did have something to do with all this

power failure and the rest of it. Meteors can do some crazy things. Like sun spots.

DON [picking up the cue]: Sure. That's the kind of thing—like sun spots. They raise Cain with radio reception all over the world. And this thing being so close—why, there's no telling the sort of stuff it can do. [He wets his lips, smiles nervously.] Go ahead, Charlie. You and Steve go into town and see if that isn't what's causing it all.

Steve and Charlie again continue to walk away from the group down the sidewalk. The people watch silently. Tommy stares at them, biting his lips and finally calling out again.

TOMMY: Mr. Brand!

The two men stop again. Tommy takes a step toward them.

TOMMY: Mr. Brand . . . please don't leave here.

Steve and Charlie stop once again and turn toward the boy. There's a murmur in the crowd, a murmur of irritation and concern as if the boy were bringing up fears that shouldn't be brought up.

TOMMY: You might not even be able to get to town. It was that way in the story. *Nobody* could leave. Nobody except—

STEVE: Except who?

TOMMY: Except the people they'd sent down ahead of them. They looked just like humans. And it wasn't until the ship landed that——[The boy suddenly stops again, conscious of his parents staring at him and of the sudden hush of the crowd.]

SALLY [in a whisper, sensing the antagonism of the crowd]: Tommy, please, son . . . honey, don't talk that way——

MAN: The kid shouldn't talk that way . . . and we shouldn't stand here listening to him. Why, this is the craziest thing I ever heard of. The kid tells us a comic-book plot, and here we stand listening——

Steve walks toward the boy.

STEVE: Go ahead, Tommy. What kind of story was this? What about the people that they sent out ahead?

TOMMY: That was the way they prepared things for the landing. They sent four people. A mother and a father and two kids who looked just like humans . . . but they weren't.

There's another silence as Steve looks toward the crowd and then toward Tommy. He wears a tight grin.

STEVE: Well, I guess what we'd better do is to run a check on the neighborhood and see which ones of us are really human.

There's laughter at this, but it's a laughter that comes from a desperate attempt to lighten the atmosphere. It's a release kind of laugh. The people look at one another in the middle of their laughter.

CHARLIE [rubs his jaw nervously]: I wonder if Floral Street's got the same deal we got. [He looks past the houses.] Where is Pete Van Horn anyway? Didn't he get back yet?

Suddenly there's the sound of a car's engine starting to turn over. Les Goodman is at the wheel of his car.

SALLY: Can you get started, Les?

Les Goodman gets out of the car, shaking his head.

GOODMAN: No dice.

As he walks toward the group, he stops suddenly. Behind him, the car engine starts up all by itself. Goodman whirls around to stare toward it. The car idles roughly, smoke coming from the exhaust, the frame shaking gently. Goodman's eyes go wide, and he runs over to his car. The people stare toward the car.

MAN: He got the car started somehow. He got *his* car started!
WOMAN: How come his car just up and started like that?
SALLY: All by itself. He wasn't anywhere near it. It started all by itself.

Don approaches the group, stops a few feet away to look toward Goodman's car and then back toward the group.

DON: And he never did come out to look at that thing that flew overhead. He wasn't even interested. [He turns to the faces in the group, his face taut and serious.] Why? Why didn't he come out with the rest of us to look?
CHARLIE: He was always an oddball. Him and his whole family. Real oddball.
DON: What do you say we ask him?

The group suddenly start toward the house. For a moment their fear almost turns their walk into a wild stampede, but Steve's voice, loud and commanding, makes them stop.

STEVE: Wait a minute . . . *wait a minute!* Let's not be a mob!

The people stop as a group, seem to pause for

a moment, and then much more quietly and slowly start to walk across the street. Goodman stands there alone, facing the people.

GOODMAN: I just don't understand it. I tried to start it, and it wouldn't start. You saw me. All of you saw me.

And now, just as suddenly as the engine started, it stops, and there's frightened murmuring of the people.

GOODMAN: I don't understand. I swear . . . I don't understand. What's happening?
DON: Maybe you better tell us. Nothing's working on this street. Nothing. No lights, no power, no radio. [And then meaningfully.] Nothing except one car—*yours!*

The people pick this up, and their murmuring becomes a loud chant filling the air with demands for action. Two of the men pass Don and head toward Goodman, who backs away, backing into his car and now at bay.

GOODMAN: Wait a minute now. You keep your distance—all of you. So I've got a car that starts by itself—well, that's a freak thing—I admit it. But does that make me some kind of a criminal or something? I don't know why the car works—it just does!

This stops the crowd, and Goodman, still backing away, goes toward his front porch. He goes up the steps and then stops to stand facing the mob.

GOODMAN: What's it all about, Steve?
STEVE [quietly]: We're all on a monster kick, Les. Seems that the general impression holds that maybe one

family isn't what we think they are. Monsters from outer space or something. Different than us. Fifth columnists[1] from the vast beyond. [He chuckles.] You know anybody that might fit that description around here on Maple Street?

GOODMAN: What is this, a gag or something? This a practical joke or something?

Suddenly the engine of the car starts all by itself again, runs for a moment, and stops. The people once again react.

GOODMAN: Now that's supposed to incriminate me, huh? The car engine goes on and off, and that really does it, doesn't it? [He looks around the faces of the people.] I just don't understand it . . . any more than any of you do! [He wets his lips, looking from face to face.] Look, you all know me. We've lived here five years. Right in this house. We're no different than any of the rest of you! We're no different at all. . . . Really . . . this whole thing is just . . . just weird—

WOMAN: Well, if that's the case, Les Goodman, explain why—[She stops suddenly, clamping her mouth shut.]

GOODMAN [softly]: Explain what?

STEVE [interjecting]: Look, let's forget this—

CHARLIE [overlapping him]: Go ahead; let her talk. What about it? Explain what?

WOMAN [a little reluctantly]: Well . . . sometimes I go to bed late at night. A couple of times . . . a couple of times I'd come out here on the porch and I'd see Mr. Goodman here in the wee hours of the morning standing out in front of his house . . . looking up at the sky. [She looks around the circle of faces.] That's right, looking up at the sky as if . . . as if he were waiting for something. [A pause.] As if he were looking for something.

There's a murmur of reaction from the crowd again. Goodman backs away.

GOODMAN: She's crazy. Look, I can explain that. Please . . . I can really explain that. . . . she's making it up anyway. [Then he shouts.] I tell you she's making it up!

He takes a step toward the crowd, and they back away. He walks down the steps after them, and they continue to back away. He's suddenly and completely left alone, and he looks like a man caught in the middle of a menacing circle.

---

[1] *Fifth columnists:* secret sympathizers and supporters of the enemy.

# Act Two

SCENE 1:

From the various houses we can see candlelight but no electricity. There's an all-pervading quiet that blankets the whole area, disturbed only by the almost whispered voices of the people as they stand around. Charlie stares across at Goodman's house. Two men stand across the street from it in almost sentrylike poses.

SALLY [a little timorously]: It doesn't seem right, though, keeping watch on them. Why, he was right when he said he was one of our neighbors. Why, I've known Ethel Goodman ever since they moved in. We've been good friends——

CHARLIE: That don't prove a thing. Any guy who'd spend his time lookin' up at the sky early in the morning—well, there's something wrong with that kind of person. There's something that ain't legitimate. Maybe under normal circumstances we could let it go by, but these aren't normal circumstances. Why, look at this street! Nothin' but candles. Why, it's like goin' back into the dark ages or somethin'!

Steve, from several yards away, walks down the steps of his porch, walks down the street over to Les Goodman's house, and then stops at the foot of the steps. Goodman stands there, Mrs. Goodman behind him, very frightened.

GOODMAN: Just stay right where you are, Steve. We don't want any trouble, but this time if anybody sets foot on my porch—that's what they're going to get—trouble!

STEVE: Look, Les——

GOODMAN: I've already explained to you people. I don't sleep very well at night sometimes. I get up and I take a walk and I look up at the sky. I look at the stars!

MRS. GOODMAN: That's exactly what he does. Why, this whole thing, it's . . . it's some kind of madness or something.

STEVE [nods grimly]: That's exactly what it is—some kind of madness.

CHARLIE'S VOICE [shrill, from across the street]: You best watch who you're seen with, Steve! Until we get this all straightened out, you ain't exactly above suspicion yourself.

STEVE [whirling around toward him]: Or you, Charlie. Or any of us, it seems. From age eight on up!

WOMAN: What I'd like to know is—what are we gonna do? Just stand around here all night?

CHARLIE: There's nothin' else we *can* do! [He turns back, looking toward Steve and Goodman again.] One of 'em'll tip their hand. They *got* to.

STEVE [raising his voice]: There's something you can do, Charlie. You could go home and keep your mouth shut. You could quit strutting around like a self-appointed hanging judge and just climb into bed and forget it.

CHARLIE: You sound real anxious to have that happen, Steve. I think we better keep our eye on you too!

DON [as if he were taking the bit in his teeth, takes a hesitant step to the front]: I think everything might as well come out now. [He turns toward Steve.] Your wife's done plenty of talking, Steve, about how odd *you* are!

CHARLIE [picking this up, his eyes widening]: Go ahead, tell us what she's said. [Steve walks toward them from across the street.]

STEVE: Go ahead, what's my wife said? Let's get it *all* out. Let's pick out every idiosyncrasy[2] of every single man, woman, and child on the street. And then we might as well set up some kind of kangaroo court.[3] How about a firing squad at dawn, Charlie, so we can get rid of all the suspects. Narrow them down. Make it easier for you.

DON: There's no need gettin' so upset, Steve. It's just that . . . well . . . Myra's talked about how there's been plenty of nights you spent hours down in your basement workin' on some kind of radio or something. Well, none of us have ever *seen* that radio——

By this time Steve has reached the group. He stands there defiantly close to them.

CHARLIE: Go ahead, Steve. What kind of "radio set" you workin' on? I never seen it. Neither has anyone else. Who do you talk to on that radio set? And who talks to you?

STEVE: I'm surprised at you, Charlie. How come you're so dense all of a sudden? [A pause.] Who do I talk to? I talk to monsters from outer space. I talk to three-headed green men who fly over here in what look like meteors.

Mrs. Brand steps down from the porch, bites her lip, calls out.

MRS. BRAND: Steve! Steve, please. [Then looking around frightened, she walks toward the group.] It's just a ham radio set, that's all. I bought him a book on it myself. It's just a ham radio set. A lot of people have them. I can show it to you. It's right down in the basement.

STEVE [whirls around toward her]: Show them nothing! If they want to look inside our house—let them get a search warrant.

CHARLIE: Look, buddy, you can't afford to—

STEVE [interrupting]: Charlie, don't start telling me who's dangerous and who isn't and who's safe and who's a menace. [He turns to the group and shouts.] And you're with him too—all of you! You're standing here all set to crucify—all set to find a scapegoat—all desperate to point some kind of a finger at a neighbor! Well now, look, friends, the only thing that's gonna happen is that we'll eat each other up alive——

He stops abruptly as Charlie suddenly grabs his arm.

CHARLIE [in a hushed voice]: That's not the only thing that can happen to us.

A figure suddenly materializes in the gloom, and in the silence we can hear the clickety-clack of

---

[2] *idiosyncrasy* (ĭd-ē-ō-sing'krə-sē): a person's habits thought to be peculiar.

[3] *kangaroo court:* court in which the principles of law and justice are disregarded or distorted.

slow, measured footsteps on concrete as the figure walks slowly toward them. One of the women lets out a stifled cry. The young mother grabs her boy as do a couple of others.

TOMMY [shouting, frightened]: It's the monster! It's the monster! [Another woman lets out a wail, and the people fall back in a group, staring toward the darkness and the approaching figure. Don Martin joins them, carrying a shotgun. He holds it up.]

DON: We may need this.

STEVE: A shotgun? [He pulls it out of Don's hand.] Will anybody think a thought around here? Will you people wise up? What good would a shotgun do against——

Charlie pulls the gun from Steve's hand.

CHARLIE: No more talk, Steve. You're going to talk us into a grave! You'd let whatever's out there walk right over us, wouldn't yuh? Well, some of us won't!

He swings the gun around to point it toward the sidewalk. The dark figure continues to walk toward them. Charlie slowly raises the gun. As the figure gets closer, he pulls the trigger. The sound explodes in the stillness. The figure lets out a small cry, stumbles forward onto his knees, and then falls forward on his face. Don, Charlie, and Steve race forward over to him. Steve is there first and turns the man over. The crowd gathers around them.

STEVE [slowly looks up]: It's Pete Van Horn.

DON [in a hushed voice]: Pete Van Horn! He was just gonna go over to the next block to see if the power was on——

WOMAN: You killed him, Charlie. You shot him dead!

CHARLIE [looks around at the circle of faces, his eyes frightened, his face contorted]: But . . . but I didn't know who he was. I certainly didn't know who he was. He comes walkin' out of the darkness—how am I supposed to know who he was? [He grabs Steve.] Steve—you know why I shot! How was I supposed to know he wasn't a monster or something? [He grabs Don.] We're all scared of the same thing. I was just tryin' to . . . tryin' to protect my home, that's all! Look, all of you, that's all I was tryin' to do. [He looks down wildly at the body.] I didn't know it was somebody we knew! I didn't know——

There's a sudden hush and then an intake of breath in the group. Across the street all the lights go on in one of the houses.

WOMAN [in a very hushed voice]: Charlie . . . Charlie . . . the lights just went on in your house. Why did the lights just go on?

DON: What about it, Charlie? How come you're the only one with lights now?

GOODMAN: That's what I'd like to know.

A pause as they all stare toward Charlie.

GOODMAN: You were so quick to kill, Charlie, and you were so quick to tell us who we had to be careful of. Well, maybe you *had* to kill. Maybe Pete there was trying to tell us something. Maybe he'd found out something and came back to tell us who there was amongst us we should watch out for——

Charlie backs away from the group, his eyes wide with fright.

CHARLIE: No . . . no . . . it's nothing of the sort! I don't know why the lights are on. I swear I don't. Somebody's pulling a gag or something.

He bumps against Steve, who grabs him and whirls him around.

STEVE: *A gag?* A gag? Charlie, there's a dead man on the sidewalk, and you killed him! Does this thing look like a gag to you?

Charlie breaks away and screams as he runs toward his house.

CHARLIE: No! No! Please!

A man breaks away from the crowd to chase Charlie. The man tackles him and lands on top of him. The other people start to run toward them. Charlie gets up on his feet, breaks away from the other man's grasp, lands a couple of desperate punches that push the man aside. Then he forces his way, fighting, through the crowd. He once again breaks free and jumps up on his front porch. A rock thrown from the group smashes a window alongside of him, the broken glass flying past him. A couple of pieces cut him. He stands there perspiring, rumpled, blood running down from a cut on the cheek. His wife breaks away from the group to throw herself into his arms. He buries his face against her. We can see the crowd converging on the porch.

FIRST VOICE: It must have been him.
SECOND VOICE: He's the one.
THIRD VOICE: We got to get Charlie.

Another rock lands on the porch. Charlie pushes his wife behind him, facing the group.

CHARLIE: Look, look, I swear to you . . .

it isn't me . . . but I do know who it is . . . I swear to you, I do know who it is. I know who the monster is here. I know who it is that doesn't belong. I swear to you I know.
DON [pushing his way to the front of the crowd]: All right, Charlie, let's hear it!
SECOND MAN [screaming]:—Go ahead, Charlie, tell us.
CHARLIE: It's . . . it's the kid. It's Tommy. He's the one!
SALLY [backs away]: That's crazy. That's crazy. He's only a boy.
WOMAN: But he knew! He was the only one who knew! He told us all about it. Well, how did he know? How *could* he have known?

The various people take this up and repeat the question aloud.

FIRST VOICE: How could he know?
SECOND VOICE: Who told him?
THIRD VOICE: Make the kid answer.

The crowd starts to converge around the mother, who grabs Tommy and starts to run with him. The crowd starts to follow, at first walking fast, and then running after Sally and Tommy. Suddenly Charlie's lights go off, and the lights in another house go on. They stay on for a moment, and then from across the street other lights go on and then off again.

MAN [shouting]: It isn't the kid . . . it's Bob Weaver's house.
WOMAN: It isn't Bob Weaver's house; its Don Martin's place.
CHARLIE: I tell you it's the kid.
DON: It's Charlie. He's the one.

Various people shout, accuse each other, scream. House lights go on and off.

SCENE 2: In a nearby field a space craft sits shrouded in darkness. An open door throws out a beam of light from the illuminated interior. Two figures silhouetted against the bright lights appear.

FIRST FIGURE: Understand the procedure now? Just stop a few of their machines and radios and telephones and lawn mowers . . . throw them into darkness for a few hours, and then just sit back and watch the pattern.

SECOND FIGURE: And this pattern is always the same?

FIRST FIGURE: With few variations. They pick the most dangerous enemy they can find . . . and it's themselves. And all we need do is sit back . . . and watch.

SECOND FIGURE: Then I take it this place . . . this Maple Street . . . is not unique.

FIRST FIGURE [shaking his head]: By no means. Their world is full of Maple Streets. And we'll go from one to the other and let them destroy themselves. One to the other . . . one to the other . . . one to the other——

SCENE 3:         The starry sky. We hear the Narrator's voice.

NARRATOR: The tools of conquest do not necessarily come with bombs and explosions and fallout. There are weapons that are simply thoughts, attitudes, prejudices—to be found only in the minds of men. For the record, prejudices can kill and suspicion can destroy, and a thoughtless, frightened search for a scapegoat has a fallout all of its own for the children . . . and the children yet unborn.

DISCUSSION      1.   "Their world is full of Maple Streets," says one of the figures from the space craft (page 343). Whose world? Do you agree? Would the outcome of the play have been different if it had happened somewhere else?

2.   The narrator at the end of the play says ". . . a thoughtless, frightened search for a scapegoat has a fallout all of its own. . . ." When did the search for a scapegoat begin? What characters in turn were suspected by the others?

3.   Which character in the play seems to be the most afraid? What effect does his fear have on the other characters? What final act does he commit because of his fear?

4.   Most of the action in the play involves the men in the neighborhood. Where are the women? Do you think the play is a true picture of the way men and women are? Explain.

5.   Who are the monsters on Maple Street?

For futher activities, see page 344.

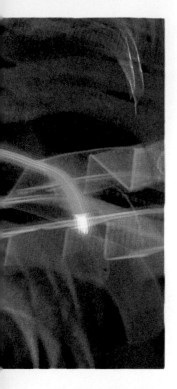

## VOCABULARY

### The Girl Who Hated Christmas (page 314)

On separate paper, write the word closest in meaning to the word in bold type in the left column.

1.  with an *eerie* sound — comical    loud    strange
2.  *diluting* the sugar — thinning    stealing    pouring
3.  a *dreary* mission — new    gloomy    old-fashioned
4.  looked in *forlornly* — sadly    enviously    cautiously
5.  shook her head *mutely* — carefully    silently    vigorously
6.  looked back *furtively* — quickly    secretly    frequently
7.  *fruitless* little errand — useless    boring    tiring
8.  old *prosperous* days — childhood    successful    sad
9.  these *transient* families — homeless    large    amusing
10. its usual *buoyancy* — anger    humor    lightness

### The Monsters Are Due on Maple Street (page 330)

Look at the stage directions below. If you were a director, how would you demonstrate these actions to your actors? How would you explain them?

he wets his lips, smiles nervously
rubs his jaw nervously
he chuckles
nods grimly
in a hushed voice

## COMPOSITION

### Florida Road Workers (page 312)

The speaker in this poem does a job that most people give little thought to. Yet the speaker likes his job and gets satisfaction from it. Think of another similar job and write about it from the point of view of a person who enjoys that job.

### The Monsters Are Due on Maple Street (page 330)

Imagine that the two creatures from outer space have returned to their home planet. Write the conversation they might have with friends, explaining what they saw on Maple Street.

# READING

## The Girl Who Hated Christmas (page 314)

**A.** The following statements are about the main characters. But which statement is about which main character? On separate paper, make three columns, one each for Araminta, Grandpa, and Mother. Then put the number of the statements in the appropriate column.

1. disapproves of drinking
2. doesn't get angry often
3. is widowed
4. longs to have fun
5. is tired and unstylish
6. is stubborn
7. believes in human dignity
8. wants warmth and comfort
9. wants things for the family only
10. believes The Folks don't appreciate what is given to them
11. thinks being poor is "fine"
12. believes Christmas is a sad time

**B.** Which two of these statements about the mission are true?

1. The mission has a plain, dull sign.
2. The mission is an orphanage.
3. The mission is located in a rundown area of the city.
4. The mission welcomes stray dogs.
5. The name of the mission is "Dog Alley."

## The Monsters Are Due on Maple Street (page 330)

The characters in this play made judgments about each other. Below are some of the reasons people gave for making their judgments. On separate paper, match the statement with the name of the appropriate character. For some characters there will be more than one statement.

1. He liked to look up at the sky in the wee hours of the morning.
2. He had a ham radio that no one had ever seen.
3. He read a story in which the invaders didn't let anyone leave except their own people.
4. His car started when no one else's would.
5. He got his gun and shot one of the neighbors.
6. He came walking slowly out of the darkness.

   Tommy   Goodman   Charlie   Pete   Steve

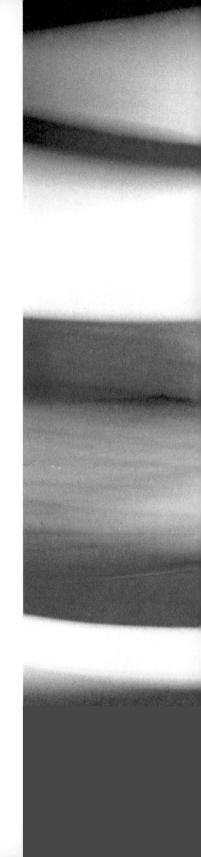

# COMPOSITION

A *paragraph* is a group of sentences unified around a single idea. The sentences being written to form *this* paragraph are centered around one thought: to help define what a paragraph is by telling how it works and what it looks like. When that definition seems complete, the paragraph will end. The beginning of the paragraph is indicated on the page by *indenting* the first sentence (bringing the first word in from the left margin or edge). Or it may be indicated by starting a new line. The final sentence of the paragraph will end where it will, but not necessarily near the righthand margin, the way other lines in the paragraph do.

A paragraph, then, is not simply a group of sentences. *Rather, it is a group of sentences exploring a single thought.* Generally, the thought is expressed directly within the paragraph. For example, the italicized sentence here expresses the central thought of the paragraph that you are reading now. Other sentences within the paragraph may give examples to make the thought clearer, they may give exceptions, or they may add information about it. But all the sentences will relate in some way to the main idea that shapes the paragraph.

When we realize that each paragraph develops one thought, we begin to see more clearly how prose is organized. (The purpose of this new paragraph will be to explain how prose is organized, or put together.) To organize prose, we group words into sentences. Sentences we then group into paragraphs. Each paragraph is like a bead on a string: it develops a single, separate idea, yet it is related to paragraphs that precede and follow it, as each bead is something complete but is tied to other beads to make a necklace.

Consider, for instance, the arrangement of the first three paragraphs of "An Unpredictable Japanese Lady" (page 298). Each develops its own idea that leads into the idea in the following paragraph. The first paragraph deals with Mother's desire to learn English. It leads to remarks in the second paragraph about her way of going about learning the language. These remarks in turn prepare for her experiences speaking English at such places as P.T.A. meetings. The third paragraph introduces those experiences. The paragraphs taken together reveal the subject in an orderly, logical way.

**BUILDING PARAGRAPHS**

## ABOUT THE SELECTIONS

1. Many selections in this section deal with life within families, among them, "Charles," "Ironman Gregory," "The Long Way Around," "An Unpredictable Japanese Lady," and "The Girl Who Hated Christmas." To which one of the families pictured here would you most like to belong? In a unified paragraph explain specifically why the family is appealing.

2. Getting along with other people isn't always easy. Which one person among the many you have come to know in these selections would you find most difficult to be with? In a paragraph mention specific characteristics, acts, and remarks of the person that have caused her or him to be chosen as your candidate for least likeable.

3. "You speak English and I speak English," Carl Sandburg writes in "Fifty-Fifty" (page 286), "and you never understand me and I never understand you." How can that be, if both speak the same language? Write a paragraph that refers to conversations or details from a selection in this section to make clear what these lines mean.

4. In a paragraph explore how the following group of sentences from "The Long Way Around" develops a single idea. What is the idea? What does each sentence within the group add to that idea?

> Actually I hated them all. I hated the teachers and the new school and my new stepmother and my father who seemed a new person too. Even my little brothers seemed to deserve a good slap for the way they had forgotten and called Alice "Mother," as if they had never had a mother of their own.

## ON YOUR OWN

1. With whom do you get along best: a classmate, a friend in the neighborhood, an older person, a relative? Write a paragraph that sketches that person for the reader. (In order to avoid embarrassing anyone, you may want to provide a name for the person different from her or his real one.)

2. We relate to each other most often through language. Try your hand at writing a dialogue that reveals two people explaining themselves to each other—or failing to. You will be writing a little play of a page or less. See how much you can reveal to the reader about the situation, about the people, and about their feelings for each other, simply through what they say.

3. What quality do you most value in people? Write a paragraph unified around explaining what that quality is (honesty? a sense of humor? courage? intelligence? generosity? concern for others?) and why it seems basic. Examples will help make your paragraph more convincing.

4. Write *two* paragraphs of three, four, or five sentences each that are related to each other in some specific way. Make sure that the first paragraph is unified around its central idea that it leads logically into the second paragraph. You may write on any reasonable subject, but choose one you know well and can write about comfortably—from sports, home life, hobbies, school, ambitions, or whatever else interests you most.

MYTHS & TALES

# THREE FABLES FROM AESOP

*(GREECE)*

JOSEPH JACOBS

# The Fox and the Crow

A fox once saw a crow fly off with a piece of cheese in its beak and settle on a branch of a tree. "That's for me, as I am a fox," said Master Reynard, and he walked up to the foot of the tree. "Good day, Mistress Crow," he cried. "How well you are looking today—how glossy your feathers, how bright your eye. I feel sure your voice must surpass that of other birds, just as your figure does; let me hear but one song from you that I may greet you as the Queen of Birds." The crow lifted up her head and began to caw her best, but the moment she opened her mouth, the piece of cheese fell to the ground, only to be snapped up by Master Fox. "That will do," said he. "That was all I wanted. In exchange for your cheese I will give you a piece of advice for the future:

*Do not trust flatterers.*"

# The Shepherd Boy

There was once a young shepherd boy who tended his sheep at the foot of a mountain near a dark forest. It was rather lonely for him all day, so he thought upon a plan by which he could get a little company and some excitement. He rushed down towards the village calling out, "Wolf, wolf," and the villagers came out to meet him, and some of them stopped with him for a considerable time. This pleased the boy so much that a few days afterwards he tried the same trick, and again the villagers came to his help. But shortly after this a wolf actually did come out from the forest, and began to worry the sheep, and the boy of course cried out, "Wolf, wolf," still louder than before. But this time the villagers, who had been fooled twice before, thought the boy was again deceiving them, and nobody stirred to come to his help. So the wolf made a good meal off the boy's flock, and when the boy complained, the wise man of the village said:

*"A liar will not be believed, even when he speaks the truth."*

# The Man, the Boy, and the Donkey

A man and his son were once going with their donkey to market. As they were walking along by its side, a countryman passed them and said, "You fools, what is a donkey for but to ride upon?"

So the man put the boy on the donkey, and they went on their way. But soon they passed a group of men, one of whom said, "See that lazy youngster; he lets his father walk while he rides."

So the man ordered his boy to get off, and got on himself. But they hadn't gone far when they passed two women, one of whom said to the other, "Shame on that lazy lout to let his poor little son trudge along."

Well, the man didn't know what to do, but at last he took his boy up before him on the donkey. By this time they had come to the town, and the passersby began to jeer and point at them. The man stopped and asked what they were scoffing at. The men said, "Aren't you ashamed of yourself for overloading that poor donkey of yours—you and your hulking son?"

The man and boy got off and tried to think what to do. They thought and they thought, till at last they cut down a pole, tied the donkey's feet to it, and raised the pole and the donkey to their shoulders. They went along amid the laughter of all who met them, till they came to Market Bridge, when the donkey, getting one of his feet loose, kicked out and caused the boy to drop his end of the pole. In the struggle the donkey fell over the bridge, and his forefeet being tied together, he was drowned.

"That will teach you," said an old man who had followed them:

*"Please all, and you will please none."*

DISCUSSION

1.  You have probably never lost a donkey or a herd of sheep. And you probably have not been outwitted by a fox. Do the lessons of these stories have meaning for you? How?

2.  The man and boy, the crow, and the shepherd all lose something through their own foolish behavior. Whose loss is the greatest?

3.  A fable is a story that teaches a moral lesson. Can we really learn from stories like these, or is personal experience the only real teacher?

# Jack's Hunting Trip

*(APPALACHIA)*

RICHARD CHASE

Back in old times there was plenty of good game back on these mountains here. And one time Jack started out real early in the mornin' on a huntin' trip. Took his daddy's old flintlock rifle down from over the fireboard, got the powder horn and some bullets, and pulled out up the river.

He traveled on through the woods a right smart ways, didn't see nothin' much for a considerable long while, till first thing he knowed he looked up ahead of him, saw a deer standin' under a big oak tree—biggest deer he'd ever seen. And right over that deer was a whole flock of wild turkeys settin' on a limb. They were a-settin' up right close together in a row, and the limb was pointin' right Jack's way.

Jack didn't know what to do. He wanted that deer, but he wanted them turkeys too. So he got out his knife and cut the ramrod in two, put one bullet on top of the powder, then he put that half-a-ramrod in the gun and put another bullet at the top end of hit. He drawed down on the deer and when he pulled the trigger he jerked up on the gun so's the bullet would go down that row of turkeys. 'Lowed maybe he'd get five or six of 'em at one shot.

Well, he got his deer all right, but that other bullet struck the limb them turkeys were settin' on, split it open, and when the split clamped back together, hit clamped down on the middle toe of ever'one of them turkeys and just helt 'em there so they couldn't fly at all. Jack saw 'em a-squawkin' and a-floppin' and knowed he had them caught, so he went on over to look at his deer. Hit was a full-grown buck, had horns on him reached about six foot from tip to tip. Jack started to walk around him, saw somethin' kickin' in the bresh. Looked and found him a big fat rabbit. That bullet had gone plumb though the deer and killed a rabbit settin' in the weeds. Then Jack saw where the bullet had glanced into a holler tree. There was somethin' sticky oozin' out the hole. Jack stuck his finger in it and tasted it. Hit was sourwood honey. That holler tree was packed full of wild honey right up to the top.

Well, Jack looked up at all them turkeys a-flutterin' and cluckin', and 'lowed he'd cut the limb off and take 'em home alive. So he scaled up the tree and com-menced cuttin' on that limb. When it came loose, he grabbed hold on it, but when he done that, them turkeys all set in to flyin' and carried Jack on off a-hangin' to the limb. Jack was mighty near scared to death. He didn't know whether he could hold on till they stopped somewhere.

Well, they kept right on up over the tops of the trees, and fin'ly Jack saw they were headed to fly right over an old stumpy tree standin' up on a ridge. So Jack said it didn't differ whether they stopped or no, he was goin' to try to drap off and light on that stumpy tree. So when they got right over it, Jack let go, but when he drapped, instead of lightin' on top of the tree, hit was holler, and Jack lit right in the mouth of the holler, went clean to the bottom. When he got up and quit staggerin' around, Jack felt somethin' come out from one side the holler and rub up against his legs. Then two more came out and got to gruntin' around and stumblin' over his feet. Jack's eyes fin'ly got used to how dark it was down there and he saw it was three young grizzly bears.

"Bedad!" says Jack. "The old bear'll be a-comin' down in here directly and she'll eat me sure!"

He couldn't figger no way in the world to get out of there. So he had to study him some plan to try and defend himself. He'd lost his knife when he grabbed that limb. He searched ever' pocket he had, and all he could find was a old table fork with only one prong on it. Well, Jack knowed that old bear 'uld have to come down back'erds, so he decided what he'd do and he just waited and started pettin' them cubs a little.

Then directly somethin' cut the light out above him all of a sudden-like and Jack heard the old grizzly bear a-scrougin' down the holler. Jumped up and reached one hand up over his head just as high as he could. And when the old bear got down close enough, Jack seized hold of her tail and com-menced gougin' her with that old table fork. The old bear went to scramblin' back out the holler and Jack he swung on tight and kept on gougin' her. When they got out at the top, Jack gave her a right quick shove and the old bear fell to the ground and broke her neck.

Jack sat there on the tree awhile and studied what he'd do next. Fin'ly he 'lowed he'd go on home and get the team to tote

in his bear and his deer so he could get 'em skinned out. Well he cloomb on down and pulled out for home. Got to the river, he saw a bunch of wild ducks a-swimmin' on the near side of a bend where it was pretty deep. Jack just had to have them ducks, and he couldn't figger out how in the world he could get 'em without no gun or nothin'. He studied about it a little; then he tied the bottoms of his overhalls so's he could swim a little better, crope up and slipped in the river, kept on easin' in till he was plumb under the water.

Then he went to swimmin' around under there, pulled out a long piece of string he had in his overhall pocket, and right easy-like so's not to scare 'em, he tied all the ducks' feet together. He didn't aim to let 'em fly off with him like the turkeys done, so he dove on down to the bottom and tied that rope to a big sycamore root. Then he popped up out the water right in amongst all them ducks, and they started in quackin' and a-floppin' to rise off the water; that rope 'uld jerk 'em back, and directly they were all tangled up in one bundle.

Jack started wadin' out, and when he got out on the bank his pants legs felt awful heavy, and he noticed somethin' kickin' around inside 'em. He'd been down there under the water so long a bunch of fish had done got tangled up inside his old baggy overhalls. So Jack ontied his legs and kicked around until he'd shook 'em all out, and when he strung 'em up they weighed about thirty pounds. Jack slung his fish across his shoulder and picked up that passel of ducks and went on. He kept on lookin' for them turkeys, but he reckoned they'd done flown clean out the country by that time.

When he got home, Will and Tom didn't believe Jack had done all that. They hitched up the team to a big sled and took two barrels to fetch the honey. They got the deer loaded on, and Jack picked up the rabbit and throwed it on the sled 'side the deer. They they cut the bee-tree, and after they'd filled both barrels, the holler was still half full. They they hauled all that back to the house, and put out after the bear. Hit weighed more'n the deer did, but they fin'ly got it loaded on. Then Will and Tom cut a hole in the bear holler and Jack caught the young'uns. They made some rope halters and tied the young bears behind the sled.

When they got out in the road again and had gone along a ways, they heard some wild turkeys a-squawkin', and there was Jack's flock still fastened on that limb and hit all tangled up on top of some bramble briars where they'd tried to light down in the bresh. Jack got him a long pole and whacked 'em all in the head to stunt 'em so's they wouldn't try to fly off no more. Then he knocked the limb loose and flung his turkeys on top of the bear.

They skinned out the deer and bear and cured the meat. Jack made him a couple of pens for his ducks and his turkeys, and his mother canned up all them fishes; and Jack and his folks had bear meat and deer meat and turkey meat and duck meat and fish meat to last 'em a right smart while.

Jack tamed up them bear cubs and carried 'em down to the King's house. The King and his folks took on so over them young bears, they paid Jack a thousand dollars a-piece for 'em. They went back and got the rest of that honey too. I forget how long it was Jack eat on that honey.

**DISCUSSION**

1. A "tall tale" is a story that takes a perfectly natural event and makes it into a fantastic adventure. Sailors tell tall tales of the sea, small children tell their parents about seeing elephants on the way to school. What kind of people would particularly enjoy Jack's hunting success? What kind of tall tales would you tell?

2. **Dialect.** The way of speaking that is peculiar to a region or group, is called dialect. This story is written in a Southern dialect. Some words have additional letters to suggest a different pronunciation (*hit* for *it*, *overhalls* for *overalls*). Some words have letters omitted (*fin'ly* for *finally*). Some words are used only in that part of the country (*a-scrougin'* for *sneaking*). Can you find other differences? How is punctuation used to show different speech patterns?

3. This story is set in Appalachia, in the southeastern United States. There are many other versions of this tale. The setting is quite different (Maine or Austria, for example), while the story is basically the same. At the end of this story Jack carried the bear cubs "down to the King's house." If the story is set in Appalachia, why is there a king?

For further activities, see page 380.

# THREE STRONG WOMEN

*(JAPAN)*

## CLAUS STAMM

Long ago, in Japan, there lived a famous wrestler, and he was on his way to the capital city to wrestle before the Emperor.

He strode down the road on legs thick as the trunks of small trees. He had been walking for seven hours and could, and probably would, walk for seven more without getting tired.

The time was autumn, the sky was a cold, watery blue, the air chilly. In the small bright sun, the trees along the roadside glowed red and orange.

The wrestler hummed to himself, "Zun-zun-zun," in time with the long swing of his legs. Wind blew through his thin brown robe, and he wore no sword at his side. He felt proud that he needed no sword, even in the darkest and loneliest places. The icy air on his body only reminded him that few tailors would have been able to make expensive warm clothes for a man so broad and tall. He felt much as a wrestler should: strong, healthy, and rather conceited.

A soft roar of fast-moving water beyond the trees told him that he was passing above a river bank. He "zun-zunned" louder; he loved the sound of his voice and wanted it to sound clearly above the rushing water.

He thought: They call me Forever-Mountain because I am such a good strong wrestler—big, too. I'm a fine, brave man and far too modest ever to say so. . . .

Just then he saw a girl who must have come up from the river, for she steadied a bucket on her head.

Her hands on the bucket were small, and there was a dimple on each thumb, just below the knuckle. She was a round little girl with red cheeks and a nose like a friendly button. Her eyes looked as though she were thinking of ten thousand funny stories at once. She clambered up onto the road and walked ahead of the wrestler, jolly and bounceful.

"If I don't tickle that fat girl, I shall regret it all my life," said the wrestler under his breath. "She's sure to go 'squeak' and I shall laugh and laugh. If she drops her bucket, that will be even funnier—and I can always run and fill it again and even carry it home for her."

He tiptoed up and poked her lightly in the ribs with one huge finger.

"Kochokochokocho!" he said, a fine, ticklish sound in Japanese.

The girl gave a satisfying squeal, giggled, and brought one arm down so that the wrestler's hand was caught between it and her body.

"Ho-ho-ho! You've caught me! I can't move at all!" said the wrestler, laughing.

"I know," said the jolly girl.

He felt that it was very good-tempered of her to take a joke so well, and started to pull his hand free.

Somehow, he could not.

He tried again, using a little more strength.

"Now, now—let me go, little girl," he said. "I am a very powerful man. If I pull too hard I might hurt you."

"Pull," said the girl. "I admire powerful men."

She began to walk, and though the wrestler tugged and pulled until his feet dug great furrows in the ground, he had to follow. She couldn't have paid him less attention if he had been a puppy—a small one.

Ten minutes later, still tugging while trudging helplessly after her, he was glad that the road was lonely and no one was there to see.

"Please let me go," he pleaded. "I am the famous wrestler Forever-Mountain. I must go and show my strength before the Emperor"—he burst out weeping from shame and confusion— "and you're hurting my hand!"

The girl steadied the bucket on her head with her free hand and dimpled sympathetically over her shoulder.

"You poor, sweet little Forever-Mountain," she said. "Are you tired? Shall I carry you? I can leave the water here and come back for it later."

"I do not want you to carry me. I want you to let me go, and then I want to forget I ever saw you. What do you want with me?" moaned the pitiful wrestler.

"I only want to help you," said the girl, now pulling him steadily up and up a narrow mountain path. "Oh, I am sure you'll have no more trouble than anyone else when you come up against the other wrestlers. You'll win, or else you'll lose, and you won't be too badly hurt either way. But aren't you afraid you might meet a really *strong* man someday?"

Forever-Mountain turned white. He stumbled. He was imagining being laughed at throughout Japan as "Hardly-Ever-Mountain."

She glanced back.

"You see? Tired already." she said. "I'll walk more slowly. Why don't you come along to my mother's house and let us make a strong man of you? The wrestling in the capital isn't due to begin for three months. I know, because Grandmother thought she'd go. You'd be spending all that time in bad company and wasting what little power you have."

"All right. Three months. I'll come along," said the wrestler. He felt he had nothing more to lose. Also, he feared that the girl might become angry if he refused, and place him in the top of a tree until he changed his mind.

"Fine," she said happily. "We are almost there."

She freed his hand. It had become red and a little swollen. "But if you break your promise and run off, I shall have to chase you and carry you back."

Soon they arrived in a small valley. A simple farmhouse with a thatched roof stood in the middle.

"Grandmother is at home, but she is an old lady and she's probably sleeping." The girl shaded her eyes with one hand. "But Mother should be bringing our cow back from the field— oh, there's Mother now!"

She waved. The woman coming around the corner of the house put down the cow she was carrying and waved back.

She smiled and came across the grass, walking with a lively bounce like her daughter's. Well, maybe her bounce was a little more solid, thought the wrestler.

"Excuse me," she said, brushing some cow hair from her dress and dimpling, also like her daughter. "These mountain paths are full of stones. They hurt the cow's feet. And who is the nice young man you've brought, Maru-me?"[1]

The girl explained. "And we have only three months!" she finished anxiously.

---

[1] *Maru-me:* pronounced mä-rōō-mā.

"Well, it's not long enough to do much, but it's not so short a time that we can't do something," said her mother, looking thoughtful. "But he does look terribly feeble. He'll need a lot of good things to eat. Maybe when he gets stronger he can help Grandmother with some of the easy work about the house."

"That will be fine!" said the girl, and she called her grandmother—loudly, for the old lady was a little deaf.

"I'm coming!" came a creaky voice from inside the house, and a little old woman leaning on a stick and looking very sleepy tottered out of the door. As she came toward them she stumbled over the roots of a great oak tree.

"Heh! My eyes aren't what they used to be. That's the fourth time this month I've stumbled over that tree," she complained and, wrapping her skinny arms about its trunk, pulled it out of the ground.

"Oh, Grandmother! You should have let me pull it up for you," said Maru-me.

"Hm. I hope I didn't hurt my poor old back," muttered the old lady. She called out. "Daughter! Throw that tree away like a good girl, so no one will fall over it. But make sure it doesn't hit anybody."

"You can help Mother with the tree," Maru-me said to Forever-Mountain. "On second thought, you'd better not help. Just watch."

Her mother went to the tree, picked it up in her two hands, and threw it—clumsily and with a little gasp, the way a woman throws. Up went the tree, sailing end over end, growing smaller and smaller as it flew. It landed with a faint crash far up the mountainside.

"Ah, how clumsy," she said. "I meant to throw it *over* the mountain. It's probably blocking the path now, and I'll have to get up early tomorrow to move it."

The wrestler was not listening. He had very quietly fainted.

"Oh! We must put him to bed." said Maru-me.

"Poor, feeble young man," said her mother.

"I hope we can do something for him. Here, let me carry him, he's light," said the grandmother. She slung him over her shoulder and carried him into the house, creaking along with her cane.

The next day they began the work of making Forever-Mountain over into what they thought a strong man should be.

They gave him the simplest food to eat, and the toughest. Day by day they prepared his rice with less and less water, until no ordinary man could have chewed or digested it.

Every day he was made to do the work of five men, and every evening he wrestled with Grandmother. Maru-me and her mother agreed that Grandmother, being old and feeble, was the least likely to injure him accidentally. They hoped the exercise might be good for the old lady's rheumatism.

He grew stronger and stronger but was hardly aware of it. Grandmother could still throw him easily into the air—and catch him again—without ever changing her sweet old smile.

He quite forgot that outside this valley he was one of the greatest wrestlers in Japan and was called Forever-Mountain. His legs had been like logs; now they were like pillars. His big hands were hard as stones, and when he cracked his knuckles the sound was like trees splitting on a cold night.

Sometimes he did an exercise that wrestlers do in Japan—raising one foot high above the ground and bringing it down with a crash. Then people in nearby villages looked up at the winter sky and told one another that it was very late in the year for thunder.

Soon he could pull up a tree as well as the grandmother. He could even throw one—but only a small distance. One evening, near the end of his third month, he wrestled with Grandmother and held her down for half a minute.

"Heh-heh!" She chortled and got up, smiling with every wrinkle. "I would never have believed it!"

Maru-me squealed with joy and threw her arms around him—gently, for she was afraid of cracking his ribs.

"Very good, very good! What a strong man," said her mother, who had just come home from the fields, carrying, as usual, the cow. She put the cow down and patted the wrestler on the back.

They agreed that he was now ready to show some *real* strength before the Emperor.

"Take the cow along with you tomorrow when you go," said the mother. "Sell her and buy yourself a belt—a silken belt. Buy the fattest and heaviest one you can find. Wear it when you appear before the Emperor, as a souvenir from us."

"I wouldn't think of taking your only cow. You've already done too much for me. And you'll need her to plow the field, won't you?"

They burst out laughing, Maru-me squealed, her mother roared. The grandmother cackled so hard and long that she choked and had to be pounded on the back.

"Oh, dear," said the mother, still laughing. "you didn't think we used our cow for anything like *work!* Why, Grandmother here is stronger than five cows!"

"The cow is our pet." Maru-me giggled. "She has lovely brown eyes."

"But it really gets tiresome having to carry her back and forth each day so that she has enough grass to eat," said her mother.

"Then you must let me give you all the prize money that I win," said Forever-Mountain.

"Oh, no! We wouldn't think of it!" said Maru-me. "Because we all like you too much to sell you anything. And it is not proper to accept gifts of money from strangers."

"True," said Forever-Mountain. "I will now ask your mother's and grandmother's permission to marry you. I want to be one of the family."

"Oh! I'll get a wedding dress ready!" said Maru-me.

The mother and grandmother pretended to consider very seriously, but they quickly agreed.

Next morning Forever-Mountain tied his hair up in the topknot that all Japanese wrestlers wear, and got ready to leave. He thanked Maru-me and her mother and bowed very low to the grandmother, since she was the oldest and had been a fine wrestling partner.

Then he picked up the cow in his arms and trudged up the mountain. When he reached the top, he slung the cow over one shoulder and waved good-bye to Maru-me.

At the first town he came to, Forever-Mountain sold the cow. She brought a good price because she was unusually fat from never having worked in her life. With the money, he bought the heaviest silken belt he could find.

When he reached the palace grounds, many of the other wrestlers were already there, sitting about, eating enormous bowls of rice, comparing one another's weight, and telling stories. They paid little attention to Forever-Mountain, except to wonder why he had arrived so late this year. Some of them noticed that he had grown quiet and took no part at all in their boasting.

All the ladies and gentlemen of the court were waiting in a

special courtyard for the wrestling to begin. They wore many robes, one on top of another, heavy with embroidery and gold cloth, and sweat ran down their faces and froze in the winter afternoon. The gentlemen had long swords so weighted with gold and precious stones that they could never have used them, even if they had known how. The court ladies, with their long black hair hanging down behind, had their faces painted dead white, which made them look frightened. They had pulled out their real eyebrows and painted new ones high above the place where eyebrows are supposed to be, and this made them all look as though they were very surprised at something.

Behind a screen sat the Emperor—by himself, because he was too noble for ordinary people to look at. He was a lonely old man with a kind, tired face. He hoped the wrestling would end quickly so that he could go to his room and write poems.

The first two wrestlers chosen to fight were Forever-Mountain and a wrestler who was said to have the biggest stomach in the country. He and Forever-Mountain both threw some salt into the ring. It was understood that this drove away evil spirits.

Then the other wrestler, moving his stomach somewhat out of the way, raised his foot and brought it down with a fearful stamp. He glared fiercely at Forever-Mountain as if to say, "Now *you* stamp, you poor frightened man!"

Forever-Mountain raised his foot. He brought it down.

There was a sound like thunder, the earth shook, and the other wrestler bounced into the air and out of the ring, as gracefully as any soap bubble.

He picked himself up and bowed to the Emperor's screen.

"The earth-god is angry. Possibly there is something the matter with the salt." he said. "I do not think I shall wrestle this season." And he walked out, looking very suspiciously over one shoulder at Forever-Mountain.

Five other wrestlers then and there decided that they were not wrestling this season, either. They all looked annoyed with Forever-Mountain.

From then on, Forever-Mountain brought his foot down lightly. As each wrestler came into the ring, he picked him up very gently, carried him out, and placed him before the Emperor's screen, bowing most courteously every time.

The court ladies' eyebrows went up even higher. The gentlemen looked disturbed and a little afraid. They loved to see fierce, strong men tugging and grunting at each other, but Forever-Mountain was a little too much for them. Only the Emperor was happy behind his screen, for now, with the wrestling over so quickly, he would have that much more time to write his poems. He ordered all the prize money handed over to Forever-Mountain.

"But," he said, "you had better not wrestle any more." He stuck a finger through his screen and waggled it at the other wrestlers, who were sitting on the ground weeping with disappointment like great fat babies.

Forever-Mountain promised not to wrestle any more. Everybody looked relieved. The wrestlers sitting on the ground almost smiled.

"I think I shall become a farmer," Forever-Mountain said, and left at once to go back to Maru-me.

Maru-me was waiting for him. When she saw him coming, she ran down the mountain, picked him up, together with the heavy bags of prize money, and carried him halfway up the mountainside. Then she giggled and put him down. The rest of the way she let him carry her.

Forever-Mountain kept his promise to the Emperor and never fought in public again. His name was forgotten in the capital. But up in the mountains, sometimes, the earth shakes and rumbles, and they say that is Forever-Mountain and Maru-me's grandmother practicing wrestling in the hidden valley.

DISCUSSION

1.   Forever-Mountain is proud of being a famous wrestler, "strong, healthy, and rather conceited" (page 359). At the end of the story he is happy even though "his name was forgotten in the capital" (p. 367). What has happened to him that he no longer needs to compete?

2.   Forever-Mountain first sees Maru-me as someone much weaker than himself. How does she change his mind? How does this affect the way he thinks of himself?

3.   **Exaggeration.**   Exaggeration is the use of overstatement to make a point or to create an effect. It is often used in tall tales to make a point or to add humor. In this story, the physical strength of the characters is much greater than human beings could actually have. When the Three Strong Women had finished training him, Forever-Mountain could stamp his foot and there would be "a sound like thunder" (p. 366). How is the strength of the women exaggerated? How do their feelings about this strength add to the humor of the story?

For further activities, see page 380.

# THE SEVEN STARS

*(CHEYENNE)*

## JOHN STANDS IN TIMBER and MARGOT LIBERTY

One time long ago a man and wife and their only child, a beautiful girl, lived in a big village in a valley. When the girl was old enough, her mother began teaching her how to use porcupine quills, sewing them onto deerskin clothing and blankets in lovely designs. The girl became good at this. Her work was among the finest done by all the people.

One day she began to work on an outfit of buckskin clothing for a man, decorating it with her best designs in dyed quills. It took her a month to finish it. When she was done she started on another, and that took a month also. And then she kept on until she had finished seven outfits in the same way. When the work was done she told her mother and father, "There are seven young men living a long journey from here. They are brothers. Since I have no brothers or sisters of my own I am going out to find them and take them for my brothers and live with them, and someday they will be known to all the people on earth."

They did not try to stop her. The girl's mother said, "I will go with you as far as the trail that leads to the lodge of the seven young men." The next morning she helped her daughter make two bags to pack the clothing in. They put three of the outfits in each of these and packed them on two dogs. The last and smallest outfit the girl carried herself.

They traveled until they came to the trail. Here the girl's mother stopped. She watched her daughter until she was out of sight and then turned and headed home. The girl kept going with the two dogs until she came to a wide river with a large tepee on its bank. As she approached, a little boy came running out, saying, "I am the youngest of the seven brothers. The rest are hunting and will be back by sundown."

The girl said, "I came to find you all. I am going to take you for my brothers." They led the dogs to the tepee and unloaded the packs. Then the girl spoke to the dogs and turned them loose, and they ran off, going home. Next she unwrapped the smallest buckskin outfit and gave it to the little boy, saying, "My brother, this is a gift from me." Right away he put on his new moccasins and leggings and shirt and a little blanket, and he was happy because of their beautiful designs.

Inside the tepee the little boy pointed to each of the beds in turn, telling to which of the brothers it belonged; and on each she put one of the buckskin outfits. Then she prepared a meal and waited until they should appear. At sundown they approached the camp, and the youngest ran out to meet them, throwing himself on the ground and kicking his legs in the air so they would be sure to see his new moccasins and leggings.

"Where did you get those things?" they asked.

"You said not to let anyone near the tepee," he said, "but a girl came, and before I could tell her to stay out she said she had brought us all some new clothes and she is taking us for brothers. She is a beautiful girl."

They were pleased with the news and went on in. In those days brothers and sisters did not talk to one another, but since the smallest had already spoken to the girl he kept on and acted as interpreter, telling the girl what the others wanted and giving them her answers. And they lived together, and were happy to have someone prepare their meals.

One morning, when the older brothers were again hunting, a yellow buffalo calf came running up to the tepee and stopped a little distance from it, looking all around.

"Buffalo Calf," said the little boy, "what do you want?"

"I am sent by the buffaloes," the calf answered. "They want your sister, and I am to take her back with me."

"No, you cannot have her," said the boy. "The older brothers are hunting and you must wait until they come back." So the calf ran away, kicking and jumping until he was out of sight. In a little while a two-year-old heifer came running up the same way and stopped outside the tepee.

"Two-Year-Old Heifer," said the little boy, "what do you want?"

"I am sent by the buffaloes," she answered. "They want your sister and I will take her back with me. If you don't let her go the Old Buffalo is coming."

"No," said the little boy. "Go back and tell them they cannot have her." So she ran away like the calf, kicking and jumping until she was out of sight. And in a little while a third buffalo came—a big cow.

"Buffalo Cow," said the little boy, "what do you want? Why are you bothering us?"

"I am sent by the buffaloes," said the cow. "They want your sister. If you don't let her go the herd is coming here after her, and you will all be killed."

"Well, you cannot have her," said the little boy. "Go back and tell them." So the buffalo cow ran away, kicking and jumping like the others. Soon the brothers returned from hunting, and when the little boy told them what had happened they were afraid. Before long they heard a noise like the earth shaking, and saw a great herd of buffalo coming toward the tepee with a big bull in the lead.

"Hurry!" cried one of the six brothers to the youngest. "You have power that can keep anything from touching you. Use it and save us!" So the little boy ran and got his bow and arrows. He aimed into the top of a tree nearby, and when the arrow hit it the tree began to grow until the top was almost out of sight. The brothers lifted the girl into the lowest branches and climbed after her, and in a minute the ground below them was covered with buffalo. All they could hear was snorting and bawling. Then the lead bull came forward and started to circle the tree trunk down below. He was angry, shaking his head and pawing the ground. Soon he charged at the tree and stopped just short of it. He did this three times, but the fourth time he struck it and cut a big piece out of it with his horn.

Four times he did the same thing, hitting the tree on the fourth charge, and cutting out a bigger piece of the trunk each

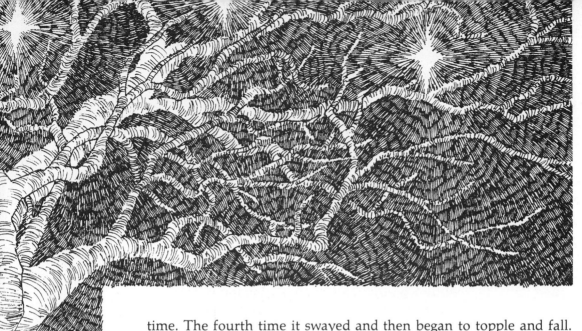

time. The fourth time it swayed and then began to topple and fall.

"Hurry!" cried the brothers to the little boy. "Save us!" Quickly he aimed and shot another arrow far into the sky. It vanished from sight and they felt the tree growing upwards after it. At last it hit the sky. They all climbed out of the branches and stayed there and turned into stars. They can still be seen at night as the Seven Stars, called by the white people the Big Dipper.

When they were all through telling that story, we boys would go out with them and look up at those stars, and we believed it. It was a story supposed to make us go to sleep, but I would lie awake thinking about those seven brothers for quite awhile, and what happened to them. I never did hear what became of the girl.

DISCUSSION

1.  Do you believe this story? What in the story is frankly not believable? Why do we tell and retell unbelievable stories?

2.  What happens to the girl? Who is the hero?

3.  Do you feel any closer to the stars if you think of them as seven brothers who would not give up their sister to the buffalo?

4.  Imagine this story changed around. Imagine seven sisters saving their little brother and becoming stars. Imagine a beautiful boy sewing deerskin clothing and cooking for his sisters. Do you feel comfortable with this version of the story? Why, or why not?

For further activities, see page 380.

# The Envious Animals

*(PUERTO RICO)*

RICARDO E. ALEGRÍA

This happened many years ago, at a time, so they say, when God walked upon the earth.

The Maker had just created animals of every kind and He delighted in contemplating them all: in the air the ones that flew; on the land those that crept, ran, and leaped; in the water, those that swam. But His happiness did not last long. Some animals were not satisfied with the form He had given them. The differences with which the Maker had endowed them to distinguish them from their fellows had begotten envy and dissatisfaction. This happened here, on the land.

One family of animals was envious of those that flew and wished to become like them. So they met with their fellows and expressed their intention of asking the Creator to change their form so that they could fly like the birds. But their fellows, who were proud to remain such as their Maker had wished them to be, refused to join in this petition. The ones who did not wish to be such as their Creator had made them were left alone and then, full of hate and rage because their fellows would not join them, they decided to take their case to God.

The Maker, saddened by what He already knew, expressed deep sorrow for the envy that led them to desire to change the form He had given them. And it was then, when the Creator refused to change their form, that they disowned their being, their fellows, and their Maker. That was the day when God, full of sorrow, left the Earth, and the Evil One, the Enemy, decided to use the passions of envy and covetousness to his own end.

The Evil One appeared before the Renegades[1] and offered to grant them their wish, granting them what the Creator had refused. The Renegades, who in their envy and rage had forgotten that only God can create, accepted the Evil One's offer to give them wings to fly like the birds. But the Evil One could not create feathers such as the birds had. He could only stretch their skin to make wings, and, believing himself a Creator, change their body in his image.

The Renegades soon realized that their wish had been granted and that, thanks to the way the Enemy had changed their bodies, they could at last fly like birds. Full of hate, their first impulse was to go find their fellows, who had refused to change their form, and proudly display what they, with the help of the Enemy, had achieved. Great was their surprise on seeing that the others, their fellows, now fled in panic on seeing them in their new shape. No longer were they recognized as brothers and the new form with which they had been endowed by the Evil One caused only horror and disgust . . . as if the rest of the animals feared that they too might suffer such a change! At first, the Renegades were surprised at the behavior of those who had formerly been their fellows. But their arrogance, and the pride they felt in their new form, made them believe that now they were superior to the others and they decided to leave their former fellows forever and go live with the birds whom they so admired. So they took to the air. When the birds saw those featherless creatures that flew and who were made in the image of the Evil One, they forbade them to approach and refused to have anything to do with them.

---

[1] *Renegades* (rĕn'ə-gādz'): deserters.

Only then did truth dawn on the Renegades. They understood that they belonged to no family: that every animal, every single one, whether it ran or flew, despised and avoided them. They realized that in trying to undo, with the aid of the Evil One, what the Creator had made, they had only achieved a monstrosity from which all fled in horror.

They had gained their end but they had not fulfilled their ambition. Everyone knew of their treason and now they were ashamed and afraid. Perpetually fearful and humiliated, they hid from everyone.

That is why, even now, they only dare leave their hiding places when the sun sets and night falls; when the other animals are asleep; when darkness hides their shape, the outward sign of their treason to God and to their fellows.

Today, in our language, we call them . . . bats. . . .

DISCUSSION      1.    Why have the Renegades become outcasts? "Every animal . . . despised and avoided them" (page 374). How do you feel about bats? Do you share these feelings of fear and disgust, or do you feel interest and sympathy, like the author of "Bat Quest" (p. 95)?

2.    How do the Renegades feel about themselves at the beginning of the story? At the end? How do envious people feel about themselves?

3.    The **plot** (see page 9) of this story follows the feelings of the envious animals. At first they feel envy and dissatisfaction, then they feel hate and rage, then arrogance and pride, and finally they feel ashamed and afraid. What are the events that result in those feelings? Is this a story about bats or about envy?

For further activities, see page 380.

# Jean Britisse, the Champion

*(HAITI)*

HAROLD COURLANDER

Jean Britisse said to his mother, "Mamma, I am going to Martinique to make my fortune."

His mother said to him, "Jean, that is fine. But without money how are you going to get there? You'll have to swim."

Jean Britisse went down to the wharf. He asked people where this ship was going and that ship was going. When he found one that was going to Martinique, he went aboard and hid himself under a pile of crates. The ship went out to sea. After two days, just before dawn, Jean Britisse heard the Captain say, "Men, as soon as we reach port, unload all these crates." Jean Britisse worried that he would be found. So he made his way to the back of the ship in the dark. Then, just as the sun was rising and the ship was sailing into port, he jumped into the water and began to swim.

"Captain, Captain!" he called out.

"Did I hear someone calling me?" the Captain said.

"Captain, Captain, slow the ship down and take me aboard!" Jean Britisse shouted.

The Captain looked over the stern.

"Who's that down there?" he said.

"Captain, take me aboard!" Jean Britisse called. "I'm getting a little tired!"

"Stop the ship!" the Captain shouted. "Take this man aboard!"

They stopped the ship. They hauled Jean Britisse out of the water.

"Wherever did you come from?" the Captain asked.

"Captain," Jean Britisse said, "I was going to Martinique, but I missed the boat. I jumped in the water, but I couldn't quite catch you. I've been swimming for two days and two nights, and at last I've made it."

*Jean Britisse:* pronounced zhôn brē-tēs'.

"Do you mean to say you swam all the way from Haiti?" the Captain said.

"Yes," Jean Britisse said, "and now I can buy a ticket and ride to Martinique with you."

"Man," the Captain said, "you don't need a ticket because you are already in Martinique."

Jean Britisse went ashore with the other passengers. Everywhere he went people said, "That's Jean Britisse, the world's champion swimmer! He swam from Haiti to Martinique, and he arrived at the same time as the ship!"

Now there were some good swimmers in Martinique, but the best of them was a man named Coqui.[1] The people went to Coqui and asked him to race against Jean Britisse. Coqui said he would race him for five hundred gourdes.[2] The people went back to Jean Britisse and said that Coqui challenged him. Jean Britisse said he would accept the challenge but not for such a little bit of money. So the people went back again, and Coqui said he would bet one thousand gourdes. And they agreed to meet on the seashore at dawn.

When daylight came, there was a crowd at the beach. Coqui arrived in his swimming suit. When Jean Britisse arrived, he was wearing a white suit, a new Panama hat, and new shoes, and he was carrying a heavy bundle. The crowd laughed.

"Is that the way you expect to swim?" people asked him.

"Just a minute," Jean Britisse said. "I am the man who was challenged, so I can set the conditions for the race, isn't that right?"

The crowd agreed.

[1] *Coqui:* pronounced kō-kē´.
[2] *gourde* (go͞ord): Haitian coin.

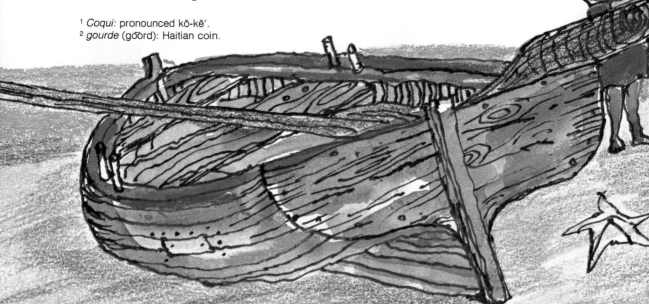

"Very well," Jean Britisse said. "The race is to be from here to Cuba. Coqui can swim a straight line if he wishes, but I have a few things here in this bundle that I bought for my mother, so I'd like to drop them off in Haiti. Since I wouldn't want to meet my old friends there in my swimming suit, I'll just go the way I am. I hope Coqui will bring enough food along to last for five or six days."

Coqui listened. He took off his swimming suit and put on his street clothes.

"Here's the thousand gourdes," he said. "I'm not going to race a man who wants to swim to Cuba."

When the carnival season arrived, there were wrestling matches in the town. The French wrestler Dumée LaFarge[3] was there. He won all the matches. They were going to give him the grand prize when someone said, "Wait, he's not the champion yet. He hasn't beaten Jean Britisse."

So Dumée LaFarge challenged him.

"Very well," Jean Britisse said. "Tomorrow morning at the wrestling court." It was arranged.

Jean Britisse didn't know how to wrestle. He sat and thought for a long time. At last he figured it out. First he went to a carpenter and ordered a coffin to be made. Then he went to a brickmason and ordered a tomb to be constructed. Then he went to the parish priest. He gave him fifty gourdes and made arrangements for him to give the last sacrament.

After that, when it was dark, Jean Britisse went to the wrestling court. There were two trees standing there, side by side. Jean Britisse dug down around the trees and chopped off all the roots. Then he put back the dirt and stamped it flat and made it look natural.

When morning came, Jean Britisse went again to the wrestling court. There was a crowd. Dumée LaFarge was waiting. Dumée LaFarge took off his shirt. He took off his shoes. Jean Britisse took off his shirt. He took off his shoes.

Just then the carpenter arrived. He was carrying a new coffin on his head. On the side of the coffin was printed the name "Dumée LaFarge."

"What kind of joke is this?" Dumée LaFarge shouted.

The carpenter put the coffin down. And he said, as he had been instructed: "What must be must be."

---

[3] *Dumée LaFarge:* pronounced dü mā′ lä-färzh′.

At that moment the brickmason came along. He went up to Dumée LaFarge and said, "Where shall I build the tomb?"

"What is going on here?" Dumée LaFarge shouted. He began to sweat.

The mason shook his head and said, "What must be must be."

And then the parish priest came walking along, reading from the Scripture in Latin. He sprinkled holy water on Dumée LaFarge.

"Stop it! I am not dead!" Dumée LaFarge said. But his legs were getting weak.

"Let the wrestling begin," the people called out.

"One moment, I must warm up a little," Jean Britisse said.

First he crouched and jumped and raced around the wrestling court. He did exercises. Then he went between the two trees he had fixed. He began to push them, one in one direction, one in the other. They leaned, and the crowd watched in astonishment. Jean Britisse pushed harder. The trees started to fall. Dumée LaFarge put on his shirt and shoes. The trees crashed to the ground. Dumée LaFarge put on his hat.

"Give him the prize money," Dumée LaFarge said. "I'm not going to wrestle a man who knocks down trees just for exercise."

"Wait," Jean Britisse said. "I'm not warmed up yet."

Dumée walked away. The parish priest followed him, sprinkling him with holy water. The carpenter followed, carrying the coffin. Behind him was the brickmason. Dumée LaFarge began to run. He went over the hill. It was the last time he was ever seen in Martinique.

DISCUSSION

1.  Three schemes work for Jean Britisse in this story. What are the three schemes and which do you think is the most clever? The most complicated?

2.  Wrestling and swimming are athletic skills that are often admired. Jean Britisse does not have much skill at either, but he is a clever trickster. Is this a skill you admire? Why, or why not?

3.  Jean Britisse tells his mother he is going to Martinique "to make my fortune." Does he?

For further activities, see page 381.

## VOCABULARY

### Jack's Hunting Trip (page 353)

People in Maine speak a dialect of English different from people who live in New Mexico, and both speak English differently from people who live in Brooklyn. Your answers for this exercise will depend on where you live. Read these expressions from this Southern dialect story and "translate" them into your own dialect.

"he cloomb on down" (p. 356)  "right easy-like" (p. 356)
"he studied about it" (p. 356)  "passel of ducks" (p. 356)
"to light down in the bresh" (p. 357)  "put out after the bear" (p. 356)

### The Envious Animals (page 372)

Copy the paragraph below, filling the blanks with these words. There is a place for each one.

humiliated    arrogant
envy          covetousness
despised      dissatisfaction

The Renegades still felt _____ toward their happier brothers. They tried to hide this by their _____ behavior. Although the Renegades knew that they were being _____ as a punishment for their _____, they still muttered their _____ with their _____ new forms.

## COMPOSITION

### Three Strong Women (page 359)

Write a brief description of a day in the life of Forever-Mountain and the Three Strong Women after he returns from the capital. What daily chores do they perform with all that exaggerated strength?

### The Seven Stars (page 368)

"The Seven Stars" tells a story of that constellation which is usually called the Big Dipper. There is another group of stars known as the Seven Sisters. Write a short story explaining how this name came to be.

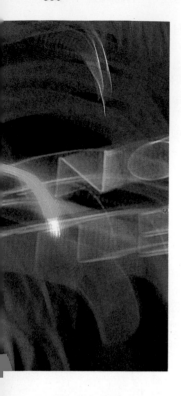

# READING

## The Seven Stars (page 368)

List the letters a through h on separate paper to represent the following events. Place a number after each letter to show the order in which these events occurred.

a. She finished seven outfits.
b. She met the little boy.
c. The buffalo calf came for her.
d. The girl learned to use porcupine quills.
e. She prepared their meals.
f. The little boy shot the arrow into the tree top.
g. The boys became the stars in the Big Dipper.
h. The little boy shot the arrow into the sky.

## Jean Britisse, the Champion (page 375)

Who is speaking? Number a paper from 1 to 6. After each number write the letter that shows which character made the statement.

A. Jean    B. Captain    C. Coqui    D. Dumée

1. "Men . . . unload all these crates."
2. "Captain, take me aboard!"
3. "I'm not going to race a man who wants to swim to Cuba."
4. "Stop it! I am not dead!"
5. "I've been swimming for two days and two nights."
6. "I'm not going to wrestle a man who knocks down trees just for ex-ercise."

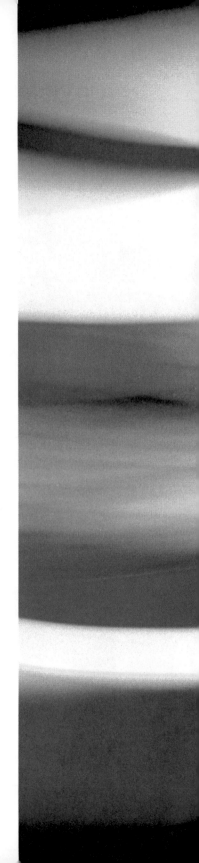

# ali baba and the forty thieves

*(MIDDLE EAST)*                                    ANDREW LANG

In a town in Persia there dwelt two brothers, one named Cassim,[1] the other Ali Baba. Cassim was married to a rich wife and lived in plenty, while Ali Baba had to maintain his wife and children by cutting wood in a neighboring forest and selling it in the town. One day when Ali Baba was in the forest, he saw a troop of men on horseback coming toward him in a cloud of dust. He was afraid they were robbers and climbed into a tree for safety. When they came up to him and dismounted, he counted forty of them. They unbridled their horses and tied them to trees.

The finest man among them, whom Ali Baba took to be their captain, went a little way among some bushes and said, "Open sesame!"[2] so plainly that Ali Baba heard him. A door opened in the rocks and, having made the troop go in, the captain followed them and the door shut again of itself.

They stayed some time inside and Ali Baba, fearing they might come out and catch him, was forced to sit patiently in the tree. At last the door opened again and the forty thieves came out. As the captain went in last, he came out first and made them all pass by him; he then closed the door, saying, "Shut sesame!" Every man bridled his horse and mounted, the captain put himself at their head, and they returned as they came.

Then Ali Baba climbed down and went to the door concealed among the bushes and said, "Open sesame!" and it flew open. Ali Baba, who expected a dull, dismal place, was greatly surprised to find it large and well lighted, and hollowed by the hand of man in the form of a vault, which received the light from an opening in the ceiling. He saw rich bales of merchandise—silk stuffs, brocades, all piled together—gold and silver in heaps, and money in leather purses. He went in and the door shut behind him. He did not look at the silver but brought out as many bags of gold as he thought his asses, which were browsing outside, could carry, loaded them with the bags, and hid it all with fagots.[3] Using the words "Shut sesame!" he closed the door and went home.

Then he drove his asses into the yard, shut the gates, carried the moneybags to his wife, and emptied them out before her. He bade her keep the secret and he would bury the gold.

---

*Ali Baba:* pronounced ä′ lē bä′ bä.
[1] *Cassim:* pronounced kä-sēm′.

[2] *sesame* (sĕs′ə-mē): seeds used for food and oil.
[3] *fagots* (făg′ ətz): bundles of sticks.

"Let me first measure it," said his wife. "I will borrow a measure from someone while you dig the hole."

So she ran to the wife of Cassim and borrowed a measure. Knowing Ali Baba's poverty, the sister was curious to find out what sort of grain his wife wished to measure, and artfully put some suet at the botton of the measure. Ali Baba's wife went home and set the measure on the heap of gold and filled it and emptied it often, to her great content. She then carried it back to her sister, without noticing that a piece of gold was sticking to it.

Cassim's wife perceived it as soon as her back was turned. She grew very curious and said to Cassim when he came home, "Cassim, your brother is richer than you. He does not count his money; he measures it!"

He begged her to explain this riddle, which she did by showing him the piece of money and telling him where she had found it. Then Cassim grew so envious that he could not sleep and went to his brother in the morning before sunrise.

"Ali Baba," he said, showing him the gold piece, "you pretend to be poor and yet you measure gold."

By this Ali Baba perceived that through his wife's folly Cassim and his wife knew his secret, so he confessed all and offered Cassim a share.

"That I expect," said Cassim, "but I must know where to find the treasure. Otherwise I will disclose all and you will lose all."

Ali Baba, more out of kindness than fear, told him of the cave and the very words to use. Cassim left Ali Baba, meaning to be beforehand with him and get the treasure for himself. He rose early next morning and set out with ten mules loaded with great chests. He soon found the place and the door in the rock. He said, "Open sesame!" and the door opened and shut behind him.

He could have feasted his eyes all day on the treasures, but he now hastened to gather together as much of it as possible; but when he was ready to go he could not remember what to say for thinking of his great riches. Instead of "sesame," he said, "Open barley!" and the door remained fast. He named several other sorts of grain, all but the right one, and the door still stuck fast. He was so frightened at the danger he was in that he had as much forgotten the word as if he had never heard it.

About noon the robbers returned to their cave and saw Cassim's mules roving about with great chests on their backs. This gave them the alarm. They drew their sabers and went to the door, which opened on their captain's saying, "Open sesame!" Cassim, who had heard the trampling of their horses' feet, resolved to sell his life dearly, so when the door opened he leaped out and threw the captain down. In vain, however, for the robbers with their sabers soon killed him. On entering the cave they saw all the bags laid ready, and could not imagine how anyone had got in without knowing their secret. They cut Cassim's body into four quarters and nailed them up inside the cave, in order to frighten anyone who should venture in, and went away in search of more treasure.

As night drew on, Cassim's wife grew very uneasy, ran to her brother-in-law, and told him where her husband had gone. Ali Baba did his best to comfort her and set out to the forest in search of Cassim. The first thing he saw on entering the cave was his dead brother. Full of horror, he put the body on one of his asses and bags of gold on the other two and, covering all with fagots, returned home. He drove the two asses laden with gold into his own yard and led the other to Cassim's house. The door was opened by the slave Morgiana, whom he knew to be both brave and cunning.

Unloading the ass, he said to her, "This is the body of your master, who has been murdered, but whom we must bury as though he had died in his bed. I will speak with you again, but now tell your mistress I am come."

The wife of Cassim, on learning the fate of her husband, broke out into cries and tears, but Ali Baba offered to take her to live with him and his wife if she would promise to keep his counsel and leave everything to Morgiana; whereupon she agreed, and dried her eyes.

Morgiana, meanwhile, sought an apothecary[4] and asked him for some lozenges. "My poor master," she said, "can neither eat nor speak and no one knows what his distemper is." She carried home the lozenges and returned next day weeping, and asked for an essence only given to those just about to die. Thus, in the evening, no one was surprised to hear the shrieks and cries of Cassim's wife and Morgiana, telling everyone that Cassim was dead.

The next day Morgiana went to an old cobbler near the gates of the town, who opened his stall early, put a piece of gold in his hand, and bade him follow her with his needle and thread. Having

---

[4] *apothecary* (ə-pŏth′ ə-kĕr ē): druggist.

bound his eyes with a handkerchief, she took him to the room where the body lay, pulled off the bandage, and bade him sew the quarters together, after which she covered his eyes again and led him home.

Then they buried Cassim. Morgiana, his slave, followed him to the grave, weeping and tearing her hair, while Cassim's wife stayed at home uttering lamentable cries. Next day Morgiana went to live with Ali Baba, who gave Cassim's shop to his eldest son.

The forty thieves, on their return to the cave, were much astonished to find Cassim's body gone, as well as some of their moneybags.

"We are certainly discovered," said the captain, "and shall be undone if we cannot find out who it is that knows our secret. Two men must have known it. We have killed one; we must now find the other. To this end one of you who is bold and artful must go into the city, dressed as a traveler, and discover whom we have killed and whether men talk of the strange manner of his death. If the messenger fails he must lose his life, lest we be betrayed."

One of the thieves started up and offered to do this and, after the rest had highly commended him for his bravery, he disguised himself and happened to enter the town at daybreak, just by Baba Mustapha's stall. The thief bade him good day, saying, "Honest man, how can you possibly see to stitch at your age?"

"Old as I am," replied the cobbler, "I have very good eyes, and you will believe me when I tell you that I sewed a dead body together in a place where I had less light than I have now."

The robber was overjoyed at his good fortune, and giving the cobbler a piece of gold, desired to be shown the house where he had stitched up the dead body. At first Mustapha refused, saying that he had been blindfolded. But when the robber gave him another piece of gold, he began to think he might remember the turnings if blindfolded as before. This means succeeded. The robber partly led him and was partly guided by him right in front of Cassim's house, the door of which the robber marked with a piece of chalk.

Then, well pleased, he bade farewell to Baba Mustapha and returned to the forest. By and by Morgiana, going out, saw the mark the robber had made, quickly guessed that some mischief was brewing, and fetching a piece of white chalk, marked two or three doors on each side of the street, without saying anything to her master or mistress.

The thief, meanwhile, told his comrades of his discovery. The captain thanked him and bade him show him the house he had marked. But when they came to it, they saw that five or six of the houses were chalked in the same manner. The guide was so confounded that he knew not what answer to make, and when they returned to the cave he was at once beheaded for having failed. Another robber was dispatched and, having won over Baba Mustapha, marked the house in red chalk; but Morgiana being again too clever for them, the second messenger was put to death also.

The captain now resolved to go himself but, wiser than the others, he did not mark the house but looked at it so closely he could not fail to remember it. He returned and ordered his men to go into the neighboring villages and buy nineteen mules and thirty-eight leather jars, all empty, except one which was full of oil. The captain put one of his men, fully armed, into each, rubbing the outside of the jars with oil from the full vessel. Then the nineteen mules were loaded with thirty-seven robbers in jars and the jar of oil, and reached the town by dusk.

The captain stopped his mules in front of the house and said to Ali Baba, who was sitting outside for coolness, "I have brought some oil from a distance to sell at tomorrow's market, but it is now so late that I know not where to pass the night, unless you will do me the favor to take me in."

Though Ali Baba had seen the captain of the robbers in the forest, he did not recognize him in the disguise of an oil merchant. He bade him welcome, opened his gates for the mules to enter, and went to Morgiana to bid her prepare a bed and supper for his guest. He brought the stranger into his hall and, after they had supped, went again to speak to Morgiana in the kitchen, while the captain went into the yard under pretense of seeing after his mules but really to tell his men what to do.

Beginning at the first jar and ending at the last, he said to each man, "As soon as I throw some stones from the window of the chamber where I lie, cut the jars open with your knives and come out, and I will be with you in a trice."

He returned to the house, and Morgiana led him to his chamber. She then told Abdallah, her fellow slave, to put on the pot to make some broth for her master, who had gone to bed. Meanwhile her lamp went out and she had no more oil in the house.

"Do not be uneasy," said Abdallah. "Go into the yard and take some out of one of those jars."

Morgiana thanked him for his advice, took the oil pot, and went into the yard. When she came to the first jar, the robber inside said softly, "Is it time?"

Any other slave but Morgiana, on finding a man in the jar instead of the oil she wanted, would have screamed and made a noise. But she, knowing the danger her master was in, bethought herself of a plan and answered quietly, "Not yet, but presently."

She went to all the jars, giving the same answer, till she came to the jar of oil. She now saw that her master, thinking to entertain an oil merchant, had let thirty-eight robbers into his house. She filled her oil pot, went back to the kitchen and, having lit her lamp, went again to the oil jar and filled a large kettle full of oil. When it boiled she went and poured enough oil into every jar to stifle and kill the robber inside. When this brave deed was done, she went back to the kitchen, put out the fire and the lamp, and waited to see what would happen.

In a quarter of an hour the captain of the robbers awoke, got up, and opened the window. As all seemed quiet, he threw down some little pebbles, which hit the jars. He listened, and as none of his men seemed to stir, he grew uneasy and went down into the yard. On going to the first jar and saying, "Are you asleep?" he smelt the hot boiled oil and knew at once that his plot to murder Ali Baba and his household had been discovered. He found all the gang were dead and, missing the oil out of the last jar, became aware of the manner of their death. He then forced the lock of a door leading into a garden and, climbing over several walls, made his escape. Morgiana heard and saw all this and, rejoicing at her success, went to bed and fell asleep.

At daybreak Ali Baba arose and, seeing the oil jars there still, asked why the merchant had not gone with his mules. Morgiana bade him look in the first jar and see if there was any oil. Seeing a man, he started in terror.

"Have no fear," said Morgiana. "The man cannot harm you; he is dead."

Ali Baba, when he had recovered somewhat from his astonishment, asked what had become of the merchant.

"Merchant!" said she. "He is no more a merchant than I am!" And she told him the whole story, assuring him that it was a plot of the robbers of the forest, of whom only three were left, and that the white and red chalk marks had something to do with it. Ali Baba at once gave Morgiana her freedom, saying that he owed

her his life. They then buried the bodies in Ali Baba's garden,
while the mules were sold in the market by his slaves.

The captain returned to his lonely cave, which seemed fright-
ful to him without his lost companions, and firmly resolved to
avenge them by killing Ali Baba. He dressed himself carefully and
went into the town, where he took lodgings at an inn. In the
course of a great many journeys to the forest he carried away
many rich stuffs and much fine linen, and set up a shop opposite
that of Ali Baba's son. He called himself Cogia Hassan[5] and as he
was both civil and well dressed he soon made friends with Ali
Baba's son and through him with Ali Baba, whom he was continually asking to sup with him.

Ali Baba, wishing to return his kindness, invited him into his
house and received him smiling, thanking him for his kindness to

[5] *Cogia Hassan:* pronounced kō-zhē′ ä hä-sän′.

his son. When the merchant was about to take his leave Ali Baba stopped him, saying, "Where are you going, sir, in such haste? Will you not stay and sup with me?"

The merchant refused, saying that he had a reason and, on Ali Baba's asking him what that was, he replied, "It is, sir, that I can eat no victuals[6] that have any salt in them."

"If that is all," said Ali Baba, "let me tell you there shall be no salt in either the meat or the bread that we eat tonight."

He went to give this order to Morgiana, who was much surprised. "Who is this man," she said, "who eats no salt[7] with his meat?"

"He is an honest man, Morgiana," returned Ali Baba. "Therefore do as I bid you."

But she could not withstand a desire to see this strange man, so she helped Abdallah carry up the dishes and saw in a moment that Cogia Hassan was the robber captain and carried a dagger under his garment. "I am not surprised," she said to herself, "that this wicked man who intends to kill my master will eat no salt with him, but I will hinder his plans."

She sent up the supper by Abdallah, while she made ready for one of the boldest acts that could be thought of. When the dessert had been served, Cogia Hassan was left alone with Ali Baba and his son, whom he thought to make drunk and then murder.

Morgiana, meanwhile, put on a headdress like a dancing-girl's and clasped a girdle round her waist, from which hung a dagger with a silver hilt, and said to Abdallah, "Take your tabor, and let us go and divert[8] our master and his guest."

Abdallah took his tabor and played before Morgiana until they came to the door, where Abdallah stopped playing and Morgiana made a low curtsy.

"Come in, Morgiana," said Ali Baba. "Let Cogia Hassan see what you can do." And turning to his guest, he said, "She is my housekeeper."

Cogia Hassan was by no means pleased, for he feared that his chance of killing Ali Baba was gone for the present, but he pretended great eagerness to Morgiana, and Abdallah began to play and Morgiana to dance. After she had performed several dances she drew her dagger and made passes with it, sometimes pointing

---

[6] *victuals* (vĭt′ lz): food.
[7] *eats no salt:* for Moslems, eating salt at table promises loyalty to host.
[8] *divert* (dĭ-vûrt′): here, to entertain.

it at her own breast, sometimes at her master's, as if it were part of the dance. Suddenly, out of breath, she snatched the tabor from Abdallah with her left hand and holding the dagger in her right, held out the tabor to her master. Ali Baba and his son put a piece of gold into it and Cogia Hassan, seeing that she was coming to him, pulled out his purse to make her a present, but while he was putting his hand into it Morgiana plunged the dagger into his heart.

"Unhappy girl!" cried Ali Baba and his son. "What have you done to ruin us?"

"It was to preserve you, master, not to ruin you," answered Morgiana. "See here," she said, opening the false merchant's garment and showing the dagger. "See what an enemy you have entertained! Remember, he would eat no salt with you; what more would you have? Look at him! He is both the false oil merchant and the captain of the forty thieves."

Ali Baba was so grateful to Morgiana for thus saving his life that he offered her to his son in marriage, who readily consented; and a few days after, the wedding was celebrated with great splendor. At the end of a year Ali Baba, hearing nothing of the two remaining robbers, judged they were dead, and set out to the cave. The door opened on his saying, "Open sesame!" He went in and saw that nobody had been there since the captain left it. He brought away as much gold as he could carry and returned to town. He told his son the secret of the cave, which his son handed down in his turn, so the children and grandchildren of Ali Baba were rich to the end of their lives.

DISCUSSION

1. Ali Baba, Cassim, and the thieves all take action because they wish for gold. Morgiana has another reason for her actions. Why does she continue to serve Ali Baba and save his life? What is her reward?

2. Ali Baba was poor, "cutting wood in a neighboring forest and selling it in the town" (page 383). His brother Cassim was a well-to-do shopkeeper. How did one brother show some generosity, and the other brother show more greed? What is the reward of each?

3. The **plot** (see page 9) of this story is built around a series of secrets. Some are better kept than secrets usually are. How many can you name? What is the final result of keeping the riches secret?

For further activities, see page 422.

# Strong Wind, the Invisible

*(ALGONQUIN)*

## CYRUS MACMILLAN

On the shores of a wide bay on the Atlantic coast there dwelt in old times a great Indian warrior. He had a very wonderful and strange power: he could make himself invisible. He could thus mingle unseen with his enemies and listen to their plots. He was known among the people as Strong Wind, the Invisible. He dwelt with his sister in a tent near the sea, and his sister helped him greatly in his work.

Many maidens would have been glad to marry him, and he was much sought after because of his mighty deeds. It was known that Strong Wind would marry the first maiden who could see him as he came home at night. Many made the trial, but it was a long time before one succeeded.

Strong Wind used a clever trick to test the truthfulness of all who sought to win him. Each evening his sister walked on the beach with any girl who wished to make the trial. His sister could always see him, but no one else could see him. And as he came home from work in the twilight, his sister would ask the girl who sought him, "Do you see him?"

And each girl would falsely answer, "Yes."

And his sister would ask, "With what does he draw his sled?"

And each girl would answer, "With the hide of a moose," or "With a pole," or "With a great cord."

And then his sister would know that they all had lied. And many tried and lied and failed, for Strong Wind would not marry any who were untruthful.

There lived in the village a great Chief
who had three daughters. Their mother had
long been dead. One of these was much younger than the others. She was very beautiful and
gentle and well beloved by all. For that reason
her older sisters were very jealous of her
charms and treated her very cruelly.

They clothed her in rags that she might be
ugly. They cut off her long black hair. They
burned her face with coals from the fire that
she might be scarred and disfigured. And they
lied to their father, telling him that she had
done these things herself.

But the young girl kept her gentle heart
and went gladly about her work.

Like other girls, the Chief's two oldest daughters tried to win Strong Wind. One evening they walked on the shore with Strong Wind's sister and waited for his coming. Soon he came home from his day's work, drawing his sled.

And his sister asked as usual, "Do you see him?"

And each one, lying, answered, "Yes."

And she asked, "Of what is his shoulder strap made?"

And each, guessing, said, "Of rawhide."

Then they entered the tent, where they hoped to see Strong Wind eating his supper. They saw nothing. Strong Wind knew that they had lied. He kept himself from their sight, and they went home.

One day the Chief's youngest daughter with her rags and her burnt face resolved to seek Strong Wind. She patched her clothes and went forth to try to see the Invisible One as all the other girls of the village had done before. And her sisters laughed at her and called her "fool." As she passed along the road, all the people laughed at her, but silently she went her way.

Strong Wind's sister received the little girl kindly, and at twilight she took her to the beach. Soon Strong Wind came home drawing his sled.

And his sister asked, "Do you see him?"

And the girl answered, "No."

His sister wondered greatly. And again she asked, "Do you see him now?"

And the girl answered, "Yes, and he is very wonderful."

And the sister asked, "With what does he draw his sled?"

And the girl answered, "With the rainbow."

And the sister asked further, "Of what is his bowstring?"

And the girl answered. "His bowstring is the Milky Way."

Then Strong Wind's sister knew that because the girl had spoken the truth at first, her brother had made himself visible to her. And she said, "Truly, you have seen him."

And she took her home and bathed her, and all the scars disappeared from her face and body. Her hair grew long and black again like the raven's wing. She gave her fine clothes to wear and many rich ornaments. Then she bade her take the wife's seat in the tent.

Soon Strong Wind entered and sat beside her and called her his bride. The very next day she became his wife, and ever afterwards she helped him to do great deeds.

The girl's two elder sisters wondered greatly at what had taken place. But Strong Wind resolved to punish them. Using his great power, he changed them both into aspen trees and rooted them in the earth. And since that day the leaves of the aspen have always trembled. They shiver in fear at the approach of Strong Wind. They are still mindful of his great power and anger because of their lies and their cruelty to their sister long ago.

**DISCUSSION**

1.  Strong Wind uses his power to both reward and punish. Whom does he reward and whom does he punish? For what reasons?

2.  How do you picture Strong Wind? Do you imagine him in his invisible form or do you see him as "a great Indian warrior" (page 392)? Which form has the greater power?

3.  The youngest sister sees Strong Wind. Imagine what she sees: the sled that is drawn by a rainbow and the bow whose string is the Milky Way. What kind of sled do you see? How large is the bow?

4.  What is beautiful about the youngest sister?

For further activities, see page 423.

# The Rabbit and the Coyote

*(MEXICO)*                                    AMÉRICO PAREDES

A man and a woman had an onion patch, and a rabbit would come and tear it up. So the woman said, "You'd better go watch for that rabbit, or he's going to make an end of our onion patch."

The man went to watch for the rabbit, but he fell asleep, and the rabbit came into the patch and ate the onions. So the woman said, "Old man, you're not good for anything. I'll go, and you'll see how I catch him."

So the woman went. She made a doll out of wax and put it right in front of the opening, right in front of the place where the rabbit came in. Then she went off a ways and watched. The rabbit came and said, "Good evening, sir."

Nothing.

"Good evening. Get out of the way and let me pass. If you don't get out of the way, I'll slap your face." So he slapped its face, and his little hand stuck.

So then he said, "Let go of my hand, or I'll slap you with the other one."

And that one stuck, so then he said, "Let go of my two hands, or I'll kick you." He said, "I'm telling you to let go, or I'll kick you." And he kicked, and his foot stuck.

"Let go of my two hands and my foot, or I'll kick you again." And his other foot stuck.

"Let go of my four feet, or I'll bite you."

Nothing.

"I'm telling you to let go of my four feet, or I'll bite you." And he got stuck.

The old woman heard him, and she came out to see. And she said, "Now I got you, you good-for-nothing rabbit. You'll see what's going to happen to you." She picked him up, doll and all, and said to the old man, "You see, husband, I did catch him. Look at him."

"Ah, the good-for-nothing!" said the man. "I'll tie him up right away," he said, "so I can put a tub of water to boil, and then we'll scald him."

Just then a coyote passed by, and the rabbit said to the coyote, "Good morning, good coyote. Do you see that tub full of boiling water? They're going to kill a lot of chickens for me, and they want me to eat them all. Why don't you tie yourself up and let me loose," he said. "You're bigger than I am."

"Is that the truth? You're not lying to me?"

"No, I'm not lying to you," he said.

So the coyote said, "Good, tie me up. Let me untie you, and then you tie me up." So he untied the rabbit, and the rabbit tied him up.

And the rabbit said, "All right now. Feet, what are you for!"

"Wife, take a look outside at the rabbit. What if he got away from us."

The woman looked out, and she said, "Husband, husband! He isn't a rabbit any more; he's a coyote now."

"More reason for scalding him. This is really bad." And no telling what else the man said. So then the man goes out, and the water was boiling. And he began to throw hot water and more hot water on the coyote. Until the coyote couldn't stand it any more; and no telling how he did it, but he managed to break the rope.

He said, "As soon as I find that good-for-nothing rabbit, I'll eat him. He won't get away from me," he said. Well, he found him way off, eating prickly pears, and he said, "Ah, you good-for-nothing rabbit! You won't get away this time. Just look how I am, all hairless and scalded. And all because of you. You lied to me."

"No, dear little coyote, don't hurt me, and I'll peel some prickly pears for you to eat."

"Is that the truth?"

"Yes, yes, I'll peel them for you," he said. And he got to work peeling prickly pears, and he also put in a few with thorns and all. Then he said, "All right, friend coyote, I think I'll go. I'm leaving you a great many prickly pears." The coyote ate until he got to the ones with thorns, and he stuck himself all over. He was very angry with the rabbit again, and he went after him once more.

After a while he found him very far away, and he said to him, "Now I got you, you good-for-nothing rabbit. You left me a lot of prickly pears with the thorns on, and I got stuck all over." And this and that and the other. . . . And that. . . .

The rabbit said, "I'm here holding up this big rock," he said. "They're going to bring me my dinner here, a great big meal."

"No, I just don't believe you any more, rabbit. You're just a big liar."

"No, this is the truth," said the rabbit. "Why don't you take my place," he said, "and you'll see." So the coyote took his place and got stuck there holding up the rock.

After a while a fox went by, and the coyote said, "Dear little fox, help me hold up this rock."

"Who left you there?"

"Why, a rabbit."

"All right. You are there, you stay there." And, "Feet. . . ." The fox ran off and didn't help him.

He managed somehow to get out from under the rock, and he caught up with the rabbit. And the rabbit said, "No, dear little coyote, don't hurt me. Look. See this little stick? I'm a schoolmaster, and these are my pupils. Be sure not to disturb them if I'm not here," he said. "They're going to pay me with a lot of chickens and other food, plenty of it. How can I eat it all? And if I don't eat it, they'll kill me."

"Well, I am hungry indeed," said the coyote.

"All right, why don't you stay here. And after a long while, one or two hours, you whip them. You whip them two or three times and tell them, 'Study, study.' "

The coyote was there for a long time, and nobody brought him chickens or food or anything else, and he said, "It's too quiet in there. I don't hear any sound." He put his ear to the hole and struck three times with his little stick. So out come all the wasps, and you should have seen them go at him. He rolled about in the dirt, and the wasps just. . . . Till he went and jumped into a lake.

He went along, and he went along, and he went along, until he caught up with the rabbit again. The rabbit got inside a cave, and the coyote came. From a distance he smelled him in the cave, and he went and knocked. But the rabbit kept quiet. Then he said, "Hello there, cave of mine." Nothing. Again, "Hello there, cave of mine. That's strange; when I call, my cave always answers." And he called again. And it answered. So he said, "What can I do? The rabbit's in there." And the coyote ran away.

He went away, and then the rabbit said, "What can I do to get rid of this coyote?" He went into a canebrake, and he cleared a spot very well, burned and cleared it all around, and the coyote found him there. The coyote said, "Now I got you, rabbit. This time you won't get away for anything at all." He said, "I'm going to eat you this time. What are you doing there?" He was always asking questions.

"I'm waiting for a wedding party. There's going to be a lot to eat, meat and plenty of everything. They'll have a lot of things."

"You're not lying to me, rabbit?"

"Of course not. When you hear the popping of the fireworks, you shut your eyes and dance and shout." That's because he meant to set fire to the cane all around, and it would pop.

"All right, but you'd better not be lying to me. I won't let you off again." Well, so the rabbit went off, but to set fire all around. The cane was thick, and it began to burn. And the coyote yelled and yelled and sang and sang, with his eyes shut. Then all of a sudden he felt the heat. Well, like it or not, he had to run through the fire. And he got out of it, anyway.

The rabbit was by the edge of a lake, looking at the moon on the water. The coyote came and said that now he had him and all that, and just look, it had been a bunch of lies, there was a big fire, and I don't know what.

"No, dear little coyote; it was the truth. I just don't know what happened. Some accident, perhaps."

"And now, what are you doing there?" the coyote said.

He said, "You know what I'm doing? I'm looking at that beautiful cheese in there. But I'm so little. If I go in after it, I'll drown."

"Is it a cheese?" the coyote said.

"Yes, it is," he said, "of course."

So the coyote jumped in the lake. And the coyote said, "I can't get to it."

"Dive deeper."

"I can't get to it."

"Dive deeper."

"I can't get to it."

"You'd better come out so I can tie a stone to you. Then, you can go all the way to the bottom, and you will get to it."

So the coyote died there. The rabbit tied a stone to him, and he went all the way down to the bottom. But he drowned and never came out again.

And colorín[1] so red, the story is finished.

---

[1] *Colorín* (kō-lō-rēn'): a red bean. From traditional Mexican story-ending verse that begins, *colorín, colorado.* . . .

**DISCUSSION**

1.  There are many tales in which rabbits outwit their natural enemies. Why do you think storytellers so often choose the rabbit as hero? What other animals could be chosen for the same reason?

2.  The coyote suffers many mishaps and finally drowns while doing something very silly. The rabbit is caught in the onion patch, also through his own stupidity, but he gets into no further trouble. Why doesn't he?

3.  The rabbit may be the leading character in this tale, but he is not the cleverest. Who is? Why?

# A TUG-OF-WAR

**(AFRICA)**     ALICE WERNER

Tortoise considered himself a great personage. He went about calling attention to his greatness. He said to people, "We three, Elephant, Hippopotamus, and I, are the greatest, and we are equal in power and authority."

Thus he boasted, and his boasts came to the ears of Elephant and Hippopotamus. They listened and then they laughed. "Pooh, that's nothing. He is a small person of no account, and his boasting can only be ignored."

The talebearer returned to Tortoise, telling him what the two great ones had said. Tortoise grew very vexed indeed. "So, they despise me, do they? Well, I will just show them my power. I am equal to them, and they will know it before long! They will yet address me as Friend." And he set off.

He found Elephant in the forest, lying down; and his trunk was eight miles long, his ears as big as a house, and his four feet large beyond measure. Tortoise approached him and boldly called out, "Friend, I have come! Rise and greet me. Your Friend is here."

Elephant looked about, astonished. Then spying Tortoise he rose up and asked indignantly, "Tortoise, small person, whom do you address as Friend?"

"You. I call you Friend. And are you not, Elephant?"

"Most certainly I am not," replied the Elephant in anger. "Besides, you have been going about and saying certain things about your great power—that it is equal to mine. How do you come to talk in such a way?"

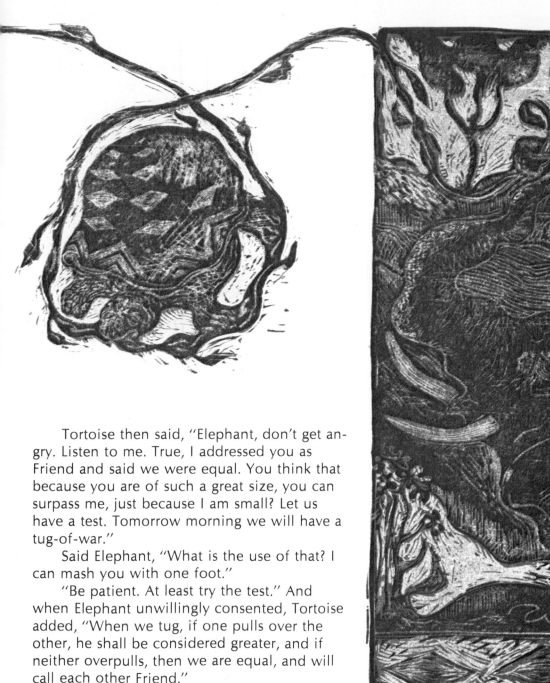

Tortoise then said, "Elephant, don't get angry. Listen to me. True, I addressed you as Friend and said we were equal. You think that because you are of such a great size, you can surpass me, just because I am small? Let us have a test. Tomorrow morning we will have a tug-of-war."

Said Elephant, "What is the use of that? I can mash you with one foot."

"Be patient. At least try the test." And when Elephant unwillingly consented, Tortoise added, "When we tug, if one pulls over the other, he shall be considered greater, and if neither overpulls, then we are equal, and will call each other Friend."

Then Tortoise cut a very long vine and brought one end to Elephant. "This end is yours. I will go off with my end to a certain spot; and we will begin to tug, and neither of us will stop to eat or sleep, until one pulls the other over, or the vine breaks." And he went off with the other end of the vine and hid it on the outskirts of the town where Hippopotamus lived.

Hippopotamus was bathing in the river and Tortoise shouted to him, "Friend, I have come! You! Come ashore! I am visiting you!"

There was a great splashing as Hippopotamus came to shore, bellowing angrily, "You are going to get it now! Whom do you call Friend?"

"Why, you, of course. There is no one else here, is there?" answered Tortoise. "But do not be so quick to fight. I do not fear your size. I say we are equals, and if you doubt me, let us have a trial. Tomorrow morning we will have a tug-of-war. He who shall overcome the other shall be the superior. But if neither is found superior, then we are equals and will call each other Friend." Hippopotamus thought the plan was absurd, but finally he consented.

Tortoise then brought his end of the vine to Hippopotamus and said, "This end is yours. And now I go. Tomorrow when you feel a pull on the vine, know that I am ready at the other end. Then you begin to tug, and we will not eat or sleep until the test is ended."

In the morning, Tortoise went to the middle of the vine and shook it. Elephant immediately grabbed his end, Hippopotamus caught up his end, and the tugging began. Each pulled at the vine mightily and it remained taut. At times it was pulled in one direction, and then in the other, but neither was overpulling the other.

Tortoise watched the quivering vine, laughing in his heart. Then he went away to seek for food, leaving the two at their tug, and hungry. He ate his bellyful of mushrooms and then went comfortably to sleep.

Late in the afternoon he rose and said, "I will go and see whether those fools are still pulling." When he went there the vine was still stretched taut, with neither of them winning. At last, Tortoise nicked the vine with his knife. The vine parted, and at their ends Elephant and Hippopotamus, so suddenly released, fell with a great crash back onto the ground.

Tortoise started off with one end of the broken vine. He came on Elephant looking doleful and rubbing a sore leg. Elephant said, "Tortoise, I did not know you were so strong. When the vine broke I fell over and hurt my leg. Yes, we are really equals. Strength is not because the body is large. We will call each other Friend."

Most pleased with this victory over Elephant, Tortoise then went off to visit Hippopotamus, who looked sick and was rubbing his head. Hippopotamus said, "So, Tortoise, we are equal. We pulled and pulled and despite my great size I could not surpass you. When the vine broke I fell and hurt my head. Indeed, strength has no greatness of body. We will call each other Friend."

After that, whenever they three and others met in council, the three sat together on the highest seats. And always they addressed each other as Friend.

Do you think they were really equal?

**DISCUSSION**

1. What does the tug-of-war demonstrate about strength? What different kinds of strength are there?

2. Does this tale remind you of other stories you have read in this unit or elsewhere? Which ones?

3. The story begins, "Tortoise considered himself a great personage." What does "great" mean to each of the animals? What does it mean to you?

# The Artist

*(CHINA)*

ISABELLE C. CHANG

There was once a king who loved the graceful
curves of the rooster. He asked the court artist to
paint a picture of a rooster for him. For one year
he waited, and still this order was not fulfilled. In
a rage, he stomped into the artist's studio and demanded to see the artist.

Quickly the artist brought out paper, paint,
and brush. In five minutes a perfect picture of a
rooster emerged from his skillful brush. The king
turned purple with anger, saying, "If you can
paint a perfect picture of a rooster in five minutes, why did you keep me waiting for over a
year?"

"Come with me," begged the artist. He led
the king to his storage room. Paper was piled
from the floor to the ceiling. On every sheet was
a painting of a rooster.

"Your Majesty," explained the artist, "it took
me more than one year to learn how to paint a
perfect rooster in five minutes."

*Life is short, art is long.*

DISCUSSION

1.  The king expected the drawing much sooner. Why didn't the artist
give the king one of his earlier drawings?

2.  The teller of the tale explains, "Life is short, art is long." What does
this mean?

# THE TIGER

*(CHINA)*

LIN YUTANG

Chang Feng was traveling in Fukien[1] in the beginning of the reign of Yuanho[2] (806–820). He was a northerner, and the luxuriant subtropical vegetation was new and interesting to him. Among other things, he had heard of tigers in the south. One day he was stopping with his servant at an inn in Hengshan, a small town near Foochow,[3] lying on the watershed of the high mountain ranges which divide Fukien from Chekiang.[4] Having deposited his luggage, he went out to take in his first impressions of the land, its people and the women's costumes. Walking alone with a cane in his hand, he went on and on, attracted by the refreshing green of the country after rain, and the bracing winds which came over the mountain. He felt strangely excited. Before him lay a landscape which was a riotous display of colors. It was autumn and the hillsides literally glowed with the gold and red of maple forests. A beautiful white temple stood half-way up the mountain above a thickly wooded slope. The golden sunset transformed the mountainside and the fields into a landscape of brilliant pastels, blue and purple and green, changing in hue every moment, mingling with the dazzling red and gold. It was like a magic land.

Suddenly he felt a fainting sensation: stars danced before his eyes and his head reeled. He thought it was due to the altitude, the overexertion, and the sudden change of climate, or perhaps he was affected by the strange light. Just a few steps before him he saw a pasture land covered with velvety lawn, lying just where the wooded slope began. He took off his gown and put it with his walking stick against a tree, and lay down to

[1] *Fukien:* pronounced foō-kyĕn'.
[2] *Yuanho:* pronounced wän-hō'.
[3] *Hengshan; Foochow:* pronounced hĕng' shän; foō' jō.
[4] *Chekiang:* pronounced chĕ' kyäng.

take a rest. He felt a little better. As he looked up at the blue
sky, he thought how beautiful and peaceful nature was. Men
fought for money and position and fame; they lied and cheated
and killed for gain; but here was peace—in nature. As he rolled
in the grass, he felt happy and relaxed. The smell of the sod and
a gentle breeze soon caressed him into sleep.

When he woke up, he felt hungry and remembered it was
evening. As he rolled his hands over his stomach, he touched a
coating of soft fur. Quickly he sat up, and he saw his body covered with beautiful black stripes, and as he stretched his arms,
he felt a delightful new strength in them, sinewy and full of
power. He yawned and was surprised at his own powerful roar.
Looking down his own face, he saw the tips of long white whiskers. Lo, he had been transformed into a tiger!

Now, that is delightful, he thought to himself. I am no
longer a man, but a tiger. It is not bad for a change.

Wanting to try his new strength, he ran into the woods and
bounced from rock to rock, delighting in his new strength. He
went up to the monastery, and pawed at the gate, seeking ad-
mittance.

"It is a tiger!" he heard a monk inside shouting. "I smell it.
Do not open!"

Now that is uncomfortable, he thought to himself. I only
intended to have a simple supper and discuss Buddhist philosophy with him. But of course I am a tiger now, and perhaps I do
smell.

He had an instinct that he should go down the hill to the
village and seek for food. As he hid behind a hedge on a country
path, he saw a beautiful girl passing by, and he thought to himself, I have been told that Foochow girls are famous for their
white complexion and small stature. Indeed it is true.

As he made a move to go up to the girl, she screamed and
ran for her life.

What kind of a life is this, when everybody takes you for
an enemy? he wondered. I will not eat her, she is so beautiful. I
will take a pig, if I can find one.

At the thought of a nice, fat pig, or a small juicy lamb, his
mouth watered, and he felt ashamed of himself. But there was
this infernal hunger gnawing at his stomach, and he knew he
had to eat something or die. He searched the village for a pig or
calf, or even a chicken, but they were all under good shelters.

All doors were shut against him, and as he crouched in a dark alley, waiting for a stray animal, he heard people talking inside their houses about a tiger in the village.

Unable to satisfy his hunger, he went back to the mountain, and lay in wait for some wayfarer in the night. All night he waited, but nothing came his way. For a while, he must have fallen asleep.

Toward dawn, he woke up. Soon travelers began to pass along the mountain road. He saw a man coming up from the city who stopped several passengers to ask whether they had seen Cheng Chiu, a bureau chief of Foochow, who was expected to return to his office today. He was evidently a clerk from the bureau who had been sent to welcome the chief.

Something told the tiger that he must eat Cheng Chiu. Just why he must eat that person he could not tell, but the feeling was very definite that Cheng Chiu was destined to be his first victim.

"He was getting up from the inn when I left. I think he is coming behind us," he heard a man reply to the clerk's question.

"Is he traveling alone, or is he accompanied by others? Tell me his dress so that I can recognize him, for I do not want to make a mistake when I go up to greet him."

"There are three of them traveling together. The one dressed in dark green is Cheng."

As the tiger listened to the conversation from his hiding place, it seemed as if it were taking place expressly for his benefit. He had never seen or heard of Cheng Chiu in his life. He crouched in a thicket and waited for his victim.

Soon he saw Cheng Chiu coming up the road with his secretaries, along with a group of other travelers. Cheng looked fat and juicy and delicious. When Cheng Chiu came within pouncing distance, the tiger, Chang, rushed out, felled him to the ground, and carried him up the mountain. The travelers were so frightened they all ran away. Chang's hunger was satisfied, and he only felt as if he had had a bigger breakfast than usual. He finished up the gentleman and left only the hair and bones.

Satisfied with his meal, he lay down to take a nap. When he woke up, he thought he must have been mad to eat a human

being who had done him no harm. His head cleared and he decided it was not such a pleasant life, prowling night after night for food. He remembered the night before, when the instinct of hunger drove him to the village and up the mountain, and he could do nothing to stop himself.

"Why do I not go back to that lawn and see if I can become a human being again?"

He found the spot where his clothing and walking stick were still lying by the tree. He lay down again, with the wish that he might wake up to be a man once more. He rolled over on the grass, and in a few seconds found that he had been restored to his human shape.

Greatly delighted, but puzzled by the strange experience, he put on his gown, took up his cane, and started back to the town. When he reached the inn, he found he had been away exactly twenty-four hours.

"Where have you been, Master?" asked his servant, "I have been out looking for you all day." The innkeeper also came up to speak to him, evidently relieved to see him return.

"We have been worried about you," said the innkeeper. "There was a tiger abroad. He was seen by a girl in the village last night, and this morning Cheng Chiu, a bureau chief who was returning to his office, was eaten by him."

Chang Feng made up a story that he had spent the night discussing Buddhist philosophy up in the temple.

"You are lucky!" cried the innkeeper, shaking his head. "It was in that neighborhood that Cheng Chiu was killed by the tiger."

"No, the tiger will not eat me," Chang Feng replied.

"Why not?"

"He cannot," said Chang Feng enigmatically.[5]

Chang Feng kept the secret to himself, for he could not afford to tell anybody that he had eaten a man. It would be embarrassing, to say the least.

He went back to his home in Honan,[6] and a few years went by. One day he was stopping at Huaiyang,[7] a city on the Huai River. His friends gave him a dinner and much wine was con-

---

[5] *enigmatically* (ĕn′ ĭg-măt′ ĭ-kəl-ē): mysteriously.
[6] *Honan:* pronounced hō′ nän.
[7] *Huaiyang:* pronounced hwī-yäng′.

sumed, as was usual on such occasions. Between the courses and
the sipping of wine, the guests were each asked to tell a strange
experience, and if in the opinion of the company the story was
not strange enough, the teller of the story was to be fined a cup
of wine.

Chang Feng began to tell his own story, and it happened
that one of the guests was the son of Cheng Chiu, the man he
had eaten. As he proceeded with his story, the young man's face
grew angrier and angrier.

"So it was you who killed my father!" the young man
shouted at him, his eyes distended and the veins standing up on
his temples.

Chang Feng hastily stood up and apologized. He knew he
had got into a very serious situation. "I am sorry. I did not
know it was your father."

The young man suddenly whipped out a knife and threw it
at him. Luckily it missed and fell with a clang on the floor. The
young man made a rush at him, and would have fallen on him,
but the guests, greatly disturbed by the sudden turn of events,
held him back.

"I will kill you to avenge my father's death. I will follow
you to the ends of the earth!" the young man shouted.

The friends persuaded Chang Feng to leave the house at
once and hide himself for a while, while they tried to calm
Cheng Chiu's son. It was conceded by everybody that to avenge
one's father's death was a noble and laudable undertaking, but
after all, Chang Feng had eaten Cheng Chiu when he was a tiger, and no one wanted to see more blood shed. It was a novel
situation and posed a complicated moral problem as to whether
revenge under such circumstances was justified. The youth still
swore murder to appease his father's spirit.

In the end, the friends spoke to the commander of the region who ordered the young man to cross the Huai River and
never return to the northern bank, while Chang Feng changed
his name and went to the northwest to keep as far away from
his sworn enemy as possible.

When the young man returned to his home, his friends said
to him, "We entirely sympathize with your determination to
avenge your father. That is a son's duty, of course. However,
Chang Feng ate your father when he was a tiger and not responsible for his action. He did not know your father and had

no purpose in killing him. That was a strange and special case, but it was not intentional murder, and if you kill him, you will be tried for murder yourself."

The son respected this advice and did not pursue Chang Feng any more.

DISCUSSION

1. Is Chang Feng a killer? Do you agree with those in the story who say to the vengeful son, "Chang Feng ate your father when he was a tiger and not responsible for his action"? Why do we excuse animals for killing and do not excuse humans?

2. Did Chang Feng really turn into a tiger in this story or did he just imagine it? What proof does the story give?

3. What did Chang Feng like about being a tiger? What did he dislike?

For further activities, see page 422.

# MIDAS

*(GREECE)*

## BERNARD EVSLIN

There was a king named Midas, and what he loved best in the world was gold. He had plenty of his own, but he could not bear the thought of anyone else having any. Each morning he awoke very early to watch the sunrise and said, "Of all the gods, if gods there be, I like you least, Apollo. How dare you ride so unthriftily in your sun-chariot scattering golden sheaves of light on rich and poor alike—on king and peasant, on merchant, shepherd, warrior? This is an evil thing, oh wastrel god, for only kings should have gold; only the rich know what to do with it."

After a while these words of complaint, uttered each dawn, came to Apollo, and he was angry. He appeared to Midas in a dream and said, "Other gods would punish you, Midas, but I am famous for my even temper. Instead of doing you violence, I will show you how gracious I can be by granting you a wish. What is it to be?"

Midas cried, "Let everything I touch turn to gold!"

He shouted this out of his sleep in a strangling greedy voice, and the guards in the doorway nodded to each other and said, "The king calls out. He must be dreaming of gold again."

Wearied by the dream, Midas slept past sunrise; when he awoke it was full morning. He went out into his garden. The sun was high, the sky was blue. A soft breeze played among the trees. It was a glorious morning. He was still half asleep. Tatters of the dream were in his head.

"Can it be true?" he said to himself. "They say the gods appear in dreams. That's how men know them. On the other hand I know that dreams are false, teasing things. You can't believe them. Let us put it to the test."

He reached out his hand and touched a rose. It turned to gold—petals and stalk, it turned to gold and stood there rigid, heavy, gleaming. A bee buzzed out of its stiff folds, furious; it lit on Midas' hand to sting him. The king looked at the heavy golden bee on the back of his hand and moved it to his finger.

"I shall wear it as a ring," he said.

Midas went about touching all his roses, seeing them stiffen and gleam. They lost their odor. The disappointed bees rose in swarms and buzzed angrily away. Butterflies departed. The hard flowers tinkled like little bells when the breeze moved among them, and the king was well pleased.

His little daughter, the princess, who had been playing in the garden, ran to him and said, "Father, Father, what has happened to the roses?"

"Are they not pretty, my dear?"

"No! They're ugly! They're horrid and sharp and I can't smell them anymore. What happened?"

"A magical thing."

"Who did the magic?"

"I did."

"Unmagic it, then! I hate these roses."
She began to cry.

"Don't cry," he said, stroking her head. "Stop crying, and I will give you a golden doll with a gold-leaf dress and tiny golden shoes."

She stopped crying. He felt the hair grow spiky under his fingers. Her eyes stiffened and froze into place. The little blue vein in her neck stopped pulsing. She was a statue, a figure of pale gold standing in the garden path with lifted face. Her tears were tiny golden beads on her

golden cheeks. He looked at her and said, "This is unfortunate. I'm sorry it happened. I have no time to be sad this morning. I shall be busy turning things into gold. But, when I have a moment, I shall think about this problem; I promise." He hurried out of the garden, which had become unpleasant to him.

On Midas' way back to the castle he amused himself by kicking up gravel in the path and watching it tinkle down as tiny nuggets. The door he opened became golden; the chair he sat upon became solid gold like his throne. The plates turned into gold, and the cups became gold cups before the amazed eyes of the servants, whom he was careful not to touch. He wanted them to continue being able to serve him; he was very hungry.

With great relish Midas picked up a piece of bread and honey. His teeth bit metal; his mouth was full of metal. He felt himself choking. He reached into his mouth and pulled out a golden slab of bread, all bloody now, and flung it through the window. Very lightly now he touched the other food to see what would happen. Meat . . . apples . . . walnuts . . . they all turned to gold even when he touched them with only the tip of his finger . . . and when he did not touch them with his fingers, when he lifted them on his fork, they became gold as soon as they touched his lips, and he had to put them back onto the plate. He was savagely hungry. Worse than hunger, when he thought about drinking, he realized that wine, or water, or milk would turn to gold in his mouth and choke him if he drank. As he thought that he could not drink, thirst began to burn in his belly. He felt himself full of hot dry sand, felt that the lining of his head was on fire.

"What good is all my gold?" he cried, "if I cannot eat and cannot drink?"

He shrieked with rage, pounded on the table, and flung the plates about. All the servants ran from the room in fright. Then Midas raced out of the castle, across the bridge that spanned the moat, along the golden gravel path into the garden where the stiff flowers chimed hatefully, and the statue of his daughter looked at him with scooped and empty eyes. There in the garden, in the blaze of the sun, he raised his arms heavenward, and cried, "You, Apollo, false god, traitor! You pretended to forgive me, but you punished me with a gift!"

Then it seemed to him that the sun grew brighter, that the light thickened, that the sun-god stood before him in the path, tall, stern, clad in burning gold. A voice said, "On your knees, wretch!"

He fell to his knees.

"Do you repent?"

"I repent. I will never desire gold again. I will never accuse the gods. Pray, revoke the fatal wish."

Apollo reached his hand and touched the roses. The tinkling stopped, they softened, swayed, blushed. Fragrance grew on the air. The bees returned, and the butterflies. He touched the statue's cheek. She lost her stiffness, her metallic gleam. She ran to the roses, knelt among them, and cried, "Oh thank you, Father. You've changed them back again." Then she ran off, shouting and laughing.

Apollo said, "I take back my gift. I remove the golden taint from your touch, but you are not to escape without punishment. Because you have been the most foolish of men, you shall wear always a pair of donkey's ears."

Midas touched his ears. They were long and furry. He said, "I thank you for your forgiveness, Apollo . . . even though it comes with a punishment."

"Go now," said Apollo. "Eat and drink. Enjoy the roses. Watch your child grow. Life is the only wealth, man. In your great thrift, you have been wasteful of life, and that is the sign you wear on your head. Farewell."

Midas put a tall pointed hat on his head so that no one would see his ears. Then he went in to eat and drink his fill.

For years he wore the cap so that no one would know of his disgrace. But the servant who cut his hair had to know so Midas swore him to secrecy, warning that it would cost him his head if he spoke of the king's ears. But the servant who was a coward was also a gossip. He could not bear to keep a secret, especially a secret so mischievous. Although he was afraid to tell it, he felt that he would burst if he didn't.

One night he went out to the banks of the river, dug a little hole, put his mouth to it, and whispered, "Midas has donkey's ears, Midas has

donkey's ears . . ." and quickly filled up the hole again, and ran back to the castle, feeling better.

But the river-reeds heard him, and they always whisper to each other when the wind seethes among them. They were heard whispering, "Midas has donkey's ears . . . donkey's ears . . ." and soon the whole country was whispering, "Have you heard about Midas? Have you heard about his ears?"

When the king heard, he knew who had told the secret and ordered the man's head cut off; but then he thought, "The god forgave me, perhaps I had better forgive this blabbermouth." Therefore he let the treacherous man keep his head.

Then Apollo appeared again and said, "Midas, you have learned the final lesson, mercy. As you have done, so shall you be done by."

And Midas felt his long hairy ears dwindling back to normal.

He was an old man now. His daughter, the princess, was grown. He had grandchildren. Sometimes he tells his smallest granddaughter the story of how her mother was turned into a golden statue, and he says, "See, I'm changing you too. Look, your hair is all gold."

And she pretends to be frightened.

DISCUSSION

1.   Apollo tells Midas he is "the most foolish of men." Why is Midas a fool? What is the punishment for his foolishness?

2.   Midas prays, "Revoke the fatal wish." Could he have died? How?

3.   Sometimes it is said that a person has "the Midas touch." What does this mean? Would you want it? Why, or why not?

For further activities, see page 423.

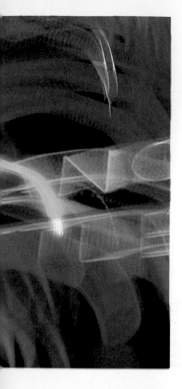

## VOCABULARY

### Ali Baba and the Forty Thieves (page 382)

| | | |
|---|---|---|
| barley | essence | suet |
| brocades | lozenges | tabor |

Are these words unfamiliar to you? Sometimes the sentence or paragraph containing an unfamiliar word will give the definition, or at least a clue. Try to write a definition for each word, using the right clue from the following list. You will need to go back and read the whole sentence or paragraph again. If you are still not sure of the meaning, use your dictionary.

"silk stuffs" (page 383)
"a piece of gold was sticking to it" (p. 384)
"he named several other sorts of grain" (p. 384)
"my poor master can neither eat nor speak" (p. 385)
"only given to those just about to die" (p. 385)
"Abdallah . . . played before Morgiana" (p. 390)

### The Tiger (page 408)

All six words in the first group below were used in this story. The second group contains words of similar meaning that could have been used in their place. Copy the first group of words and write next to each its matching word from the second group.

1. laudable     enigmatically     conceded
   distended     luxuriant         infernal

2. abominable    admitted          praiseworthy
   abundant      protruding        mysteriously

## COMPOSITION

### The Tiger (page 408)

Suppose that when you go home today you stop to rest in a park or field near your home. The sun is warm and you feel drowsy. Suddenly, like Chang Feng, you wake up and find that you have turned into—what? Write a short story from this new point of view, describing your new form, how you feel, and how others react to you.

## Midas (page 415)

When everything Midas touched turned into gold, he soon found this a terrible experience. Suppose he had discovered that objects he touched became alive. What kind of experience would this be? Write a story in which this happens, and see what kind of problems your Midas has.

## READING

### Strong Wind, the Invisible (page 392)

Do you always read carefully and remember the action of a story? On separate paper, indicate whether these statements are true or false.

1. Strong Wind would marry the first maiden who could see him.
2. The Chief's daughters were beautiful and loved by all.
3. Strong Wind draws his sled with the Milky Way and his bowstring is the rainbow.
4. The youngest daughter cut her long, stringy hair when she became his wife.
5. No one ever dared lie to Strong Wind.
6. Strong Wind lived with his sister in a tent on the mountain top.
7. The two elder sisters became trees as a result of their lies and cruelty.
8. In winter their needles are covered with snow and they shiver with cold when Strong Wind is in the North.

### The Tiger (page 408)

Some of the following statements describe Chang Feng the man; some describe Chang Feng the tiger. On a separate paper write the number of each statement, indicating whether it describes (a) the man or (b) the tiger.

1. He felt happy.
2. He had choices.
3. He was led by his instincts.
4. He was lonely.
5. He appreciated beauty.
6. He was uncomfortable.
7. He had a gnawing hunger.
8. He felt a new strength.

# COMPOSITION

**WRITING
FICTION**

*Fiction* (page 103) refers to "made-up" stories, stories that come out of an author's imagination. Long John Silver, Ali Baba, Dorothy in *The Wizard of Oz,* Gulliver, Frankenstein, Scrooge, Becky Thatcher are all fictional characters. So are the great majority of characters whom actors play on television and so are the characters you have met in this section of myths and tales. None really lived. Each one was born in some author's imagination.

It can be exciting, creating on paper a character where none existed before. Try it. Draw, as always, on your own experience—on what you know best. But use your imagination to go beyond the present and near at hand, into the past, into the far away, even into the future. How, for instance, do you imagine that the neighbor who moved away from your school three years ago, and who hasn't been seen or heard of since, would look and act by now?

Give your character a fictional name, then set her or him in motion. Always draw, to start with, on what you know best. Is it life in the country? In a town? In the suburbs? In the city? Wherever, start your character moving through that world, inventing place names but describing the world with words that let your reader see it clearly.

Having created a convincing character *(characterization)*, and described the world the character is a part of *(description)*, you will have to attend to two other matters. You must tell what happens to the character. The technical word for this is *narration.* You will need to develop the knack of narrating a story in an interesting way, keeping the plot moving forward, cutting out unnecessary details, bringing in other characters to heighten tension that may lead to conflict. Finally, you must listen to how people speak, so that the *dialogue*—those words your characters utter—will sound believable.

As you see, the task of writing fiction is challenging. It involves paying attention to a number of different matters at the same time. But so does driving a car. So does any sport or skill. Try it. As with your first time bowling, your first time on a skateboard, the effort may feel odd at the start, until you discover those hidden talents within you.

## ABOUT THE SELECTIONS

1.   Which myth or tale in this section did you enjoy most? In a unified paragraph try as specifically as possible to account for your choice. Did you find most appealing the *idea* (as in "The Artist"), or the *humor* (as in "Three Strong Women"), or the *plot* (as in "The Tiger"), or something else?

2.   "Strong Wind, the Invisible" offers an explanation for why aspen leaves tremble. Write a paragraph pointing out other facts of nature "explained" in the course of these selections. How, for example, did bats come to be? Mention the selections specifically, and tell in the paragraph which explanation appealed to you most— and why.

3.   Jean Britisse is a clearly developed character. We come to know a lot about him: how he looks, talks, thinks. What other character or characters in the section do you get to know well? Choose the one you can see most clearly, then write a paragraph describing that character as you picture her or him. How has the author helped you picture the character clearly?

4.   As in Bugs Bunny cartoons, so in "The Rabbit and the Coyote." Someone who thinks and talks fast can often get the better of her or his opponents, even when the opponents are stronger. Which characters in the section win out because they use their heads rather than their muscles? Write a unified paragraph that mentions those characters and suggests which one is cleverest of all.

## ON YOUR OWN

1.   Create a character by combining traits from several different people whom you have known at different times and places in your life. Let us see how the person looks and moves, hear how he or she speaks. The person may be doing nothing more exciting than washing dishes or waiting on a corner, but let us get to know the character by the way you describe her or him.

2.   Write a myth that briefly accounts for how something came to be—what caused the Grand Canyon or Niagara Falls or the Sahara Desert, or how the giraffe's neck was stretched or the porcupine got its quills or the elephant got its trunk. Use your imagination—and the myths in this section for models.

3.   "Jack's Hunting Trip" is told in dialect (p. 357). Write a sample of dialect that reproduces the speech of someone you know in real life or from television. Make up a name for the person, then try to capture her or his way of speaking exactly. Have the person talk about something that may be of interest to your reader, an adventure or skill or opinion.

4.   Think of an everyday saying that tells a truth about life. ("Better safe than sorry." "He who hesitates is lost." "Absence makes the heart grow fonder." "Don't put all your eggs in one basket.") Then invent a fable that illustrates the saying you have chosen, creating animal characters in the manner of the fables in this section. See if you can make the characters seem real, each with a personality and her or his own way of speaking. Include the saying you have chosen as the moral at the end.

TURNING POINTS

# The Turtle

GEORGE VUKELICH

They were driving up to fish the White Creek for German Browns and the false dawn was purpling the Wisconsin countryside when they spotted the huge hump-backed object in the middle of the sandroad and Jimmy coasted the station wagon to a stop.

"Pa," he said. "Turtle. Lousy snapper."

Old Tony sat up.

"Is he dead?"

"Not yet," Jimmy said. "Not yet he isn't." He shifted into neutral and pulled the handbrake. The snapper lay large and dark green in the headlight beams, and they got out and went around to look at it closely. The turtle moved a little and left razorlike clawmarks in the wet sand, and it waited.

"Probably heading for the creek," Jimmy said. "They kill trout like crazy."

They stood staring down.

"I'd run the wagon over him," Jimmy said. "Only he's too big."

He looked around and walked to the ditchway, and came back with a long finger-thick pine branch. He jabbed it into the turtle's face and the snakehead lashed out and struck like spring-steel and the branch snapped like a stick of macaroni, and it all happened fast as a matchflare.

"Looka that!" Tony whistled.

"You bet, Pa. I bet he goes sixty pounds. Seventy maybe."

The turtle was darting its head around now in long stretching movements.

"I think he got some branch stuck in his craw," Jimmy said. He got out a cigarette and lighted it, and flipped the match at the rockgreen shell.

"I wish now I'd brought the twenty-two," he said. "The pistol."

"You going to kill him?"

"Why not?" Jimmy asked. "They kill trout, don't they?"

They stood there smoking and not talking, and looking down at the unmoving shell.

"I could use the lug wrench on him," Jimmy said. "Only I don't think it's long enough. I don't want my hands near him."

Tony didn't say anything.

"You watch him," Jimmy said. "I'll go find something in the wagon."

Slowly Tony squatted down onto his haunches and smoked and stared at the turtle. Poor Old One, he thought. You had the misfortune to be caught in the middle of a sandroad, and you are very vulnerable on the sandroads, and now you are going to get the holy life beaten out of you.

The turtle stopped its stretching movements and was still. Tony looked at the full webbed feet and the nail claws and he knew the truth.

"It would be different in the water, turtle," he said. "In the water you could cut down anybody."

He thought about this snapper in the water and how it would move like a torpedo and bring down trout, and nobody would monkey with it in the water—and here it was in the middle of a

sandroad, vulnerable as a baby and waiting to get its brains beaten out.

He finished his cigarette and field-stripped it[1] and got to his feet and walked to the wagon and reached into the glove compartment for the thermos of coffee. What was he getting all worked up about a turtle for? He was an old man and he was acting like a kid, and they were going up to the White for German Browns, and he was getting worked up about a God-forsaken turtle in the middle of a God-forsaken sandroad. *God-forsaken.* He walked back to the turtle and hunched down and sipped at the strong black coffee and watched the old snapper watching him.

Jimmy came up to him holding the bumper jack.

"I want to play it safe," he said. "I don't think the lug wrench is long enough." He squatted beside Tony. "What do you think?"

"He waits," Tony said. "What difference what I think?"

Jimmy squinted at him.

"I can tell something's eating you. What are you thinking, Pa?"

"I am thinking this is not a brave thing."

"What?"

"This turtle—he does not have a chance."

Jimmy lit a cigarette and hefted the bumper jack. The turtle moved ever so slightly.

"You talk like an old woman. An old tired woman."

"I can understand this turtle's position."

"He doesn't have a chance?"

"That's right."

"And that bothers you?"

Tony looked into Jimmy's face.

"That is right," he said. "That bothers me."

"Well of all the dumb stupid things," Jimmy said. "What do you want me to do? Get down on all fours and fight with him?"

"No," Tony said. "Not on all fours. Not on all fours." He looked at Jimmy. "In the water. Fight this turtle in the water. That would be a brave thing, my son."

Jimmy put down the bumper jack and reached for the thermos jug and didn't say anything. He drank his coffee and smoked his cigarette, and he stared at the turtle and didn't say anything.

"You're crazy," he said finally.

---

[1] *field-stripped it:* tore it apart to prevent an accidental fire.

"It is a thought, my son. A thought. This helpless plodding old one like a little baby in this sandroad, eh? But in the water, his home. . . ." Tony snapped his fingers with the suddenness of a switchblade. "In the water he could cut down anyone, anything . . . any man. Fight him in the water, Jimmy. Use your bumper jack in the water. . . ."

"I think you're nuts," Jimmy said. "I think you're honest to goodness nuts."

Tony shrugged. "This does not seem fair for you, eh? To be in the water with this one." He motioned at the turtle. "This seems nuts to you. Crazy to you. Because in the water he could cripple you. Drown you. Because in the water you are not a match."

"What are you trying to prove, Pa?"

"Jimmy. This turtle is putting up his life. In the road here you are putting up nothing. You have nothing to lose at all. Not a finger or a hand or your life. Nothing. You smash him with a long steel bumper jack and he cannot get to you. He has as much chance as a ripe watermelon."

"So?"

"So I want you to put up something also. You should have something to lose or it is no match."

Jimmy looked at the old man and then at the turtle.

"Any fool can smash a watermelon," Tony said. "It does not take a brave man."

"Pa. It's only a turtle. You're making a federal case."

Old Tony looked at his son. "All right," he said. "Finish your coffee now and do what you are going to do. I say nothing more. Only for the next five minutes put yourself into this turtle's place. Put yourself into his shell and watch through his eyes. And try to think what he is thinking when he sees a coward coming to kill him with a long steel bumper jack."

Jimmy got to his feet and ground out his cigarette.

"All right, Pa," he said. "All right. You win."

Tony rose slowly from his crouch.

"No," he said. "Not me. You. You win."

"But Pa, they do kill trout."

"So," Tony said. "They kill trout. Nature put them here, and they kill trout. To survive. The trout are not extinct, eh? We kill trout also, we men. To survive? No, for sport. This old one, he takes what he needs. I do not kill him for being in nature's plan. I do not play God."

Jimmy walked to the rear of the wagon then and flung down the bumper jack and closed up the door and came back.

"Pa," he said. "Honest to goodness you got the nuttiest ideas I ever heard."

Old Tony walked around behind the snapper and gently prodded it with his boot toe, and the turtle went waddling forward across the road and toppled over the sand shoulder and disappeared in the brushy growth of the creek bank. Tony and his son climbed into the wagon and sat looking at each other. The sun was coming up strong now and the sky was cracking open like a shell and spilling reds and golds and blues, and Jimmy started the engine.

Tony put the thermos away and got out his cigarettes and stuck one in his son's mouth.

"So?" he said.

They sat smoking for a full minute watching each other, and then Jimmy released the emergency and they rolled slowly along the drying sandroad and down past the huge cleansing dawn coming, and the pine forests growing tall in the rising mists, and the quickly quiet waters of the eternal creek.

DISCUSSION

1. When Jimmy sees the turtle, he wants to kill it. Why? While Jimmy is going for the bumper jack, Tony, his father, studies the turtle in the roadway. "I can understand this turtle's position," he remarks when Jimmy returns (page 430). What similarities between himself and the creature in the road have led Tony to that understanding?

2. Was Tony serious when he suggested that his son get into the water with the bumper jack and fight the turtle? Why did he make such a suggestion?

3. Theme. The main thought or meaning of a story is its theme. These questions will help you understand the theme. The turtle kills trout; but so do men. How do the two kinds of killing differ? "I don't play God," Old Tony insists (p. 431). What does he mean? What would you say is the theme of the story?

For further activities, see page 479.

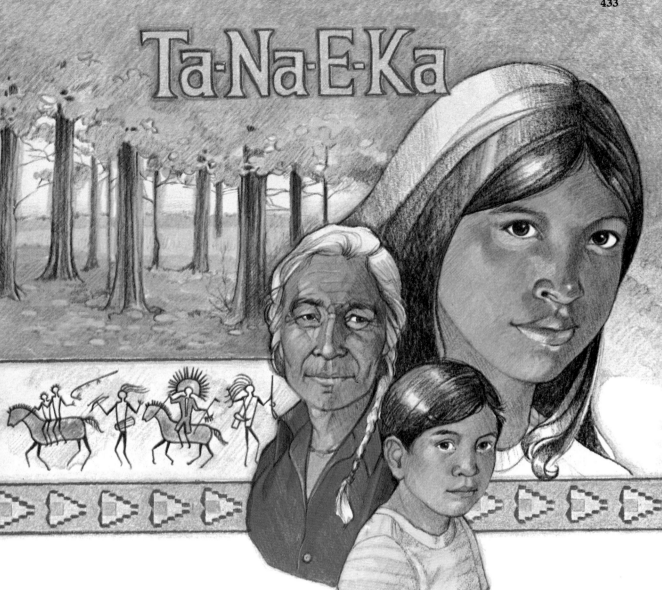

# Ta-Na-E-Ka

MARY WHITEBIRD

As my birthday drew closer, I had awful nightmares about it. I was reaching the age at which all Kaw Indians had to participate in Ta-Na-E-Ka. Well, not all Kaws. Many of the younger families on the reservation were beginning to give up the old customs. But my grandfather, Amos Deer Leg, was devoted to tradition. He still wore handmade beaded moccasins instead of shoes, and kept his iron-gray hair in tight braids. He could speak English, but he spoke it only with white men. With his family he used a Sioux dialect.

Grandfather was one of the last living Indians (he died in 1953 when he was eighty-one) who actually fought against the U.S. Cavalry. Not only did he fight, he was wounded in a skirmish at Rose Creek—a famous encounter in which the celebrated Kaw Chief Flat Nose lost his life. At the time, my grandfather was only eleven years old.

Eleven was a magic word among the Kaws. It was the time of Ta-Na-E-Ka, the "flowering of adulthood." It was the age, my grandfather informed us hundreds of times, "when a boy could prove himself to be a warrior and a girl took the first steps to womanhood."

"I don't want to be a warrior," my cousin, Roger Deer Leg, confided to me. "I'm going to become an accountant."

"None of the other tribes make girls go through the endurance ritual," I complained to my mother.

"It won't be as bad as you think, Mary," my mother said, ignoring my protests. "Once you've gone through it, you'll certainly never forget it. You'll be proud."

I even complained to my teacher, Mrs. Richardson, feeling that, as a white woman, she would side with me.

She didn't. "All of us have rituals of one kind or another," Mrs. Richardson said. "And look at it this way: How many girls have the opportunity to compete on equal terms with boys? Don't look down on your heritage."

Heritage, indeed! I had no intention of living on a reservation for the rest of my life. I was a good student. I loved school. My fantasies were about knights in armor and fair ladies in flowing gowns, being saved from dragons. It never once occurred to me that being an Indian was exciting.

But I've always thought that the Kaw were the originators of the women's liberation movement. No other Indian tribe—and I've spent half a lifetime researching the subject—treated women more "equally" than the Kaw. Unlike most of the subtribes of the Sioux Nation, the Kaw allowed men and women to eat together. And hundreds of years before we were "acculturated," a Kaw woman had the right to refuse a prospective husband even if her father arranged the match.

The wisest women (generally wisdom was equated with age) often sat in tribal councils. Furthermore, most Kaw legends revolve around "Good Woman," a kind of Joan of Arc of the high plains. Good Woman led Kaw warriors into battle after battle from which they always seemed to emerge victorious.

And girls as well as boys were required to undergo Ta-Na-E-Ka.

The actual ceremony varied from tribe to tribe, but since the Indians' life on the plains was dedicated to survival, Ta-Na-E-Ka was a test of survival.

"Endurance is the loftiest virtue of the Indian," my grandfather explained. "To survive, we must endure. When I was a boy, Ta-Na-E-Ka was more than the mere symbol it is now. We were painted white with the juice of a sacred herb and sent naked into the wilderness without so much as a knife. We couldn't return until the white had worn off. It took almost eighteen days, and during that time we had to stay alive, trapping food, eating insects and roots and berries, and watching out for enemies. And we did have enemies—both the white soldiers and the Omaha warriors, who were always trying to capture Kaw boys and girls undergoing their endurance test. It was an exciting time."

"What happened if you couldn't make it?" Roger asked. He was born only three days after I was, and we were being trained for Ta-Na-E-Ka together. I was happy to know he was frightened too.

"Many didn't return," Grandfather said. "Only the strongest and shrewdest. Mothers were not allowed to weep over those who didn't return. If a Kaw couldn't survive, he or she wasn't worth weeping over. It was our way."

"What a lot of hooey," Roger whispered. "I'd give anything to get out of it."

"I don't see how we have any choice," I replied.

Roger gave my arm a little squeeze. "Well, it's only five days."

Five days! Maybe it was better than being painted white and sent out naked for eighteen days. But not much better.

We were to be sent, barefoot and in bathing suits, into the woods. Even our very traditional parents put their foot down when Grandfather suggested we go naked. For five days we'd have to live off the land, keeping warm as best we could, getting food where we could. It was May, but on the northernmost reaches of the Missouri River the days were still chilly and the nights were fiercely cold.

Grandfather was in charge of the month's training for Ta-Na-E-Ka. One day he caught a grasshopper and demonstrated how to pull its legs and wings off in one flick of the fingers and how to swallow it.

I felt sick, and Roger turned green. "It's a darn good thing it's 1947," I told Roger teasingly. "You'd make a terrible warrior." Roger just grimaced.

I knew one thing. This particular Kaw Indian girl wasn't going to swallow a grasshopper no matter how hungry she got. And then I had an idea. Why hadn't I thought of it before? It would have saved nights of bad dreams about squooshy grasshoppers.

I headed straight for my teacher's house. "Mrs. Richardson," I said, "would you lend me five dollars?"

"Five dollars!" she exclaimed. "What for?"

"You remember the ceremony I talked about?"

"Ta-Na-E-Ka. Of course. Your parents have written me and asked me to excuse you from school so you can participate in it."

"Well, I need some things for the ceremony," I replied, in a half truth. "I don't want to ask my parents for the money."

"It's not a crime to borrow money, Mary. But how can you pay it back?"

"I'll babysit for you ten times."

"That's more than fair," she said, going to her purse and handing me a crisp new five-dollar bill. I'd never had that much money at once.

"I'm happy to know the money's going to be put to a good use," Mrs. Richardson said.

A few days later, the ritual began with a long speech from my grandfather about how we had reached the age of decision, how we now had to fend for ourselves and prove that we could survive the most horrendous of ordeals. All the friends and relatives who gathered at our house for dinner made jokes about their own Ta-Na-E-Ka experiences. They all advised us to fill up now, since for the next five days we'd be gorging ourselves on crickets. Neither Roger nor I was very hungry. "I'll probably laugh about this when I'm an accountant," Roger said, trembling.

"Are you trembling?" I asked.

"What do you think?"

"I'm happy to know boys tremble too," I said.

At six the next morning we kissed our parents and went off to the woods. "Which side do you want?" Roger asked. According to the rules, Roger and I would stake out "territories" in separate areas of the woods and we weren't to communicate during the entire ordeal.

"I'll go toward the river, if it's okay with you," I said.

"Sure," Roger answered. "What difference does it make?"

To me, it made a lot of difference. There was a marina a few miles up the river and there were boats moored there. At least, I hoped so. I figured that a boat was a better place to sleep than under a pile of leaves.

"Why do you keep holding your head?" Roger asked.

"Oh, nothing. Just nervous," I told him. Actually, I was afraid I'd lose the five-dollar bill, which I had tucked into my hair with a bobby pin. As we came to a fork in the trail, Roger shook my hand. "Good luck, Mary."

"N'ko-n'ta," I said. It was the Kaw word for *courage.*

The sun was shining and it was warm, but my bare feet began to hurt immediately. I spied one of the berry bushes Grandfather had told us about. "You're lucky," he had said. "The berries are ripe in the spring, and they are delicious and nourishing." They were orange and fat and I popped one into my mouth.

*Argh!* I spat it out. It was awful and bitter, and even grasshoppers were probably better tasting, although I never intended to find out.

I sat down to rest my feet. A rabbit hopped out from under the berry bush. He nuzzled the berry I'd spat out and ate it. He picked another one and ate that too. He liked them. He looked at me, twitching his nose. I watched a redheaded woodpecker bore into an elm tree, and I caught a glimpse of a civet cat waddling through some twigs. All of a sudden I realized I was no longer frightened. Ta-Na-E-Ka might be more fun than I'd anticipated. I got up and headed toward the marina.

"Not one boat," I said to myself dejectedly. But the restaurant on the shore, Ernie's Riverside, was open. I walked in, feeling silly in my bathing suit. The man at the counter was big and tough looking. He wore a sweatshirt with the words "Fort Sheridan, 1944," and he had only three fingers on one of his hands. He asked me what I wanted.

"A hamburger and a milk shake," I said, holding the five-dollar bill in my hand so he'd know I had money.

"That's a pretty heavy breakfast, honey," he said.

"That's what I always have for breakfast," I lied.

"Forty-five cents," he said, bringing me the food. (Back in 1947, hamburgers were twenty-five cents and milk shakes were twenty cents.) "Delicious," I thought. "Better 'n grasshoppers—and Grandfather never once mentioned that I couldn't eat hamburgers."

While I was eating, I had a grand idea. Why not sleep in the restaurant? I went to the ladies' room and made sure the window was unlocked. Then I went back outside and played along the river bank, watching the water birds and trying to identify each one. I planned to look for a beaver dam the next day.

The restaurant closed at sunset, and I watched the three-fingered man drive away. Then I climbed in the unlocked window. There was a night light on, so I didn't turn on any lights. But there was a radio on the counter. I turned it on to a music program. It was warm in the restaurant, and I was hungry. I helped myself to a glass of milk and a piece of pie, intending to keep a list of what I'd eaten so I could leave money. I also planned to get up early, sneak out through the window, and head for the woods before the three-fingered man returned. I turned off the radio, wrapped myself in the man's apron, and, in spite of the hardness of the floor, fell asleep.

"What the heck are you doing here, kid?"

It was the man's voice.

It was morning. I'd overslept. I was scared.

"Hold it, kid. I just wanna know what you're doing here. You lost? You must be from the reservation. Your folks must be worried sick about you. Do they have a phone?"

"Yes, yes," I answered. "But don't call them."

I was shivering. The man, who told me his name was Ernie, made me a cup of hot chocolate while I explained about Ta-Na-E-Ka.

"Darnedest thing I ever heard," he said, when I was through. "Lived next to the reservation all my life and this is the first I've heard of Ta-Na whatever-you-call-it." He looked at me, all goosebumps in my bathing suit. "Pretty silly thing to do to a kid," he muttered.

That was just what I'd been thinking for months, but when Ernie said it, I became angry. "No, it isn't silly. It's a custom of the Kaw. We've been doing this for hundreds of years. My mother and my grandfather and everybody in my family went through this ceremony. It's why the Kaw are great warriors."

"Okay, great warrior," Ernie chuckled, "suit yourself. And, if you want to stick around, it's okay with me." Ernie went to the broom closet and tossed me a bundle. "That's the lost-and-found closet," he said. "Stuff people left on boats. Maybe there's something to keep you warm."

The sweater fitted loosely, but it felt good. I felt good. And I'd found a new friend. Most important, I was surviving Ta-Na-E-Ka.

My grandfather had said the experience would be filled with adventure, and I was having my fill. And, Grandfather had never said we couldn't accept hospitality.

I stayed at Ernie's Riverside for the entire period. In the mornings I went into the woods and watched the animals and picked flowers for each of the tables in Ernie's. I had never felt better. I was up early enough to watch the sun rise on the Missouri, and I went to bed after it set. I ate everything I wanted— insisting that Ernie take all my money for the food. "I'll keep this in trust for you, Mary," Ernie promised, "in case you are ever desperate for five dollars." (He did too, but that's another story.)

I was sorry when the five days were over. I'd enjoyed every minute with Ernie. He taught me how to make western omelets and to make Chili Ernie Style (still one of my favorite dishes). And I told Ernie all about the legends of the Kaw. I hadn't realized I knew so much about my people.

But Ta-Na-E-Ka was over, and as I approached my house, at about 9:30 in the evening, I became nervous all over again. What if Grandfather asked me about the berries and the grasshoppers? And my feet were hardly cut. I hadn't lost a pound and my hair was combed.

"They'll be so happy to see me," I told myself hopefully, "that they won't ask too many questions."

I opened the door. My grandfather was in the front room. He was wearing the ceremonial beaded deerskin shirt which had belonged to *his* grandfather. "N'g'da'ma," he said. "Welcome back."

I embraced my parents warmly, letting go only when I saw my cousin Roger sprawled on the couch. His eyes were red and swollen. He'd lost weight. His feet were an unsightly mass of blood and blisters, and he was moaning: "I made it, see. I made it. I'm a warrior. A warrior."

My grandfather looked at me strangely. I was clean, obviously well-fed, and radiantly healthy. My parents got the message. My uncle and aunt gazed at me with hostility.

Finally my grandfather asked, "What did you eat to keep you so well?"

I sucked in my breath and blurted out the truth: "Hamburgers and milk shakes."

"Hamburgers!" my grandfather growled.

"Milk shakes!" Roger moaned.

"You didn't say we *had* to eat grasshoppers," I said sheepishly.

"Tell us all about your Ta-Na-E-Ka," my grandfather commanded.

I told them everything, from borrowing the five dollars, to Ernie's kindness, to observing the beaver.

"That's not what I trained you for," my grandfather said sadly.

I stood up. "Grandfather, I learned that Ta-Na-E-Ka *is* important. I didn't think so during training. I was scared stiff of it. I handled it my way. And I learned I had nothing to be afraid of. There's no reason in 1947 to eat grasshoppers when you can eat a hamburger."

I was inwardly shocked at my own audacity. But I liked it. "Grandfather, I'll bet you never ate one of those rotten berries yourself."

Grandfather laughed! He laughed aloud! My mother and father and aunt and uncle were all dumbfounded. Grandfather never laughed. Never.

"Those berries—they are terrible," Grandfather admitted. "I could never swallow them. I found a dead deer on the first day of my Ta-Na-E-Ka-—shot by a soldier, probably—and he kept my belly full for the entire period of the test!"

Grandfather stopped laughing. "We should send you out again," he said.

I looked at Roger. "You're pretty smart, Mary," Roger groaned. "I'd never have thought of what you did."

"Accountants just have to be good at arithmetic," I said comfortingly. "I'm terrible at arithmetic."

Roger tried to smile, but couldn't. My grandfather called me to him. "You should have done what your cousin did. But I think you are more alert to what is happening to our people today than we are. I think you would have passed the test under any circumstances, in any time. Somehow, you know how to exist in a world that wasn't made for Indians. I don't think you're going to have any trouble surviving."

Grandfather wasn't entirely right. But I'll tell about that another time.

DISCUSSION

1.   When the Ta-Na-E-Ka is over, what does Mary's family feel about her? How do you think Roger feels?

2.   What are some lessons that Mary learns about respect for her Indian heritage? What other lessons does she learn?

3.   The things Mary says help us to understand her more fully. Find lines in the story that show her unconcern for Ta-Na-E-Ka, her foresight, her fear, and her nerve.

For further activities, see page 478.

# Knoxville, Tennessee

NIKKI GIOVANNI

I always like summer
best
you can eat fresh corn
from daddy's garden
and okra                                        5
and greens
and cabbage
and lots of
barbecue
and buttermilk                                  10
and homemade ice-cream
at the church picnic
and listen to
gospel music
outside                                         15
at the church
homecoming
and go to the mountains with
your grandmother
and go barefooted                               20
and be warm
all the time
not only when you go to bed
and sleep

DISCUSSION

1. What do you think the speaker likes best of all about summer?

2. **Image.** This poem is full of images, or word pictures that appeal to our senses. They let us *imagine* not just the *sight* of daddy's garden, but also the *taste* of corn and okra, the *sound* of gospel music, the *feel* of summer warmth and bare feet on the earth. What do all the images in this poem have in common?

For further activities, see page 478.

# The WIShING WELL

### PHILLIP BONOSKY

Beezie went home that night after listening to the caddy and
lay awake thinking of the bottom of the well building higher
and higher with dimes, nickels, quarters, and half dollars. That
had been going on for years, the caddy had guessed; for years—
the guys and girls would throw money into the water and make
wishes.

"Will you come with me?" he said to Kozik. "Will you
come? Just watch, I'll go down. But will you come?"

"If they catch us?"

"Kick us in the pants and let us go. We're just kids," he
explained.

"How can we get in?"

"I'll find a way, but will you come?"

Kozik's yellow eyes considered. Over them his lids fell and
opened like the lazy wings of a moth.

"How much will you give me?"

"A third," Beezie said.

"No, a half."

"You'll just watch. *I'll* go down the well!"

Kozik stared away.

"How much you think is down there?"

"A hundred dollars!"

"Gee!" His lids opened wide. "A hundred dollars!" he
echoed. "You're crazy! Who'd let all that money lay down that
old well? *Somebody* would take it! You're crazy!"

"You don't *know!*" Beezie replied. "You don't know *them!*
They're rich!"

They pooled their money and took two streetcars—the first
one carried them out of town; the second one, ten miles into the
country, through the little hamlets, until up on a green hill, like
a pearl, sat the big white house, partly screened by elm trees. It
was late afternoon, and they were hungry but had no money to
buy food. They ate sour-grass. They had no money either to
ride back home again in case they failed. They hadn't thought
about that.

"We'll wait until it gets dark," Beezie said.

"Then the fellas come down," Kozik protested.

"That's why you gotta watch. They'd see us in the day-time."

"How about dogs?"

"Dogs?"

"Yeah, how about dogs?"

But Beezie didn't answer.

They sat on a rock at the point where the driveway divided from the road. They stared solemnly as the bright sports cars loaded with strange women and stranger-looking men drove up. The cars were jagged with tennis rackets, golf clubs, polo sticks—the unrecognizable tools of their living. The women's hair didn't look like hair to the boys, and the hair on the men was odd too. They wore sunglasses—tortoise shelled or pink coral, in every shape. They also spoke differently, and though the boys heard whole phrases, they understood nothing that was said.

They watched them like exotic birds from a green jungle.

"Besides," Beezie said, remembering the final proof, "it was in the papers—about their doing it; the wishing well, throwing money in it."

"How you going to find where it is?"

"Down there," Beezie said mysteriously, pointing to a clump of trees down the hill from the house. "Down there. That's where."

They were both hungry but didn't realize it. Their hunger was trapped inside their excitement. They lay beside the road, munching sour-grass or chewing orchard grass; they picked off the green haws from the bushes and threw them at ants and at birds. Cars came and went, and each time one arrived, both fell silent and stared at its strange cargo.

"Suppose they catch us?" Kozik echoed.

It was still less than dark when, worn out with waiting, Beezie cried: "Let's start!"

"They'll see us!"

"No," he fired back. "Hear the music!"

They stood to listen. From the house on the hill came music. Lights had begun to shine, too. But the music, most of all, came; it made the house seem like a handful of another world set down on top of the hill in the middle of the woods and fields, being by itself.

"They're listening to that. They won't hear us."

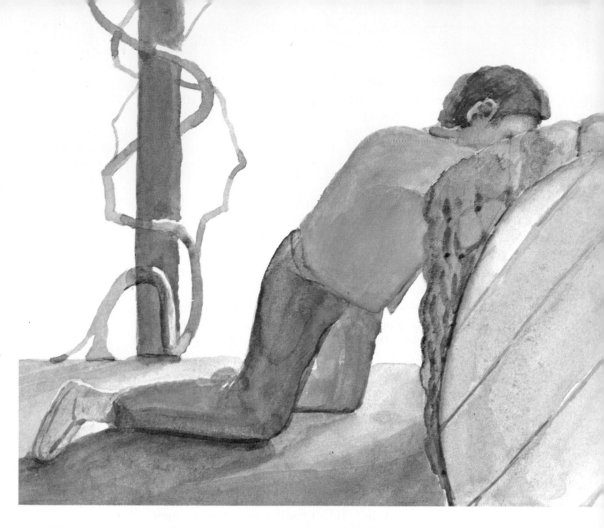

There was a wire fence running along the road. It was tipped with sharpened, turned-over naked ends. When they touched it with their hands, they jumped back.

"Oh!" Kozik cried, backing away from it and staring at it with horror. His lids fell heavily and then opened.

From behind the charged fence the music came. Beezie's hands tingled and his scalp had grown cold. It seemed to him for a moment that they had taken the wrong streetcar and this was the wrong place, it wasn't even in the same country.

Away from them the fence crossed a creek, and between the creek and the bottom of the fence was a foot and a half of space. They stood above it debating silently for a long time before taking the risk of climbing under the fence. But they only wet their shoes.

Inside the fence it felt different. Now even the music seemed nearer and clearer. Beezie felt his heart pounding right

under his shirt; he wanted to still it with his hand.

The music charged on them. They could distinguish a cymbal clash; even, for one brief moment that made them stand still with cold, the crystal laugh of a girl; then it was shut off.

The creek led through thicker and thicker bushes. Beezie could smell crushed blackberries. A bridle path followed along, but they did not dare to walk the path; instead, they threaded themselves through the bushes. When they arrived, at first they didn't recognize the spot. The well was under a pergola, over which grapes grew. There were stone seats around, off a little; inside the pergola was the stone well. It had an old wooden handle, an old green-mossy axle around which the rope wound which let down a wooden bucket into the well. A wooden lid with a hand-carved handle stood beside it, green with faint moss.

Kozik's moth-lids blinked. "How deep is it?" he asked.

Beezie looked at the well, then leaned over into it. He threw a pebble down and listened. A *plunk* followed, and he said, thoughtfully, "It's pretty far down, but not *deep,* I think."

He stood silent. Neither did Kozik speak. Fireflies suddenly swarmed out of the bushes and flew in and out. The music was faint again, but through the trees they could see the lighted windows; then the music, flung at them suddenly, crashed through and jarred him.

"Well," Beezie said, remotely, "I'll go down. You unwind it, slow."

"All right."

"And watch."

"All right."

"When I'm down, you put in the peg in there." He showed how to peg the winder so that it would no longer turn.

He took off his shoes and stockings and rolled up his trouser legs above his knees. The moonlight made his legs look pale. He climbed into the bucket. His white face hovered over the rim of the well for a moment and, hushed, he said: "We'll be rich, Kozik!"

"We'll count it when we get home," Kozik said.

"Yes," Beezie answered. Kozik began to unwind. His white face staring at him, Beezie disappeared.

The wood creaked loud in the stillness. It unwound slowly, and the bucket bumped solemnly from side to side of the well. Looking up, he could see only gray, and with an upward leap of his heart, a single shining star. Kozik he could not see.

*If the rope broke,* he thought; but he gripped it and felt its strength. Suddenly the unwinding stopped and he dangled in the middle of the well. Looking up, he saw silhouettes. Then heard voices. Suddenly money began to fall past him, plunking into the water; there was laughter upstairs. "I was right," he whispered to himself.

He sat twirling slowly, lazily, round and round. As he came near the wall of the well, he gently kicked it and swung away. The wall was slimy and cold to the touch of his bare toes; the well smelled of moss and frogs and salamanders.

Then the rope began to unwind again, its creaking sounding wooden and old, like an ungreased wheel. Abruptly he landed on the water and cried out: "Down!" and the creaking stopped. Kozik leaned his head over and cried: "Down?"

"Down," he answered.

He dangled his feet over into the water and began to reach through it for footing. The water was so cold he gasped. He hunted with his foot but found nothing to stand on.

Now he took his trousers off and let himself over the rim of the bucket into the water, shuddering as he sank, and hanging onto the bucket stretched his feet as far as they could go. Still there was no footing. Now, closing his eyes, he let go of the bucket and sank down over his head. Touching bottom, he fell to his knees and began to grope along the pebbled bottom picking up coins. Then he shot to the water top, and his lungs beating, and his teeth beginning to chatter slightly, he dumped the coins into the bucket. Again he let go of it and sank to the bottom; underneath he worked furiously, with slow motions, as in a dream, holding his breath until his head blew up with blood; then he burst to the surface again, and again dumped the coins into the wooden bucket. And again he sank down.

He seemed to rise out of the water like an icicle. His teeth were clenched in his frozen mouth. It was too dark to see what coins he had brought up; his head was so filled with cold he could not hear what Kozik shouted down to him. He heard a cry, but dived down again to the bottom of the well, scratched desperately, then, both fists clutched with coins, rose again to the surface.

He reached for the bucket—treaded water reaching for it, his eyes still closed. Then, looking up suddenly, he saw it whirling slowly upward, and beyond it, over the rim of the well, the white face of a girl looking down.

Treading water, he only watched it, unable to think. His head was growing cold from the inside. His feet seemed to tread as if forgotten by him. Then he heard them.

"Look at that!" the man cried. "Money!"

"Oh," the girl said.

"It must have fallen into the bucket instead," the man said.

"This is our lucky night!" the girl cried, laughing.

"Throw it back in," the man ordered.

"No," she said. "If we were smart enough to bring the bucket up—we *win*!" she cried.

"Some of it, anyhow," the man said.

Money spattered down beside him, hitting him, falling around him.

He suddenly began to sink. Loosening one of his fists spasmodically and letting the coins sink, he flung a hand toward the wall and there caught onto a crack filled with moss. Holding onto it, he rested. He smelled worms in the well.

Now the cold grew in his body; he felt it touch his bones, get into his stomach, encase his lungs with a film of ice. Like a sound over mountains, he felt the first pangs of cramps gathering in his loins, begin slightly to clutch at his stomach. "Let them go away," he said.

In his other fist the coins felt jagged. His hand was shut so tightly over them it seemed to be locked. Trying to open it slightly, he discovered that he could not. He laughed at it, surprised, at his fist.

Above him they were still talking; no longer arguing, they were talking to each other. Where was Kozik? *Where are you, Kozik?* he cried. Did he run home, did he get scared and run home? *No money for you, Kozik,* he cried; *no money for you, you lost your share for running away! You're yellow; you won't get any at all. I'll keep it; I'll learn you to be yellow, Kozik,* he cried. *You'd better come back!*

He felt that his fingers holding the crack were losing sensation. Now, remotely, he felt his legs again. They were still treading, had been treading all the time. He felt grateful to them that they were still treading, because at this point he felt that they didn't need to if they didn't want to. Parts of his body became objectified: his fist was one, his legs were another, his free hand holding to the crack was another, his stomach was another; *himself* was in his head. He promised the parts things and chided them too; he also reasoned with them. "Hold on tighter," he admonished his hand. To his fist he said: "You hurt."

The water was up to his neck. He had left his shirt on and it was soaked. Suddenly he thought of his pants. Did they throw them away? He cried, "My pants!" He was cold now; it would be cold; how could he go anywhere without pants? He wanted to laugh, thinking of himself going home without pants; then his father whipping him—he wanted to cry now; then suddenly his body began to ache from head to foot. His head began to give in; it began to grow colder and colder and throb, it began to collect cold behind his eyes, at the back of his nose. All over it began to attack at once, and he saw himself shutting his eyes and slipping swiftly to the bottom of the well.

"Oh, Kozik!" he cried. "Kozik!"

He lifted his head to stare at the top of the well. The open circle of the well was gone. He couldn't see the star! They had put the lid over him! He was dead. *I'm in my grave without a coffin,* he said.

Suddenly he began to scream, pulling himself out of the water and falling back again. His feet thrashed beneath him as he screamed. His free hand searched the entire slimy wall for a place to put his feet.

Then he heard the clunk of the bucket against the side of the well. He saw a rim of light, a nimbus, around the bucket; then he caught a glimpse of the star again. It was the bucket coming down. Suddenly he began to sob for it. *Come down, come down,* he cried. *Oh, come down, come down!*

It hit beside him, tilting in the water. It was too far away to reach with his fist; the fist was clenched shut, it could not open. The coins were jagged inside. He let go of the crack with his other hand and fell forward into the water, catching the bucket. It swung toward him and hit his nose, bringing cold tears. He pulled his arm over it, pulled himself half over on it, and lay still. In his mouth he felt the loud chatter of his teeth; they went so fast they began to hurt.

Now, slowly, the bucket began to rise. He lay half across it, his legs dangling, his head pointed downward, his eyes closed. He felt the thick rope throb against his neck. Then he was there; he felt hands, heard a voice.

Kozik struggled with him, finally pulled him off the bucket and fell to the ground with him. He was crying, "Beezie, what's the matter, Beezie? Can't you talk, Beezie? They didn't go away! They kept talking and talking, Beezie, and kissing—they wouldn't go away! They kept kissing, Beezie!"

He looked down; he stared into the blue face of his friend and cried: "Beezie! Beezie! You look sick! What's the matter, Beezie; can't you talk?"

Beezie rolled over face down onto the grass. He gripped his teeth into the grass and bit. His shoulders began to shake. The other stared at him with horror and fear. "Beezie!" he kept crying. "It's not my fault, Beezie! It's not my fault! I didn't say to come out here!" Then, suddenly, freshly: "They threw your pants away and I saved them!"

Bit by bit the quaking died down; he felt his separate feet and hands and stomach come together again. The ache subsided behind his eyes; the pain slowly dwindled.

The first thing he said: "Did you get the pants, you said?"

"Yes," the other replied, holding them up. "They're not even wet!"

Beezie stood up and put his trousers on. His fist was still closed. "Let's go home," he said.

They began to walk through the woods; suddenly they began to run. When they came to the fence, they crawled under it, drenching themselves; and on the other side they kept running until they reached the car stop.

Beezie stretched his fist over to Kozik.

"Open it," he ordered.

Finger by finger Kozik pulled the paralyzed fingers apart and unfolded the fist. In it lay four dimes and two quarters. They both stared at it for a long time.

Slowly Beezie took one of the quarters and gave it to Kozik.

"This is your share," he said.

The other looked at the quarter. Then, taking a dime, Beezie said, "This is because you didn't run away."

As they waited for the car to take them home, Kozik asked: "Shall we come back again?"

Beezie thought a long time before he finally answered.

"No," he said.

DISCUSSION

1. Beezie has learned a lesson from the wishing well experience. What is that lesson?

2. Is this story of the two boys' experience seen as a happy adventure, a foolish quest, or a dangerous mission? Why do you think so?

3. Find lines in the story that show the relationship between Beezie and Kozik at the beginning and at the end of the story. How has that relationship changed?

For further activities, see page 479.

# THE BIG WAVE

PEARL BUCK

A TELEVISION PLAY

| CHARACTERS | | |
|---|---|---|
| | NARRATOR | JIYA'S FATHER, the fisherman |
| | KINO UCHIYAMA, a farmer's son | OLD GENTLEMAN, a wealthy landowner |
| | kē-nō ōo-chē-yä-mä | GARDENER |
| | MOTHER | FIRST MAN |
| | FATHER, the farmer | SECOND MAN |
| | SETSU, Kino's sister | WOMAN |
| | sĕ-tsōo | CHILD |
| | JIYA, a fisherman's son | |
| | jē-yä | |

# Act I

A scene in Japan, sea and mountainside, and in the distance Mount Fuji.

Dissolve To: A small farmhouse, built on top of the terraces. This, as the Narrator speaks, dissolves to the inside of the house, a room with the simplest of Japanese furniture.

NARRATOR: Kino lives on a farm. The farm lies on the side of a mountain in Japan. The fields are terraced by walls of stone, each of them like a broad step up the mountain. Centuries ago, Kino's ancestors built the stone walls that hold up the fields. Above the fields stands this farmhouse, which is Kino's home. Sometimes he feels the climb is hard, especially when he has been working in the lowest field and is hungry.

Dissolve To: Kino comes into the room. He is a sturdy boy of about thirteen, dressed in shorts, and a Japanese jacket, open on his bare chest.

Mother hurries in. She is a small, serious-looking woman dressed in an everyday cotton kimono, sleeves tucked up. She is carrying a jar of water.

MOTHER: Dinner is ready. Where is your father?

KINO: Coming. I ran up the terrace. I'm starving.

MOTHER: Call Setsu. She is playing outside.

KINO [turning his head]: Setsu!

FATHER: Here she is. [He comes in, holding by the hand a small roguish girl.] Getting so big! I can't lift her anymore. [But he does lift her so high that she touches the rafters.]

SETSU: Don't put me down; I want to eat my supper up here.

FATHER: And fall into the soup?

KINO: How would that taste?

SETSU [willfully]: It would taste nice.

MOTHER: Come, come—[They sit on the floor around the little table. The mother serves swiftly from a small bucket of rice, a bowl of soup, a bowl of fish. She serves the father first, then Kino, then Setsu, then herself.]

FATHER: Kino, don't eat so fast.

KINO: I have promised Jiya to swim in the sea with him.

MOTHER: Obey your father.

FATHER [smiling]: Let him eat fast. [He puts a bit of fish in Setsu's bowl.] There—that's a good bit.

KINO: Father, why is it that Jiya's father's house has no window to the sea?

FATHER: No fisherman wants windows to the sea.

MOTHER: The sea is their enemy.

KINO: Mother, how can you say so? Jiya's father catches fish from the sea and that is how his family lives.

FATHER: Do not argue with your mother. Ask Jiya your question. See what he says.

KINO: Then may I go?

FATHER: Go.

Montage: Film. A sandy strip of seashore at the foot of the mountain. A few cottages stand there. Dissolve to: Jiya, a tall slender boy. He stands at the edge of the sea, looking up the mountain.

JIYA [calling through his hands]: Kino!
KINO: Coming. [He is running and catches Jiya's outstretched hand, so that they nearly fall down. They laugh and throw off their jackets.]
KINO: Wait—I am out of breath. I ate too much.
JIYA [looking up the mountain]: There's Old Gentleman standing at the gate of his castle.
KINO: He is watching to see whether we are going to the sea.
JIYA: He's always looking at the sea—at dawn, at sunset.

Dissolve To: Old Gentleman, standing on the rock, in front of his castle, halfway up the mountain. The wind is blowing his beard. He wears the garments of an aristocrat. Withdraw the cameras to the beach again.

JIYA: He is afraid of the sea—always watching!
KINO: Have you ever been in his castle?
JIYA: Only once. Such beautiful gardens—like a dream in a fairy tale. The old pines are bent with the wind, and under them the moss is deep and green and so smooth. Every day men sweep the moss with brooms.
KINO: Why does he keep looking to the sea?
JIYA: He is afraid of it, I tell you.
KINO: Why?
JIYA: The sea is our enemy. We all know it.
KINO: Oh, how can you say it? When we have so much fun. . . .
JIYA: It is our enemy. . . .
KINO: Not mine—let's swim to the island.
JIYA: No. I must find clams for my mother.
KINO: Then let's swim to the sandbar. There are millions of clams there.
JIYA: But the tide is ready to turn. . . .
KINO: It's slow—we'll have time.

They plunge into the sea and swim to the sandbar. Jiya has a small, short-handled hoe hanging from his girdle. He digs into the sand. Kino kneels to help him. But Jiya digs for only a moment; then he pauses to look out over the sea.

KINO: What are you looking for?
JIYA: To see if the sea is angry with us.
KINO [laughing]: Silly—the sea can't be angry with people.
JIYA: Down there, a mile down, the old sea god lives. When he is angry he heaves and rolls, and the waves rush back and forth. Then he gets up and stamps his foot, and the earth shakes at the bottom of the sea. . . . I wish I were a farmer's son, like you. . . .

KINO: And I wish I were a fisherman's son. It is stupid to plow and plant and cut
sheaves, when I could just sit in a boat and reap fish from the sea!

JIYA: The earth is safe.

KINO: When the volcano is angry the earth shakes too.

JIYA: The angry earth helps the angry sea.

KINO: They work together.

JIYA: But fire comes out of the volcano.

Meanwhile, the tide is coming in and swirls about their feet.

JIYA [noticing]: Oh—we have not half enough clams. . . . [They fall to digging fanatically].

Dissolve To: The empty seashore and the tide rushing in. A man paces the sand
at the water's edge. He wears shorts and a fisherman's jacket, open above his
bare breast. He calls, his hands cupped about his mouth.

JIYA'S FATHER: Ji————ya!

There is only the sound of the surf. He wades into the water, still calling. Suddenly he sees the boys,
and he beckons fiercely. They come in, and he gives a hand to each one and pulls them out of the
sea.

JIYA'S FATHER: Jiya! You have never been so late before.

JIYA: Father, we were on the sand bar, digging clams. We had to leave them.

JIYA'S FATHER [shaking his shoulders]: Never be so late!

KINO [wondering]: You are afraid of the sea, too?

JIYA'S FATHER: Go home, farmer's boy. Your mother is calling you.

In the distance a woman's voice is calling Kino's name. He hears and runs toward the mountain.

JIYA: Father, I have made you angry.

JIYA'S FATHER: I am not angry.

JIYA: Then why do you seem angry?

JIYA'S FATHER: Old Gentleman sent down word that a storm is rising behind the horizon. He sees the clouds through his great telescope.

JIYA: Father, why do you let Old Gentleman make you afraid? Just because he is rich
and lives in a castle, everybody listens to him.

JIYA'S FATHER: Not because he is rich—not because he lives in a castle, but because he
is old and wise and he knows the sea. He doesn't want anybody to
die. [He looks over the sea, and his arm tightens about his son, and he mutters
as though to himself.] Though all must die. . . .

JIYA: Why must all die, Father?

JIYA'S FATHER: Who knows? Simply, it is so.

They stand looking over the sea.

# Act 2

Montage. Film of the Japanese scene as in Act 1.

NARRATOR: Yet there was much in life to enjoy. Kino had a good time every day. In the winter he went to school in the fishing village, and he and Jiya shared a bench and writing table. They studied reading and arithmetic and learned what all children must learn in school. But in the summer Kino had to work hard on the farm. Even Setsu and the mother had to help when the rice seedlings were planted in the watery terraced fields. On those days Kino could not run down the mountainside to find Jiya. When the day was ended he was so tired he fell asleep over his supper.

There were days when Jiya, too, could not play. Schools of fish came into the channel between the shore and the island, and early in the morning Jiya and his father sailed their boats out to sea to cast their nets at dawn. If they were lucky, their nets came up so heavy with fish that it took all their strength to haul them in, and soon the bottom of the boat was flashing and sparkling with wriggling fish.

Sometimes, if it were not seedtime or harvest, Kino went with Jiya and his father. It was exciting to get up in the night and put on his warm padded jacket; for even in summer the wind was cool over the sea at dawn. However early he got up, his mother was up even earlier to give him a bowl of hot rice soup and some bean curd and tea before he went. She packed him a lunch in a clean little wooden box—cold rice and fish and a radish pickle. Down the stone steps of the mountain path, Kino ran straight to the narrow dock where the fishing boats bobbed up and down with the tide. Jiya and his father were already there, and in a few minutes their boat was nosing its way past the sandbar toward the open sea. Sails set, and filling with wind, they sped straight into the dawnlit horizon. Kino crouched down in the bow, and his heart rose with joy and excitement. It was like flying into the sky. The winds were so mild, the sea lay so calm and blue, that it was hard to believe that it could be cruel and angry. Actually it was the earth that brought the big wave.

One day, as Kino helped his father plant turnips, a cloud came over the sun.

Dissolve To: A field, and Kino and his father. The volcano is in the background.

KINO: Look, Father, the volcano is burning again!

FATHER [straightens and gazes anxiously at the sky]: It looks very angry. I shall not sleep tonight. We must hurry home.

KINO: Why should the volcano be angry, Father?

FATHER: Who knows? Simply, the inner fire burns. Come—make haste.

They gather their tools.

> Dissolve To: Night. The threshing floor outside the farmhouse. Kino's Father sits on a bench outside the door. He gets up and walks to and fro and gazes at the red sky above the volcano. The Mother comes to the door.

MOTHER: Can you put out the volcano by not sleeping?

FATHER: Look at the fishing village! Every house is lit. And the lamps are lit in the castle. Shall I sleep like a fool?

MOTHER: I have taken the dishes from the shelves and put away our good clothes in boxes.

FATHER [gazing down at the village]: If only I knew whether it would be earth or sea. Both work evil together. The fires rage under the sea, the rocks boil. The volcano is vent unless the sea bottom breaks.

KINO [coming to the door]: Shall we have an earthquake, Father?

FATHER: I cannot tell.

MOTHER: How still it is. There's no wind. The sea is purple.

KINO: Why is the sea such a color?

FATHER: Sea mirrors sky. Sea and earth and sky—if they work against man, who can live?

KINO [coming to his Father's side]: Where are the gods? Do they forget us?

FATHER: There are times when the gods leave men alone. They test us to see how able we are to save ourselves.

KINO: What if we are not able?

FATHER: We must be able. Fear makes us weak. If you are afraid, your hands tremble, your feet falter. Brain cannot tell hands what to do.

SETSU [her voice calling from inside the house]: Mother, I'm afraid!

MOTHER: I am coming. [She goes away.]

FATHER: The sky is growing black. Go into the house, Kino.

KINO: Let me stay with you.

FATHER: The red flag is flying over the castle. Twice I've seen that red flag go up, both times before you were born. Old Gentleman wants everybody to be ready.

KINO [frightened]: Ready for what?

FATHER: For whatever must be.

A deep-toned bell tolls over the mountainside.

KINO: What is that bell? I've never heard it before.

FATHER: It rang twice before you were born. It is the bell inside Old Gentleman's temple. He is calling to the people to come up out of the village and shelter within his walls.

KINO: Will they come?

FATHER: Not all of them. Parents will try to make their children go, but the children will not want to leave their parents. Mothers will not want to leave fathers, and the fathers will stay by the boats. But some will want to be sure of life.

The bell continues to ring urgently. Soon from the village comes a straggling line of people, nearly all of them children.

KINO [gazing at them]: I wish Jiya would come. [He takes off his white cloth girdle and waves it.]

Dissolve To: Jiya and his Father by their house. Sea in the background, roaring.

JIYA's FATHER: Jiya, you must go to the castle.

JIYA: I won't leave you and mother.

JIYA'S FATHER: We must divide ourselves. If we die, you must live after us.

JIYA: I don't want to live alone.

JIYA'S FATHER: It is your duty to obey me, as a good Japanese son.

JIYA: Let me go to Kino's house.

JIYA'S FATHER: Only go—go quickly.

Jiya and his Father embrace fiercely, and Jiya runs away, crying, to leap up to the mountainside.

Dissolve To: Terrace and farmhouse, and center on Kino and his Father, who put out their hands to help Jiya up the last terrace. Suddenly Kino screams.

KINO: Look—at the sea!

FATHER: May the gods save us.

The bell begins to toll, deep, pleading, incessant.

JIYA [shrieking]: I must go back—I must tell my father. . . .

FATHER [holding him]: It is too late. . . .

Film. The sea rushes up in a terrible wave and swallows the shore. The water roars about the foot of the mountain.

Jiya, held by Kino and his Father stares transfixed, and then sinks unconscious to the ground. The bell tolls on.

# Act 3

NARRATOR: So the big wave came, swelling out of the sea. It lifted the horizon while the people watched. The air was filled with its roar and shout. It rushed over the flat, still waters of the sea; it reached the village and covered it fathoms deep in swirling, wild water—green, laced with fierce white foam. The wave ran up the mountainside until the knoll upon which the castle stood was an island. All who were still climbing the path were swept away, mere tossing scraps in the wicked waters. Then with a great sucking sigh, the wave ebbed into the sea, dragging everything with it—trees, rocks, houses, people. Once again it swept over the village, and once again it returned to the sea, sinking into great stillness.

Upon the beach, where the village stood, not a house remained, no wreckage of wood or fallen stone wall, no street of little shops, no docks, not a single boat. The beach was as clean as if no human being had ever lived there. All that had been was now no more.

Dissolve To: Inside the farmhouse. The farm family is gathered about the mattress on which Jiya lies.

MOTHER: This is not sleep. . . . Is it death?

FATHER: Jiya is not dead. His soul has withdrawn for a time. He is unconscious. Let him remain so until his own will wakes him.

MOTHER [rubbing Jiya's hands and feet]: Kino, do not cry.

Kino cannot stop crying, although silently.

FATHER: Let him cry. Tears comfort the heart. [He feels Kino's hands and cheeks.] He is cold. Heat a little rice soup for him and put some ginger in it. I will stay with Jiya.

Mother goes out. Setsu comes in, rubbing her eyes and yawning.

FATHER: Sleepy eyes! You have slept all through the storm. Wise one!

SETSU [coming to stare at Jiya]: Is Jiya dead?

FATHER: No, Jiya is living.

SETSU: Why doesn't he open his eyes?

FATHER: Soon he will open his eyes.

SETSU: If Jiya is not dead, why does Kino stand there crying?

FATHER: As usual, you are asking too many questions. Go back to the kitchen and help your mother.

Setsu goes out, staring and sucking her thumb. Father puts his arm around Kino.

FATHER: The first sorrow is the hardest to bear.

KINO: What will we say to Jiya when he wakes? How can we tell him?

FATHER: We will not talk. We will give him warm food and let him rest. We will help him to feel he still has a home.

KINO: Here?

FATHER: Here. I have always wanted another son, and Jiya will be that son. As soon as he knows this is his home, we must help him to understand what has happened. Ah, here is Mother, with your hot rice soup. Eat it, my son—food for the body is food for the heart, sometimes.

Kino takes the bowl from his Mother with both hands and drinks. The parents look at each other and at him, sorrowfully and tenderly. Setsu comes in and leans her head toward her Mother.

Dissolve To: The same room, the same scene except that Mother and Setsu are not there. Father sits beside Jiya's bed, Kino is at the open door.

KINO: The sky is golden, Father, and the sea is smooth. How cruel. . . .

FATHER: No, it is wonderful that after the storm the sea grows calm again, and the sky is clear. It was not the sea or sky that made the evil storm.

KINO [not turning his head]: Who made it?

FATHER: Ah, no one knows who makes evil storms. [He takes Jiya's hand and rubs it gently.] We only know that they come. When they come we must live through them as bravely as we can, and after they are gone we must feel again how wonderful life is. Every day of life is more valuable now than it was before the storm.

KINO: But Jiya's father and mother—and the other fisherfolk—so good and kind—all of them—lost. [He cannot go on].

FATHER: We must think of Jiya—who lives. [He stops. Jiya has begun to sob softly in his unconsciousness.]

FATHER: Quick, Kino—call your mother and Setsu. He will open his eyes at any moment, and we must all be here—you to be his brother, I, his father, and the mother, the sister——

Kino runs out, Father kneels beside Jiya, who stirs, still sobbing. Kino comes back with Mother and Setsu. They kneel on the floor beside the bed. Jiya's eyelids flutter. He opens his eyes and looks from one to the other. He stares at the beams of the roof, the walls of the room, the bed, his own hands. All are quiet except Setsu, who cannot keep from laughing. She claps her hands.

SETSU: Oh, Jiya has come back. Jiya, did you have a good dream?

JIYA [faintly]: My father, my mother——

MOTHER [taking his hands in both hers]: I will be your mother now, dear Jiya.

FATHER: I will be your father.

KINO: I am your brother now, Jiya. [He falters.]

SETSU [joyfully]: Oh, Jiya, you will live with us.

Jiya gets up slowly. He walks to the door, goes out, and looks down the hillside.

> Dissolve To: The peaceful empty beach. Then back to the farmhouse and Jiya, standing outside and looking at the sea. Setsu comes to him.

SETSU: I will give you my pet duck. He'll follow you—he'll make you laugh.

MOTHER [leaving the room]: We ought all to eat something. I have a fine chicken for dinner.

KINO [coming to Jiya]: Mother makes such good chicken soup.

SETSU: I'm hungry, I tell you.

FATHER: Come, Jiya, my son.

Jiya stands still dazed.

KINO: Eat with us, Jiya.

JIYA: I am tired—very tired.

KINO: You have been sleeping so long.

JIYA [slowly]: I shall never see them again. [He puts his hands over his eyes]. I shall keep thinking about them—floating in the sea.

MOTHER [coming in]: Drink this bowl of soup at least, Jiya, my son.

Jiya drinks and lets the bowl fall. It is wooden and does not break.

JIYA: I want to sleep.

FATHER: Sleep, my son. Sleep is good for you. [He leads Jiya to the bed and covers him with a quilt.]

FATHER [to them all]: Jiya is not yet ready to live. We must wait.

KINO: Will he die?

FATHER: Life is stronger than death. He will live.

# Act 4

NARRATOR: The body heals first, and the body heals the mind and the soul. Jiya ate food, he got out of bed sometimes, but he was still tired. He did not want to think or remember. He only wanted to sleep. He woke to eat, and then he went to sleep again. In the quiet, clean room Jiya slept, and the mother spread the quilt over him and closed the door and went away.

All through these days Kino did not play about as he once had. He was no longer a child. He worked hard beside his father in the fields. They did not talk much, and neither of them wanted to look at the sea. It was enough to look at the earth, dark and rich beneath their feet.

One evening Kino climbed the mountain behind the house and looked up at the volcano. The heavy cloud of smoke had gone away, and the sky was clear. He was glad that the volcano was no longer angry, and he went down again to the house. On the threshold his father was smoking his usual evening pipe. In the house his mother was giving Setsu her evening bath.

KINO [dropping down on the bench beside his father]: Is Jiya asleep, again?

FATHER: Yes, and it is a good thing for him. When he sleeps enough, he will wake and remember.

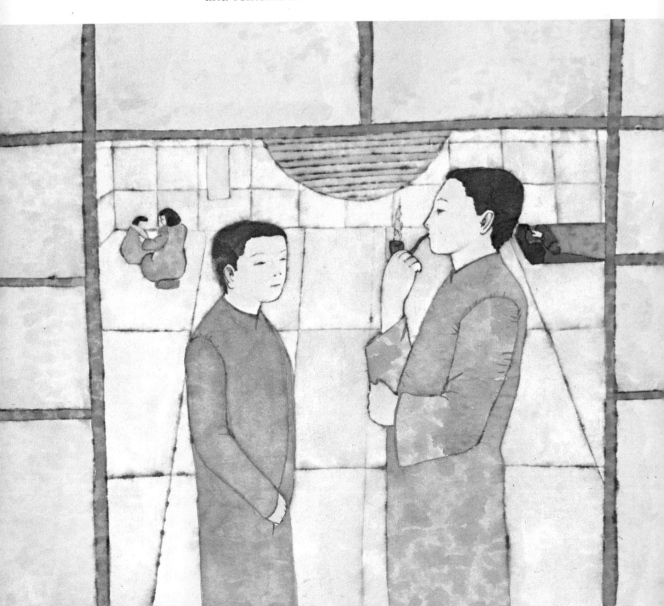

KINO: But should he remember?

FATHER: Only when he dares to remember his parents will he be happy again.

> [A silence]

KINO: Father, are we not very unfortunate people to live in Japan?

FATHER: Why do you think so?

KINO: The volcano is behind our house and the sea is in front. When they work together to make earthquake and big wave, we are helpless. Always, many of us are lost.

FATHER: To live in the presence of death makes us brave and strong. That is why our people never fear death. We see it too often, and we do not fear it. To die a little sooner or a little later does not matter. But to live bravely, to love life, to see how beautiful the trees are and the mountains—yes, and even the sea—to enjoy work because it produces food—in these ways we are fortunate people. We love life because we live in danger. We do not fear death, for we understand that death and life are necessary to each other.

KINO: What is death?

FATHER: Death is the great gateway.

KINO: The gateway—where?

FATHER: Can you remember when you were born?

KINO: I was too small.

FATHER [smiling]: I remember very well. Oh, hard you thought it was to be born. You cried and you screamed.

KINO [much interested]: Didn't I want to be born?

FATHER: You did not. You wanted to stay just where you were, in the warm dark house of the unborn, but the time came to be born, and the gate of life opened.

KINO: Did I know it was the gate of life?

FATHER: You did not know anything about it, and so you were afraid. But see how foolish you were! Here we were waiting for you, your parents, already loving you and eager to welcome you. And you have been very happy, haven't you?

KINO: Until the big wave came. Now I am afraid again because of the death the big wave brought.

FATHER: You are only afraid because you don't know anything about death. But someday you will wonder why you were afraid, even as today you wonder why you once feared to be born.

KINO: I think I understand—I begin to understand. . . .

FATHER: Do not hurry yourself. You have plenty of time. [He rises to his feet.] Now what do I see? A lantern coming up the hill.

KINO [running to the edge of the threshold]: Who can be coming now? It is almost night.

FATHER: A visitor—ah, why, it's Old Gentleman!

Old Gentleman indeed is climbing the hill. He is somewhat breathless in spite of his long staff. His manservant carries the lantern, and, when they arrive, steps to one side.

OLD GENTLEMAN [to Manservant]: Is this the house of Uchiyama, the farmer?

MANSERVANT: It is—and this is the farmer himself and his son.

FATHER [bowing deeply]: Please, Honored Sir, what can I do for you?

OLD GENTLEMAN: Do you have a lad here by the name of Jiya?

FATHER: He lies sleeping in my house.

OLD GENTLEMAN: I wish to see him.

FATHER: Sir, he suffered the loss of his parents when the big wave came. Now sleep heals him.

OLD GENTLEMAN: I will not wake him. I only wish to look at him.

FATHER: Please come in.

> Dissolve To: Jiya asleep. The Manservant holds the lantern so that the light does not fall on Jiya's face directly. Old Gentleman looks at him carefully.

OLD GENTLEMAN: Tall and strong for his age—intelligent—handsome. Hm—yes. [He motions to the Manservant to lead him away, and the scene returns to the dooryard.]

OLD GENTLEMAN [to Father]: It is my habit, when the big wave comes, to care for those who are orphaned by it. Thrice in my lifetime I have searched out the orphans, and I have fed them and sheltered them. But I have heard of this boy Jiya and wish to do more for him. If he is as good as he is handsome, I will take him for my own son.

KINO: But Jiya is ours!

FATHER [sternly]: Hush. We are only poor people. If Old Gentleman wants Jiya, we cannot say we will not give him up.

OLD GENTLEMAN: Exactly. I will give him fine clothes and send him to a good school, and he may become a great man and an honor to our whole province and even to the nation.

KINO: But if he lives in the castle we can't be brothers!

FATHER: We must think of Jiya's good. [He turns to Old Gentleman.] Sir, it is very kind of you to propose this for Jiya. I had planned to take him for my own son, now that he has lost both his parents; but I am only a poor farmer, and I cannot pretend that my house is as good as yours or that I can afford to send Jiya to a fine school. Tomorrow when he wakes I will tell him of your fine offer. He will decide.

OLD GENTLEMAN: Very well. But let him come and tell me himself.

FATHER [proudly]: Certainly. Jiya must speak for himself.

Old Gentleman bows slightly and prepares to depart. Father bows deeply and taps Kino on the head to make him bow. Old Gentleman and his manservant return down the mountain.

KINO: If Jiya goes away, I shall never have a brother.

FATHER: Kino, don't be selfish. You must allow Jiya to make his own choice. It would be wrong to persuade him. I forbid you to speak to him of this matter. When he wakes, I will tell him myself.

KINO [pleading]: Don't tell him today, Father.

FATHER: I must tell him as soon as he wakes. It would not be fair to Jiya to let him grow used to thinking of this house as his home. He must make the choice today, before he has time to put down his new roots. Go now, Kino, and weed the lower terrace.

> Dissolve To: Kino working in the terrace, weeding. It is evident that he has worked for some time. He looks hot and dusty, and he has quite a pile of weeds. He stops to look up at the farmhouse, but sees no one and resigns himself again to his work. Suddenly his name is called.

FATHER: Kino!

KINO: Shall I come?

FATHER: No, I'm coming—with Jiya.

Kino stands waiting. Father and Jiya come down the terraces. Jiya is very sad. When he sees Kino, he tries not to cry.

FATHER [putting his arm about Jiya's shoulder]: Jiya, you must not mind that you cry easily. Until now you couldn't cry because you weren't fully alive. You had been hurt too much. But today you are beginning to live, and so your tears flow. It is good for you. Let your tears come—don't stop them. [He turns to Kino.] I have told Jiya that he must not decide where he will live until he has seen the inside of the castle. He must see all that Old Gentleman can give him. Jiya, you know how our house is—four small rooms, and the kitchen, this farm, upon which we have to work hard for our food. We have only what our hands earn for us. [He holds out his two workworn hands.] If you live in the castle, you need never have hands like this.

JIYA: I don't want to live in the castle.

FATHER: You don't know whether you do or not; you have never seen the castle inside. [He turns to Kino.] Kino, you are to go with Jiya, and when you reach the castle you must persuade him to stay there for his own sake.

KINO: I will go and wash myself—and put on my good clothes.

FATHER: No—go as you are. You are a farmer's son.

Kino and Jiya go, reluctantly, and Father stands looking after them.

> Dissolve To: The mountainside and the two boys nearing the gate of the castle.

> The gate is open, and inside old gardener is sweeping moss under pine trees. He sees them.

GARDENER: What do you want, boys?

KINO: My father sent us to see the honored Old Gentleman.

GARDENER: Are you the Uchiyama boy?

KINO: Yes, please, and this is Jiya, whom Old Gentleman wishes to come and live here.

GARDENER [bowing to Jiya]: Follow me, young sir.

> They follow over a pebbled path under the leaning pine trees. In the distance the sun falls upon a flowering garden and a pool with a waterfall.

KINO [sadly]: How beautiful it is—of course you will want to live here. Who could blame you?

> Jiya does not answer. He walks with his head held high. They come to a great door where a Man-servant bids them to take off their shoes. The Gardener leaves them.

MANSERVANT: Follow me.

> They follow through passageways into a great room decorated in the finest Japanese fashion. In the distance at the end of the room, they see Old Gentleman, sitting beside a small table. Behind him the open panels reveal the garden. Old Gentleman is writing. He holds his brush upright in his hand, and he is carefully painting letters on a scroll, his silver rimmed glasses sliding down his nose. When the two boys approach, the Manservant announces them.

MANSERVANT: Master, the two boys are here.

OLD GENTLEMAN [to boys]: Would you like to know what I have been writing?

> Jiya looks at Kino, who is too awed to speak.

JIYA: Yes, Honored Sir, if you please.

OLD GENTLEMAN [taking up the scroll]: It is not my own poem. It is the saying of a wise man of India, but I like it so much that I have painted it on this scroll to hang it there in the alcove where I can see it every day.
[He reads clearly and slowly.]
"The children of God are very dear,
But very queer—
Very nice, but very narrow."
[He looks up over his spectacles.] What do you think of it?

JIYA [looking at Kino who is too shy to speak]: We do not understand it, Sir.

OLD GENTLEMAN [shaking his head and laughing softly]: Ah, we are all children of God! [He takes off his spectacles and looks hard at Jiya]. Well? Will you be my son? [Jiya, too embarrassed to speak, bites his lip and looks away, etc.]

OLD GENTLEMAN: Say yes or no. Either word is not hard to speak.

JIYA: I will say—no. [He feels this is too harsh, and he smiles apologetically.] I thank you, sir, but I have a home—on a farm.

KINO [trying to repress his joy and speaking very solemnly as a consequence.]: Jiya, remember how poor we are.

OLD GENTLEMAN [smiling, half sad]: They are certainly very poor and here, you know, you would have everything. You can invite this farmboy to come and play, sometimes, if you like. And I am quite willing to give the family some money. It would be suitable as my son for you to help the poor.

JIYA [suddenly, as though he had not heard]: Where are the others who were saved from the big wave?

OLD GENTLEMAN: Some wanted to go away, and the ones who wanted to stay are out in the back yard with my servants.

JIYA: Why do you not invite them to come into the castle and be your sons and daughters?

OLD GENTLEMAN [somewhat outraged by this]: Because I don't want them for my sons and daughters. You are a bright, handsome boy. They told me you were the best boy in the village.

JIYA: I am not better than the others. My father was a fisherman.

OLD GENTLEMAN [taking up his spectacles and brush]: Very well—I will do without a son.

The Manservant motions to the boys to come away, and they follow.

MANSERVANT [to Jiya]: How foolish you are! Our Old Gentleman is very kind. You would have everything here.

JIYA: Not everything. . . .

KINO: Let's hurry home—let's hurry—hurry——

They run down the mountainside and up the hill to the farmhouse. Setsu sees them and comes flying down to meet them, the sleeves of her bright kimono like wings, and her feet clattering in their wooden sandals.

SETSU: Jiya has come home—Jiya, Jiya——

Jiya sees her happy face and opens his arms and gives her a great hug.

# Act 5

NARRATOR: Now happiness began to live in Jiya, though secretly and hidden inside him, in ways he did not understand. The good food warmed him, and his body welcomed it. Around him the love of four people who received him for their own glowed like a warm and welcoming fire upon his heart.

Time passed. Eight years. Jiya grew up in the farmhouse to be a tall young man, and Kino grew at his side, solid and strong, but never as tall as Jiya. Setsu grew too, from a mischievous child, into a gay, willful, pretty girl. But time, however long, was split in two parts, the time before and the time after the big wave. The big wave had changed everybody's life.

In all these years no one returned to live on the empty beach. The tides rose and fell, sweeping the sands clear every day. Storms came and went, but there was never such a wave as the big one. At last people began to think that never again would there be such a big wave. The few fishermen who had listened to the tolling bell from the castle, and were saved with their wives and children, went to other shores to fish and they made new fishing boats. Then, as time passed, they told themselves that no beach was quite as good as the old one. There, they said, the water was deep and great fish came close to shore. They did not need to go far out to sea to find booty.

Jiya and Kino had not often gone to the beach, either. At first they had walked along the empty sands where once the street had been, and Jiya searched for some keepsake from his home that the sea might have washed back to the shore. But nothing was ever found. So the two boys, as they grew to be young men, did not visit the deserted beach. When they went to swim in the sea, they walked across the farm and over another fold of the mountains to the shore.

Yet Jiya had never forgotten his father and mother. He thought of them every day, their faces, their voices, the way his father talked, his mother's smile. The big wave had changed him forever. He did not laugh easily or speak carelessly. In school he had earnestly learned all he could, and now he worked hard on the farm. Now, as a man, he valued deeply everything that was good. Since the big wave had been so cruel, he was never cruel, and he grew kind and gentle. Jiya never spoke of his loneliness. He did not want others to be sad because of his sadness. When he laughed at some mischief of Setsu's when she teased him, his laughter was wonderful to hear because it was whole and real. And, sometimes, in the morning, he went to the door of the farmhouse and looked at the empty beach below, searching with his eyes as though something might one day come back. One day he did see something. . . .

JIYA: Kino, come here! [Kino comes out, his shoes in his hand.]

JIYA: Look—is someone building a house on the beach?

KINO: Two men—pounding posts into the sand——

JIYA: And a woman—yes, and even a child.

KINO: They can't be building a house.

JIYA: Let's go and see.

Dissolve To: The beach. The two Men, Jiya and Kino, Woman and Child.

JIYA [out of breath]: Are you building a house?

FIRST MAN [wiping sweat from his face]: Our father used to live here, and we with him. We are two brothers. During these years we have lived in the houses of the castle, and we have fished from other shores. Now we are tired of having no homes of our own. Besides, this is still the best beach for fishing.

KINO: What if the big wave comes again?

SECOND MAN [shrugging his shoulders]: There was a big wave, too, in our great-grandfather's time. All the houses were swept away. But our grandfather came back. In our father's time there was again the big wave. Now we return.

KINO [soberly]: What of your children?

The Men begin to dig again. The Woman takes the Child into her arms and gazes out to the sea. Suddenly there is a sound of a voice calling. All look up the mountain.

FIRST MAN: Here comes our Old Gentleman.

SECOND MAN: He's very angry or he wouldn't have left the castle. [Both throw down their shovels and stand waiting. The Woman sinks to a kneeling position on the sand, still holding the Child. Old Gentleman shouts as he comes near; his voice is high and thin. He is very old now, and is supported by two Manservants. His beard flies in the wind.]

OLD GENTLEMAN: You foolish children! You leave the safety of my walls and come back to this dangerous shore, as your father did before you! The big wave will return and sweep you into the sea.

FIRST MAN: It may not, Ancient Sir.

OLD GENTLEMAN: It will come, I have spent my whole life trying to save foolish people from the big wave. But you will not be saved.

JIYA [stepping forward]: Sir, here is our home. Dangerous as it is, threatened by the volcano and the sea, it is here we were born.

OLD GENTLEMAN [looking at him]: Don't I know you?

JIYA: Sir, I was once in your castle.

OLD GENTLEMAN [nodding]: I remember you. I wanted you for my son. Ah, you made a great mistake, young man. You could have lived safely in my castle all your life, and your children would have been safe there. The big wave never reaches me.

KINO: Sir, your castle is not safe, either. If the earth shakes hard enough, even your castle will crumble. There is no refuge for us who live on these islands. We are brave because we must be.

SECOND MAN: Ha—you are right.

The two men return to their building.

OLD GENTLEMAN [rolling his eyes and wagging his beard]: Don't ask me to save you the next time the big wave comes!

JIYA [gently]: But you will save us, because you are so good.

OLD GENTLEMAN [looking at him and then smiling sadly]: What a pity you would not be my son! [He turns and, leaning on his Manservants, climbs the mountain.]

Fade To: His arrival at the castle gate. He enters, and the gates clang shut.

Dissolve To: The field where Father and Jiya and Kino are working.

FATHER [to Jiya]: Did you soak the seeds for the rice?

JIYA [aghast]: I forgot.

KINO: I did it.

JIYA [throwing down his hoe]: I forget everything these days.

FATHER: I know you are too good a son to be forgetful on purpose. Tell me what is on your mind.

JIYA: I want a boat. I want to go back to fishing.

Father does not pause in his hoeing; but Kino flings down his hoe.

KINO: You, too, are foolish!

JIYA [stubbornly]: When I have a boat, I shall build my own house on the beach.

KINO: Oh, fool, fool!

FATHER: Be quiet! Jiya is a man. You are both men. I shall pay you wages from this day.

JIYA: Wages! [He falls to hoeing vigorously.]

Dissolve To: The beach, where the two young men are inspecting a boat.

JIYA: I knew all the time that I had to come back to the sea.

KINO: With this boat, you'll soon earn enough to build a house. But I'm glad I live on the mountain. [They continue inspecting the boat, fitting the oars, etc., as they talk].

JIYA [abruptly]: Do you think Setsu would be afraid to live on the beach?

KINO [surprised]: Why should Setsu live on the beach?

JIYA [embarrassed but determined]: Because when I have my house built, I want Setsu to be my wife.

KINO [astonished]: Setsu? You would be foolish to marry her.

JIYA [smiling]: I don't agree with you.

KINO [seriously]: But why—why do you want her?

JIYA: Because she makes me laugh. It is she who made me forget the big wave. For me, she is life.

KINO: But she is not a good cook. Think how she burns the rice when she runs outside to look at something.

JIYA: I don't mind burned rice, and I will run out with her to see what she sees.

KINO [with all the gestures of astonishment and disbelief]: I can't understand. . . .

Dissolve To: The farmhouse, and Father who is looking over his seeds.

KINO [coming in stealthily]: Do you know that Jiya wants to marry Setsu?

FATHER: I have seen some looks pass between them.

KINO: But Jiya is too good for Setsu.

FATHER: Setsu is very pretty.

KINO: With that silly nose?

FATHER [calmly]: I believe that Jiya admires her nose.

KINO: Besides, she is such a tease.

FATHER: What makes you miserable will make him happy.

KINO: I don't understand that, either.

FATHER [laughing]: Someday you will understand.

Dissolve To: Narrator.

NARRATOR: One day, one early summer, Jiya and Setsu were married. Kino still did not understand, for up to the last, Setsu was naughty and mischievous. Indeed on the very day of her wedding she hid Kino's hairbrush under his bed. "You are too silly to be married," Kino said when he had found it. "I feel sorry for Jiya," he said. Setsu's big brown eyes laughed at him, and she stuck out her red tongue. "I shall always be nice to Jiya," she said.

But when the wedding was over and the family had taken the newly married pair down the hill to the new house on the beach, Kino felt sad. The farmhouse was very quiet without Setsu. Already he missed her. Every day he could go to see Jiya, and many times he would be fishing with him. But Setsu would not be in the farmhouse kitchen, in the rooms, in the garden. He would miss even her teasing. And then he grew very grave indeed. What if the big wave came again?

Dissolve To: The new house. Kino turns to Jiya.

KINO: Jiya, it is all very pretty—very nice. But Setsu—what if the big wave comes again?

JIYA: I have prepared for that. Come—all of you. [He calls the family in]. This is where we will sleep at night, and where we will live by day. But look——

The family stands watching, and Jiya pushes back a long panel in the wall. Before their eyes is the sea, swelling and stirring under the evening wind. The sun is sinking into the water.

JIYA: I have opened my house to the sea. If ever the big wave comes back, I shall be ready. I face it, night and day. I am not afraid.

KINO: Tomorrow I'll go fishing with you, Jiya—shall I?

JIYA [laughing]: Not tomorrow, brother!

Setsu comes to his side and leans against him, and he puts his arm around her.

FATHER: Yes, life is stronger than death. [He turns to his family.] Come, let us go home.

Father and Mother and Kino bow and leave. Jiya and Setsu stand looking out to the sea.

JIYA: Life is stronger than death—do you hear that, Setsu?

SETSU: Yes. I hear.

Curtain

DISCUSSION    1.    In Act Four the father says, ''To live in the presence of death makes us brave and strong'' (page 467). How does his statement apply to Kino and Jiya?

2.    The big wave changes the lives of both Kino and Jiya. What is the most important change in Jiya as he grows up? In Kino?

3.    In Act One Jiya says, ''I wish I were a farmer's son like you'' and Kino replies, ''And I wish I were a fisherman's son'' (p. 458). Why do the boys envy each other?

4.    What is the **setting** (see page 12) of ''The Big Wave''? In what way does the setting determine the plot?

For further activities, see page 478.

478

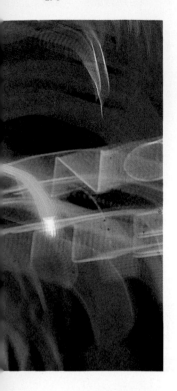

## VOCABULARY

### The Wishing Well (page 444)

Look at the description (in italics) in each of these sentences. See if you can think of one word for each sentence that will take the place of the description but mean the same thing: 1. Kozik's yellow eyes considered. Over them his lids fell and opened *like the lazy wings of a moth.* 2. They watched them *like exotic birds from a green jungle.* 3. . . . it made the house seem *like a handful of another world set down on top of the hill.* . . .

### The Big Wave (page 455)

On separate paper, write the characters' names as they appear below. Then from the second column, find the adverbs that describe each character's manner of speaking. Find the exact lines in the play that support your answers. Then see if you can read the line in the way described by the adverb. Look up any adverb you don't know.

| *Characters* | *Adverbs* | |
|---|---|---|
| Jiya | willfully | slowly |
| Kino | sternly | faintly |
| Father | joyfully | proudly |
| Setsu | sadly | soberly |

## COMPOSITION

### Ta-Na-E-Ka (page 433)

Roger's reactions to Ta-Na-E-Ka are different from Mary's. So are his experiences. Imagine you are Roger and write a letter to a friend, describing what happened to you during Ta-Na-E-Ka.

### Ta-Na-E-Ka and Knoxville, Tennessee (pages 433 and 443)

Both selections deal with appreciation of our homes and traditions—our heritages. Write a short composition in which you discuss the appreciation of heritage in "Ta-Na-E-Ka" and "Knoxville, Tennessee" and appreciation of your own heritage.

# READING

## The Turtle (page 428)

Tony and Jim express conflicting views about the turtle and what its fate should be. Here are some statements from or about the story. On separate paper, indicate which statements reflect Tony's way of thinking and which reflect Jim's. You'll have two statements left over.

1. The turtle should be killed.
2. The turtle should be captured, taken home, and used for soup.
3. To fight the turtle in the water is the only fair way.
4. "I'd run the wagon over him, only he's too big."
5. "Poor Old One. You had the misfortune to be caught."
6. "This turtle—he does not have a chance."
7. It's crazy to identify with the turtle.
8. The type of killing the turtle does is part of nature's plan—it's survival.
9. "I could use the lug wrench . . . I don't want my hands near him."
10. Even if he is not killed, the turtle will die soon.

## Ta-Na-E-Ka (page 433)

Though Mary did not exactly break the rules, she "stretched" them a bit, proving that she knew "how to exist in a world that wasn't made for Indians." List *three* things she did which "stretched" the rules.

## The Wishing Well (page 444)

On separate paper, write these statements in the order in which they happened in the story.

1. Beezie sees the face of the girl at the well.
2. Beezie and Kozik stare at the ninety cents in change.
3. Beezie panics, thinking that he has been abandoned.
4. The boys sneak under the electrified fence.
5. Beezie starts putting money in the bucket.
6. Beezie lies—blue, frozen, and sick—on the ground.
7. The couple takes the money.
8. Beezie feels the cold growing in his body—his hand is locked shut.

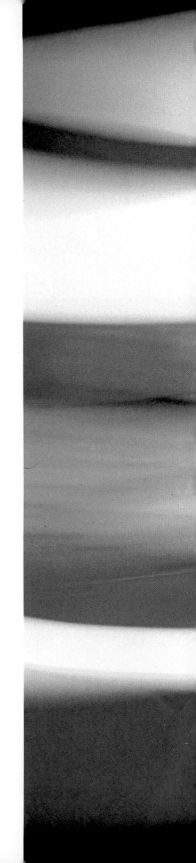

# ROBERTO

OSCAR LEWIS

When I was about eleven years old and still in the first grade, I ran away for the first time. I went to Veracruz with no more than the clothes on my back. I had no money to start out with. In those days, I never got to have a whole *peso*[1] in my pocket all at once. I was limited to the five *centavos*[2] my father would put under our pillows each morning before he went to work. On Sundays, we got twenty *centavos* each. But I usually spent my money right away and never had any in my pocket. On the road all the money I had was what one driver gave me.

My excuse for running away was that my father scolded me, but in reality, he always scolded me. The main reason was that I heard the boys talking about their adventures and I wanted to find out for myself. So I went to Veracruz. I chose that place because I had been to Veracruz once with my father and mother, Manuel and Consuelo, who was a nursing baby then. My grandfather had died and some uncles of mine had put my father in jail and had taken away his inheritance. Just to think of it made my blood boil! Imagine, my uncles had done this to my father! Such shameless, materialistic people! Money was everything to them! But my uncles were dead and I didn't know about my other relatives until later.

Right off the bat, I walked about twenty-three kilometers on the Mexico-Puebla highway. I have always liked the road; walking is my life. I've walked from Maltrata all the way along the railroad tracks as far as Orizaba (about seventy kilometers), just to see the vegetation and the fantastic view. The train would pass by and I could have jumped it (I don't have the old-fashioned bad habit of paying fares) but I preferred to walk along, admiring the scenery. I like to walk day and night, until I fall down with exhaustion. Then I go to sleep at the side of the highway. I can find grass anywhere and I'd cut a pile of it for my bed.

On the highway I felt happy and carefree. The problem of food didn't worry me. It was easy for me to go up to a shack and ask for work to do in exchange for a *taco*. Everybody gave me something to do, draw water from the well, chop wood, or

---

[1] *peso* (pĕ'sŏ): Mexican coin, equal to about eight cents.
[2] *centavos* (sĕn·tä'vōs): coins worth one hundredth of a peso.

any simple thing like that, and then they'd give me something to eat. Lots of people would tell me to sit down to eat first, and then they wouldn't let me do anything for them. They would fix up a pack of *tortillas* and salt and off I'd go.

I had laid out a route and went as I had planned. From Los Reyes, I walked as far as the crossroads, where the highways to Texcoco, Puebla, and Veracruz meet. No car would stop for me, even though they saw I was a kid. A bus picked me up and they asked where I was from. If I had known that saying you are from Mexico City closed doors to you, I would have said I was from somewhere else. People from the capital have a very bad reputation. At the carnivals and *fiestas,* whenever they catch anybody stealing or doing something wrong, he turns out to be from there.

I traveled alone. I never wanted to take along friends because I have always preferred to go on my own. It is easier for me to get around by myself. I would ask people the way. By asking, you can get to Rome.

When I left home, I felt as though a great weight was lifted off me. To live with other people is hard. I never wanted to be tied to the family again. Sometimes I would ask for lodging for a night and I would stay with a family for a few days. But I wasn't comfortable because what I was looking for was to be free. And so I went, like the air, without difficulty, without direction, free. . . . People would ask, "Why did you leave home?"

"Because my father scolded me. I have a stepmother." How I used Elena as an excuse! I think that was why I was always making her mad, so that I could use her as a pretext for my lies. I had the luck of a canaille,[3] for I achieved my ends for the moment. I call myself canaille, because I used another person to cover up my lies. What I have gone through is nothing, compared to what I deserve.

Like all adventurers, when I arrived in Veracruz, I asked the way to the sea. I reached it and sat on a navy dock all day looking at its vastness. The sea was beautiful, overpowering. I was there all day and saw how the tourists and the watchmen, who guard the docks and the cargoes, had nothing else to do but fish. When it was nightfall I wondered where I was going to

---

[3] *canaille* (kə·nī′): scoundrel.

sleep. That is the least problem there, because it is very hot. I decided to stay on one of the beaches, the best and softest one. At night the tide rises, so I stayed some distance from the sea.

The next day I felt like eating. I hadn't eaten anything the day before. I was so entranced, watching the sea and the fishing. I went over to the docks, because of the cargo boats anchored there. I saw a lot of people walking back and forth. They were a rough bunch, husky, dark-skinned guys. I approached the boat cook and asked if he didn't have any work for me in exchange for a *taco*. He felt sorry for me and it was because of that cook that I worked as a longshoreman for the first time in my life. I carried any little stuff and they would give me meals in return. We started work at eight and stopped at twelve, then began at twelve-thirty and quit at four-thirty. That was the way I got my food and lodging, for they gave me permission to sleep on the boat.

After a while, it didn't look like such a good setup for me. A boat would come in and I would stick to it like a leech. But the next day it would pull out and I would be homeless and without food again. I was always having to look for a place to eat and sleep. But I knew that if anybody died of hunger it was because he was lazy. If you helped the fishermen on the free beaches pull in their nets, you wouldn't get money but they'd give you a few fish. In one casting, they get all kinds of things, from sharks to turtles. I sold the fish, keeping one or two which I'd ask the fishermen's wives to cook for me.

I was willing to work at whatever came along, so I could eat. I never earned a copper working, they just gave me fruit, for the most part. I even ate wild greens and there were times when I didn't taste bread for two weeks. When I had nothing to eat, I would ask the watchmen to let me take a few pieces of coconut. When ships came in from Tabasco, or from places where they grew fruit, I had a feast day!

I began to have worries about a place to sleep because I heard that the police van was going around the beaches, where all the riffraff of Veracruz gathered. Anyone found sleeping on the sand would be taken off to jail. Nothing happened to me, but I slept with less calm, and went further away from the beach, toward the mountains. I didn't dare go away from the docks in the daytime—they were the source of life for me.

About three months passed like this. The time came when I felt like going home. I thought of the family only once in a while, but when I did, I felt like getting back home as fast as I could. There were moments when I felt brave enough to leave, then I would lose heart. I never wrote home, because I didn't know how to write a letter and I didn't want them to know where I was. I imagined that if my *papá* found out he would come and beat me to death. That is what I thought, but I went home anyway.

The return trip was hard because I had to walk from Veracruz to Puebla. It took me eight or nine days. I walked day and night, as no truck would pick me up. I took the Córdoba road and came to the police booth at the entrance of the city of Puebla. My shoes were all worn out, strong miner's boots that my father always bought for us. I asked the truck drivers for a lift, but they refused. Some of them made fun of me. I paid no attention to them but I felt lonely for the first time, alone as a feather flying through the air. I sat at the side of the road, crying.

Finally, the police stopped a truck and said, "Take care of this kid adventurer. He is headed for Mexico City." I got on and we arrived late at night, at the Merced Market, near the Zócalo, the central square of Mexico City. Imagine, it was my first time there. I had been to Veracruz but had never seen the Zócalo! When I crossed in front of the National Palace, I saw the great big clock in the Cathedral as it struck three. There I was, all alone in the plaza. I hurried home, knocked at the *vecindad* [4] gate and the *portera* [5] let me in.

Outside our door I sat, wondering whether or not to go in. I expected a terrific beating. I started to knock, but sat down again. Then something strange occurred. I am not superstitious, but if you had seen what I have, you would consider me a superior being. Sitting there, at that hour, I saw someone dressed like a *charro,* a cowboy, came down from the roof near the water tank. He lit something, a cigar, I think, because the fire was so big. I kept staring and wondering what the man was looking for. Then the cigar fell to the ground and the man disappeared . . . just like that. I figured he must have been kidding around . . . but where did he go?

[4] *vecindad* (vā•sĭn•thad′): neighborhood.
[5] *portera* (pôr•târ′ä): gatekeeper.

I have always liked danger and strong emotions and when there is something unfamiliar, I want to know more about it. So I climbed up to the water tank, way up to the top. I went to the little garden and to the bathhouse. Rumors had gone around the *vecindad* that these places were haunted. Well, if I were superstitious, I would be dead now, because as I went to the bathhouse I heard a tremendous noise, a crash, as though something had broken. I got panicky and ran back to our door and knocked. They called out, "Who is it?" and I said, "Me, *papá.*"

My father opened the door immediately. "So you finally got back, son. Well, come on in." He was very nice. I thought he would meet me with a belt in his hand and give me the hiding of the ages. But he said to me, "Did you have any supper?" We had no kerosene stove then, just a charcoal brazier, so he got himself to work and lit a fire. He heated the beans and coffee and said, "Eat. When you are finished turn out the light." Then he went back to bed. As I knew he left for work early and that he was a light sleeper, I turned out the light and there I was eating in the dark. Then I went to sleep . . . and he hadn't scolded me or hit me or anything.

**DISCUSSION**

1. Why does Roberto return home? Why do you think his father doesn't punish him?

2. On page 482 Roberto says that when people asked why he'd left home he would say "Because my father scolded me." But that was not his real reason. What was his reason?

3. Roberto tells many things about himself after he ran away. For example, on page 483 he shows that he was resourceful when he says, "I was willing to work at whatever came along." Find lines that show he was also lonely and afraid.

For further activities, see page 510.

# Conversation with Myself

EVE MERRIAM

This face in the mirror
stares at me
demanding *Who are you? What will you become?*
and taunting, *You don't even know.*
Chastened, I cringe and agree
and then
because I'm still young,
I stick out my tongue.

# Locomotive 38, the Ojibway

WILLIAM SAROYAN

One day a man came to town on a donkey and began loafing around in the public library where I used to spend most of my time in those days. He was a tall young Indian of the Ojibway tribe. He told me his name was Locomotive 38. Everybody in town believed he had escaped from an asylum.

Six days after he arrived in town his animal was struck by the Tulare Street trolley and seriously injured. The following day the animal passed away, most likely of internal injuries, on the corner of Mariposa and Fulton streets. The animal sank to the pavement, fell on the Indian's leg, groaned and died. When the Indian got his leg free he got up and limped into the drug store on the corner and made a long distance telephone call. He telephoned his brother In Oklahoma. The call cost him a lot of money, which he dropped into the slot as requested by the operator as if he were in the habit of making such calls every day.

I was in the drug store at the time, eating a Royal Banana Special, with crushed walnuts.

When he came out of the telephone booth he saw me sitting at the soda fountain eating this fancy dish.

Hello, Willie, he said.

He knew my name wasn't Willie—he just liked to call me that.

He limped to the front of the store where the gum was, and bought three packages of Juicy Fruit. Then he limped back to me and said, What's that your eating, Willie? It looks good.

This is what they call a Royal Banana Special, I said.

The Indian got up on the stool next to me.

Give me the same, he said to the soda fountain girl.

That's too bad about your animal, I said.

There's no place for an animal in this world, he said. What kind of an automobile should I buy?

Are you going to buy an automobile? I said.

I've been thinking about it for several minutes now, he said.

I didn't think you had money, I said. I thought you were poor.

That's the impression people get, he said. Another impression they get is that I'm crazy.

I didn't get the impression that you were crazy, I said, but I didn't get the impression that you were rich, either.

Well, I am, the Indian said.

I wish I was rich, I said.

What for? he said.

Well, I said, I've been wanting to go fishing at Mendota for three years in a row now. I need some equipment and some kind of an automobile to get out there in.

Can you drive an automobile? the Indian said.

I can drive anything, I said.

Have you ever driven an automobile? he said.

Not yet, I said. So far I haven't had any automobile to drive, and it's against my family religion to steal an automobile.

Do you mean to tell me you believe you could get into an automobile and start driving? he said.

That's right, I said.

Remember what I was telling you on the steps of the public library the other evening? he said.

You mean about the machine age? I said.

Yes, he said.

I remember, I said.

All right, he said. Indians are born with an instinct for riding, rowing, hunting, fishing, and swimming. Americans are born with an instinct for fooling around with machines.

I'm no American, I said.

I know, the Indian said. You're an Armenian. I remember. I asked you and you told me. You're an Armenian born in America. You're fourteen years old and already you know you'll be able to drive an automobile the minute you get into one. You're a typical American, although your complexion, like my own, is dark.

Driving a car is no trick, I said. There's nothing to it. It's easier than riding a donkey.

All right, the Indian said. Just as you say. If I go up the street and buy an automobile, will you drive for me?

Of course, I said.

How much in wages would you want? he said.

You mean you want to give me wages for driving an automobile? I said.

Of course, the Ojibway said.

Well, I said, that's very nice of you, but I don't want any money for driving an automobile.

Some of the journeys may be long ones, he said.

The longer the better, I said.

Are you restless? he said.

I was born in this little old town, I said.

Don't you like it? he said.

I like mountains and streams and mountain lakes, I said.

Have you ever been in the mountains? he said.

Not yet, I said, but I'm going to reach them some day.

I see, he said. What kind of an automobile do you think I ought to buy?

How about a Ford roadster? I said.

Is that the best automobile? he said.

Do you want the *best?* I said.

Shouldn't I have the best? he said.

I don't know, I said. The best costs a lot of money.

What is the best? he said.

Well, I said, some people think the Cadillac is the best. Others like the Packard. They're both pretty good. I wouldn't know which is best. The Packard is beautiful to see going down the highway, but so is the Cadillac. I've watched a lot of them fine cars going down the highway.

How much is a Packard? he said.

Around three thousand dollars, I said. Maybe a little more.

Can we get one right away? he said.

I got down off the stool. He sounded crazy, but I knew he wasn't.

Listen, Mr. Locomotive, I said, do you really want to buy a Packard right away?

You know my animal passed away a few minutes ago, he said.

I saw it happen, I said. They'll probably be arresting you any minute now for leaving the animal in the street.

They won't arrest me, he said.

They will if there's a law against leaving a dead donkey in the street, I said.

No, they won't, he said.

Why not? I said.

Well, he said, they won't after I show them a few papers I carry around with me all the time. The people of this country have a lot of respect for money, and I've got a lot of money.

I guess he is crazy after all, I thought.

Where'd you get all this money? I said.

I own some land in Oklahoma, he said. About fifty thousand acres.

Is it worth money? I said.

No, he said. All but about twenty acres of it is worthless. I've got some oil wells on them twenty acres. My brother and I.

How did you Ojibways ever get down to Oklahoma? I said. I always thought the Ojibways lived up north, up around the Great Lakes.

That's right, the Indian said. We used to live up around the Great Lakes, but my grandfather was a pioneer. He moved west when everybody else did.

Oh, I said. Well, I guess they won't bother you about the dead donkey at that.

They won't bother me about anything, he said. It won't be because I've got money. It'll be because they think I'm crazy.

Nobody in this town but you knows I've got money. Do you know where we can get one of them automobiles right away?

The Packard agency is up on Broadway, two blocks beyond the public library, I said.

All right, he said. If you're sure you won't mind driving for me, let's go get one of them. Something bright in color, he said. Red, if they've got red. Where would you like to drive to first?

Would you care to go fishing at Mendota? I said.

I'll take the ride, he said. I'll watch you fish. Where can we get some equipment for you?

Right around the corner at Homan's. I said.

We went around the corner to Homan's and the Indian bought twenty-seven dollars' worth of fishing equipment for me. Then we went up to the Packard agency on Broadway. They didn't have a red Packard, but there was a beautiful green one. It was light green, the color of new grass. This was back there in 1922. The car was a beautiful sports touring model.

Do you think you could drive this great big car? the Indian said.

I *know* I can drive it, I said.

The police found us in the Packard agency and wanted to arrest the Indian for leaving the dead donkey in the street. He showed them the papers he had told me about and the police apologized and went away. They said they'd remove the animal and were sorry they'd troubled him about it.

It's no trouble at all, he said.

He turned to the manager of the Packard agency, Jim Lewis, who used to run for Mayor every time election time came around.

I'll take this car, he said.

I'll draw up the papers immediately, Jim said.

What papers? the Indian said. I'm going to pay for it now.

You mean you want to pay three thousand two hundred seventeen dollars and sixty-five cents *cash*? Jim said.

Yes, the Indian said. It's ready to drive, isn't it?

Of course, Jim said. I'll have the boys go over it with a cloth to take off any dust on it. I'll have them check the motor too, and fill the gasoline tank. It won't take more than ten minutes. If you'll step into the office I'll close the transaction immediately.

Jim and the Indian stepped into Jim's office.

About three minutes later Jim came over to me, a man shaken to the roots.

Aram, he said, who is this guy? I thought he was a nut. I had Johnny telephone the Pacific-Southwest and they said his bank account is being transferred from somewhere in Oklahoma. They said his account is something over a million dollars. I thought he was a nut. Do you know him?

He told me his name is Locomotive 38, I said. That's no name.

That's a translation of his Indian name, Jim said. We've got his full name on the contract. Do you know him?

I've talked to him every day since he came to town on that donkey that died this morning, I said, but I never thought he had any money.

He says you're going to drive for him, Jim said. Are you sure you're the man to drive a great big car like this, son?

Wait a minute now, Mr. Lewis, I said. Don't try to push me out of this chance of a lifetime. I can drive this big Packard as well as anybody else in town.

I'm not trying to push you out of anything, Jim said. I just don't want you to drive out of here and run over six or seven innocent people and maybe smash the car. Get into the car and I'll give you a few pointers. Do you know anything about the gear shift?

I don't know anything about anything yet, I said, but I'll soon find out.

All right, Jim said. Just let me help you.

I got into the car and sat down behind the wheel. Jim got in beside me.

From now on, son, he said, I want you to regard me as a friend who will give you the shirt off his back. I want to thank you for bringing me this fine Indian gentleman.

He told me he wanted the best car on the market, I said. You know I've always been crazy about driving a Packard. Now how do I do it?

Well, Jim said, let's see.

He looked down at my feet.

Son, he said, your feet don't reach the pedals.

Never mind that, I said. You just explain the gear shift.

Jim explained everything while the boys wiped the dust off the car and went over the motor and filled the gasoline tank.

When the Indian came out and got into the car, in the back where I insisted he should sit, I had the motor going.

He says he knows how to drive, the Indian said to Jim Lewis. By instinct, he said. I believe him, too.

You needn't worry about Aram here, Jim said. He can drive all right. Clear the way there, boys, he shouted. Let him have all the room necessary.

I turned the big car around slowly, shifted, and shot out of the agency at about fifty miles an hour, with Jim Lewis running after the car and shouting, Take it easy, son. Don't open up until you get out on the highway. The speed limit in town is twenty-five miles an hour.

The Indian wasn't at all excited, even though I was throwing him around a good deal.

I wasn't doing it on purpose, though. It was simply that I wasn't very familiar with the manner in which the automobile worked.

You're an excellent driver, Willie, he said. It's like I said. You're an American and you were born with an instinct for mechanical contraptions like this.

We'll be in Mendota in an hour, I said. You'll see some great fishing out there.

How far is Mendota? the Indian said.

About ninety miles, I said.

Ninety miles is too far to go in an hour, the Indian said. Take two hours. We're passing a lot of interesting scenery I'd like to look at a little more closely.

All right, I said, but I sure am anxious to get out there and fish.

Well, all right then, the Indian said. Go as fast as you like this time, but some time I'll expect you to drive a little more slowly, so I can see some of the scenery. I'm missing everything. I don't even get a chance to read the signs.

I'll travel slowly *now* if you want me to, I said.

No, he insisted. Let her go. Let her go as fast as she'll go.

Well, we got out to Mendota in an hour and seventeen minutes. I would have made better time except for the long stretch of dirt road.

I drove the car right up to the river bank. The Indian asked if I knew how to get the top down, so he could sit in the open and watch me fish. I didn't know how to get the top down, but I got it down. It took me twenty minutes to do it.

I fished for about three hours, fell into the river twice, and finally landed a small one.

You don't know the first thing about fishing, the Indian said.

What am I doing wrong? I said.

Everything, he said. Have you ever fished before?

No, I said.

I didn't think so, he said.

What am I doing wrong? I said.

Well, he said, nothing in particular, only you're fishing at about the same rate of speed that you drive an automobile.

Is that wrong? I said.

It's not exactly wrong, he said, except that it'll keep you from getting anything to speak of, and you'll go on falling into the river.

I'm not falling, I said. They're pulling me in. They've got an awful pull. This grass is mighty slippery, too. There ain't nothing around here to grab hold of.

I reeled in one more little one and then I asked if he'd like to go home. He said he would if I wanted to, too, so I put away the fishing equipment and the two fish and got in the car and started driving back to town.

I drove that big Packard for this Ojibway Indian, Locomotive 38, as long as he stayed in town, which was all summer. He stayed at the hotel all the time. I tried to get him to learn to drive, but he said it was out of the question. I drove that Packard all over the San Joaquin Valley that summer, with the Indian in the back, chewing eight or nine sticks of gum. He told me to drive anywhere I cared to go, so it was either to some place where I could fish, or some place where I could hunt. He claimed I didn't know anything about fishing or hunting, but he was glad to see me trying. As long as I knew him he never laughed, except once. That was the time I shot at a jack-rabbit with a 12-gauge shotgun that had a terrible kick, and killed a crow. He tried to tell me all the time that that was my average. To shoot at a jack-rabbit and kill a crow. You're an American, he said. Look at the way you took to this big automobile.

One day in November that year his brother came to town from Oklahoma, and the next day when I went down to the hotel to get him, they told me he'd gone back to Oklahoma with his brother.

Where's the Packard? I said.

They took the Packard, the hotel clerk said.

Who drove? I said.

The Indian, the clerk said.

They're both Indians, I said. Which of the brothers drove the car?

The one who lived at this hotel, the clerk said.

Are you sure? I said.

Well, I only saw him get into the car out front and drive away, the clerk said. That's all.

Do you mean to tell me he knew how to shift gears? I said.

It *looked* as if he did, the clerk said. He looked like an expert driver to me.

Thanks, I said.

On the way home I figured he'd just wanted me to *believe* he couldn't drive, so *I* could drive all the time and feel good. He was just a young man who'd come to town on a donkey, bored to death or something, who'd taken advantage of the chance to be entertained by a small town kid who was bored to death, too. That's the only way I could figure it out without accepting the general theory that he was crazy.

DISCUSSION

1.  Locomotive 38 had known how to drive a car all along. Why do you suppose he pretended that he did not? "Everybody in town believed he had escaped from an asylum" (page 488). What was there about Locomotive 38 that led the townspeople to feel that way?

2.  This story is told from Aram's point of view. What is his reaction when Locomotive 38 offers him the chance to drive? What does he finally come to understand to be Locomotive 38's reasons for using him?

3.  There are many examples of humor in this story. Although Locomotive 38 has left a dead donkey lying in the street, he escapes arrest by showing the police "a few papers"—perhaps the bankroll which he later produces when paying for the car. What other scenes or remarks struck you as funny?

For further activities, see page 510.

# Primer Lesson CARL SANDBURG

Look out how you use proud words.
when you let proud words go,
   it is not easy to call them back.
They wear long boots, hard boots;
   they walk off proud; they can't hear you
   calling—
Look out how you use proud words.

DISCUSSION

1.  What is a primer? Why should the idea in this poem be a "primer lesson" for everyone?

2.  What do you think the speaker means by "proud words"? Give some examples.

# The Apprentice

DOROTHY CANFIELD FISHER

The day had been one of the unbearable ones, when every sound had set her teeth on edge like chalk creaking on a blackboard, when every word her father or mother said to her or did not say to her seemed an intentional injustice. And of course, it would happen as the end to such a day, that just as the sun went down back of the mountain and the long twilight began, she noticed that Rollie was not around.

Tense with exasperation at what her mother would say, she began to call him in a carefully casual tone—she would simply explode if Mother got going—"Here, Rollie! He-ere, boy! Want to go for a walk, Rollie?" Whistling to him cheerfully, her heart full of wrath at the way the world treated her, she made the rounds of his haunts; the corner of the woodshed, where he liked to curl up on the wool of Father's discarded old windbreaker; the hay barn, the cow barn, the sunny spot on the side porch—, no Rollie.

Perhaps he had sneaked upstairs to lie on her bed where he was not supposed to go—not that *she* would have minded! That rule was a part of Mother's fussiness, part too of Mother's bossiness. It was *her* bed, wasn't it? But was she allowed the say-so about it? Not on your life. They *said* she could have things the way she wanted in her own room, now she was in her teens, but—her heart raged against unfairness as she took the stairs stormily, two steps at a time, her pigtails flopping up and down on her back. If Rollie was on her bed, she was just going to let him stay right there, and Mother could say what she wanted to.

But he was not there. The bedspread and pillow were crumpled, but not from his weight. She had flung herself down to cry there that afternoon. And then she couldn't. Every nerve in her had been twanging discordantly, but she couldn't cry. She could only lie there, her hands doubled up hard, furious that she had nothing to cry about. Not really. She was too big to cry just over Father's having said to her, severely, "I told you if I let you take the chess set you were to put it away when you got through with it. One of the pawns was on the floor of our bedroom this morning. I stepped on it. If I'd had my shoes on, I'd have broken it."

Well, he *had* told her to be sure to put them away. And although she had forgotten and left them, he hadn't said she mustn't ever take the set again. No, the instant she thought about that, she knew she couldn't cry about it. She could be, and she was, in a rage about the way Father kept on talking, long after she'd got his point, "It's not that I care so much about the chess set," he said, just leaning with all his weight on being right, "it's because if you don't learn how to take care of things, you yourself will suffer for it, later. You'll forget or neglect something that will be really important, for *you*. We *have* to try to teach you to be responsible for what you've said you'll take care of. If we . . ." on and on, preaching and preaching.

She heard her mother coming down the hall, and hastily shut her door. She had a right to shut the door to her own room, hadn't she? She had *some* rights, she supposed, even if she was only thirteen and the youngest child. If her mother opened it to say, smiling, "What are you doing in here that you won't want me to see?" she'd say—she'd just say—

She stood there, dry-eyed, by the bed that Rollie had not crumpled, and thought, "I hope Mother sees the spread and says something about Rollie—I just hope she does."

But her mother did not open the door. Her feet went steadily on along the hall, and then, carefully, slowly, down the stairs. She probably had an arm full of winter things she was bringing down from the attic. She was probably thinking that a tall, thirteen-year-old daughter was big enough to help with a chore like that. But she wouldn't *say* anything. She would just get out that insulting look of a grown-up silently putting up with a crazy unreasonable kid. She had worn that expression all day; it was too much to be endured.

Up in her bedroom behind her closed door the thirteen-year-old stamped her foot in a rage, none the less savage and heart-shaking because it was mysterious to her.

But she had not located Rollie. Before she would let her father and mother know she had lost sight of him, forgotten about him, she would be cut into little pieces. They would not scold her, she knew. They would do worse. They would look at her. And in their silence she would hear droning on reproachfully what they had said when the sweet, woolly collie-puppy had first been in her arms and she had been begging to keep him for her own.

How warm he had felt! Astonishing how warm and alive a puppy was compared to a doll! She had never liked her dolls much, after she had held Rollie, feeling him warm against her

breast, warm and wriggling, burstling with life, reaching up to lick her face—he had loved her from that first instant. As he felt her arms around him, his beautiful eyes had melted in trusting sweetness. As they did now, whenever he looked at her. "My dog is the only one in the whole world who *really* loves me," she thought passionately.

Even then, at the very minute when as a darling baby dog he was beginning to love her, her father and mother were saying, so cold, so reasonable—gosh! how she *hated* reasonableness!—"Now, Peg, remember that, living where we do, with sheep on the farms around us, it is a serious responsibility to have a collie dog. If you keep him, you've got to be the one to take care of him. You'll have to be the one to train him to stay at home. We're too busy with you children to start bringing up a puppy, too." Rollie, nestling in her arms, let one hind leg drop awkwardly. It must be uncomfortable. She looked down at him tenderly, tucked his dangling leg up under him and gave him a hug. He laughed up in her face—he really did laugh, his mouth stretched wide in a cheerful grin.

Her parents were saying, "If you want him, you can have him. But you must be responsible for him. If he gets to running sheep, he'll just have to be shot, you know that."

They had not said, aloud, "Like the Wilsons' collie." They never mentioned that awfulness—her racing unsuspectingly down across the fields just at the horrible moment when Mr. Wilson shot their collie caught in the very act of killing sheep. They probably thought that if they never spoke about it, she would forget it—*forget* the crack of that rifle, and the collapse of the great beautiful dog! Forget the red red blood spurting from the hole in his head. She hadn't forgotten. She never would. She knew as well as they did, how important it was to train a collie-puppy about sheep. They didn't need to rub it in like that. They always rubbed everything in. She had told them, fervently, indignantly, that of *course* she would take care of him, be responsible for him, teach him to stay at home. Of course, of course. *She* understood!

And now, this afternoon, when he was six months old, tall, rangy, powerful, standing up far above her knee, nearly to her waist, she didn't know where he was. But of course he must be somewhere around. He always was. She composed her face to look natural and went downstairs to search the house. He was probably asleep somewhere. She looked every room over carefully. Her mother was nowhere visible. It was safe to call him again, to give the special piercing whistle which always brought him racing to her, the white-feathered plume of his tail waving in elation that she wanted him.

But he did not answer. She stood still on the front porch to think.

Could he have gone up to their special place in the edge of the field where the three young pines, their branches growing close to the ground, make a triangular, walled-in space, completely hidden from the world. Sometimes he went up there with her. When she lay down on the dried grass to dream, he too lay down quietly, his head on his paws, his beautiful eyes fixed adoringly on her. He entered into her every mood. If she wanted to be quiet, all right, he did too.

It didn't seem as though he would have gone alone there. Still——She loped up the steep slope of the field rather fast, beginning to be anxious.

No, he was not there. She stood, irresolutely, in the roofless, green-walled triangular hide-out, wondering what to do next.

Then, before she knew what thought had come into her mind, its emotional impact knocked her down. At least her knees crumpled under her. Last Wednesday the Wilsons had brought their sheep down to the home farm from the upper pasture! She herself had seen them on the way to school, and like an idiot had not thought of Rollie. She had seen them grazing on the river meadow.

She was off like a racer at the crack of the starting pistol, her long, strong legs stretched in great leaps, her pigtails flying. She took the short cut down to the upper edge of the meadow, regardless of the brambles. Their thorn-spiked, wiry stems tore at her flesh, but she did not care. She welcomed the pain. It was something she was doing for Rollie, for her Rollie.

She was tearing through the pine woods now, rushing down the steep, stony path, tripping over roots, half-falling, catching herself just in time, not slackening her speed. She burst out on the open knoll above the river meadow, calling wildly, "Rollie, here, Rollie, here, boy! here! here!" She tried to whistle, but she was crying too hard to pucker her lips. She had not, till then, known she was crying.

There was nobody to see or hear her. Twilight was falling over the bare knoll. The sunless evening wind slid down the mountain like an invisible river, engulfing her in cold. Her teeth began to chatter. "Here, Rollie, here boy, here!" She strained her eyes to look down into the meadow to see if the sheep were there. She could not be sure. She stopped calling him as if he were a dog, and called out his name despairingly, as if he were her child, "Rollie! oh, *Rollie,* where are you!"

The tears ran down her cheeks in streams. She sobbed loudly, terribly. Since there was no one to hear, she did not try to control herself. "Hou! hou! hou!" she sobbed, her face contorted grotesquely. "Oh, Rollie! Rollie! Rollie!" She had wanted something to cry about. Oh, how terribly now she had something to cry about.

She saw him as clearly as if he were there beside her, his muzzle and gaping mouth all smeared with the betraying blood (like the Wilsons' collie). "But he didn't *know* it was wrong!" she screamed like a wild creature. "Nobody *told* him it was wrong. It was my fault. I should have taken better care of him. I will now. I will!"

But no matter how she screamed, she could not make herself heard. In the cold gathering darkness, she saw him stand, poor, guiltless victim of his ignorance, who should have been protected from his own nature, his soft eyes looking at her with love, his splendid plumed tail waving gently. "It was my fault. I promised I would bring him up. I should have *made* him stay at home. I was responsible for him. It was my fault."

But she could not make his executioners hear her. The shot rang out, Rollie sank down, his beautiful liquid eyes glazed, the blood spurting from the hole in his head—like the Wilsons' collie. She gave a wild shriek, long, soul-satisfying, frantic. It was the scream at sudden, unendurable tragedy of a mature, full-blooded woman. It drained dry the girl of thirteen. She came to herself. She was standing on the knoll, trembling and quaking with cold, the darkness closing in on her.

Her breath had given out. For once in her life she had wept all the tears there were in her body. Her hands were so stiff with cold she could scarcely close them. How her nose was running! Simply streaming down her upper lip. And she had no handkerchief. She lifted her skirt, fumbled for her slip, stopped, blew her nose on it, wiped her eyes, drew a long quavering breath—and heard something! Far off in the distance, a faint sound, like a dog's muffled bark.

She whirled on her heels and bent her head to listen. The sound did not come from the meadow below the knoll. It came from back of her higher up, from the Wilsons' maple grove. She held her breath. Yes, it came from there.

She began to run again, but now she was not sobbing. She was silent, absorbed in her effort to cover ground. If she could only live to get there, to see if it really were Rollie. She ran steadily till she came to the fence and went over this in a great plunge. Her skirt caught on a nail. She impatiently pulled at it, not hearing or not heeding the long sibilant tear as it came loose. She was in the dusky maple woods, stumbling over the rocks as she ran. As she tore on up the slope, she heard the bark again, and knew it was Rollie's.

She stopped short and leaned weakly against a tree. She was sick with the breathlessness of her straining lungs, sick in the reaction of relief, sick with anger at Rollie, who had been here having a wonderful time while she had been dying, just dying in terror about him.

For she could now not only hear that it was Rollie's bark. She could hear, in the dog language she knew as well as he, what he was saying in those excited yips—that he had run a woodchuck into a hole in the tumbled stone wall, that he almost had him, that the intoxicating wild-animal smell was as close to him—almost—as if he had his jaws on his quarry. Yip! Woof! Yip! Yip!

The wildly joyful quality of the dog-talk enraged the girl. She had been trembling in exhaustion. Now it was indignation. So that was where he had been—when *she* was *killing* herself trying to take care of him. Plenty near enough if he had paid attention to hear her calling and whistling to him. Just so set on having his foolish good time, he never thought to listen for her call.

She stooped to pick up a stout stick. She would teach him. She was hot with anger. It was time he had something to make him remember to listen. She started forward on a run.

But after a few steps she stopped, stood thinking. One of the things to remember about collies, everybody knew that, was that a collie who had been beaten was never "right" again. His spirit was broken. "Anything but a broken-spirited collie," she had often heard a farmer say that. They were no good after that.

She threw down her stick. Anyhow, she thought, he was really too young to know that he had done wrong. He was still only a puppy. Like all puppies, he got perfectly crazy over wild-animal smells. Probably he truly hadn't heard her calling and whistling.

All the same, all the same—she stood stock-still, staring intently into the twilight—you couldn't let a puppy grow up just as he wanted to. It wouldn't be safe—for *him.* Somehow she would

have to make him understand that he musn't go off this way, by himself. He must be trained to know how to do what a good dog does—not because *she* wanted to, but for his own sake.

She walked on now, steady, purposeful, gathering her inner strength together, Olympian in her understanding of the full meaning of the event.

When he heard his own special young god approaching, he turned delightedly and ran to meet her, panting, his tongue hanging out. His eyes shone. He jumped up on her in an ecstasy of welcome and licked her face.

She pushed him away. Her face and voice were grave. "No, Rollie, *no!*" she said severely, "you're *bad.* You know you're not to go off in the woods without me! You are—a—*bad—dog.*"

He was horrified. Stricken into misery. He stood facing her, frozen. The gladness went out of his eyes, the waving plume of his tail slowly lowered to slinking, guilty dejection.

"I know you were all wrapped up in that woodchuck. But that's no excuse. You *could* have heard me, calling you, whistling for you, if you'd paid attention," she went on. "You've got to learn, and I've got to teach you."

With a shudder of misery he lay down, his tail stretched out limp on the ground, his head flat on his paws, his ears drooping— ears ringing with the doomsday awfulness of the voice he loved and revered. To have it speak so to him, he must have been utterly wicked. He trembled, he turned his head away from her august look of blame, he groveled in remorse for whatever mysterious sin he had committed.

As miserable as he, she sat down by him. "I don't *want* to scold you. But I have to! I have to bring you up right, or you'll get shot, Rollie. You mustn't go away from the house without me, do you hear, *never.*"

His sharp ears, yearning for her approval, caught a faint overtone of relenting affection in her voice. He lifted his eyes to her, humbly, soft in imploring fondness.

"Oh, Rollie!" she said, stooping low over him, "I *do* love you. I do. But I *have* to bring you up. I'm responsible for you, don't you see."

He did not see. Hearing sternness, or something else he did not recognize, in the beloved voice, he shut his eyes tight in sorrow, and made a little whimpering lament in his throat.

She had never heard him cry before. It was too much. She sat down by him and drew his head to her, rocking him in her arms, soothing him with inarticulate small murmurs.

He leaped in her arms and wriggled happily as he had when he was a baby, he reached up to lick her face as he had then. But he was no baby now. He was half as big as she, a great, warm, pulsing, living armful of love. She clasped him closely. Her heart was brimming full, but calmed, quiet. The blood flowed in equable gentleness all over her body. She was deliciously warm. Her nose was still running, a little. She sniffed and wiped it on her sleeve.

It was almost dark now. "We'll be late to supper, Rollie," she said, responsibly. Pushing him gently off she stood up. "Home, Rollie, home."

Here was a command he could understand. At once he trotted along the path towards home. His tail, held high, waved plume-like. His short dog-memory had forgotten the suffering just back of him.

Her human memory was longer. His prancing gait was as carefree as a young child's. She plodded behind him like a serious adult. Her very shoulders seemed bowed by what she had lived through. She felt, she thought, like an old, old woman of thirty. But it was all right now, she knew she had made an impression on him.

When they came out into the open pasture, Rollie ran back to get her to play with him. He leaped around her in circles, barking in cheerful yawps, jumping up on her, inviting her to run a race with him, to throw him a stick, to come alive.

His high spirits were ridiculous. But infectious. She gave one little leap to match his. Rollie took this as a threat, a pretend, play-threat. He planted his forepaws low and barked loudly at her, laughing between yips. He was so funny, she thought, when he grinned that way. She laughed back, and gave another mock-threatening leap at him. Radiant that his sky was once more clear, he sprang high on his steel-spring muscles in an explosion of happiness, and bounded in circles around her.

Following him, not noting in the dusk where she was going, she felt the grassy slope drop steeply. Oh, yes, she knew where she was. They had come to the rolling-down hill just back of the house. All the kids rolled down there, even the little ones, because it was soft grass without a stone. She had rolled down that slope a million times—years and years before, when she was a kid herself, six or seven years ago. It was fun. She remembered well the whirling dizziness of the descent, all the world turning crazily over and over. And the delicious giddy staggering when you first stood up, the earth still spinning under your feet.

"All right, Rollie, let's go," she cried, and flung herself down in the rolling position, her arms straight up over her head.

Rollie had never seen this skylarking before. It threw him into almost hysterical amusement. He capered around the rapidly rolling figure, half scared, mystified, enchanted.

His wild frolicsome barking might have come from her own throat, so accurately did it sound the way she felt—crazy, foolish—like a little kid, no more than five years old, the age she had been when she had last rolled down that hill.

At the bottom she sprang up, on muscles as steel-strong as Rollie's. She staggered a little, and laughed aloud.

The living-room windows were just before them. How yellow lighted windows looked when you were in the darkness going home. How nice and yellow. Maybe Mother had waffles for supper. She was a swell cook, Mother was, and she certainly gave her family all the breaks, when it came to meals.

"Home, Rollie, home!" She burst open the door to the living room. "Hi, Mom, what you got for supper?"

From the kitchen her mother announced coolly, "I hate to break the news to you, but it's waffles."

"Oh, *Mom!*" she shouted in ecstasy.

Her mother could not see her. She did not need to. "For goodness' sakes, go and wash," she called.

In the long mirror across the room she saw herself, her hair hanging wild, her long bare legs scratched, her broadly smiling face dirt-streaked, her torn skirt dangling, her dog laughing up at her. Gosh, was it a relief to feel your own age, just exactly thirteen years old.

**DISCUSSION**

1. "And now, this afternoon, when he was six months old, tall, rangy, powerful, standing up far above her knee, nearly to her waist, she didn't know where he was" (page 502). Why is Peg frightened because she cannot find Rollie? When she does find the dog, what is he doing? Peg picks up a stick. Why? Why does she throw the stick down?

2. What is an apprentice? In what sense is Peg an apprentice? Might the word refer to Rollie as well? Explain.

3. At the end of the story, Peg's attitude toward her parents has changed. How has it changed? Why has it changed?

For further activities, see page 511.

510

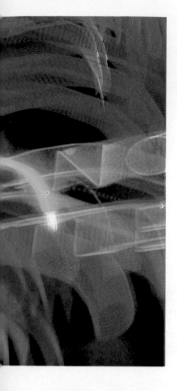

## VOCABULARY

### Roberto (page 480)

Many Spanish words in our language are associated with the Old West and Western movies. Write the definitions of the words below. Look up any you don't know.

| | |
|---|---|
| mustang | rodeo |
| loco | corral |
| lariat | adobe |
| vamoose | chaps |

### Locomotive 38, the Ojibway (page 488)

There are also many Indian words in our language. Do you know what the following Indian words mean? Do you know how to pronounce them? Look up any you don't know.

| | |
|---|---|
| succotash | hominy |
| mackinaw | terrapin |
| persimmon | hickory |

## COMPOSITION

### Roberto (page 480)

Roberto tells his story about running away and returning home from his own point of view. He says little about his father. But from what he does say, you must have some idea of what his father was like. In a short composition, tell the story of Roberto's running away and his return home from his father's point of view. To help you in writing this composition imagine that you *are* Roberto's father, that Roberto is *your* son.

### Primer Lesson (page 498)

Carl Sandburg tells us "look out how you use proud words." From your own reading or experience, what other primer lessons could you suggest to us? Present them in either a composition or a short poem.

## READING

### Locomotive 38, the Ojibway (page 488)

Below are statements from or about the story. Some of the statements are facts; some are opinions. On separate paper, list the numbers of the facts, then the numbers of the opinions. Be prepared to support your answers with references to the story, if necessary.

1. The Indian stayed at the hotel all summer.
2. The donkey died from injuries suffered in an accident.
3. Locomotive 38 had lots of money.
4. He had escaped from an asylum.
5. "Americans are born with an instinct for fooling around with machines."
6. The Indian bought an expensive car.
7. Locomotive 38 learned how to drive by watching Aram.
8. "Indians are born with an instinct for hunting, riding, rowing, fishing, and swimming."
9. Aram spent the summer driving around the San Joaquin Valley with Locomotive 38.
10. Locomotive 38 could not hunt or fish.

### The Apprentice (page 499)

Sometimes Peg expresses childlike, immature feelings. Other times her attitudes are quite mature. Below are a number of attitudes Peg expressed. On separate paper make two columns, one labeled "Immature" and one labeled "Mature." Then put the number of the statement in the right column.

1. "My dog is the only one in the whole world who really loves me."
2. Peg was just waiting to get into a tiff with her mother.
3. She knew that she had been irresponsible for having lost sight of Rollie.
4. Peg realized the seriousness and import of her responsibility to Rollie.
5. Though Rollie had not known he had done wrong, she knew it was up to her to teach him.
6. Hearing Rollie's joyful bark, she became "hot with anger" and was ready to beat him mercilessly.
7. Peg's experience gave her insight into her parents' responsibilities.
8. She was looking for something to be angry about—to express her mood.

# COMPOSITION

**WRITING
NONFICTION**

"Roberto," the selection on page 480, is an example of nonfiction, prose that is factually, historically true. There lives in Mexico now, or somewhere on earth if fate has been kind, a man whose past includes precisely those details of the walk to Veracruz that Roberto took when he was eleven years old and described in words of his own, recorded in the selection. The events really happened some fifteen or twenty years ago. The author did not make them up out of his imagination.

A great deal of what we read from day to day is nonfiction. Almost everything in a newspaper (except the comics) is. Indeed, most of us in the course of our lives will be called on to read (and write) nonfiction far more often than fiction: notes and recipes and instructions and school schedules and job applications and geography textbooks and bank statements and explanations of whatever kinds. Many such kinds of writing you will be called on to read, and some you will write yourself. Specifically, you will most often be called on to write nonfiction for two purposes. You will need to *explain* something to somebody. Or you will need to *persuade* somebody about something.

How do you *explain* the way to put a monster model together, or bake brownies, or do a magic trick, or find your way around a space craft? The best way is to take matters a step at a time. Start at the beginning and proceed logically, using words that are precise and accurate, defining any words in your explanation that your reader may not know. Try, as you write, to put yourself in the reader's place. Think about what parts of the process that you are explaining will be most difficult for her or him to understand, then explain those parts with particular care.

And how do you *persuade* someone that one movie is better than another, that a certain football team is going to win, that a certain person—you—should be hired for the summer job? Not by yelling in print, or begging, or bullying. You persuade with facts. The more facts—solid, specific, convincing facts—that you can bring to bear on the point you are making, the more likely is the chance that what you write will convince others that they ought to change their minds and share your opinion.

## ABOUT THE SELECTIONS

1.  Many different lives, in many different worlds, are described in the course of this unit. In which world would you most like to grow up? Write a paragraph that explains what there is about that world that appeals to you, whether it is Japan or Mexico or the Far West or wherever.

2.  A number of characters in this section learn something important that will probably change their lives. What was the most important single idea or insight that a character discovered in the unit? Write a paragraph that makes clear how that insight may change that person's life. How, for instance, will Peg be changed by her new awareness of the responsibilities of masters to their pets, of parents to their children?

3.  What is a Ta-Na-E-Ka? How do you drive a car, for Locomotive 38 or anyone else? How do you train a collie or any other dog to stay off a neighbor's property? How do you plant a garden? Choose some question that a selection in this section raises. Then carefully explain, step by step, in a paragraph or two, what you have chosen to write about.

4.  Choose from among these selections some question about which there might be a difference of opinion. Is Locomotive 38 really crazy? Should Kozik have stayed at the top of the wishing well, no matter what? Should Jiya have moved to the seashore, within range of the big waves? Write a paragraph that persuades the reader to accept your opinion on the question. Remember that the more facts you can include in support of your views, the more persuasive your remarks will be.

## ON YOUR OWN

1.  The descent into the wishing well (page 448) is described so vividly that we can imagine it all: the slimy feel of the wall, the smell of moss and salamanders, the sound of the rope creaking around the wood overhead, the look of the single star beyond the mouth of the well. Try your hand at describing an unusual location, maybe inside a chimney, or in a cave, or high, high in the branches of a tree. Use your imagination, and let us see, hear, smell, feel how it would be to be there.

2.  What is the single most important insight or idea you have ever heard? Think hard. What advice or motto or comment has meant most to you? In a paragraph that contains specific facts or examples, persuade your reader that the insight may be as important for her or him as it has been for you.

3.  Try your hand at writing a poem like "Knoxville, Tennessee." Write it, of course, about a place you know well. Decide what feelings that place awakens in you. Then try to awaken the same feelings in your reader by including specific details—of sight and sound and taste and smell and touch—that let the readers know the place as you do.

4.  How do you repair a broken window pane? Do a card trick? Scramble eggs? Fix a flat tire on a bicycle? Choose a task (make it a fairly simple one) and explain, step by step, how to do it. Make your explanation so clear that someone who has never tried the task before can do it successfully just by following your directions.

# ABOUT THE authors

**Ricardo E. Alegría** (born 1921) After receiving a master's degree from the University of Chicago and doing further graduate work at Harvard, Ricardo Alegría returned to Puerto Rico, where he was born. There he became an associate professor of history, then a professor of anthropology and history, and director of the archeological museum and research center at the University of Puerto Rico at Río Piedras. Since 1955 he has acted as director of the Institute of Puerto Rican Culture in San Juan. His books include historical studies written in Spanish, and collections of Puerto Rican folktales, one of which, *The Three Wishes,* has been translated into English.

**Richard Armour** (born 1906) Armour once described himself as the wearer of two costumes: "a cap and gown and a cap and bells." He holds a Ph.D. degree from Harvard University and as a scholar, he writes serious books. As an entertainer, he is known as one of the country's liveliest writers of light verse and humorous prose. In particular he has delighted many readers with his irreverent approach to history and literature in such books as *It All Started with Columbus* and *Twisted Tales from Shakespeare.*

**Rosemary Carr Benét** (1898–1962) A translator and critic as well as a poet, Rosemary Carr married the poet Stephen Vincent Benét a year after their meeting in Paris. She lived most of her life in New York with her husband and three children. The Benéts' interests in American history led to their collaboration on *A Book of Americans,* in which Mrs. Benét wrote the portraits of the women and her husband those of the men.

**Scott Blaine** (born 1956) In 1972, *Scholastic* Magazine chose Scott Blaine as a winner of its Creative Writing Awards for poetry. At the time he was a student at Hillside Junior High School in Salt Lake City, Utah. From there, he went to Utah State University at Logan, Utah.

**Phillip Bonosky** (born 1916) Son of a Lithuanian immigrant steel worker in Pennsylvania, Bonosky for a time also worked in the steel mill. After graduating from high school and college, he turned to writing. His stories have appeared in *Story* magazine, *New Masses, Colliers,* and *Today.* Bonosky wrote the biography of one of the founders of the United Auto Workers Union, two travel books, and two novels, *Burning Valley* and *The Magic Fern.*

**Pearl Buck** (1892–1973) Pearl Buck grew up in China, where her parents were missionaries. She learned the Chinese language and customs. After attending school in America, she returned to China to teach. Over the years, she wrote more than forty books, many of them based on her experiences in China and one of which, *The Good Earth,* won a Pulitzer Prize. Pearl Buck was later awarded the Nobel Prize for Literature (in 1938) for her entire body of literature.

**Norah Burke** This British writer spent most of her childhood in India, as her father was a British officer assigned there. She was educated in both England and Switzerland and made her home in Suffolk, England. Although the author of several short stories, she is primarily known in England for her novels.

**Isabelle Chang** (born 1924) Daughter of a tea merchant from Boston's Chinatown, Isabelle Chang as a child learned many stories from her Chinese teacher. Later she wrote down these stories for her children. She earned a bachelor's degree and worked in libraries in Boston and at Harvard and Yale universities. In 1967 she earned an M.A. degree. Since then she has toured the country interviewing Chinese Americans for a book about the Chinese outside China.

**Richard Chase** (born 1904) Richard Chase grew up near Huntsville, Alabama. A chance visit to Pine Mountain Settlement School in the Kentucky mountains helped him to discover his life's work—collecting English and Appalachian ballads and folktales. There he heard his first ballad and saw his first country dance and began immediately studying Appalachian folk art. Many of the tales collected in his books came to him by chance. The "Jack Tales," for instance, were first mentioned to him by a teacher at a conference in North Carolina. Chase spent seven years researching and tracking down the tales before publishing them.

**Elizabeth Coatsworth** (born 1893) Before she was six years old, Elizabeth Coatsworth had traveled with her family to Egypt and the Alps. The taste for travel stayed with her; in her twenties she spent a year in the Orient. Popular first as a poet, Coatsworth later took up what she calls "the pleasant habit" of writing books for young people. These include *Here I Stay* and *The Cat Who Went to Heaven,* which won a Newbery award.

**Harold Courlander** (born 1908) Harold Courlander feels that the folktales from Africa, Indonesia, and Haiti, which he collects and retells, are as suitable and enriching for adults as for children. What he likes especially about these tales is their "immediacy to life" in contrast to the European type folktales. Courlander has held a variety of jobs, including chief of news broadcasts for Voice of America. In addition to his folktales, he has published black folk plays and two books on Haitian art and life.

**W. H. Davies** (1871–1940) William Henry Davies was born in Newport, Wales, and was brought up by his grandparents. In his twenties he went to America and wandered all over the United States and Canada as a tramp, losing his leg in a jump from a moving train. Back in England living in poverty, he began to write poems, first peddling them door to door, then publishing them at his own expense. Bernard Shaw admired his work and brought him to critical attention. Later Davies wrote *The Autobiography of a Super-Tramp* at Shaw's suggestion. His poems have been collected and published in *The Complete Poems of W.H.D.*

**Borden Deal** (born 1922) A writer of novels as well as short stories, Borden Deal has also fought forest fires, worked for a circus, and been a government skip tracer (tracer of people who fail to pay bills). Born and reared in Mississippi, he served in the navy during World War II and now lives in Florida. Deal began his writing career when he won first prize in a short-story contest while a student at the University of Alabama.

**Gerald Durrell** (born 1925) At the age of six, Gerald Durrell decided that he would someday have his own zoo. Even then he was an avid collector, and life for the rest of the Durrell family was full of surprises: snakes in the bathtub, scorpions in match boxes, etc. Following his informal education by private tutors, Durrell made several expeditions to Africa and South America to collect animals for British zoos. In 1958 he founded his own zoo on Jersey Island in the English Channel, protecting and preserving animal life of all sorts. Books such as *The Drunken*

*Forest, A Zoo in My Luggage,* and *The Overloaded Ark* describe his many adventures while collecting wild animals.

**Alan Devoe** (1909–1955) "Down to Earth," the title of the monthly column Alan Devoe edited for *American Mercury* for many years, indicates the direction of the author's interests. A naturalist and a writer, Devoe wrote lively studies of animal life geared to the nonscientist reader. Some of his book titles are *Lives Around Us, Our Animal Neighbors,* and *Mind in Nature.* Born in Montclair, New Jersey, Devoe ended his days in a house in Hillsdale, New York, called Phudd Hill, which was the subject of one of his books.

**Mari Evans** A native of Toledo, Ohio, Mari Evans was a John Hay Whitney Fellow, 1965–66, and a Consultant for the National Endowment of the Arts. Her poetry has been used extensively in textbooks and anthologies. Formerly producer/director of a weekly half-hour television series "The Black Experience," she is Writer-in-Residence and assistant professor in Black Literature at Indiana University, Bloomington, Indiana. She is the author of several juvenile books and her poems have been collected in two volumes, *Where Is All the Music,* and *I Am a Black Woman.*

**Bernard Evslin** (born 1922) Writing documentary films for television, plays for Broadway, and books of mythology for adults and young people has filled Bernard Evslin's career with distinction. Born in Philadelphia, Evslin was educated at Rutgers University. The National Education Association gave him an award for best television documentary on an educational theme in 1961. His play *Step on a Crack* was produced on Broadway.

**Dorothy Canfield Fisher** (1879–1958) Born in Kansas, the daughter of an educator and an artist, young Dorothy was sent to Paris at age ten for a year of school. Later she attended Ohio State University while her father was president of the college. Afterward she studied at the Sorbonne in France and then at Columbia University in New York. She wrote several books about education. She also translated works from French to English, and French characters (along with New Englanders) played an important role in her novels and stories. Some of her works include *The Deepening Stream, Understood Betsy,* and *Seasoned Timber.*

**Mona Gardner** Although she was born in Seattle and graduated from Stanford, Mona Gardner is known for her novels and stories of the Orient. She has lived in Hong Kong, Canton, Shanghai, Thailand, Malaysia, Java, and India. Her stories have been published in *The New Yorker* and *Reader's Digest.* Her novels *Middle Heaven*—about a modern Japanese peasant family—and *Hong Kong*—about the opening of China to foreign trade—have found a wide audience.

**Nikki Giovanni** (born 1943) A popular poet who has read her poetry on television and put out a best-selling album, Giovanni continues to search for individual values in the black community. She was born in Knoxville, Tennessee, studied with John Killens at Fisk University, and attended the University of Pennsylvania school of social work, and Columbia University. Her books of poetry include *Black Feeling, Black Talk, Black Judgement, Spin a Soft Black Song,* and *My House.*

**Dick Gregory** (born 1932) From a career as a popular nightclub and television entertainer Dick Gregory turned, in the 1960s, to political involvement. His deep concern for equal rights led him to accept the presidential nomination from the Peace and Freedom Party in 1968, and he has been active in other causes. As an undergraduate at Southern Illinois University, he was named outstanding athlete and won the

Missouri Mile championship twice. His books include *No More Lies: The Myth and Reality of American History* and *Dick Gregory's Political Primer.*

**Arthur Hailey** (born 1920) Hailey was born in Luton, England, but became a Canadian citizen in 1952 after taking air force training there during World War II. His early career included work as an office boy and clerk in England, and editor and sales promotion manager in Canada. His first television play, ''Flight into Danger,'' was a success and was later turned into a novel and a motion picture. Since then Hailey has written numerous television plays, film scripts, and novels, some of the best known of which are *Airport, Hotel,* and *The Moneychangers.*

**Sandra Hochman** (born 1936) Following a New York acting career, Sandra Hochman turned to writing poetry. She has been poet-in-residence at Fordham University and has produced a weekly poetry program for a New York radio station. Her second book of poems, *Manhattan Pastures,* won the Yale Younger Poets Award, and her later volumes have aroused much critical interest. Educated at Bennington College, the Sorbonne, the University of Paris, and Columbia University, Sandra Hochman has lived in Paris, London, and Athens.

**Edwin A. Hoey** (born 1930) After graduating from Swarthmore College in Pennsylvania, Edwin Hoey joined the army. He has had a diversified writing career, publishing not only poetry but also articles on topics as widely varied as slavery and skiing. His work has appeared in a variety of journals. He has worked as an editor in a publishing house.

**Frank Horne** (born 1899) Frank Horne has had a diversified career, as both an optometrist and a poet. He was born in New York City and attended the College of the City of New York, where he distinguished himself as a track athlete. He later attended Northern Illinois College of Ophthamology, and has practiced optometry in both Chicago and New York. His poems have been widely anthologized and his collected poetry was first published in England.

**Langston Hughes** (1902–1967) When Langston Hughes finished college in 1929, jobs of any kind were scarce, and he was forced, as he said, to ''turn poetry into bread. It was a question of writing or starving.'' What he wrote was ''largely concerned with the depicting of Negro life in America.'' The rhythms of his verse were compounded of a jazz beat and the street sounds of Harlem. His poetry, sometimes written in dialect, conveys a warm, inexhaustible sympathy for the people whose lives he interpreted and celebrated. In addition to poetry, Hughes produced short stories, novels, travel articles, autobiography, song lyrics, essays, plays, and humorous pieces.

**Ted Hughes** (born 1930) English-born Ted Hughes is the author of several books of poetry and the editor of poetry anthologies. He has won various awards for his poetry, including the Somerset Maugham Award and the Hawthornden Prize, as well as a Guggenheim fellowship. He has also written plays, stories, and poems for children. A graduate of Cambridge University, he was married to Sylvia Plath, a well-known American poet who died in 1963. Hughes's work has been collected in the volume *Selected Poems 1957–1967.*

**Shirley Jackson** (1919–1965) ''Mothers,'' Shirley Jackson once said, ''are harried creatures, haunted by all sorts of terror—rusty nails, the rising cost of sneakers, rain on Class Picnic Day. . . . Over and above such trials most mothers are called upon, from time to time, to endure periods of such unnerving strain that only a heroine could meet them.'' She herself was the mother of several children, including a boy named Laurence. In a humorous book entitled

*Life Among the Savages* she described her family's life in their rural Vermont home. Shirley Jackson was also known for her serious writing, which includes many short stories and several novels. Her horror story "The Lottery" has become a modern classic, appearing many times in print and on television.

**Dorothy M. Johnson** (born 1905) After a fifteen-year career as a magazine editor in New York, Dorothy Johnson moved to Montana and began to write the western novels for adults and young people which have won her renown. Among these are *Lawmen of the Old West*, *Some Went West*, and *A Biography of Sitting Bull*. The movies *The Hanging Tree*, *The Man Who Shot Liberty Valance* and *A Man Called Horse* were based on her stories.

**Elsie Katterjohn** (born 1904) After receiving her B.A. from Oxford College for Women and her M.A. from the University of Iowa, Elsie Katterjohn began a thirty-three year career as a teacher. She taught mainly in Illinois but briefly in Indiana, Minnesota, Wisconsin, and California. At each school she was primarily concerned with making English classes interesting to reluctant students and she later helped write and edit text books aimed at this goal. In her retirement she does free-lance writing for newspapers and magazines, and works for animal welfare.

**Rudyard Kipling** (1865–1936) The son of British parents, Rudyard Kipling was born and reared in India and it was his familiarity with India that made him famous. When his first stories and poems of that far-off land reached England in 1884, they were an immediate success. By the time he was twenty-five, Kipling was one of the most widely read authors in the world. His autograph was so prized that people often kept as souvenirs the checks he wrote—or sold them at a profit. In 1907 he became the first

Englishman ever to be awarded the Nobel Prize for literature.

**Andrew Lang** (1844–1912) Andrew Lang was born in Scotland. As a young man, he moved to London and began to write. He published verses, articles, and literary reviews. But he was most fascinated by the Scottish ballads and folktales he had absorbed in his youth. He began to write stories based on traditional fairy tales. He called his books simply the "Red Fairy Book" or the "Yellow Fairy Book" (ten colors in all). Later he turned to Greek myths and wrote *Tales of Troy and Greece* and *The Story of the Golden Fleece*.

**Virginia Layefsky** (born 1927) A student at the Juilliard School of Music in New York, Virginia Layefsky later married a violinist with the Pittsburgh Symphony Orchestra. "Moonlight—Starlight" is one of the first stories she wrote. She now lives with her husband, a teenaged daughter, a dog, a cat, and "other live transients like frogs" half the year in Pittsburgh and the other half in the British Virgin Islands.

**Oscar Lewis** (1914–1970) When he wrote of people trapped by poverty, Oscar Lewis combined humane understanding with scientific knowledge. He held a Ph.D. in anthropology from Columbia University, and taught at the University of Illinois. Lewis was involved in field studies from 1940 and wrote books about Mexican and Puerto Rican life. These books focus on particular families and use the words of the people themselves as much as possible. *La Vida,* his account of a Puerto Rican family in San Juan and New York won the National Book Award for nonfiction in 1967.

**Lin Yutang** (1895–1976) Lin Yutang was born in Amoy, Fukien Province, China, where he studied English and Western subjects at a mission school. After his marriage, he and his wife set out to study abroad, attending Harvard, Jena, and Leipzig universities. Returning to China, Lin became a professor of English Philology at Peking National University and joined the radical movement. He became disillusioned with politics ("I always like a revolution," he said, "but never the revolutionists.") and moved to the United States. Here he founded and edited literary and humor magazines. His book *My Country and My People* was criticized in China as being unpatriotically harsh, but Lin Yutang said "I have never written a line that pleased the authorities, nor have I said anything that would please everybody, or tried to."

**Frank Linderman** (1869–1938) A desire to get away from what he called "contaminating civilization" was a determining factor in Linderman's life. When his family moved to Chicago he could not stand city life and left for western Montana. There he got to know the Flathead Indians very well. Later he developed a long-term interest in the Cree and Chippewa and that interest led him to lobby for many years for a government reservation for these tribes, an effort that was finally successful. During this time he learned many of the Cree myths, tales, and legends, which he wrote down in *Indian Why Stories*. His knowledge of sign language helped him interview Plenty-coups, chief of the Crows, and to write a book about him.

**Cyrus Macmillan** (1882–1953) Born on Prince Edward Island off the coast of Canada, Cyrus Macmillan studied first at McGill University in Montreal and then at Harvard where he wrote his thesis on the ballads and fables of Canada. World War I interrupted his teaching career at McGill and it was in the trenches in France that Macmillan corrected proofs for his book *Canadian Wonder Tales*. Returning to McGill, Macmillan became dean of the faculty of arts and wrote a history of the university. He was later elected to a seat in the Canadian House of Commons and served for a short period as Minister of Fisheries.

**Daniel P. Mannix** (born 1911) Fond of animals since his childhood, Mannix returned to his original interest after a varied career as a professional magician, fire-eater, and sword swallower for a sideshow. He was born in Pennsylvania. At the University of Pennsylvania he studied first zoology, then journalism, and finally witchcraft. Publishing articles in the *Saturday Evening Post* and *Esquire* drew him toward a career in journalism and encouraged him to write *All Creatures Great and Small*. The novel was a success, for as Mannix says "as long as there are children, there will always be someone who loves animals."

**Jean McCord** (born 1924) After losing her parents when she was twelve, Jean McCord led a highly mobile life. She completed high school at fifteen, after attending sixteen different schools, and has engaged, by her count, in forty-five different occupations since graduation from college. Her love of books was a constant factor in her change-filled life and when she turned to writing she based her stories on recollections of her adolescent years.

**Phyllis McGinley** (born 1905) "The vanishing West had not quite vanished," recalls Phyllis McGinley about her childhood on a Colorado ranch. She and her brother rode ponies three miles to a school at which they were sometimes the only students. Later McGinley spent a year in Utah as a teacher. Today, however, she and her husband live in the suburbs of New York City. Much of her poetry, which has been collected in *Times Three,* she describes as "outwardly amusing, but inwardly serious."

**Irene Rutherford McLeod** (1891–1968) English poet Irene Rutherford McLeod burst onto the

London literary scene in 1915 with the publication of her book of poems *Songs to Save a Soul,* soon followed by *Before Dawn* and *Swords for Life.* Critics said of her work ''Miss McLeod sees magic even in a London fog'' and called *Songs to Save a Soul* ''the very credo of ardent and idealistic youth.'' Her poems were published in many English magazines including *The Nation, Votes for Women,* and *The Smart Set.* She later wrote a novel called *Graduation.*

**Eve Merriam** (born 1916) ''A poem . . . is very much like you, and that is quite natural, since there is a rhythm in your own body: in your pulse, in your heartbeat, in the way you breathe, laugh, or cry,'' says Eve Merriam. She describes growing up in the suburbs of Philadelphia, ''surrounded by beautiful birch trees, dogwood trees and rock gardens. . . .'' She moved to New York City where she worked in advertising and as a fashion editor for a magazine. She has published several books of poetry, for both children and adults.

**Edna St. Vincent Millay** (1892–1950) By the time she was twenty, Edna St. Vincent Millay had achieved fame with her poem ''Renascence.'' The poem marked the beginning of a career that was to see her become probably the most popular poet in America between the two World Wars. Her poems expressed the disillusionment of the postwar generation and struck a tone that appealed to public tastes. Although usually working within traditional stanza forms, she often expressed a romantic protest against traditions and conventions. Her early concern with her own identity—her relationship to others and to the universe—gradually shifted to a concern with broader social issues.

**Rosalie Moore** (born 1910) Rosalie Moore is known for her poetry and children's books. Her book *The Grasshopper Man and Other Poems* was selected by W. H. Auden for inclusion in the Yale Poetry Series. She is the recipient of two Guggenheim Fellowships for creative writing.

**Ogden Nash** (1902–1971) America's best-known writer of humorous verse, Nash didn't start out to be a poet. After a year at Harvard he went to New York City and worked for two years as a bond salesman. ''I sold one bond—to my godmother,'' he recalled. Nash then tried his hand at advertising, at book publishing, and at magazine work. On those jobs he discovered that misspellings often made a story or article unintentionally funny. Accordingly, he began writing verse with deliberate misspellings and unexpected rhymes. Out of those first attempts grew poems that have been described as ''the most original light verse written in America.'' His poetry now fills more than twenty books.

**Robert Nathan** (born 1894) A native New Yorker, Robert Nathan lectured at the New York University School of Journalism for a year before going to Hollywood to become a screen writer. He is the author of more than thirty novels, spanning the years from 1919 to 1973, including *The Elixer* and *Mia.* His several books of poems have been assembled in *The Green Leaf: The Collected Poems of Robert Nathan.* During his varied career, Nathan contributed to magazines such as *The New Yorker.* He wrote songs and composed a violin sonata. His book of children's stories, *The Snowflake and the Starfish,* has been compared to the work of Hans Christian Andersen.

**Alfred Noyes** (1880–1958) One of the most popular of modern English poets, Noyes was for several years professor of modern English literature at Princeton University. He wrote ''The Highwayman'' one night after standing in the blustery wind on the edge of Bagshot Heath, a deserted spot in England that two centuries before had often been the scene of highwaymen's exploits. As a boy the poet had devoured adventure stories of America's Wild West, and he once said that his boyhood reading may have given him the idea for what was to become his most famous poem, ''The Highwayman.''

**Mary O'Hara** (born 1885) *My Friend Flicka,* Mary O'Hara's best-known work, began as a short story, written while the author was living on a ranch in Wyoming. Expanded into a full-length novel, the story became a best seller. It was later made into a movie. Later, *My Friend Flicka* was followed by a sequel novel, *Thunderhead.* The author grew up in Brooklyn Heights, New York, where her father was a minister. She attended Packer Institute in Brooklyn and studied music and languages in Europe. Before becoming a novelist, she composed music and adapted many well-known stories for the screen, including *Prisoner of Zenda.*

**Américo Paredes** (born 1915) A descendant of the settlers who colonized the Rio Grande area, Américo Paredes was born in Brownsville, Texas. After graduating from the University of Texas, he returned to earn his M.A. and Ph.D. in English and Spanish and is now professor of English and anthropology at the same university. Dr. Paredes is a contributing editor for the Chicano journal *Aztlán* and writes short stories and poems. Two of his books are *With His Pistol in His Hand* and *Folktales of Mexico.*

**Ann Petry** (born 1911) Following her father's example, Ann Petry began a career in pharmacy after graduation from the University of Connecticut. Later, when she moved to New York, she left pharmacy and engaged in a succession of interesting occupations. She worked as a newspaper reporter, a social worker, and as a participant in an elementary school educational project. The field of writing, however, was Petry's major interest. She studied creative writing at night and produced her first novel, *The Street,* while on a Houghton Mifflin fellowship. As her writing style developed, she focused her efforts on writing about black people as human

beings, not as stereotypes. Ann Petry has also written *The Narrows, Country Place,* and several books for children.

**Edgar Allan Poe** (1809–1849) In his short life, Poe achieved fame, but his story is tragic, full of frustration and sadness, poverty and loneliness. He lost both of his parents before he was three, one by death and the other by desertion. Foster parents brought him up, but as he grew older there were many quarrels at home. After a short stay at the University of Virginia he began a career as a soldier, then as a writer and editor. While Poe was writing his tales of the supernatural and suspense, his young wife was hopelessly ill. In 1874 she—like his mother—died of tuberculosis. Two years later Poe was found unconscious on a Baltimore street and taken to the charity hospital where he died. ''The saddest and strangest figure in American literary history,'' one biographer has said of Poe.

**Anthony Quinn** (born 1915) The star of such movies as *Zorba the Greek, The Guns of Navarone,* and *La Strada,* Quinn made his acting debut in 1937 after several years of working as a boxer, carpenter, fruit picker, writer, painter, and ditch digger. He was born in Mexico, to a Mexican mother and an Irish father. Quinn has received Academy Awards for his performances in *Viva Zapata!* and *Lust for Life.*

**Quentin Reynolds** (1902–1965) An outstanding newspaper reporter, Quentin Reynolds covered World War II in North Africa, Sicily, Salerno, Teheran, Palestine, and the Southwest Pacific. He published a book about wartime England called *The Wounded Don't Cry* which became a best seller. When Dwight Eisenhower became president, Reynolds was the only reporter the president would allow to write a personal story about him for *Life* magazine. Reynolds grew up in Brooklyn, went to Brown University where he became heavyweight boxing champion, and earned his law degree at night while writing for the New York *Evening World.*

**Barbara Ritchey** (born 1949) The poem "Question" was based on Barbara Ritchey's experience as a high-school English teacher in a small town near Jacksonville, Florida. She says that "although teaching is very rewarding, a frustrating part of it, I think, is never being quite sure that one is reaching one's students." Ritchey's father was an army officer and she spent her childhood traveling "as an army brat." Her family finally settled in a small Kansas town when she was in her teens and she attended Kansas State University, majoring in secondary English education. Then she married and moved to Jacksonville where she continues to teach and to write.

**Theodore Roethke** (1908–1963) A teacher throughout much of his adult life, Theodore Roethke was also a fine athlete and an excellent coach. "It took me ten years to complete one little book," he confessed about his first volume of verse. That book and the six that followed have earned him many literary honors, including the 1954 Pulitzer Prize. Many of his poems reflect his professional knowledge of flowers, gained from a childhood spent in and around a greenhouse owned by his father and uncle. "Who else," a reviewer commented in amazement, "would know that tulips 'creak'?" Roethke's style is original and powerful, striving—as he once explained—to "permit many ranges of feeling, including humor."

**Carl Sandburg** (1878–1967) Milkman, dishwasher, harvest hand, sign painter, brickmaker, and barbershop porter—all these jobs Carl Sandburg had tried before enrolling in Lombard College not far from his Illinois home. With the publication of "Chicago" in 1914, Sandburg at last found the role for which he had unconsciously been preparing all his life. In many books which followed, Sandburg demonstrated his remarkable command of American speech, rhythms, and colloquial idiom, as well as an uncanny ability to convey what it feels like to live in a modern industrial civilization.

**William Saroyan** (born 1908) Author of the widely read *My Name Is Aram,* Saroyan was born in California of Armenian parents. He early displayed a spirit of independence. Before he went to work to help his mother support the family, he earned himself a reputation for playing hooky from school. But books appealed to him, even if school did not, and his wide reading encouraged him to write his own stories. Saroyan has tried almost every kind of writing: stories, plays, novels. It is the writing itself, not the various forms, that interests him: "What difference does it make what you call it, just so it breathes?" he once asked. His most recent book is *Sons Come & Go, Mothers Hang In Forever.*

**Sir Walter Scott** (1771–1832) Scott created in words the landscape and life of his homeland, the border region of Scotland. He won his first fame as a poet, but later became an equally successful novelist, the first writer in English literature to place fictional characters in a historical setting. In 1820, his genius in both poetry and prose received royal recognition; he was knighted as a baronet. Even today, his novels *Ivanhoe* and *Rob Roy* capture the imagination of readers much as they did in Scott's own time.

**Rod Serling** (1924–1975) Prejudice and fear are two recurring themes in Rod Serling's work. He explained, "I've always tried to attack prejudice more than any other social evil. I've always felt that prejudice is probably the most damaging, the most jeopardizing, the most fruitless of human frailties. I think prejudice is a waste, and its normal end is violence.'' Rod Serling was a television writer whose name became synonymous with stories of the eerie unknown. Before creating his famous series ''The Twilight Zone,'' he wrote both radio and television dramas. Four times he received the Emmy award for best television play.

**Celestine Sibley** (born 1917) Celestine Sibley began her career in journalism as a five-dollar-a-week general assignment reporter for the *Mobile Press-Register*. She has won numerous awards for journalism including Associated Press Awards. Her mystery novel *The Malignant Heart* was a popular success and was followed by *Peachtree Street U.S.A.: An Affectionate Portrait of Atlanta*.

**Henry Slesar** (born 1927) Slesar has divided his life between advertising and creative writing, with notable success in both fields. He is president of his own New York advertising firm. In 1959 he received the Edgar Award for the best first mystery novel, *The Gray Flannel Shroud*. Since that time, by his own count, he has written 550 short stories, novelettes, and novels, as well as fifty plays for television and four motion pictures. In his free time he is fond of listening to music, both jazz and classical.

**Edward Rowe Snow** (born 1902) A daily columnist for the *Patriot Ledger* in Quincy, Massachusetts, since 1957, Edward Rowe Snow is also known as a lecturer throughout New England and a radio and television speaker for Boston stations. He was once a high school teacher, but in recent years has concentrated on writing about Boston and New England, sailing, shipwrecks, pirates, lighthouses, and sea tales and legends of the Atlantic coast. His books include *Secrets of North Atlantic Islands* and *Great Sea Rescues and Tales of Survival*.

**Monica Sone** (born 1919) Brought up in a hotel managed by her father on the Seattle waterfront, Monica Sone attended both American schools and Nihon Gakko, a special Japanese school. When World War II broke out she and her family were relocated to a camp for Japanese and Japanese-Americans, first in Washington and then in Idaho. She worked as a secretary until she was released from the camp in the care of a Presbyterian minister in Chicago. After a period of working as a dental assistant, she won a scholarship to Hanover College in Indiana. Later she wrote a book describing those early experiences, called *Nisei Daughter*.

**Claus Stamm** (born 1929) Although born in Germany and fluent in German, Claus Stamm was assigned the job of Japanese language specialist when he enlisted in the U.S. Army just after World War II. There, in small Japanese villages throughout the country, he heard the *dowa,* or Japanese legends told to children. After graduating from Columbia University as an English composition major with a minor in Japanese, he began to write down some of the *dowa* stories he remembered, adding characters here and there and sometimes inventing new endings. *Three Strong Women* is one of these tales, originally illustrated by Stamm's wife.

**John Stands In Timber** (1883?–1967) A member of the Northern Cheyenne tribe, John Stands In Timber was born a few years after his grandfather was killed in the Custer battle. During his childhood he absorbed the Cheyenne traditions and after returning from school he dedicated himself to collecting and preserving the oral literature of his people. He sought out older members of his tribe who could add to his store of knowledge of Cheyenne culture and history. Wishing to communicate the truth about his people to the whites, he collaborated with

Margo Liberty, an anthropologist, on *Cheyenne Memories,* a book which was praised as a classic.

**Jesse Stuart** (born 1907) "I was born in this wonderful country," writes Jesse Stuart. "Here I grew from boyhood to manhood." Stuart's wonderful country was Greenup County, Kentucky, so remote from city life that the boy never saw a telephone or an electric light until after he was fifteen. The son of a farmer, young Jesse often stayed out of school to help support his family, working on neighboring farms for twenty-five or thirty cents a day. Many of his stories recreate incidents from those boyhood years. After working his way through college, Stuart became a teacher and superintendent of Greenup County Schools. *The Thread That Runs So True* describes his efforts to give the hill children a better education.

**Ernest Lawrence Thayer** (1863–1940) While a student at Harvard, Ernest Lawrence Thayer edited the student humor magazine, *The Lampoon,* and met William Randolph Hearst who persuaded him to leave school to write for the *San Francisco Examiner.* That newspaper was the first to publish his famous poem "Casey at the Bat." Thayer later returned to his birthplace of Worcester, Massachusetts, to operate his father's textile business, but continued writing. Many baseball players have claimed to have been the model for the famous "Casey" poem but the author denied that it was based on any one player. Thayer died in Santa Barbara, California.

**George Vukelich** (born 1927) Born in South Milwaukee, Wisconsin, of immigrant parents, George Vukelich majored in English at the University of Wisconsin. His short stories and poetry have appeared in the *Atlantic Monthly* and other magazines, and he has written television scripts for the Canadian Broadcasting System and National Educational Television.

**Donald E. Westlake** (born 1933) Donald Westlake has written more than a dozen novels dealing in one way or another with crime. His early works were of the serious crime novel genre; his later novels treat crime in a comic farce manner. Before becoming a full-time writer, Westlake worked at odd jobs and served in the air force. His novels include *The Hot Rock, Bank Shot,* and *Cops and Robbers,* all of which were produced as movies.

## AUTHORS AND TITLES

Titles of selections are in italics. Biographical information for the authors can be found in *About the Authors,* beginning on page 514.

## W

## LITERARY SKILLS

The page number given indicates where the term is introduced and defined.

Credits continued

Sandburg, Carl. ''Fifty-Fifty,'' from *Honey and Salt,* copyright, © 1963 by Carl Sandburg. Reprinted by permission of Harcourt Brace Jovanovich, Inc. ''Primer Lesson,'' from *Slabs of the Sunburnt West* by Carl Sandburg, copyright, 1922, by Harcourt Brace Jovanovich, Inc., copyright, 1950, by Carl Sandburg. Reprinted by permission of the publishers.
Saroyan, William. ''Locomotive 38, the Ojibway,'' from *My Name Is Aram.* Copyright William Saroyan. Adapted and reprinted by permission of the author.
Serling, Rod. ''The Monsters Are Due on Maple Street,'' slightly adapted and reprinted by permission of International Creative Management. Copyright © 1960 by Rod Serling.
Slesar, Henry. ''Examination Day,'' © 1966. HMH Publications, Inc.
Snow, Edward Rowe. ''The Light at South Point,'' reprinted by permission of Dodd, Mead & Company, Inc., from *Incredible Mysteries and Legends of the Sea* by Edward Rowe Snow. Copyright © 1967 by Edward Rowe Snow.
Sone, Monica. ''An Unpredictable Japanese Lady,'' excerpted from *Nisei Daughter* by Monica Sone. Copyright 1953 by Monica Sone. By permission of Little, Brown and Co., in association with the Atlantic Monthly Press.
Stamm, Claus. ''Three Strong Women,'' copyright © 1962 by Claus Stamm and Kazue Mizumura. Reprinted by permission of The Viking Press.
Stands In Timber, John. ''The Seven Stars,'' by John Stands In Timber and Margot Liberty from *Cheyenne Memories,* copyright 1967. By permission of Yale University Press.
Stuart, Jesse. ''Old Ben,'' from *Clearing in the Sky* by Jesse Stuart. Copyright 1950 by Jesse Stuart. Used with permission of McGraw-Hill Book Company.
Vukelich, George. ''The Turtle,'' from *The University Review* (Summer, 1958) of The University of Missouri at Kansas City. Reprinted by permission of the author.
Werner, Alice. ''Tug-of-War,'' from *Myths and Legends of the Bantu* by Alice Werner. Published by George G. Harrap & Company Ltd. Reprinted by permission of the publisher.
Westlake, Donald E. ''Just One of Those Days,'' copyright © 1966 by Donald Westlake. Reprinted from *The Curious Facts Preceding My Execution,* by Donald Westlake, by permission of Random House, Inc.
Whitebird, Mary. ''Ta-Na-E-Ka,'' adapted and reprinted by permission from *Scholastic Voice,* © 1973 by Scholastic Magazines, Inc.

# GLOSSARY OF LITERARY TERMS

**Alliteration**   Repetition of the same beginning sound in words close together. The repeated sound is usually a consonant sound. A good example of alliteration is Coleridge's lines:

> The fair breeze blew, the white foam flew,
> The furrow followed free.

**Allusion**   A reference to a person or place or thing that the writer expects the reader to recognize.

**Autobiography**   An account of a person's life written by herself or himself.

**Biography**   An account of a person's life written by another person.

**Characterization**   The ways a writer helps you to see and know the characters in a story. This can be done by describing how characters speak and act and look and by showing them through the eyes of other characters.

**Comparison**   Points out what is similar between two things. Writers often use comparison to make a point clear or to help us visualize what they see.

**Conflict**   A struggle of some kind. Conflict is a major part of almost all plots; it can take a number of forms. One character or group of characters may conflict with another; a character may be in conflict with nature; or a character may have an inner conflict. Several conflicts are often present in one work of literature.

**Dialect**   The way of speaking that is peculiar to a region or group.

**Dialogue**   Conversation carried on among characters. Except for stage directions, the body of a play is made up entirely of dialogue.

**Exaggeration**   Use of overstatement to make a point or create an effect. Exaggeration is often used in tall tales to make a point or to add humor.

**Fiction**   Prose writing that tells a story drawn from the author's imagination. Fiction usually refers to novels, short stories, and plays.

**Flashback**   An episode that interrupts the present action to relate something that happened earlier. A flashback usually explains something necessary to understand the characters or plot.

**Foreshadowing**   Clues that a writer places early in a selection to hint at or warn of events that will occur later.

**Image**   A word picture that appeals to the senses. An image creates a picture or suggests a sensation of sound, smell, taste, or touch. Whitman appeals to the sense of smell as well as that of sight in the following lines:

> The sniff of green leaves and dry leaves,
> and of the shore and dark-color'd sea-
> rocks, and of hay in the barn . . .

**Nonfiction**   Prose writing that describes only real people and true events.

**Plot**   The arrangement of events in a story. It is the bare outline of what happens in the order that the events occurred.

**Point of view**   The vantage point from which a story is told. The point of view depends on *who* tells the story. The author may stand outside the story and view what happens from a distance or enter into the story and tell what happens from the point of view of one of the characters.

**Rhyme**   Repetition of the same sound or sounds at the ends of words. Usually when rhyme is used in a poem, the end of one line will rhyme with the end of another line nearby.

**Rhythm**   The beat of prose or poetry. Rhythm is the melody of language—the flowing sound of words together, as distinguished from their meaning.

**Setting**   The time and place of the action.

**Stanza**   Lines of poetry grouped together and printed as a unit. Each stanza is usually like the others in number of lines and rhyme scheme. The beginning of a new stanza is usually indicated by skipping a line.

**Theme**   The main thought or meaning in a literary work. The theme is not usually stated directly, although all parts of the work contribute to the theme in some way.

# ART CREDITS

## ILLUSTRATIONS

pp. 2, 6–7 Jon Goodell
p. 10 Jane Clark
pp. 15, 18 Tony Spengler
pp. 26, 28 29 Jeremy Elkin
pp. 33, 36–37, 41 Valdis Kupris
pp. 47, 49, 51 Eric Spencer
pp. 74, 78–79, 82, 85 Robert Lo Grippo
pp. 86, 90 Sal Barracca
pp. 92–93 Marc Brown
pp. 104, 105 Details from murals by Ugo Mochi, courtesy of the American Museum of Natural History
p. 107 Candy Ann Kaihlanen
pp. 110, 111 Mark Fisher
pp. 118–119, 120 Dorothea Sierra
pp. 130–131 Jill Entis
pp. 136, 140–141, 145 Carole Kowalchuk
pp. 156–157 Ann Toulmin-Rothe
pp. 163, 168–169 Jon Goodell
p. 186 Herb Rogalski
p. 193 Ann Grifalconi
pp. 196, 201, 206, 213, 218, 225 William Carroll
pp. 231, 236 John Walley
pp. 240–241 detail from "Midnight Ride of Paul Revere," Grant Wood, 1931, oil on composition board, The Metropolitan Museum of Art, Arthur H. Hearn Fund, 1950
pp. 244–245 Carol Schwartz
pp. 250, 257 Bob Dacey
p. 266 David Frampton
p. 275 Annie Gusman
pp. 276, 283 George Ulrich
pp. 290, 294 Laura Blacklow
p. 297 David Garland
pp. 298, 299, 302, 305 Tomie Arai
pp. 316, 323 Joan Hall
p. 329 Gian Calvi
pp. 330–331, 336–337, 342 Joseph Warner

pp. 350, 351 from *Aesop's Fables with Upwards of One Hundred and Fifty Emblematical Devices,* John Locken, Philadelphia, 1842. Engravings
p. 355 Rick Brown
pp. 358, 365 Kyuzo Tsugami
pp. 370–371 David Garland
pp. 376–377 Bill Negron
pp. 382, 389 Nahid Haghighat
pp. 396–397 Marc Brown
pp. 402–403 David Frampton
p. 408 Chiang Kai Chung
p. 411 "Tiger," attributed to Mu Ch'i, Chinese, Sung Dynasty, one of a pair of hanging scrolls, ink on silk, The Cleveland Museum of Art, Purchase from the J.H. Wade Fund
pp. 416, 420 Bill Greer
pp. 433, 438 Meryl Henderson
pp. 442–443 Joan Paley
pp. 446–447, 451 John Walley
pp. 454–455, 461, 466, 473 Frank Bozzo
pp. 490, 495 Dennis Hughes
p. 498 Sabra Segal
pp. 501, 506 Jim Kingston

## PHOTOGRAPHS

Cover: Jim Elder, The Image Bank
Title page: Cliff Feulner, The Image Bank
p. i (24, 58, 108, 150, 194, 260, 308, 344, 380, 422, 478, 510) Al Rubin, Stock/Boston
p. iv (25, 59, 109, 151, 195, 261, 309, 345, 381 423, 479, 511) Erik Anderson, Stock/Boston
pp. xiv-1 Arthur Tress
p. 21 Ira Gavrin
pp. 22–23 Bob Evans, Peter Arnold
pp. 44–45 Inge Morath, Magnum
p. 54 Ingbert Gruttner
pp. 62–63 Mark Godfrey, Magnum

p. 65 Brown Brothers
p. 68 Alfreda Pieuch, Panopticon Gallery
p. 70 Frank Siteman, Stock/Boston
p. 94 Ira Gavrin
p. 101 J.R. Eyerman
p. 113 Ylla, Photo Researchers
pp. 122–123 Rene Burri, Magnum
p. 126 Tom McHugh, Photo Researchers
pp. 154–155 Rebecca Wall, Sports Camera West
p. 175 Bobbi Carrey
p. 178 United Artists Corp.
p. 182 Library of Congress
p. 185 Philip Jon Bailey
p. 189 Boston University Photo Services
p. 190 Jerry Berndt, Stock/Boston
pp. 248–249 Christopher Johnson, Stock/Boston
pp. 264–265 Mitchell Funk, The Image Bank
p. 271 Mike Mazzaschi, Stock/Boston
p. 286 Andrew Brilliant
p. 310 Ira Gavrin
pp. 312–313 Dan Seymour, Magnum
pp. 348–349 S. J. Kraseman, Peter Arnold
p. 393 Bill Finch, Stock/Boston
p. 406 Rene Burri, Magnum
p. 417 Madeline Grimoldi
pp. 426–427 John Running, Stock/Bosto1n
p. 429 Eugene Richards
p. 480 Owen Franken, Stock/Boston
p. 484 Peter Menzel, Stock/Boston
p. 487 Andrew Brilliant